The Treasury of Inspirational Anecdotes, Quotations, and Illustrations

The Treasury of Inspirational Anecdotes, Quotations, and Illustrations

1875 Illustrations on Nearly 250 Topics

Compiled by E. Paul Hovey

Fleming H. Revell
A Division of Baker Book House
Grand Rapids, Michigan 49516

First paperback edition 1994

Published by Fleming H. Revell
a division of Baker Book House Company
P.O. Box 6287, Grand Rapids, MI 49516-6287

Printed in the United States of America

Library of Congress Catalog Card Number: 59-8725

ISBN 0-8007-5539-1

ACKNOWLEDGMENTS

Acknowledgment is made to the following, who have granted permission for the reprinting of copyrighted material:

ABINGDON PRESS for selections from *The Interpreter's Bible,* copyright, 1952–1957, by Abingdon Press, by the following contributors: George A. Buttrick, Sherman E. Johnson, Paul W. Hoon, Arthur John Gossip, Halford E. Luccock and Lynn Harold Hough; for selections from the following: *Preaching* by Walter Russell Bowie, copyright, 1954, by Abingdon Press; *Who Speaks for God?* by Gerald Kennedy, copyright, 1954, by Abingdon Press; *So We Believe, So We Pray* by George A. Buttrick, copyright, 1951, by Abingdon Press; *Heaven and Hell* by John S. Bonnell, copyright, 1956, by Abingdon Press; *Christian Ethics* by Georgia Harkness, copyright, 1957, by Abingdon Press; *The American Canon* by Daniel L. Marsh, copyright, 1939, by Abingdon Press; *This Is the Victory* by Leslie Weatherhead, copyright by Abingdon Press; *Sermons from the Mount* by Charles W. Crowe, copyright, 1954, by Abingdon Press.

Advance for selection from "Are You Prepared for Christmas?" by James Willis Lenhart, in December 13, 1954, issue.

AMERICAN BIBLE SOCIETY for selection from "The Power of the Bible" by John Mott in Bible Society *Record,* January, 1946, issue.

RICHARD ARMOUR for selections from two poems.

ASSOCIATION PRESS for selection from *Rediscovering the Church* by George L. Hunt.

The Atlantic Monthly for selection from "The Valor of Teaching" by Agnes de Mille, June, 1955, issue.

Better Homes & Gardens for quotations from Burton Hillis.

JOE DAVID BROWN for selection from *Stars in My Crown* © 1946, 1947 by The Curtis Publishing Corp. Copyright © 1947 by Joe David Brown.

CAMBRIDGE UNIVERSITY PRESS for excerpt from *Christian Doctrine* by J. S. Whale.

Chicago Tribune for selection by John Evans.

THE CHRISTIAN SCIENCE PUBLISHING SOCIETY for excerpt from an editorial in *The Christian Science Monitor.*

Christianity and Crisis for selection from "A Church Speaks Its Mind" by Dr. John C. Bennett, from issue of June 10, 1957, Vol. XVII, No. 10.

CITY NEWS PUBLISHING CO. for excerpts from *Vital Speeches.*

NEIL M. CLARK for excerpt from "The Country Church Comes Back to Life."

The Commonweal for short excerpts.

The Congregational Way for selections by Archie H. Hook.

THE CURTIS PUBLISHING COMPANY for excerpt from January, 1946, editorial, "Last Trump" by Bruce Gould in *Ladies' Home Journal,* copyright, 1945, by The Curtis Publishing Company (also permission of Bruce Gould); for excerpts by Marcelene Cox appearing in 1956 and 1957 issues of *Ladies' Home Journal,* copyright by The Curtis Publishing Company; for excerpt from "The White Sofa" by Dorothy Thompson, copyright, 1951, by The Curtis Publishing Company (also permission of Dorothy Thompson).

Daily Idahonian (News Review Publishing Co., Inc., Moscow, Idaho) for excerpt from editorial.

DOUBLEDAY & COMPANY, INC. for selection from *The Restoration of Meaning to Contemporary Life* by Paul Elmen. Copyright © by Paul Elmen. Reprinted by permission of Doubleday & Company, Inc.; selection from *Naught for Your Comfort* by Trevor Huddleston. Copyright, 1956, by Ernest Urban Trevor Huddleston. Reprinted by permission of Doubleday & Company, Inc.

E. P. DUTTON & CO., INC. for selections from *How You Can Find Happiness* by Samuel M. Shoemaker; for excerpt from *No Mean City* by Simeon Strunsky.

PRESIDENT DWIGHT D. EISENHOWER for excerpt from Second Inaugural Address, January 21, 1957.

CLARENCE W. HALL for excerpts from his Commencement address, "Our Imprisoned Splendor," at the University of Idaho.

HARCOURT, BRACE AND COMPANY, INC., for selection from *Reflections on the Psalms,* © 1958 by C. S. Lewis. Reprinted by permission of Harcourt, Brace and Company, Inc.; for selection from *North to the Orient,* copyright, 1935, by Anne Morrow Lindbergh. Reprinted by permission of Harcourt, Brace and Company, Inc.; for excerpts from *Common Sense and World Affairs,* copyright © 1955, by Dorothy Fosdick. Reprinted by permission of Harcourt, Brace and Company, Inc.

HARPER & BROTHERS for selection from *Re-port to the Creator* by Jerome E. Ellison; for selection from *The Christian Faith* by Nels F. S. Ferré.

J. EDGAR HOOVER for quotation from "Religion in American Life."

HERBERT HOOVER for quotation from *Facts Forum News,* January, 1956.

HOUGHTON MIFFLIN COMPANY for excerpt from *The World, the Flesh and Father Smith* by Bruce Marshall. For selection from *Book of Friendship* by Elizabeth Selden.

House & Garden for excerpts from "The Anniversary" by William H. Lowe, Jr., copyright, 1956, the Condé Nast Publications Inc.

ALFRED A. KNOPF, INC. for selection from *The Fountain* by Charles Morgan. Copyright, 1932, by Charles Morgan; for a selection reprinted from *The Prophet* by Kahlil Gibran.

Lewiston (Idaho) *Tribune* for quotation from article by Dr. H. L. Talkington.

Look magazine for selection from "All Ball Players Are Afraid" by George Tebbetts, May 14, 1957, issue.

THE MACMILLAN COMPANY for selections from the following: *New Testament Christianity* by J. B. Phillips, copyright, 1956; *God with Us* by J. B. Phillips, copyright, 1957; *The Screwtape Letters* by C. S. Lewis; *The Art of Dodging Repentance* by D. R. Davies; *Science and the Modern World* by Alfred N. Whitehead, copyright, 1925; *Toward the Understanding of Jesus* by V. G. Simkhovitch, copyright, 1947; *The Quest of the Historical Jesus* by Albert Schweitzer; *Autobiography* of William Allen White, copyright, 1946.

McCall's magazine for selections by the following: Dwight D. Eisenhower, Harry and Bonaro Overstreet, Norman Vincent Peale, Elizabeth Pope and Joseph P. Welch.

MC GRAW-HILL BOOK CO., INC. for selection from Catherine Marshall, *A Man Called Peter,* McGraw-Hill Book Co., Inc.

Monday Morning for selections from "Captured But Free" by Harold L. Bowman in November 27, 1944, issue; for selection by Paul S. Wright.

The Nation for excerpt from "The Misuses of History" by Godfrey Barraclough, November 10, 1956, issue.

National Parent-Teacher for selection from "The Great Wall" by Pauline Frederick; for quotation by Bonaro Overstreet in May, 1957, issue.

Newsweek for material, identified in the text, reprinted from its columns.

The New Leader for selection from "Reflections at 80" by Upton Sinclair, in September 8, 1958, issue; for quotation by Benjamin H. Brown, in September 26, 1955, issue; for quotations by Jawaharlal Nehru; for selection from "The Cool Approach" by Richard L. Schoenwald in September 5, 1955, issue; for quotation from Robert E. Fitch in December 10, 1956, issue; for quotation from Daniel Bell, in February 11, 1957, issue; for selection from "Legislating Union Democracy" by J. B. S. Hardman, in December 2, 1957, issue.

The New York Times Magazine and the writers indicated for excerpts from September 30, 1956, issue by Henry T. Heald and Dorothy Barclay; for selections from "Epic of Liberty Island" by Allan Nevins, October, 1958, issue.

PANTHEON BOOKS INC. for selections from *Dr. Zhivago* by Boris Pasternak.

DANIEL A. POLING for excerpt from "The Call of the Church" from *Association Men.*

PRENTICE-HALL, INC. for selection from *Try Giving Yourself Away* by David Dunn, © 1956 by Prentice-Hall, Inc.

Presbyterian Life for selection from "Faith in Jesus Christ" by George Buttrick, reprinted by permission from *Presbyterian Life,* Witherspoon Building, Philadelphia 7, Pa.; for selection from "The Bible Is a One World Book" by Calvin T. Ryan, reprinted from the *The Presbyterian* by permission of *Presbyterian Life, Inc.*

G. P. PUTNAM'S SONS for selection from *East River* by Sholem Asch. Reprinted by permission of publisher.

RANDOM HOUSE INC. for excerpt from *Man on Earth* by Jacquetta Hawkes, copyright by Jacquetta Hawkes, 1955; for selection from *Savrola* by Winston Churchill; for quotation from *Seven Gothic Tales* by Isak Dinesen.

The Reader's Digest for selection from "How Wonderful You Are" by Arthur Gordon (and *Woman's Day,* October, 1956); for selection from "I Am for the Churches" by Roger William Riis, copyright, 1951, by Reader's Digest Association, Inc.

WILL ROGERS, JR. for quotations from Will Rogers.

The Rotarian for selection from "Paradox" by Richard Wheeler; for selections from "Ten Marks of a Good Citizen" by Herbert J. Taylor; for quotation from R. C. Wallace, in October, 1956, issue; for quotation from Kenneth McFarland in July, 1951, issue; for quotation from Clarence B. Randall in June, 1957, issue.

ROSALIND RUSSELL for quotation.

CULBERT G. RUTENBER for selection from "Christ or Karl Marx," published by American Baptist Home Mission Societies.

SIMON AND SCHUSTER, INC. for selections from *Peace of Mind* by Joshua Loth Liebman.

THE SOCIETY OF AUTHORS, AND THE PUBLIC TRUSTEE, LONDON, for selection from *Candida* by Bernard Shaw, and for other quotations from the same author.

ADLAI STEVENSON for excerpt from acceptance speech of August 17, 1956.

This Week magazine, and authors indicated, for a quotation from "The Way to Greatness" by Herbert Hoover, copyright 1958 by the United Newspapers Magazine Corporation; for a quotation from "My Key to Success" by Samuel Goldwyn, copyright 1956 by the United Newspapers Magazine Corporation; for a quotation from "Don't Get Too Comfortable" by Carl Sandburg, copyright 1956 by the United Newspapers Magazine Corporation; for a quotation from "The Greatest Commandment" by Cecil B. De Mille, copyright 1957 by the United Newspapers Magazine Corporation.

Time magazine for selection from story "The U.S. Air Force," in March 5, 1956, issue.

DOROTHY THOMPSON and *Ladies' Home Journal* for selection from "The White Sofa" from February, 1951, issue.

THE UNITED PRESBYTERIAN CHURCH IN THE UNITED STATES OF AMERICA, Commission on Ecumenical Mission and Relations, for selection from *Ten More Stories of World Communion* by Roy S. Lautenschlager.

MARK VAN DOREN for selection from *Liberal Education,* Henry Holt and Company, Inc., copyright © 1943, 1948 by Mark Van Doren.

THE VIKING PRESS INC. for selections from *Now Is the Time* by Lillian Smith; for selection from *The Meaning of Treason* by Rebecca West; for selections from *My Lord, What a Morning* by Marian Anderson.

THE WARTENBURG PRESS and the author for "A Twentieth-Century Papyrus to the Most Reverend Paul" by Wilson C. Egbert, from the *Lutheran Standard,* March 17, 1956, issue.

THE WESTMINSTER PRESS for selection from *The Significance of the Church* by Robert McAfee Brown. Copyright, 1956, W. L. Jenkins, The Westminster Press. Used by permission. For selection from *Faith, Hope and Love* by Emil Brunner. Copyright, 1956, by W. L. Jenkins, The Westminster Press. Used by permission. For selections from *Smoke on the Mountain* by Joy Davidman. Copyright, 1953, 1954, by Joy Davidman, The Westminster Press. Used by permission. For selection from *Mrs. Minister* by Olive Knox. Copyright, 1956, by Olive Knox, The Westminster Press. Used by permission. For selections from *How Christian Parents Face Family Problems* by John C. Wynn. Copyright, 1955, W. L. Jenkins, The Westminster Press. Used by permission. For selection from *The Altar Fire* by Olive Wyon, The Westminster Press. Used by permission. For quotation from article by Elliot Porter from *Forward.* Copyright by The Westminster Press. Used by permission. For selection from *The Prospectus, Christian Faith and Life,* October, 1949, the Presbyterian Board of Christian Education. Used by permission.

To my wife, Barbara, and my children, Roy and Linda, whose opinions of my clippings, filing system, and accumulation through the years have not always been "fit to be quoted."

PREFACE

THERE WAS a time when the craftsman did all his work with a minimum
of tools. For instance, a carpenter could go to work with a saw, a hammer
and a keg of nails—and complete the job. This is no longer true. Today
a veritable chest of tools and gadgets is necessary, and the average job
will call for the use of most of them. What is true of the carpenter is
also true of the doctor, the farmer, the mechanic, in fact, of man in
almost every line of work.

Once the public speaker and the preacher, by reading in the classics
and the Bible, could speak with regularity and authority because thus
he possessed more information than his audience. But today's speaker
and preacher has need of a more elaborate chest of tools, if he is to be
proficient in his task. Indeed, Robert Gunderson tells us that "the stock-
pile of quotations ("commonplaces," Aristotle called them) which American leaders glean from their schooling is so inadequate that of course
they must rely upon ghost writers."

The Treasury of Inspirational Anecdotes, Quotations and Illustrations
is a tool for speakers. A tool is something the worker masters and then
employs with skill in his chosen work. The compiler would make no
such sweeping claims for *The Treasury* as were made in the advertisement of a book which stated that "B—'s book . . . is uniquely organized
to deliver instantly the exact . . . anecdote . . . for the subject, the
occasion, or the audience . . . (it) gives . . . infallible rules for picking
the *right* story. . . . You can't miss!" The person who needs that kind
of tool had better not be speaking at all.

The compiler does, however, feel that *The Treasury of Inspirational
Anecdotes, Quotations and Illustrations* can be a valuable and helpful
tool to almost anyone who engages in the art of public speaking. No one
can read everything. But in the works of others the speaker finds ideas
fit to be quoted. *The Treasury* attempts to gather and classify certain
quotations, anecdotes, and illustrations—tools which sharpen, interpret,

polish, clinch, and convey the speaker's thoughts. If the book can thus serve, its mission will have been fulfilled.

Beyond being a tool in the hands of the speaker, it should prove a fertile field of sources for those radio and TV announcers who use quotes, "thoughts for the day," or fill-in material when "conditions beyond local control" prevail. They will find material for adding that human, spiritual or humorous touch to their programs. The same qualities are available to the editor and writer.

Although *The Treasury* was not intended primarily as a devotional book, there is much in it that is devotional in nature. By making use of the special day index, the person who would like a fresh and different approach to his devotional reading can find within these pages much that is inspiring and refreshing for daily or occasional devotional reading.

Many feel that they do not have time to read long articles, and to such this book should have a strong appeal. It might well grace the table of the professional man's waiting room.

In *The Treasury* I am sharing that which captured my imagination when I first read or heard the statement, and I hope that much of it will capture yours. My only plea is that you use the book. It cannot speak to you from the shelf, but used at odd moments or in concentrated study it may enrich each speech you are called upon to deliver.

The preparation of any book of this kind involves the meeting of many minds, directly or indirectly, and its breadth of interest is the result of these many influences. I am well aware of many debts, some of them to persons whom I have never met and to others whose lives have at various times touched mine very closely. The invitation to edit *The Treasury* came as my family was beginning a vacation visit in Cambridge, Mass., in the interesting and motivating, comfortable and relaxing atmosphere of the residence of Dean and Mrs. Douglas Horton of the Harvard Divinity School. The welcome respite from regular duties coupled with their delightful hospitality afforded the opportunity of giving the book its initial organization, and the libraries of the Harvard Yard of securing much of its contents. The kindness of Charles L. Wallis, editor of *Pulpit Preaching* and author of many helpful books, in granting opportunities and encouragement, paved the way for the building up of my files of material, from which these pages were drawn. One owes a tremendous debt to his teachers; in my case they were Earl F. Zeigler, editor of *Today;* Mrs. Evelyn C. King, formerly of the Presbyterian College of Christian Education; John Frederick Lyons, James W. Clarke,

Floyd V. Filson, Robert Worth Frank, G. Ernest Wright, Joseph Haroutunian, William H. Hudnut, Marshal Scott, and the late Jesse Halsey all of McCormick Seminary, Chicago, whose instruction opened to me the wide vistas of Christianity and life; each in some specific way pointed out to me ways of illustrating its truths and teachings.

One is always influenced by his colleagues, and I am indebted to them for many of the items in *The Treasury* which came from their lips as we sat together in the various meetings of the Black Hills Presbytery; the Black Hills Baptist Association; the Dakota Conference of the Methodist Church; the Northern Idaho Presbytery; the Washington-North Idaho Congregational Christian Conference and the Lewiston Ministerial Association.

Similar debts are due members of the churches I have served: Central Presbyterian, Denver, Colorado; First Presbyterian, Amarillo, Texas; Austin Presbyterian, Chicago; The United Churches (Baptist, Presbyterian, Methodist), Hot Springs, South Dakota; and the Congregational Presbyterian (Federated), Lewiston, Idaho.

I have not found the fitting quotation which expresses my debt to Dr. Frank Mead and Donald T. Kauffman of the Fleming H. Revell Company whose skillful and friendly direction brought *The Treasury* into being. To them I sincerely say, "Thank you."

E. Paul Hovey

CONTENTS

Alphabetically arranged by subject

(ITEMS ARE LISTED BY PAGE NUMBER)

THE TREASURY OF
Inspirational Anecdotes, Quotations and Illustrations

ABILITY

1

The ablest men in all the walks of modern life are men of faith. Most of them have much more faith than they themselves realize.—Bruce Barton

2

Among men of outstanding ability and accomplishment are many who possess a significant characteristic. They have a measuring rod, so to speak, by which they test values. They do not work to passing purposes, but in terms which will continue their influence.

This is what makes us revere distinguished men. No one today can seriously study the life of Abraham Lincoln without being—in one way or another—emancipated. Such men are not confined in their thinking by threescore and ten years. They simply do the best that is in them and then leave it to time to determine its value. —J. C. Penney

3

I have never doubted that God created man for great purposes nor that man has the potentiality within himself to achieve God's goal for him. —Preston Bradley

4

Man's ability is derived from God and does not have to be acquired, as is commonly thought, but becomes apparent as consciousness is illumined by the divine light of Christ.—James Harry McReynolds

5

The nation is beset with difficulties and confusions. Many of us have doubt and grave concern for the future. But no one who reviews the past and realizes the vast strength of our people can doubt that this, like a score of similar experiences in our history, is a passing trial. From this knowledge must come the courage and wisdom to improve and strengthen us for the future.

We must not be misled by the claim that the source of all wisdom is in the Government. Wisdom is born out of experience, and most of all out of precisely such experiences as are brought to us by the darkest moments. It is in the meeting of such moments that are born new insights, new sympathies, new powers, new skills.

Such conflicts as we are in the midst of today cannot be won by any single stroke, by any one strategy sprung from the mind of any single genius. Rather must we pin our faith upon the inventiveness, the resourcefulness, the initiative of every one of us. That cannot fail us if we keep faith in ourselves and our future, and in the constant growth of our intelligence and ability to cooperate with one another. . . . The way to greatness is the path of self-reliance, independence and steadfastness in time of trial and stress.—Herbert Hoover

6

It is not given to everyone to be a great or even an outstanding Christian. But many more could be if they would make the effort. The tragedy is that so

19

few individuals exert themselves to be even reasonably good Christians. No one grows up automatically to be a strong Christian, let alone a great Christian. No one can inherit or drift casually into greatness in Christ's kingdom. . . . The source of spiritual greatness lies in the Word of God. For there the living God speaks to us. Through the Word the Holy Spirit nourishes a growing faith. A great Christian may arise.

ACHIEVEMENT

7

When the great doctor-missionary, Albert Schweitzer, announced at the age of thirty his decision to study medicine and enter the African mission field, his dismayed family and friends protested strongly. He was already renowned throughout Europe as a musician, philosopher, and theologian. It was almost beyond belief that such a man, established in a distinguished career and in the late days of his youth, should enter medical school as a freshman, and then bury himself in the jungle.

But Albert Schweitzer replied, "I can do it—I must do it." Today the world recognizes him as one of its greatest men.

Dr. Schweitzer has given a message to all who would take a definite stand for the betterment of humanity. He says: "Anyone who proposes to do good must not expect people to roll stones out of his way, but must accept his lot calmly if they even roll a few more upon it."—Jack Kytle

8

When nothing else seems to help, I go and look at a stonecutter hammering away at his rock, perhaps a hundred times without a crack showing in it. Yet at the hundred-and-first blow the rock will split in two, and I know that

it was not only that blow which split it, but all that had gone before.—Jacob A. Riis

9

The mode by which the inevitable comes to pass is effort.—Justice Oliver Wendell Holmes

10

All that a comedian has to show for his years of work and aggravation is the echo of forgotten laughter.—Fred Allen

11

The greatest argument for Christianity is not in its appeal to the reason. It is the simple fact that it works.—Stuart Nye Hutchison

12

Dean Sperry of Harvard . . . tells the story of the president of the Blue Funnel Line of steamships. . . . Called as a young man to the presidency, he said in the course of his address of acceptance, "I hope to run this line in a way acceptable to my directors and stockholders, to my passengers, to my employees, and to my God." At this one of the directors was heard to remark that if he pleased the first four, they would not trouble about the last. In twenty years the line had grown in every branch, and the president, now in middle life, had become one of the significant personalities of his city. A banquet was tendered him at which the toastmaster recalled his words of acceptance. "Perhaps," said he, "you would be willing to tell us now what you meant by running the line acceptably to God." "Gladly," said the president. "I know that this is a moral world. Some day I must give an account of myself. God will say to me, 'Who are you?' And for answer I want to have run the line in such a way that I can look at Him confidently and make the simple answer, 'I have been the president of the Blue Funnel Line!' "—Douglas Horton, *The Art of Living Today*

13

Nothing will ever be attempted if all possible objections must be first overcome.—Samuel Johnson, *Rasselas*

14

When "Boss" Kettering, for years vice president of General Motors and director of their research laboratories, was just beginning his inventive career in Ashland, Ohio, he worked out a central battery telephone exchange which did away with the nuisance of cranking the phone in rural communities. It seemed like a huge success but at one point it was in danger of being scrapped because for about two hours every afternoon the whole thing went dead. Kettering worked frantically for several weeks to locate the trouble. He finally discovered that out on one of the farms a certain grandfather had the habit of laying his spectacles on top of the telephone box every afternoon while he took a nap, thus short-circuiting the system.

In a measure that is a picture of the world into which the graduates of today are moving. A world of unbelievable wonders—wonders in atomic science, medicine, industrial management and political organization, but so many short circuits because some oldsters in my generation and those ahead of us have gone to sleep and laid down our aids to living at the wrong places. A large part of your opportunity in the years that lie ahead is to discover the cause of those short circuits, and to clear the lines of communication make the world today a better world tomorrow.—W. Ralph Ward, Jr., *Vital Speeches*

15

A man who has tried to play Mozart and failed, through that vain effort comes into position better to understand the man who tried to paint the Sistine Madonna, and did.—Gerald W. Johnson, *A Little Night-Music*

16

An eighteen-year-old Canadian girl, Barbara Ann Scott, won the skating championship in the winter Olympics. Many an eighteen-year-old must have read the story of her triumph and envied the acclaim she would receive. . . . But I wonder how many skipped over one important line in the newspaper account. Barbara estimated that in preparation for this event, she had spent 20,000 hours in practice. She was already the greatest skater in Canada but she went on and spent 20,000 hours in preparation for this one event! Small wonder she won! She was talented but she added to her talent the essential ingredient of hard work and continual practice.

Fritz Kreisler said that even after he had reached world fame he still spent eight hours a day in practice. He said, "If I neglect my practice for a day I can tell the difference. If I neglect it for a week my wife can notice the difference; but if I were to neglect it for a month my audiences could tell the difference."

Whether in the field of skating, playing a violin, or in prayer, one great truth stands out. Nothing great was ever achieved without effort and perseverance.

Someone has said that life is like having to play the violin before an audience and having to *learn* to play it as you go on the stage. He was suggesting that we are *on* the stage, in full view, before we acquire the techniques for living. How true!—Cecil G. Osborne

17

Paradox

The person who
Would like to make

His dreams come true
Must stay awake!
—Richard Wheeler, *Rotarian*

18

If your determination is fixed, I do not counsel you to despair. Few things are impossible to diligence and skill. . . . Great works are performed, not by strength, but perseverance.—Samuel Johnson

19

Most of us live too near the surface of our abilities, dreading to call upon our deeper resources. It is as if a strong man were to do his work with only one finger.—John Charles Wynn, *How Christian Parents Face Family Problems*

20

To *believe* in sensible ideas is easy, but to *implement* them involves sacrifice. To allocate time, money, effort, or concentration for one purpose diminishes their availability for other purposes. To accomplish something, as distinct from being in favor of it, confronts us with losses as well as returns, pains as well as gains. No wonder we are inclined to speak up for many good ideas, only to fail to come to terms either with thinking them through or carrying them out.—Dorothy Fosdick, *Common Sense and World Affairs*

21

I have sometimes said of the people of my own denomination that in our support of colleges for Negroes we continually *act* better than we *are,* and in acting better than we are we tend somewhat to *become* better than we *were.* Put it this way. Left to ourselves, as individuals and as local congregations, we should not have either the grace or the staying power to keep patiently working at this responsibility of opening doors of equal opportunity to these fellow Americans. . . . If the church is to penetrate the community with the redemptive power of the gospel it must recognize that there is a wider community into which local congregations cannot go alone. One route of access to this larger culture is through Christian institutions.—Truman B. Douglass

22

I cannot read the story of the anointing of Christ in the home of Simon without recalling the time my brother came home from Sunday school reciting the memory verse of that lesson. In his childish speech the verse became, "She 'half' done what she could." This incident, however, has reinforced the message of that story for me. In praising the woman, Jesus revealed that many of the others had only half done their work.

How much half-done work exists in this world! How many seem to have heard one half of Jesus' command: "Thou shalt love the Lord thy God with all thy heart, and with all thy soul, and with all thy mind, and with all thy strength. . . . Thou shalt love thy neighbor as thyself," and proceeded to love God or neighbor but not both. . . . Our job is only half done when we learn of the needs of people in other lands and of the needs of our nearer neighbors. Our job is only half done when we do it because we know it is the right thing to do. Our task becomes fully done when we see in our fellow man his need of God and of us, and when we minister unto those needs because we love God *and* our neighbor.—E. Paul Hovey, *The Westminster Adult Bible Class*

ACTION

23

You cannot build a reputation on things you are going to do.

24

There is an old military maxim: "If you don't know what to do, do something." It is a good rule, because in a time of danger, doing something is almost always better than doing nothing.

25

It is more important to know where you are going than to get there quickly. Do not mistake activity for achievement.—Mabel Newcomber

26

Every man feels instinctively that all the beautiful sentiments in the world weigh less than a single lovely action.—James Russell Lowell

27

From Australia a few years ago came amazing stories of a kindly nurse who was doing wonderful things to enable children who had been crippled with infantile paralysis to walk. The name of Sister Elizabeth Kenny became known all around the world. Sister Kenny visited the United States and gave her treatments in several large hospitals. To one who spoke to her admiringly, one day Sister Kenny said quietly, "I'm no genius. I'm just a very ordinary person who still remembers and puts into action the stories my mother told me from the Bible." Sister Kenny had learned about Jesus, and had come to desire above everything else to live as He lived, and to love as He loved. Friends of Jesus can always be identified by the fact that they are interested in the happiness, health, spiritual well-being of all. They are like Jesus in spirit and purpose.

28

During the war the brave people of the Danish underground had a motto: "Do it well, and do it now." What better motto could we have as Christians? Christian happiness lies not in merely knowing what Christ would want us to do, but in actually doing it!

29

In the old China the religions never demanded much from the laity—never much in time, talent, or money. The layman faced no challenge to win others to his faith, or educate them to its truer meanings. Moral and social reform, with the laymen bearing a major responsibility to create new ways of life, were almost unknown. . . . But the Christian church comes with its call to new life, a more abundant life for all. Not only is this a gift of God, but it is a creation of society, inspired by the spirit and power of Christ. If it comes to pass, all Christians, layman and pastor alike, must sacrifice for its coming.—F. Olin Stockwell

30

The true friends of Christ are active. "Ye are my friends if ye do . . . my commandments." Christ did not save us to sit down. As one has said: "The symbol of Christianity is not a rocking chair, but a cross." A small boy in church with his parents listened to the minister describe his visit to a poor home. The minister pictured the bare rooms, the ragged clothing, the empty dishes on the table, the pale, hungry children. When he had finished his story, he announced the closing hymn. But the little boy, with tears in his eyes, cried out to his father, "But, Daddy, aren't we going to *do* anything about it?"

31

Suppose the next time the good Samaritan went down the road to Jericho he found another man robbed and beaten and lying half-dead by the roadside. Suppose he became a frequent traveler on that dangerous road and on each of his travels he stopped to minister to other victims of assault. Would not something be lacking in his mercy if he did not inquire about highway patrols? Would not his feeling against such injustice lead him to join with other Samaritans in instigating proper police protection for the road?—William Miller

32

There is no place of active life on which thought is negligible, except that of the merest automatic execution of orders; and . . . no species of thinking which can be quite without effect upon action.—T. S. Eliot

ADVERTISING

33

Bruce Barton once made a great speech pointing out how Joseph grew to be a foremost figure in ancient Egypt, only to die, and how Exodus reports "there arose in Egypt a new king who knew not Joseph." This story led Bruce Barton to a conclusion: "A good product, a good service, a good organization, a good individual, or a good idea must be sold all the time. Because every day Joseph dies and there arise new 'kings which know not Joseph.' "—Kenneth McFarland, *Rotarian*

34

The function of advertising is to seduce people, to make them dissatisfied with their standard of living, to make them want more and to make them work for it. Does not everybody want more? Not really. The desire for a high standard of living is a relatively modern, largely Western, and until recently, mostly urban desire. Almost all human societies, traditionalist and habit-ridden as they have been, tend to resist change. The "social function" of advertising is to stimulate wants, to make people work harder and earn more. In that sense, advertising, and its helpmate the instalment plan, are

the two most fearsome social inventions of man since the discovery of gunpowder.

Yet, this function—to stimulate dissatisfaction—is relatively recent, for the goods that people want—the automobile, the washing machine, the radio, television, electric iron, electric toaster, refrigerator, vacuum cleaner, dishwasher—are all products of the last forty years or less. All this is part of the transformation, of the Western world at least, to a high-consumption society.—Daniel Bell, "The Impact of Advertising," *The New Leader*

35

The American citizen lives in a state of siege from dawn to bedtime. Nearly everything he sees, hears, touches, tastes and smells is an attempt to sell him something. . . . To break through his protective shell, the advertisers must continuously shock, tease, tickle or irritate him, or wear him down by the drip-drip-drip of Chinese water-torture methods of endless repetition. Advertising is the handwriting on the wall, the sign in the sky, the bush that burns regularly every night.—*Fortune*

36

Advertising nourishes the consuming power of man . . . sets up the goal of a better home, better clothing, better food for himself and his family. It spurs individual exertion and greater production. It brings together in fertile union those things which otherwise would not have met.—Winston Churchill

37

The trade of advertising is now so near to perfection that it is not easy to propose any improvement. But as every art ought to be exercised in due subordination to the public good, I cannot but suppose it as a moral question to those masters of the public ear, whether they do not sometimes play too wantonly with our passions?—Samuel Johnson

38

"Unforgettable Memories," is the title of a most excellent folder advertising life insurance. As the title indicates, it depicts the most memorable events in the life of an American—a girl, of course. It is written in the very best literary style and illustrated with appealing photographs showing a little girl eating a strawberry soda, graduating from college, throwing her bridal bouquet from a stairway, etc. Not a single one of the "unforgettable memories," however, have to do with church school or the worship in God's house. The ad writer truly reflects our time and nation. The church is a side issue in the lives of the vast majority of the American people. To many, the church and its message are matters of almost complete indifference. A few of our citizens hate the church, but the majority are just indifferent.

The great danger the church faces today is the fact that it is ignored, as if it were an institution that had outlived its usefulness, whose "remains" historians and philosophers are now busy gathering in proper museums, that is, inside the covers of their dry and voluminous works, which they hope will be read by scholars a thousand years hence.

39

Let the seller be aggressive, according to the ethics of our business tradition, and let the buyer beware. Let him beware also lest he take everything he reads in his big-circulation newspapers or magazines as guileless truth, for the goods merchant and the printer are organically one. Much true and helpful material appears in our press, but that which might embarrass an influential seller is doctored or deleted. When there are daring exceptions to this rule, the effect is almost absurd. I recall one issue of a magazine whose dignified editorial page carried a persuasive essay on our national need for individual and group self-restraint, while in all the colors available to the modern printshop a hundred advertising pages bound between the same covers shouted self-indulgence unlimited.

It is on this issue of restraint, I think, that the philosophies of religion and of modern American commerce become irreconcilable. . . . Advertising men, bellwethers of the consumption frenzy, grow ever more hysterical in their efforts to goad, tease, scare, bully, wheedle, entice or argue us into slopping up mayonnaise, face cream, beer, prunes, peanut butter . . . in ever greater quantity, disregarding need. . . . It is most deadly effective. It contributes more than any other single factor . . . toward making us the nation of nervous, overpressured, apprehensive near-neurotics that we are. . . . Religion, as it has filtered down to us, speaks a great deal about forbearance and restraint, self-deprivation and self-sacrifice, and hardly at all of unlimited multiplication of material wants, or of their prompt gratification. . . . We are rapidly advertising ourselves out of the spiritual treasures of our culture. We have all but sold our heritage for a mess of plumbing. Help us rediscover the rewards of voluntarily going without!—Jerome Ellison, *Report to the Creator*

40

Advertising is no longer a mere announcement of goods or services for sale. It has adopted the ways of education and the arts and accepted the obligations of democratic economy.

The evidence of this is everywhere: In the tools, utilities, textiles and appliances we use; in our automobiles, our entertainment, medicines, books and cosmetics—everything, in short, that makes "the American standard of living" not only a goal achieved but a promise of the same abundance to all men.—*Los Angeles Examiner*

41

A hundred years ago, Ralph Waldo Emerson wrote, "If a man has good corn, or wood, or boards, or pigs to sell, or can make better chairs or knives, crucibles or church organs than anybody else, you will find a broad, hard-beaten road to his house, though it be in the woods."

That's the origin of the much more familiar "If you build a better mousetrap" proverb that has long been cited to prove that action is more important than advertising. But the adapter of Emerson's words forgot the sentence just before that quoted above: "I trust a good deal to common fame, as we all must." For "common fame" read "advertising" and you will see that the better mousetrap theory doesn't hold much water. Nobody's going into the woods after mousetraps unless he knows why he's going.

That's the essential service of advertising—to tell which is the better mousetrap. Advertising tells you which mousetrap—whether it be an automobile or a can opener—has the best construction, the most efficient operation and the best adaptability to your needs and pocketbook. Only when you know that are you going to head for the woods—if you have to.

All the advertising in the world isn't going to sell an inferior product, and there's a long list of failures to prove it. But good products don't sell if people don't know about them, and there's almost as long a list of failures to prove that, too.

Advertising is probably the most insistent profession there is. There's hardly an hour of the day when our eyes or ears don't encounter some aspect of advertising—in newspapers, in magazines, in store windows. You can't get away from it.

And it's a good thing you can't. Ad-

vertising gives you an essential service . . . advertising plays a pretty important role in your life. In short, advertising has helped you to buy wisely, because advertising has given you essential information about the quality, the prices and the advantages of the things you need.—*Daily Idahonian*

ALONE

42

Everyone should try to find a spot to be alone, in order to have a proper opportunity to concentrate and to think. We have too little space and too little time, and therefore the tension on our nerves becomes too great.—Queen Juliana of the Netherlands

43

We have lost the habit of thinking quietly, of trying to know ourselves and our friends, and the world around us, and the God who is above and within us. We are looking in the wrong places for happiness. We are so exclusively occupied with material things and with their accumulation that the higher values are crowded out.—Robert J. McCracken

44

In these days the practice of withdrawing from the presence of men and from the ordinary activities . . . for the purpose of going alone with God and with His truth, is absolutely necessary.—John R. Mott

45

Admiral Byrd lived by himself for five months in a small shack in the Antarctic zone. Blizzards blew all around his hut, and the temperature was sometimes as cold as eighty-two degrees below zero.

Then he was terrified by a sudden discovery: carbon dioxide was escaping from his stove. Try as hard as he could,

Byrd was unable to fix it; when he attempted to make a repair, he would be almost overcome by the fumes. He could not turn off the stove for fear he would freeze. The nearest help, which was 123 miles away, could not reach him for months. He lost his ability to eat or to sleep, and he was so weak that he stayed in bed.

Admiral Byrd was forced to seek a power that was higher than his own. He reached out with his prayers and experienced the loving touch of the presence of God. In his diary he wrote, "I am not alone." Admiral Byrd knew that One who loved him deeply was with him all the time, bringing him an experience of peace which would lead him to face the future with true spiritual strength.

46

I find it wholesome to be alone the greater part of the time. . . . I love to be alone. . . . A man thinking or working is always alone, let him be where he will.—Henry David Thoreau

47

Shakespeare, Leonardo da Vinci, Benjamin Franklin, and Lincoln never saw a movie, heard a radio or looked at TV. They had "loneliness" and knew what to do with it. They were not afraid of being lonely because they knew that was when the creative mood in them would work.—Carl Sandburg

48

I can amuse my solitude by the renovation of the knowledge which begins to fade from my memory, and by recollection of the incidents of my past life.—Samuel Johnson

49

The world . . . has formed a habit of thinking in groups . . . masses; and civilization is breaking down under the burden of that error. . . . Birth and death are solitary, thought and growth

are solitary; every final reality of man's life is his alone . . . as soon as he ceases to be alone, he moves away from realities.—Charles Morgan, *The Fountain*

50

One of the important words for life is "alone." Yet instead of welcoming it we run from it in fear. Jesus was able to give others life because His own spiritual energy was always at the brim and overflowing from long periods of aloneness . . . "in the morning, long before daylight, he got up and left the house and went off to a lonely spot, and prayed there."—Rae Noel

AMBITION

51

The child without ambition is like a watch with a broken spring.—Ralph W. Sockman

52

Frances Willard was great. Babies have been named for her, and her statue stands in the Capitol at Washington. When she was only eighteen, Frances Willard made this resolution: "I will spend my coming years in being somebody and in doing something for somebody." Years later, when her enemies were criticizing her mercilessly, she said: "I have been called ambitious, and so I am, if to have had from childhood the sense of being born for a great purpose is an element of ambition. For I never knew what it was not to aspire, not to believe myself capable of heroism. I have always wanted to react upon the world about me to the utmost ounce of my power, to be widely known, loved and believed in. Every life has its master passion; this has been mine. I did not wish to climb by [the overthrow of others], and I laid no schemes to undermine them, but I wanted to be my very utmost. I felt that a woman owed it to all other women to live as bravely and as helpfully and grandly as she could, and to let the world know it."

53

Was it worth it? The struggle, the labor, the constant rush of affairs, the sacrifice of so many things that make life easy, or pleasant—for what? A people's good! That, he could not disguise from himself, was rather the direction than the cause of his efforts. Ambition was the motive force, and he was powerless to resist it.—Winston Churchill, *Savrola*

54

Throw away all ambition beyond that of doing the day's work well.—Sir William Osler

55

The way people feel about ambition is plain in the way they say: "He's a go-getter"; "I'm a go-getter"; in a tone of respect, pride, self-satisfaction. Obviously ambition is a greatly admired expression of energy. That's why the more there is of it the more it needs to be examined. Every doctor's and psychiatrist's office is crowded with people who are sick because they are, as Shakespeare said, "Chok'd with ambition of the meaner sort." Or, to see it from another angle, because they are self-frustrated by the too limited goals described by Pearl S. Buck, "A winged ambition limited to the attainable never reaches its height." And all ambition centered in *self* is like that. Seeking self-security and self-prestige, it binds itself more and more tightly by conformity to a social status, an organization, the State:

I had Ambition, by which sin
  The angels fell;
I climbed and, step by step, O Lord,
  Ascended into Hell. (William Henry
    Davies)
          —Rae Noel, *Classmate*

56

All ambitions are lawful except those which climb upward on the miseries or credulities of mankind.—Joseph Conrad

57

Shakespeare's Macbeth is a young man going places. He is already a success . . . and greedy of greater success. Any man going ahead is in danger, if he has strong ambition without strong principles. . . . Macbeth is evil, not in ambition, but in the willingness to pay too great a price. He does not know how to put first things first.—Ernest Marshall Howse, *Spiritual Values in Shakespeare*

AMERICA

58

Free to speak, write and vote for my rights; free to compete with everyone, protected by both public sentiment and law which I help to make; with education free and religion unfettered; freedom's soil beneath me, freedom's government over me, and the sustaining brotherhood of freedom around me—I love America.—Paul Patton Faris

59

U. S. means United States, not Uniform States. We have in-groups, out-groups, marginal men; ethnic, class, linguistic, regional variations; an incredibly divine culture. Look closely, and you can find in America every conceivable type of man—and some inconceivable ones . . . the chief characteristic of the American pattern is a lack of pattern.—Marshall Fishwick, *Saturday Review*

60

Nothing annoys me so much as all this talk that Americans are money grubbers, and all they care about is money. Of course we work hard. We are industrious. We want our children to have a good education. But this idea of our not having any interest in spiritual things is wrong. This is just what America stands for: good will and freedom and justice.—Harold R. Medina, "A Look at America," *Vital Speeches*

61

We are on the threshold of another great, decisive era. History's headlong course has brought us, I devoutly believe, to the threshold of a new America—to the America of the great ideals and noble visions which are the stuff our future must be made of.

I mean a new America where poverty is abolished and our abundance is used to enrich the lives of every family.

I mean a new America where freedom is made real for all without regard to race or belief or economic condition.

I mean a new America which everlastingly attacks the ancient idea that men can solve their differences by killing each other.

These are the things I believe in and will work for with every resource I possess.—Adlai E. Stevenson

62

Before all else we seek, upon our common labor as a nation, the blessings of Almighty God. And the hopes in our hearts fashion the deepest prayers of our whole people.

May we pursue the right—without self-righteousness.

May we know unity—without conformity.

May we grow in strength—without pride in self.

May we, in our dealings with all peoples of the earth, ever speak truth and serve justice. . . .

May the light of freedom, coming to all darkened lands, flame brightly—until at last the darkness is no more.

May the turbulence of our age yield to a true time of peace, when men and nations shall share a life that honors the dignity of each, the brotherhood of all.—Dwight D. Eisenhower, Second Inaugural Address

63

We in the United States are amazingly rich in the elements from which to weave a culture; we have the best of man's past on which to draw, brought to us by our native folk from all parts of the world. In binding these elements into a national fabric of beauty and strength, let us keep the original fibers so intact that the fineness of each will show in the completed handiwork.—Franklin D. Roosevelt

64

The American pioneer . . . faced the forest and the future with three powerful weapons in his hands: he carried an axe, a gun, and a Book.

With the axe he attacked the forests, hewed logs for his house, his school, and his church. With the gun he hunted game for his table and animal pelts for a livelihood, and protected himself against the predatory forces of the wilderness. The Book was the center of his personal devotions, the inspiration of his institutions and the textbook of his education.—Edward L. R. Elson, *America's Spiritual Recovery*

65

American history may be regarded as shaped by the frontier; a new frontier in every generation, steadily receding westward. It may equally be regarded as shaped by immigration; a new wave from the eastward in each generation. As the Atlantic frontier, the Appalachian frontier, the prairie frontier and the plains frontier were all different, yet in vital elements the same, so the British waves of immigration, the German wave, the Irish wave, the Italian and Slav waves, all differed in salient respects, yet in other ways had an identical impact. Each brought to the New World its special traditions, aptitudes and gifts, which were all transmuted into something fresh and peculiarly American.—Allan Nevins, "Epic of Liberty Island," *The New York Times Magazine*

66

America does not consist of groups. A man who thinks of himself as belonging to a particular national group in America has not yet become an American.—Woodrow Wilson

67

India is an old nation but a young republic. We, in comparison, are a young nation but an old republic.

This truth is pointed up in the story of a U. S. tourist who visited an Indian village. "Have you ever heard of America?" he asked an old peasant.

The Indian scratched his head. "America?" he replied. "Oh, I guess you mean the country Columbus found when he was looking for India."— *Senior Scholastic*

68

Americans have a great heritage of religious faith closely allied with their patriotic history. The Mayflower Compact, drawn up before the Pilgrims had firmly established themselves on these shores, begins, "In the Name of God." The Constitution of the United States, while providing for the separation of Church and State, fully guarantees to every citizen the right to exercise that religious faith which is most meaningful to him.

Our leaders have often looked to the Bible as the source of divine guidance for the life of the nation, as well as their personal lives. The "salt" that has preserved our nation and given her progress and glory is from the Bible. The "light" that has shone to mark a pathway to leadership among the nations of the world is from the Bible.

We recall the profound religious awareness of our great presidents and national leaders; for example, Washington on his knees at Valley Forge, and Lincoln deeply concerned that the nation should be "on God's side."

69

Nobody in this world is more secure than a man in a penitentiary. He is fed, clothed and housed. But he is not free to go and come as he pleases. He is watched, guarded and disciplined. There are millions of people in other lands who have that same kind of security. But we Americans have always believed that the only real security lies in liberty and opportunity.—Harvey S. Firestone, Jr.

70

Americans hold a political philosophy which maintains that the state is the possession of its citizens. The state is set up by the people as the organization through which they can best work for the good of all. We believe that the government is a convenient tool for doing collectively what we cannot do individually. This is the one and only proper function of the government. The state should protect us against invasion, for that must be a collective effort, but it must not prescribe our beliefs, for that is a personal responsibility.

This is the political philosophy written into the Bill of Rights. The Bill of Rights is the pillar supporting this philosophy in America. It protects us from an oppressive government not so much by its specific provisions, but by its act of keeping a proper concept of government uppermost in the minds of Americans.—Roy P. Hovey

71

With the unprecedented material advantages of today, an attitude of complacency seems to have permeated the national mind to an almost unbelievable extent. There is a trend of softness toward wrongdoing which can cause irreparable harm. We are being stifled by technicalities and by the throwing of roadblocks in the pathway of our traditional methods of justice.

We need to dedicate ourselves anew to the perpetuation of our American heritage, and to a nationwide recognition campaign to bring about a renewed appreciation of this heart-stirring heritage. It is disheartening that more young people appear to know the words of popular "soap-jingles" than the meaningful words of "The Starspangled Banner." It is time for all of us to reacquaint ourselves with our historical treasures and the moral values which inspired our forefathers to lead our country to the pinnacle of world leadership. . . .

We must pass on to our young people the greatness that is America's. We must remind all our citizens of the wealth of our Nation's moral and spiritual treasures. By reflecting upon the glories of our past, we can advance together to' even greater heights of achievement in the future. We can eradicate the blighting slums of juvenile crime and repel, by our own example of united strength, the threats of subversive destruction. In moral and spiritual issues, there can be no neutrality. —J. Edgar Hoover, *Vital Speeches*

72

America is a symbol—a generous symbol, which we, as a Nation, translate into a way of life, of liberty and the pursuit of happiness. This eventually, I believe, will be attained for all by the collective effort of mankind seeking freedom from the nameless, and unexplainable myriad of human fears— attained by first dissolving, through understanding, the fear of man for man. That is what America means to me.—Major Thomas A. Palmer

73

An American's day begins when he gets out of bed in his pajamas, *a gar-*

ment of East Indian origin; drinks his breakfast coffee, *grown on an Abyssinian plant first discovered by the Arabs;* places upon his head a molded piece of felt, *invented by the nomads of eastern Asia;* and, if it looks like rain, puts on outer shoes of rubber, *discovered by the ancient Mexicans;* and takes his umbrella, *invented in India.* He then sprints for his train, *an English invention.* At the station he pauses to buy a newspaper with coins, *invented in ancient Lydia.* Once on board he settles back to read the news imprinted in characters, *invented by the ancient Semites;* by a process *invented in Germany;* upon a material *invented in China.* As he scans the latest editorial pointing out the dangers of accepting foreign ideas, he thanks a God *he got from the Hebrews*—using a language of *Indo-European origin*—that he is "ONE HUNDRED PER CENT AMERICAN."

ANGER

74

Medicine has discovered that anger can do as much damage to the body as bacteria, the loss of a limb and loss of a loved one may be equally traumatic, and that we sometimes eat too much because we do not get on well with others. Bacteria, shattered limbs, and diet are the concern of medicine. But anger, sorrow, and loneliness are plainly in the sphere of religion.—J. Carter Swaim, *Body, Soul and Spirit*

75

As a boy, the gifted Negro tenor Roland Hayes heard an old Negro minister preach a sermon on Christ before Pilate. The preacher contrasted two kinds of power confronting each other. Pilate, irked by the silence of Jesus, cried, "Why don't you answer me? Don't you know I have power?" The illiterate old preacher went on to say, "No matter how angry the crowd got, He never said a mumberlin' word, not a word." Years later, at the peak of fame with his golden voice, Roland Hayes stood before a Nazi audience in Berlin's Beethoven Hall. The audience was hostile, ugly, scornful of a Negro daring to sing at the center of Aryan culture. He was greeted with a chorus of Nazi hisses, growing louder and more ominous; for ten minutes Hayes stood there in silence at the piano, resentment swelling up in him like an irresistible tide. And then he remembered the sermon of long ago—"He never said a mumberlin' word, not a word." He shouted back no words born in anger; he kept his head, for he knew that the ultimate power was on his side, not theirs. He stood there and prayed, silently, and the quiet dignity of his courage conquered the savage spirits in his audience, and in hushed pianissimo he began to sing a song of Schubert's. He won, without so much as "a mumberlin' word."

"He that is slow to anger is better than the mighty, and he that ruleth his spirit than he that taketh a city."—J. Wallace Hamilton, *Ride the Wild Horses!*

76
Anger is, usually, a label of a lack. We have a shortcoming. Someone says or does something and our shortcoming is revealed. We flame into hot anger. If we were strong and confident; if we were the truly superior beings we want others to think we are, we would not become angry.

Anger, in addition to proving our weakness, makes us perform ridiculous or harmful acts. We close our eyes and open our mouths. This is bad enough when we sleep because it makes us snore. But when we are awake, such an action is certain to make us appear foolish. Anger may be an excuse. It is seldom a reason.—Fred Dodge

77
An angry man opens his mouth and shuts his eyes.—Cato

78
Reckon the days in which you have not been angry. I used to be angry every day; now every other day; then every third and fourth day; and if you miss it so long as thirty days, offer a sacrifice of thanksgiving to God.—Epictetus

ANTAGONISM

79
People are not antagonistic to religion. They just don't know. But they'd like to know.—*Newsweek*

80
Your temper is the only thing that doesn't get better with use.

81
The fact that Pashhur, the priest and chief officer of the temple, both struck Jeremiah and confined him overnight in the stocks signifies that opposition to the prophet had at last lost patience and broken out into overt opposition. As in a drama, certain well-defined developments of the antagonistic forces may be observed: first the entrenched powers are indifferent to the challenger; then they are restively tolerant; then at some moment entirely unforeseen, and frequently around some incident otherwise of no great importance, the mounting irritation and uneasy concern of the challenged interests declares its hand through some passionate and ill-considered act, thus dignifying and defining the ultimate symbolic significance of the protagonist; thereafter these contending forces clash as principles, and demand a reconciliation and catharsis at a higher, and a deeper, level than either, taken by itself, fore-

sees. Jeremiah now has thrust upon him all the reflex power of these national and religious policies catapulting to a fall. And Pashhur—a name obscure and otherwise unknown—acquires a place in history, because he materializes, and henceforth typifies, the animus of the official orthodoxy of the temple against the word of God proclaimed by Yahweh's prophet.—Stanley Romaine Hopper

82

Why would we kill off a good watch dog just because he could not fly?—Frank Mar

83

How can you be boss and still be one of the boys? When we British were top dogs, we were represented by a ruling class that was arrogantly self-sufficient, not caring . . . whether they were liked or not. But the American, when he finds out that he is not liked just because he is top dog, is shocked, bewildered, saddened and occasionally very angry.—J. B. Priestley

84

No one ever won an argument that lost a friend.

APPRECIATION

85

In the moment of appreciation we live again the moment when the Creator saw and held the hidden likeness.—J. Bronowski, "Science and Human Values," *The Nation*

86

No man has really lived until he has looked into the heart of Nature and learned to appreciate the magnificent world on which he has been created. —Frank S. Smythe

87

We must have a weak spot or two in a character before we can love it much. People that do not laugh or cry, or take more of anything than is good for them, or use anything but dictionary words are admirable subjects for biographies. But we don't always care most for those flat-pattern flowers that press best in the herbarium.—Oliver Wendell Holmes

ASPIRATION

88

Mountain climbing has always fascinated me. As a small boy I looked up at the peaks . . . and longed for the day when I would grow up and could climb to their very summits. . . . The impulse to climb is always preceded by the sight of the mountain itself. A great mountain has a hypnotic message which it conveys to the one who gazes with admiration at its glory and majesty. The opportunities that are in the range of our immediate vision are great enough to inspire all our energy, talents and will. . . . My second observation is that there are no short cuts. We cannot skip up a mountain. It is a step by step process. . . . An old motto remains as I think of the patient, persistent climbing that is necessary—"Not at the top but climbing." Another observation is that there are always higher mountains. This is not a discouragement but a challenge. The discouraging thing would be to have reached the summit of the highest mountain with none higher to climb. Dr. Douglas Horton gave a pungent answer to the question, "Why do men climb mountains?" After telling why they do not climb them, he said, "There is no logical answer to the question, for the reason is deeper than logic. It is the way God made us—He made us to aspire."—Archie H. Hook

89

Take from the people of our country the source of initiative and the opportunity to aspire and to struggle in order that that aspiration may become a reality, and though you couch your action in any sympathetic terms, it will fail of its purpose and be the undoing of the vital forces that go to make up a virile people.—Samuel Gompers

ATOM

90

Two thousand years ago an event fully as epoch-making as the birth of the atomic bomb occurred, when Christ was born and pronounced the principles of what was to become Christianity.

What Jesus had to pronounce was that the world could be saved only by love. Today the world has once again been shaken to its foundations—this time by the birth of the atomic bomb. What the atomic bomb means to humanity is that the world can be saved only by love.

Because human beings fear love—so recently have we emerged from the jungle—only a handful of the great religious geniuses have understood Jesus and followed Him. A handful of religious geniuses and those many loving women who through care and sacrifice have nurtured humanity from the cradle to the grave. But many, fearing love, have, down through the centuries, put off until tomorrow what should have been today's imperative. In fear, we have lived and fought who might, in love, have created God's world.

Now the atomic bomb, born in hate, has been released on a world appalled at the destruction which awaits us all unless we learn to love one another enough to trust one another.

Suddenly we find ourselves our brothers' keeper. Suddenly our great fear is not to love. Will humanity, which would not choose love, be forced by the basic primal law of self-preservation to accept love as its only choice save destruction? Out of the crucifixion of those who died at Nagasaki and Hiroshima may come the final redemption of the world. If not, we cannot, like Jesus, cry, "My God, my God, why hast thou forsaken me?" But only, in the agony of the world's death, after two thousand years of patience, "Why, in Christ's name, have we, by our final choice, forsaken God?"—Bruce Gould

91

Man now can make weapons capable of reducing the world to the primitive conditions of the time of Cain and Abel. He even has, within the range of his grasp, means to completely exterminate the human race. Today, scientists can make a good educated guess as to the number of [bombs] needed for total world catastrophe—to scatter to the four winds, in a matter of seconds, the civilization it has taken man so many centuries to put together. No wonder some ask, "Are we not playing with things that belong to God?" The concerted, atheistic threat against all we hold dear has increased and grown bolder in the ratio that the hydrogen bomb has surpassed the rifle. We, in turn, must remain armed to the teeth to contain that threat.

I believe that God meant us to find the atom. Admittedly, we are wrestling with the greatest alteration in man's relation with Nature since the upheaval at the time of the Garden of Eden. But his fundamental relation with God has not changed one whit. The same trial that tested the first man in Eden, and every man since, challenges us in the atomic problem. It is the exercise of choice, the dangerous freedom to use God-given power for good or ill. I do not mean for a moment that science is wrong, but only man's worship of it. Surely, a part of our duty, the effect of the primal urge implanted by our

Creator, is to discover more and more of the world we live in. But science can give man mastery only over matter. It never reaches ultimates. . . . Some leading nonreligious scientists are beginning to acknowledge that the concept of divine creation should no longer be dogmatically excluded from rational speculation about the origin of the universe. To my mind, there are today startling possibilities for a religious breakthrough into the secular mind. The time is ripening for a marriage of religion and science.—Thomas E. Murray, Atomic Energy Commissioner

92

The awareness that we are all human beings together has become lost in war and politics. . . . At this stage we have the choice of two risks. The one consists in continuing the mad atomic arms race with the danger of unavoidable atomic war in the near future. The other is in the renunciation of nuclear weapons, and the hope that America and the Soviet Union, and the peoples associated with them, will manage to live in peace. The first holds no hope of a prosperous future; the second does. We must risk the second.—Albert Schweitzer, "Obligation to Tomorrow"

93

The thing for us to fear today is not the atom, but the nature of man, lest he lose either his conscience or his humility before the inherent mystery of things.—Life

94

The man who made the greatest contribution to the American development of the atom bomb was Adolf Hitler. For it was his racial theories which drove such men and women as Einstein, Meitner, Bohr, Fermi and countless others from Germany and its allies, or conquered countries. The theoretical physicists, chemists and mathematicians who were exiled . . . provided the nucleus around which the American and British teams rallied to produce the atom bomb. As anyone who has even skimmed through the name index . . . must know, the Manhattan Project was truly an international accomplishment.—James B. Kelley, "Moon We Never Made," Commonweal

95

There is a remarkable revelation of God in the atomic bomb for those who have the imagination to see. The terrible explosion was a result of the release of energy from uranium, but similar vast stories of atomic energy are resident in all atoms.

This means that inside the atoms which compose the rose that a beautiful woman wears in her hair, there is a store of energy beyond any man's ability to compute. The pencil we handle as we write a letter to a friend is vibrant with energy. The ink that flows from our fountain pen is pulsing with power.

Never have we had any revelation of nature which has made the might of God more intimate. The ring we wear upon our finger and the very food we eat are packed with divine resources. The holy word, "in him we live, and move, and have our being," is a stark and vivid reality.

Let any man who wishes to sense the nearness of God sit down and contemplate a bit of material which he may hold in his hand. Even so lowly a "something" as a lump of coal tar is full of the incredible energies which have come from God.

The bomb which completely destroyed a city was carried in a container that was floated to earth on the frail support of a parachute. It was so small that it could have been carried easily by a small plane. Yet it shook the earth.

If so tiny an amount of God's power is capable of so great a task, what are we to think of the might of our universe in the midst of which we live, every atom of which is alive with God?—Roy L. Smith, *The Christian Advocate*

96

The real problem is in the hearts and minds of men. It is not a problem of physics but of ethics. It is easier to denature plutonium than to denature the evil spirit of man.—Albert Einstein

ATTEMPT

97

We are attempting great things for God, and we expect great things of Him. We believe in a big God; big enough to once again shake the world with His power. God is ready to move, we are ready to move, the world is waiting to be moved—to the task and to God be the glory.—Buckner Fanning

98

There's no sort of work that could ever be done well if you minded what fools say. You must have it inside you that your plan is right, and that plan you must follow.—George Eliot

99

Ways of making mountain peaks serve as radio booster stations are now common knowledge to radio engineers. That which makes this possible is known as "obstacle gain." It was discovered by military operators during the Korean War. The discovery was that a signal could be sent direct from one valley to another, even though a peak stood in the way. The fact established is that when a radio signal of the proper frequency hits a suitable mountain peak, it is apparently reradiated in all directions. Naturally, the finding was a source of comfort to the operators who otherwise would have had to put relay stations on the peaks. "Obstacle gain" is not a reason-

ably sounding name for any situation. But when we think it through, it has much reason on its side.

We encounter obstacles all our lives, and we know that but for many of them we would not grow in stature, in wisdom and in skill. The psalmist was impressed with this fact when he cried: "It is good for me that I have been afflicted; that I might learn thy statutes." Paul also knew the buffetings of infirmity which by grace and faith were transformed into "obstacle gain" for him. Aldous Huxley, in the spirit of turning obstacles into "obstacle gain," asserts: "Experience is not what happens to a man. It is what man does with what happens to him."—J. Marvin Rast

ATTENDANCE

100

It took time for country people to realize what not going to church did to them. It showed visibly on the countryside and in their children. Often, less care was taken of homes, and gullies deepened in the fields. Brought up with no particular faith to tie to, no God they felt close to, with only self-interest as a guide, many of the youngsters lacked any vital sense of responsibility to themselves, to others or to God's greatest material gift, the land. Many were unwilling to take on duties as leaders or even as followers in necessary causes. When whole communities were affected with this kind of root-rot, progress was blighted.—Neil M. Clark, "The Country Church Comes Back to Life," *Saturday Evening Post*

101

A full church gives me the sense of fighting with a victorious host in the battles of the Lord. A half empty church immediately symbolizes the fact that Christianity is very much of a minority movement in a pagan world and that it can be victorious only by snatching victory out of defeat.—Reinhold Niebuhr, *Leaves from the Notebook of a Tamed Cynic*

102

There is a vast distinction between an audience and a Christian church at worship. An audience is simply an assembly of "auditors" or "observers. . . ." But a Christian church at worship is a corporate fellowship taking common or united action.—Edward L. R. Elson, *America's Spiritual Recovery*

103

One afternoon in "Bughouse Square," Chicago, a group stood about a soap box occupied by a man who was just standing looking them over. One of the group shouted out, "Give us a speech, Tony. You've got a crowd." His reply was rapid, "I don't want a crowd. I want an audience."—E. Paul Hovey

AVERAGE

104

In the intention of Jesus, to be a Christian obviously involved being above the average and ahead of the time.—Harry Emerson Fosdick

105

The effort is to cut everyone down to size who stands up or stands out in any direction.—David Riesman

106

Whenever the human adventure reaches great and complete expression, we can be sure it is because someone has dared to be his *un*average self. A St. Francis, a Van Gogh, an Abe Lincoln, or a Thoreau are proof in point. Instead of trying to look for the average, we might do better to follow Chesterton's example. He never even tried to see what everyone else saw. All the time he was seeing qualities in his friends, ideas in literature, and possibilities in life.—Rae Noel

107

As it has its being from God, and as God sees it, there is nothing—from the greatest human intellect to the tiniest blade of grass—that is not its individual, different self. God sees nothing average.

BAPTISM

108

A part of the act of baptism in the Church of India is for the candidate to place his own hand on his head and say, "Woe is me if I preach not the gospel."

This is part of the baptismal service of new members, not the ordination of ministers!

109

Little Richie, who had recently been baptised, was asked by his father if he wanted to go to church.

"Yes," he promptly replied, "and let's take Stevie (his new brother) and get him advertised."—E. Paul Hovey

BEAUTY

110

Beauty is the gift of God.—Aristotle

111

Beauty is not caused. It is.—Emily Dickinson

112

That which is striking and beautiful is not always good; but that which is good is always beautiful.—Ninon de l'Enclos

113

I pray thee, O God, that I may be beautiful within.—Socrates

BELIEF

114

Paul was the first of the followers of Christ to point out that in order to be Christians they had to stop being Jews. By insisting that the Messiah's message was supernational as well as supernatural, he helped to prevent the young Christian religion from becoming a captive sect of Judaism.—*Newsweek*

115

Nothing great is achieved in history without passion and the most powerful passions are those which have been rationalized by the ideologies. But the relation between the great revolutionary ideologies and the Christian message is a very strange one; they are very close to it, and at the same time entirely different from it. The superficial resemblance between them is just as disturbing as the apparent antithesis between them. In fact they are very close to the Christian message when they attack the churches for the conservative attitude they have adopted for the last three centuries, and when they denounce the hypocrisy of a piety which is divorced from justice and love. In this they seem to echo the great prophets, the Sermon on the Mount, or the social message of the apostles. But these ideologies are very far from the Christian message even when they most resemble it, for instance, in their belief in the redemption of history and the reconciliation of men, for the simple reason that this redemption and this reconciliation do not pass through Jesus Christ but through the sacrifice of a social class, which is (as it were) a purely human and collective Christ. This type of humanized Christology can be heard running like an undertone through all the revolutionary ideologies of the nineteenth century.—P. Ricoeur, *The Ecumenical Review*

116

One person with a belief is equal to a force of ninety-nine who have only interests.—John Stuart Mill

117

My childhood mind was not troubled by doubts of God's existence. I would have been much more comfortable at times had I not believed in Him. Hence when I hear cynical critics say that belief in God is only wishful thinking, I know it was not so in my case, for I believed in God even when I wished there were no such Being to see what I was doing.—Ralph W. Sockman

118

When Dr. A. Powell Davies says, "The right to disbelieve is inherent in the right to believe," he implies that rights come in contrary pairs. Thus, Americans have the right to protect their country and if Dr. Davies is correct, the right to betray it. Isn't he confusing the ability to choose between good and evil with the idea of right?

With equal justification we should insist that every business concern employ a few dishonest clerks to keep the others on their toes.

119

Recognize your dignity and the differences which flow from it. Repudiate the blasphemous notion that it makes no difference what a man believes, or what he does, or by what road he seeks his heaven, or with whom he associates or how he lives, or whom he loves, so long as he does not interfere with the other fellow's rights or offend the other fellow's feelings. It makes all the difference in the world, all the difference in time and eternity what you believe and what you love, for the things men do are only the outward expression of the things they believe, and the practical expression of their ideal loves.—John J. Wright, *Vital Speeches*

120

I have a firm conviction, which is to me an article of faith, that no conscious effort toward the better, whether individual or collective, is ever lost. It is held in the lap of time.—R. C. Wallace, *Rotarian*

121

One of the questions a would-be member of my church often asks is this: "If I join the church, what have I got to believe?" The answer I give appears sometimes to startle the questioner, for I say to him, "Nothing." Then I take up his surprise and ask him whether he can believe anything because he is told to believe it. . . .

My attitude has been criticized. Some people have made the false deduction that it doesn't matter what a man believes. Who would like to do business with a man who believed one thing but said another? My attitude is rather this: What a man believes is too important to be imposed upon him by some alleged outward authority. . . .

The Church of Jesus Christ started with a group of sincere people who wanted to learn how to live and felt that if they could be with Him, they could do it. That is why when a man asks me, "What have I got to believe?" I say: "Nothing. Come and try out with us a way of life which Jesus started and which we believe He still sustains. And as you come into the fellowship, you will gradually make your creed. . . ." The laws of our mind show us that while we can assent to what another says, we cannot believe it unless it appears true to us. If you say to me threateningly, "You must believe so and so," I may assent through fear or in order to please you; but I cannot believe.—Leslie D. Weatherhead

122

On the wall of a cellar in Cologne, where a number of escaped prisoners hid out for the duration, there was found this inscription: "I believe in the sun, even when it is not shining. I believe in love, even when feeling it not. I believe in God, even when He is silent."—Louis Binstock, *The Power of Faith*

123

Belief means that the truth has made a conquest in personality.—Leslie D. Weatherhead

124

While I was in America, a witness who happened to be called at the Sessions of the county of Chester declared that he did not believe in the existence of God or in the immortality of the soul. The judge refused to admit his evidence on the ground that the witness had destroyed beforehand all the confidence of the court in what he was about to say. The newspapers related the fact without any further comment.—Tocqueville, *Democracy in America*

125

In an article in *The New Yorker*, A. J. Liebling relates an incident which happened as he sought to get a visa at the Lebanese Embassy. Having received his visa, he was called by the Embassy, and told that he had failed to fill in the blank regarding his religion and without it the visa would have to be revoked. Liebling told the girl in charge that he was not devout, not an observer, not even a believer, but that he would make trouble if his visa were revoked. She replied: "If you don't believe then you have no religion. Put down 'Without Religion.' " He received his visa and was allowed to sail.

Can we, however, sail through life without belief, without religion?

126

Who . . . has ever seen an idea? . . . Who has ever seen love? . . . Who has ever seen faith? . . . The real things in the world are the invisible spiritual realities. Is it so difficult, then, to believe in God?—Charles Templeton, *Life Looks Up*

127

It makes all the difference in the world what one believes. For our conceptions of what is right or wrong depend upon our beliefs about ultimate truths concerning God, man, this life, and the life to come. The Nazis in Germany had their own particular ideas about all these questions, and these ideas led them to believe that they did the right thing when they murdered millions of Jews and other people in concentration camps and gas chambers. It was all part of their religion. In fact, people only deceive themselves when they think that they have no religion and that they can get along without it.—Herbert Gezork

128

Reichel was conducting a rehearsal of *The Messiah*. The chorus had sung through to the point where the soprano solo takes up the refrain, "I know that my Redeemer liveth." The soloist's technique was perfect—she had faultless breathing, flawless enunciation. After the final note, all eyes were fixed on the conductor to catch his look of approval.

Instead he silenced the orchestra, walked up to the singer with sorrowful eyes, and said, "My daughter, you do not really know that your Redeemer liveth, do you?" "Why, yes," she answered, flushing, "I think I do."

"Then sing it," cried Reichel. "Tell it to me so that I will know and all who hear you will know that you know the joy and power of it."

He motioned the orchestra to play again. This time she sang the truth as she knew it in her own soul and all who heard wept under the spell. The old master approached her with tear-dimmed eyes and said, "You do know, for you have told me."

BEST

129

Only a mediocre person is always at his best.—Somerset Maugham

130

The greatest thing you can do for any individual or any group in your day is to help them find the best.—Katherine Logan, *The Call of the Upper Road*

131

One of the rarest things that a man ever does is to do the best he can.—Josh Billings

132

I don't do the best I know how, but I do the best I can.—Joseph Nelson, *Backwoods Teacher*

THE BIBLE

133

In the first volume of sermons of the theologian, Karl Barth, which were translated into English, there is a great sermon entitled, "The Strange New World Within the Bible." Karl Barth takes the position in that sermon that in the Bible we are indeed in a different world, and then defines it as a world "in which everybody is looking up."

In that sense, the Bible does introduce us to another world. It is the world in which all of us need to learn to live. The Bible introduces us to the world in which, moment by moment, we are dependent on God.

What the world needs is not to expect God to do for us what we ought to do for ourselves, but to be under-girded with a mighty faith that God is on the throne of the universe and that He does work in the affairs of the world. This faith the Bible has.—Lowell B. Hazzard

134

The Bible is not merely a book of texts, but a textbook. It contains the truths we have to teach, the laws which we have to illustrate in their relations to the lives of our people, the divine promises by which we are to console them in trouble and to strengthen their faith in the love and power of God.—R. W. Dale, *Nine Lectures on Preaching*

135

It is impossible to mentally or socially enslave a Bible-reading people. —Horace Greeley

136

The Word of God is in the Bible as the soul is in the body.—Peter Taylor Forsyth

137

The Scriptures principally teach what man is to believe concerning God, and what duty God requires of man. —*Westminster Shorter Catechism*

138

If I were a dictator, the first book I would exterminate would be the Bible. I would destroy it because I realize that our whole concept of democracy came from the Book.

In the Bible, and particularly in Jesus' spiritual concepts of God and man, all men can find the key to victory, not only over one evil system, but in the greater crusade against all falsehood. Mankind, however, appears to come slowly to the realization that Freedom is not won and held solely by material means.—Admiral Arthur Radford, "Battle for Freedom," *Vital Speeches*

139

Read Demosthenes or Cicero; read Plato, Aristotle, or any others of that class; I grant you that you will be attracted, delighted, moved, enraptured by them in a surprising manner; but if, after reading them, you turn to the perusal of the sacred volume, whether you are willing or unwilling, it will affect you so powerfully, it will so penetrate your heart, and impress itself so strangely on your mind that, compared with its energetic influence, the beauties of rhetoricians and philosophers will almost entirely disappear; so that it is easy to perceive something divine in the sacred Scriptures, which far surpasses the highest attainments and ornaments of human industry.—John Calvin, *The Institutes*

140

The Word of God cannot be turned into a closed system of "Body of Divinity." God speaks to each generation according to its situation and its need. The living God is a free God, and He addresses Himself to minds which are free and open to hear His Word. Jesus Christ at the right hand of the Father reigns over His kingdom with a freedom which will not permit the legalism implicit in closed systems of theology. The Holy Spirit works in the church to make us free to meet new occasions and opportunities with relevant and creative action. The Bible itself, which is no system, speaks to us the Word of God for an obedience of faith and hope.—Joseph Haroutunian, *McCormick Speaking*

141

After seeing a pile of new books about how to succeed in marriage and avoid divorce, I asked my ninety-year-old Grannie how she and Granddad ever managed without such valuable helps. She looked scornfully at me and held out her Bible.—James J. O'Reilly, *Your Life*

142

Have you found difficulty in reading your Bible profitably? Try skimming through it somewhat as you would go touring through a lovely countryside this summer.

When you set out for a drive in the country, you do not stop at every turn of the road to investigate, study and analyze the scenery or the situation. Instead, you drive along watching for the thing that may invite your interest. When you come to a spot of surpassing beauty, you stop, take time to enjoy it and then drive on when your inclination suggests.—Roy L. Smith

143

The basis of Calvin's theology is the belief that through the Bible alone can God be known in His wholeness as the Creator, Redeemer and Lord of the world. He is not so discernible in any other place—in the creation, or in man's conscience, or in the course of history and experience. And since, if we are to know of God, we must go to the place where He is to be found, it is to the Scriptures that we must go, and there we shall find Him as He is. . . . The Scriptures are not man's guesses about the mystery of God, nor are they the conclusions that men have drawn from certain data at their disposal. On the contrary, they are the unveiling of the mystery of God by God Himself; God's gracious revelation of Himself to ignorant and sinful men. Far from being a stage, even the last stage, of man's quest for the well at the world's end, the Bible is the place where God comes from above and beyond the world to show Himself to His people.—T. H. L. Parker, *Portrait of Calvin*

144

The Bible, more than any other book or collection of books, has power to enlighten. . . . In all the many centuries the thinkers and teachers of the human race have not been able to exhaust even one of its great truths and set that truth to one side. The Bible has power to emancipate. It has burst more shackles and liberated more millions of human beings than all other influences combined. . . . Christianity as set forth in the Scriptures is the best means of overcoming all forms of exploitation of life. . . . The Bible as no other book has power to console and deeply satisfy. . . . On every hand the world over are evidences that the Bible has power to transform (or civilize). . . . It would be difficult to overstate the vital part the circulation and study of the Bible have had in the uplift of backward parts of the world. . . . As no other writings, the Bible has power to enrich. Jesus Christ declared that He came that we might have life, and that we might have it more abundantly. . . . The Bible also has the marvelous power, so imperatively needed in these days, to unify. It has power to insure good will and right relations between the nations. It is a most striking fact that international law is a product of Christian nations. . . . Increasingly . . . the Bible has become the symbol and safeguard of Christian unity and of the genuine ecumenical movement. It is the fountainhead of spiritual life. It is the Deathless Book. "Heaven and earth shall pass away; but my words shall not pass away."—John R. Mott, "The Power of the Bible," *Adult Class*

145

The Bible is the story not of what a people desired and might have done, but rather of what God's unwearying purpose wrought in them.—Walter Russell Bowie, *Preaching*

146

Don't forget the Bible. I was a poor boy, but I was rich because I had the Bible.—H. M. Tomlinson

147

One of the vivid memories of my youth is that of the period at the age of eight when, in the normal course of events in childhood, I became an atheist. Along with other philosophers of about the same age, I longed to make one grand gesture of heroic impiety, to do the wickedest thing we could imagine. We decided that would be to burn a Bible.

So we got from my father's table a large book bound in leather and a public burning of the Book was celebrated in the back yard. It was interrupted by the arrival of my father, who was a preacher. He did the meanest thing which possibly could be done to spoil the party there at the burning. He gently pointed out that what we had on the fire and which, like the burning bush, refused to be consumed, was not the Bible but the dictionary! And all the thrill was gone when we discovered that it was not God we were defying, but merely Noah Webster.

Yet I have often thought since that there is a close relation between the Bible and the dictionary. The dictionary depends upon the Bible for the highest meaning of its greatest words. We cannot throw away the Bible without at the same time doing something destructive to the dictionary. Cast away the Bible and every word of the dictionary shrinks! The great words are not the long words, but the short ones —life, man, love, child, home, country, death, friend, hope.—Halford E. Luccock, *Christianity and the Individual*

148

"The Book of Life" is the Bible. With singular significance it begins and ends with a reference to "the tree of life" (Genesis 2:9; Revelation 22:2).

So far as form and materials are concerned, books once claimed kinship with trees. Several well-known words survive which etymologically testify to a common derivation. For example, *liber* in Latin originally meant the bark of a tree, and *codex* meant the trunk; while the English word *book* is itself only the Anglo-Saxon form of *beech* (originally Saxon books were usually made from beech trees), and we still speak of binding books in *boards;* the word *leaf* being common to both.

Yet, not all books are living books any more than all trees are living trees. Most ancient books are either already dead or dormant . . . every real book embodies the best of real man . . . "the precious life-blood of a master-spirit. . . ." Christianity is the living expression of a living Book!— George L. Robinson, *The Book of Life*

149

I get many requests to mention new books but there's one book no publisher need ask me to boost, which I'm going to mention. . . . It's a book you can borrow from any library or buy at any bookstand. It's the book-of-the-month for every month of the year, the best seller for all time. At any price, it's priceless. For it brings solace to the sick, spiritual strength to the strong, has given hope to the poor, humility to the proud. It has touched the heart of king and commoner. It was written for all nations and is banned by only one nation. In it the money changers of our own . . . markets find their counterpart driven from the Temple, and . . . recognize their own technique in the unjust steward of another day. Too many of us make a Bible of the *Wall Street Journal* or the daily racing form, while the greatest investment guide of all time points the way to spiritual wealth that never can be taxed, and to eternal dividends that never will be passed. This Book is our legacy from the greatest Teacher the world has ever known . . . if we live by His teachings, we cannot fail to make Democracy live.

150

The Bible is filled with big ideas, ready to give men and women the courage to live. How often it seems, like empty vessels, they wait the filling. They need the constant, daily reminder that these big ideas are God's gift for every day.

151

When Theodore Roosevelt gives an account of crossing the Andes, and meeting one night with a group of men of different nationalities, he speaks of their inability to find something of common interest to talk about. But in time the men hit upon great literature. The Italian laborer could talk about and quote Dante. The Spaniard knew Cervantes. Each man could talk about his country's great writer, and all the others would be sufficiently acquainted to make interesting conversationalists. . . . Great books are great civilizing forces. If each one is written in the life-blood of some man, as Milton said, then in those books one finds the life-blood of a nation, of all nations.

If this is true of the classics, great literature by great men, it is even more true of the Bible. While Goethe and Shakespeare, for instance, are for all time and all people, while they were geniuses unconfined by any country's borders, they were nevertheless circumscribed in their thoughts and attitudes. Shakespeare was an Englishman, as well as an internationalist. Goethe was a German, as well as an internationalist.

This is not true of the Bible. It is the book best suited for the One World we talk about so glibly. No boundaries of country or time circumscribe it. . . . Jesus died for all mankind, and before His leaving the disciples, He gave them the Great Commission to go into all the world and teach and preach. Obviously, what they were to teach is what the present world is to teach and be taught. It is the same old story, suitable for any part of the One World. —Calvin T. Ryan, "The Bible Is a One World Book," *The Presbyterian*

152

One day I was sitting beside a young composer at work on a new selection. He was trying out different chords and as he ran some parallel fifths and octaves, he turned to me and said, "They never sound quite right to me."

He had learned through hard experience what he might have learned in a first lesson in harmony that "The first, and most important, absolute prohibition which we meet in composition is this: consecutive octaves, unisons, and fifths are forbidden" (Foote and Spalding, *Modern Harmony*).

Some stumble upon the great truths and facts of the Christian faith, and tell us of their discoveries, discoveries which they would have known as facts had they studied the Book.—E. Paul Hovey

153

To study the Bible as the history of men and nations—and the Bible is full of history—unless it is the study of God's activity in history is to miss its significance entirely. It is often the tendency of the student to regard events which happened long ago with some degree of detachment, as if those events are unrelated to the present— interesting but somehow irrelevant. Actually, this is a distortion of history because one age emerges from the one preceding and merges into the one following in one continuous process. Therefore, even on the human plane, historical events are relevant. But the assumption that man lives a one-dimension existence, i.e., that history is merely the record of human striving, provides the greatest problem in the study of the Bible as history. God is the central figure of history. It is His activity in the lives of men which must be seen and understood, not only long ago but now. History is never static, nor has it ever been completed. It goes on and on and God's activity is continuous, purposeful, ever present. It is with the assurance that in its pages can be found God's will for our lives that the Bible should be studied. This is the primary purpose. All else is secondary. . . .

It is only when we read the Bible with humble and receptive hearts, in a spirit of prayer, that God, through the Holy Spirit, makes clear to us His word to us. But we must be ready not only to hear what God says, we must yield ourselves to His rule in our lives in faith and obedience.

It is through God's word to us in the Bible that we become conscious of our need, that we recognize that the real reason for our estrangement from God lies in our own self-will, that in the acceptance of Jesus Christ as Lord of our lives, our reconciliation with God is effected, and that in the eternal purpose of God, as revealed in the life of the fellowship of the saints, we find our destiny.—*Christian Faith and Life*

154

Dickens was asked for the most pathetic story in literature, and he said it was that of the Prodigal Son. Coleridge was asked for the richest passage in literature, and he said that it was the first sixteen verses of the fifth chapter of Matthew. Another asked Daniel Webster for the greatest legal digest, and he replied that it was the Sermon on the Mount. No one has equaled David for poetry, nor Isaiah for vision, nor Jesus for His moral and ethical teachings, nor Peter for holy zeal, nor Apollos for fiery oratory,

nor Paul for logic, nor John for statements of sanctified love. What a ridiculous statement that to study the Bible "marks a step backward in education"! God's Word is the very greatest of all the books. We do well to stay close to its pages. It is the Book.

155

The Bible is a great library of books, written by different people, at different times, and in many different situations. While it reflects the changing fortunes of a people—their hopes and their fears, their joys and their sorrows, their periods of prosperity and their periods of misery, times of war and times of peace—the central character in this divine-human drama is God. There are many minor characters—people as generous, as envious, as acquistive, as self-centered as we know ourselves to be—some good, some bad. Here is the written record of God's activity in the lives of a people, calling them to great ventures of faith, giving them over to the consequences of their folly, patient with them, yet firm with them, loving them, yet chastening them, but seeking always to restore them to complete fellowship with Him, which by their own self-will they had broken. This is the record of a divine, self-giving love so great that it could not stop short of the Cross.—*Christian Faith and Life*

156

Unesco's *Index Translationum*, 9th edition, lists the "world's most translated authors in 1956." It reveals that 331 translations of the works of Lenin led the list, but 257 were made in the Soviet Republic and none in the United States or the United Kingdom. Jules Verne was the next most translated author with 143 translations, 31 of them being made in Spain and 5 in the United States. Tolstoy was next with 134 translations; 36 were made in the Soviet Republic and 5 in the United States. The Bible stood in sixth place, so far as the number of translations made was concerned with 99. Only one of these was in the Soviet Republic while 11 were made in the United States, with Germany leading with 28.

157

Those who talk of reading the Bible "as literature" sometimes mean, I think, reading it without attending to the main thing it is about; like reading Burke with no interest in politics, or reading the *Aeneid* with no interest in Rome. That seems to me to be nonsense. But there is a saner sense in which the Bible, since it is after all literature, cannot properly be read except as literature; and the different parts of it as the different sorts of literature they are. Most emphatically the Psalms must be read as poems; as lyrics, with all the licenses and all the formalities, the hyperboles, the emotional rather than logical connections, which are proper to lyric poetry. They must be read as poems if they are to be understood; no less than French must be read as French or English as English. Otherwise we shall miss what is in them and think we see what is not.—C. S. Lewis, *Reflections on the Psalms*

BIGNESS

158

What lies ahead, it's not given to us to know. Certainly many of you are marked for leadership of widest responsibility. But your world need not be large geographically to be of infinite importance.

Your world of the future may be marked only by the boundaries of a borough, the streets of a community, perhaps only the four walls of a home.

But there—supremely there—what you do is going to count. There you will be either part and parcel of the whole world's big problem—or part of the solution to that problem.

We Americans are accused (and often rightly) of being obsessed by size—of thinking that the Big Act is the only act, the High Place the only significant place.

Samuel Goldwyn once remarked that he wanted a film which "begins with an earthquake and works up to a climax." He rightly assessed the popular appeal of the colossal.

Remember always that vitality is of vaster importance than size. Remember always that first mathematical principle that "the whole is the sum of its parts" —and every part can be vital, must be vital.

I learned that anew one day in June, 1945. As a war correspondent, I had flown down from Manila to join the U. S. Fleet for the amphibious assault on Borneo, then in Japanese hands.

On the evening before the landings, while we were steaming toward Brunei Bay, we correspondents were called in for briefing by General MacArthur and Admiral Royal.

Great maps were unrolled—and the whole strategy of the big operation was carefully explained. On the Big Maps, we saw clearly why Borneo had to be taken. We saw its relation to other parts of the Pacific War—and to the entire global conflict of freedom against tyranny.

And on the Big Maps the operation looked vast and complicated. The war was an immense thing.

But when we leaped out of the landing boats at dawn next morning, splashed through the surf, and hit the beaches, the war suddenly shrank. It was no longer the vast, impersonal thing of the Maps. It was intensely personal, intensely concentrated. For each a tiny patch of beach, a hastily dug foxhole.

Yet every man of us knew, somehow, that for us *this was THE WAR*. It would have been easy for any soldier to say to himself: "One man doesn't matter. I can run out on this thing, and nobody will be hurt, no ground lost."

But every man knew—and knew well—that such thinking and such acting would be disastrous. A tiny hole opened in the advance here, a little ground given there, would matter—terribly.

And we knew that—however corny it all had sounded in those orientation lectures—the outcome of that operation, and of the whole Allied effort, did actually depend to an important degree on how well every man carried out his assignment, no matter how small.

Big Maps . . . and *Little Beachheads!* War is like that. Life is like that. Life is always like that.

. . . whether it becomes yours to design and unroll the Big Maps . . . or yours to be faithful on the Beachheads . . . your winning in the battle of life . . . is going to be in direct ratio to how well you learn the technique, and practice the high art of "opening out a way whence the imprisoned splendor" in you may escape! —Clarence W. Hall, "Our Imprisoned Splendor"

159

We must never lose sight of the fact that ours is a country that has grown because of our belief in ideas, not because of our belief in things. As things become more available, as they become more pleasant, ideas tend to fade away a little. We've got to be sure that we always remember that it is the idea— the big, clean idea and not the thing —that makes us and our country bigger.—Frank Pace, Jr.

160

By faith Abraham . . . went out, not knowing whither he went. This ancient and dim figure of Abraham

leads a procession which in some measure we all join. It is the Big Parade of our time, indeed, of every time. We are conscripted into an expedition beyond familiar landmarks, a thrust outward into new and uncharted territory. . . . Harold Lamb's life of Alexander the Great . . . describes memorably the consternation which came upon the Greek army following Alexander across Asia Minor, when they discovered that they had marched clear off the map. The only maps they had were Greek maps, showing only a part of Asia Minor. The rest was blank space . . . our world has marched off many maps, and new ones must be drawn . . . more true to the realities of the present situation.—Halford E. Luccock, *Marching Off the Map*

BIRTH

161

High birth is a thing which I never knew anyone to disparage except those who had it not; and I never knew anyone to make a boast of it who had anything else to be proud of.—Warburton

162

Whenever I hear people discussing birth control, I always remember that I was the fifth.—Clarence Darrow, *The Story of My Life*

163

I have learned to judge of men by their own deeds, and not to make the accident of birth the standard of their merit.—Mrs. Hale

BLAME

164

The seven-year-old son of a friend of ours was recently rebuked for making designs in clay upon the newly painted walls of his playroom. "I'm getting sick of this," the boy complained. "Everything I do, you blame on me."—*The New Yorker*

165

Learn from your mistakes, but don't cry over them. We best redeem the past by forgetting it.—Elbert Hubbard

166

All of us, whether we realize it or not, have a tendency to like or dislike, to praise or blame, to believe or doubt, to radiate cheerfulness or spread gloom. These tendencies are characteristic of the way we think or feel, and represent our attitudes. Sooner or later we are known and classified by our particular attitudes.—Carl Holmes

167

Last week I saw a man who had not made a mistake in 4,000 years. He was a mummy in the British Museum.—H. L. Wayland

168

The men who are lifting the world upward and onward are those who encourage more than criticize.—Elizabeth Harrison

BLESSINGS

169

The missionaries made the fatal mistake of telling the African child that he was a child of God, that he had skills, abilities and talents which he ought to develop; that he should look forward, even if not in the context of his own life span, to that day when he should be allowed to develop those skills and abilities and talents in the service of his country. That was the mistake the missionary made. He dared to proclaim that education was something which belonged to the whole process of civilization, that it was not the right of the European to bring the treasures that they had in the way of culture to another land, and to keep those treasures solely for themselves.—Trevor Huddleston, *Christianity and Crisis*

170

Reflect upon your present blessings, of which every man has many; not on your past misfortunes, of which all men have some.—Charles Dickens

BOOKS

171

There are more books about books than about any other subject.—Montaigne

172

Books are the legacies that genius leaves to mankind, to be delivered down from generation to generation, as presents to those that are yet unborn.—Addison

173

Reading Christians are growing Christians. When Christians cease to read, they cease to grow.—John Wesley

174

Reading without purpose is sauntering, not exercise. More is got from one book, on which the thought settles for a definite end in knowledge, than from libraries skimmed over by a wandering eye.—Lord Lytton

175

The man who does not read good books has no advantage over the man who can't read them.—Mark Twain

176

Be sure to read no mean books. Shun the spawn of the press on the gossip of the hour. Do not read what you shall learn, without asking, in the street and the train.—Ralph Waldo Emerson

177

Good books are to pore over, to be discussed, criticized and debated, to be read with one's children, to be re-read and cherished and owned. Book-shelves are a symbol of the inquiring mind.—Elmo Roper

178

If you cannot enjoy reading a book over and over again, there is no use reading it at all.—Oscar Wilde

179

Never read any book that is not a year old.—Ralph Waldo Emerson

180

Get a habit, a passion for reading; not flying from book to book, with the squeamish caprice of a literary epicure, but reading systematically, closely, thoughtfully, analyzing every subject as you go along, and laying it up care-fully and safely in your memory.—William Wirt

181

Reading is a joy not dulled by age, a polite and unpunishable vice, a selfish, serene, life-long intoxication.—Logan Pearsall Smith

182

Reading is the work of the alert mind, is demanding, and under ideal conditions produces finally a sort of ecstasy. This gives the experience of reading a sublimity and power un-equaled by any other form of com-munication.—E. B. White

183

People automatically believe in books. Messages come from behind the controlled and censored areas of the world and they do not ask for radios, for papers and pamphlets. They invariably ask for books. They believe books when they believe nothing else.

184

We almost always underestimate the book. All of our wisdom, generation after generation, every bit of us that is good and great and fine, not only can be wrapped up in board covers, but is.—William C. Rogers

185

The pleasure of reading with applica-tion is a dangerous pleasure. Useless books we should lay aside, and make all possible good use of those from which we may reap some fruit.—John Foster

186

Some read books only to find fault, while others read only to be taught. The former are like venomous spiders, extracting a poisonous quality, where the latter, like bees, sip a sweet and profitable juice.—Sir Roger L'Estrange

187

Every library should try to be com-plete on something, even if it were only the history of pin-heads.—Oliver Wendell Holmes

188

Truly each new book is as a ship that bears us away from the fixity of our limitations into the movement and splendor of life's infinite ocean.—Helen Keller

189

There are four kinds of readers. The first is like the hourglass; their reading being as the sand, it runs in and runs out, and leaves not a vestige behind. The second is like a sponge, which imbibes everything and returns it in nearly the same state, only a little dirtier. The third is like a jelly-bag, allowing all that is pure to pass away, and retaining only the refuse and the dregs. And the fourth is like the slaves in the diamond mines of Golconda who, casting aside all that is worthless, retain only the pure gems. —Samuel Taylor Coleridge

190

Let us read nothing that bores us. It should go without saying that if we are going to read deliberately for the sake of the profit which we may derive from our reading, we shall need to find the reading pleasurable.—Montgomery Belgion

191

For the overwhelming majority, the quickest and easiest access to the world's best thought is through the public library. To maintain this source of information open to all and unpolluted by any self-seeking interest is a task important beyond all computation, not to ourselves alone but to the world.—Gerald W. Johnson

192

In the flush of TV spectaculars, wider and wider screeneramas, and all the rest of our frightful, fruitful mechanical advancements, the book is still the essential civilizing influence, able to penetrate the unknowns of human aspiration.—Budd Schulberg

193

Skipping intelligently when you read is ridiculous; you never know what to skip till you've read it.—Bergen Evans

194

Goethe once said that there are three classes of readers; some enjoy without judgment, others judge without enjoyment, and some judge while they enjoy and enjoy while they judge. All that mankind has done, thought, gained, or been is lying in magic preservation in the pages of books, said

Carlyle. So help yourself by reading books.—Adolph A. Kroch

195

Give me a condor's quill! Give me Vesuvius's crater for an inkstand! To produce a mighty book, you must choose a mighty theme.—Herman Melville

196

Books give a deeper meaning and interest to living. There is nothing in daily work, in the most humdrum occupation, that cannot be made more interesting or more useful through books. They are means to proficiency in every calling. They are inexhaustible sources of pleasure. They bring to us the life of the world as it was and as it is now. They supply increased resources. Those able to turn to books for companionship are seldom lonely; nor do they suffer from the need of finding some action, however trivial, to fill an empty hour. They have friends who will come when desired, bringing amusement, counsel or some absorbing confidence; friends who, unlike the human variety, may be dismissed when their conversation palls, and who may be chosen to suit whatever mood or interest is uppermost.—Helen E. Haines

197

The greatest tribute that a writer can earn is not that we keep our eye fast upon his page, forgetting all else, but that sometimes, without knowing that we have ceased to read, we allow his book to rest, and look out over and beyond it with newly opened eyes.—Charles Morgan

198

To read well is to think well; the eye is merely the servant of the alert mind.—R. L. Lyman

199

'Tis the good reader that makes the good book; in every book he finds passages which seem confidences or asides hidden from all else and unmistakably meant for his ear. The profit of books is according to the sensibility of the reader; the profoundest thought or passion sleep as in a mine, until it is discovered by an equal mind and heart.—Ralph Waldo Emerson

200

The principal purpose of reading should be to lead people into mature development, almost the way we would lead a very young child into the business of getting acquainted with books. —Harold K. Guinzburg

201

Reading good books is like having a conversation with the highly worthy persons of the past who wrote them; indeed, it is like having a prepared conversation in which those persons disclose to us only their best thinking. —Descartes

202

If the riches of the Indies, or the crowns of all the kingdoms of Europe, were laid at my feet in exchange for my love of reading, I would spurn them all.—François Fénelon

203

Reading serves for delight, for ornament, for ability. The crafty condemn it; the simple admire it; the wise use it.—Francis Bacon

204

Literature flourishes best when it is half a trade and half an art.—R. W. Inge

205

A novel was once written around the idea of how the reading of a book changed a woman's life, made her feel a certain dignity and worth. There is a Book which has changed the lives of countless readers. It is, of course, the Bible.—E. Paul Hovey

206

All books will become light in proportion as you find light in them.— Mortimer J. Adler

207

Library catalogue files have an odd fascination. They are a testimonial to patience, creativity, and frustration.

The librarian faithfully records the work of the creative writer who becomes buried under the avalanche of the constant piling up of new works. The frequency of the thumbmarks testify mutely to the law of the survival of the fittest.—John G. Fuller, *Saturday Review*

208

Books are to be called for and supplied on the assumption that the process of reading is not a half-sleep, but in the highest sense an exercise, a gymnastic struggle—that the reader is to do something for himself.—Walt Whitman

209

Books extend our narrow present back into a limitless past. They show us the mistakes of the men before us and share with us recipes for human success. There's nothing to be done which books will not help us do better. —T. V. Smith

210

The voice of a man when he reads reveals not what he is, but what he wants to be. It is the voice of the personage whom he visualizes when he thinks of himself.—André Maurois

211

Think as well as read, and do it while you read. Yield not your minds to the passive impressions which others may make upon them. Hear what they have to say; but examine it, weigh it, and judge for yourselves. This will enable you to make a right use of books —to use them as helpers, not as guides to your understanding: as counsellors, not as dictators of what you are to think and believe.—Tryon Edwards

212

Books are the key to man's culture. If they vanished overnight and could not be replaced, our culture and civilization would disappear within two generations. The most significant thing man has ever learned to do with his hands, since he stopped walking on all fours or swinging from trees, is to use them to write books and to open their pages in order to read them.—Richard Powell

213

In books, you gain friends—real people—who will be your companions forever. Books will take you places that you cannot otherwise visit, places that have never existed on this earth, real places that no longer exist. Books will bring you ideas that men of all nations have considered and evolved since the beginning of history. Books will tell you how other men have met life's problems. . . . Books will excite you, amuse you, rest you, inspire you. Books will give you courage, fortitude, patience, tolerance, wisdom, hope, insight, skill, perseverance, sympathy. Books will make you grow . . . deeper, broader, taller. Books will help you to understand other men—and to know yourself . . . when you find and finish a book . . . that suits and satisfies your own special appetite . . . you can hold it for a moment in your hand and say, "Here is something that has added to my knowledge and my life."—Edward Prager, *Coronet*

214

Books are a series of windows opening on the strangeness of the world— the physical world, which we are finding more intricate than we ever dreamed; the world of the emotions, which the novelist knows is of equal intricacy; and the world of the spirit, where all of us need as much light as we can get.—Marchette Chute

215

The printed word is the very stuff of power. We are the sum total of what we read.—Saxton Bradford

216

A good book is the precious life blood of a master spirit, embalmed and treasured up on purpose to a life beyond life.—John Milton

217

A great library contains the diary of the human race.—George Dawson

218

The writings of the wise are the only riches our posterity cannot squander.—Walter Savage Landor

219

Is it not strange that the two greatest classics of our tongue, Shakespeare and the English Bible, are just the two books that editorial stupidity, bad arrangements, and perverse traditions, have made the hardest for the general reader to enjoy with understanding? —Frederick Pollock

220

Close familiarity with a few great books will do more than anything else to enrich and discipline your mind.— R. W. Dale, *Nine Lectures on Preaching*

221

The books you read may have much to do with your choosing of the road.

Good books are wonderfully helpful and intimate friends. Through them others pass on their best thoughts.— Katherine Logan

222

A man who buys a book is not only buying a few ounces of paper, string and printer's ink; he may be buying a whole new life.

223

I have always had poor eyes and I couldn't read a lot—I think I have been spared a lot of confusion.— Charles F. Kettering

224

A man ought to read just as his inclination leads him; for what he reads as a task will do him little good. A young man should read five hours a day, and so may acquire a great deal of knowledge.—Samuel Johnson

225

For a person to read his own works over with delight, he ought first to forget that he ever wrote them.—William Hazlitt

226

Read the best books first, or you may not have a chance to read them at all.—Henry David Thoreau

227

Take up a book because it will tell you something of the world; read what you want to read, not what you think you should read. This is the frame of mind that makes reading worth while and deeply rewarding.—Weller B. Embler

228

There is a wonderful charm in reading a book every line of which is familiar to you. It is like talking over school days and college days with an old friend. You have heard him tell every one of his tales a dozen times; you know as soon as he begins a story how it will end; you anticipate his look when he comes to his comic passages, and the tone in which he will tell them, and the precise point at which he will explode in irrepressible laughter; but the old stories from the old friend have a greater charm than the fresh wit of a stranger.—R. W. Dale, *Nine Lectures on Preaching*

229

To a bookish household, reference books are as important as salt to a cook. They make for peace by settling arguments, and they are a blessing to the school child with homework.

230

I have tired of the look of many things, but never of books. I have kept them always in my bedroom so I could see them from my bed as I used to in this attic room. They still surround me at night, and I look at them tenderly and without thought as I fall asleep. They are the mind of man arrayed like dragoons and Javanese dancers. They are as symmetrical as ripples on a river. When there is only moonlight on them, they shine with mystic life. They are the only real ghosts. How dead the world would be without these dead ones! I sometimes say aloud the names of the authors on my shelves, as I do of loved ones who have died. They dreamed of being remembered. There is as deep a charm in conferring immortality as in achieving it.—Ben Hecht

231

I forget the greater part of what I read, but all the same it nourishes my mind.—G. C. Lichtenberg

232

In the course of a reasonably long life I must have read many hundreds of books, some of which I have forgotten, but most of which I remember, and all of which, remembered or forgotten, must have left some mental deposit, so that in a sense I am mentally as much the books I have read as I am chemically the foods I have eaten.—Sheila Kaye-Smith

233

When I am reading a book, whether wise or silly, it seems to me to be alive and talking to me.—Jonathan Swift

234

It takes two to speak truth—one to speak it and one to hear it. Is this not the way in which any living book must be read—any book, indeed, that contains the essence, or the extension, of a distinct identity?—Ellen Glasgow

235

Good as it is to inherit a library, it is better to collect one.—Augustine Birrell

236

When we teach a child to read, our primary aim is not to enable it to decipher a waybill or receipt, but to kindle its imagination, enlarge its vision, and open for it the avenues of knowledge.—Charles W. Eliot

BOYS

237

During his presidency we heard little of Woodrow Wilson's brilliant wit but he was a master of the pointed remark. Addressing a group of alumni when he was president of Princeton University, he said that he intended to devote a portion of the time to answering some of the questions written him by those whose sons were currently enrolled at the University. He proceeded to take care of the more academic queries, then exploded a bombshell in their midst. "Quite a few of you," said Wilson, "keep asking us why we don't make more of your boys. The main reason is just this—because they are *your* boys."—Mary Alkus

238

Man was made before woman. When God looked at Adam, He said to Himself: "Well, I think I can do better if I try again," and then He made Eve. God liked Eve so much better than Adam that He has made more women than men ever since.—A little girl's essay on "Boys"

239

I have in my study a placard with the picture of a boy on it and underneath are these words: "A good man dies when a boy goes wrong. . . ." We see many boys, of all ages, all types, good, bad and indifferent. Do we seriously think of them as men and as the coming generation?

On . . . the Archives Building in Washington is carved: "The heritage of the past is the seed that brings forth the harvest of the future." The boys on the streets and elsewhere are the seeds that will bring forth the harvest of the future. What will our boys be? What is our responsibility toward them? J. Edgar Hoover says, "We must teach boys to be honest, responsible boys who will protect and not destroy our great American heritage."—Herbert W. Ludwig, *Baptist Leader*

240

"The Man and Boy Movement" is an effort to interest a man in taking a boy who is not in Sunday school to some Sunday school for four Sundays. We believe the boy will go alone thereafter, very likely become a Christian, and influence other members of his family to go with him.—*Baptist Brotherhood*

241

Between the innocence of babyhood and the dignity of manhood we find a delightful creature called a boy. Boys come in assorted sizes, weights, and colors, but all boys have the same creed: To enjoy every second of every minute of every hour of every day and to protest with noise when their last minute is finished. . . .

A boy is a composite—he has the appetite of a horse, the digestion of a sword swallower, the energy of a pocket-size atomic bomb, the curiosity of a cat, the lungs of a dictator, the imagination of a Paul Bunyan, the shyness of a violet, the audacity of a steel trap, the enthusiasm of a fire cracker, and when he makes something he has five thumbs on each hand. . . .

A boy is a magical creature—you can lock him out of your workshop, but you can't lock him out of your heart. You can get him out of your study, but you can't get him out of your mind. Might as well give up—he is your captor, your jailer, your boss, and your master—a freckled-faced, pint-sized, cat-chasing, bundle of noise. But when you come home at night with only the shattered pieces of your hopes and dreams, he can mend them like new with the two magic words—"Hi Dad!"—Alan Beck

BRAINS

242

I not only use all the brains I have, but all I can borrow.—Woodrow Wilson

243

Since the nation was shocked when some of our Korean P. O. W.'s confessed shamelessly to acts they never committed, a hunt has been on for ways and means of preparing men to stand up to that mental torture known as "brainwashing. . . ." the defenses . . . are formed early in life in the home,

the church, the school and the community. . . . Christian missionaries, who had spent their lives in China doing good works for the people, had their faith, but it was sorely tried before they were freed. Young Corporal Claude Batchelor, who didn't want to come home and then changed his mind, had no faith, no convictions to cling to. Colonel Frank Schwable, who confessed to . . . germ warfare, said that if he had only known what the Chinese were up to, he might have acted otherwise. The brainwashers don't tell you what they're up to. They starve you until the mind is foggy and confused. . . . It is in this long waiting-starving process that prayer, faith and conviction come to the aid of the tortured. —Melvin Whiteleather, "Outwitting Brainwashing"

244

A Negro cook told her children, "When you don't have an education, you've got to use your brains."

BROTHERHOOD

245

If we do not go out into the world and call every man our brother, there are those who will go out and call him "comrade."

246

Brotherhood, according to the dictionary, is the relationship of two male persons having the same parents—or the members of a fraternity or organization.

I don't think the dictionary goes far enough. To me brotherhood isn't just something you're born with or something you join. It's something deep inside you, like love or loyalty, that reaches out to all the world and everybody in it—men, women, children.

Just the thought of brotherhood has a sobering effect on me, for it reminds me that I am only a transitory member of a very large family called Humanity. —Bellamy Partridge

247

The challenge of brotherhood may be illustrated in . . . socio-economic . . . relations. . . . The question, "Am I my brother's keeper?" became one of great insistence with the advent of the Industrial Revolution, a time of crowding into cities and the dependence of many on a few men or, worse yet, on machines. Writing at that time, Thomas Carlyle tells of an Irish widow who, for the support of her three children, appealed to charitable establishments in Edinburgh, where her husband died. Continually rebuffed, she fell exhausted, contracted typhus fever, died, and infected her street. Seventeen others perished as a consequence. Am I my brother's keeper? Carlyle concludes, "Had human creature ever to go lower for proof?"

We have come a long way since that day; society has a conscience; our economic brothers are not so selfishly overlooked in the free world.—Eldon L. Johnson, "The Challenge of Brotherhood"

248

It is increasingly evident that only brotherhood has survival value. Good will among men will be preserved; but by whom? It is not enough to equate God and the church. That is a proper equation as long as the church is God's church, recognizable to Him and employable by Him. There is no magic in the name church if it has become only a cloak for human desires and earthly purposes. The tyranny of words deludes us into thinking that what Christ calls His church is what we call the church. The church is the church when it is the continuing and unfailing fellowship of men filled with the Spirit and dominated by the life of Christ, when it is brotherhood alive and at work in the

midst of a flood of denial and distrust. This will survive!—John Gray Rhind, *Westminster Adult Bible Class*

249

The churches will take longer to achieve integration because they are undertaking a much greater accomplishment. Worshiping together is a more personal thing than riding trains or attending movies together. Tolerance is not enough; it must be real brotherhood or nothing.—Frank T. Wilson

250

The high moral values of the ages have grown and been preserved in the great religions. Christian teachings are among the finest expression of human relationships. The brotherhood of man, equality before God, the common Father, the dignity of human personality, the Golden Rule—these central teachings of Jesus embrace most of what good men have been striving for through the ages.—Edwin R. Embree, *Color and Christianity*

251

"You Can't Be Human Alone" is the provocative title of a booklet by Margaret Kuhn.

252

What must be the general character of coexistence between the primitive people and the educated ones? Am I to treat a primitive man as an equal or as my inferior? I must show him that I can respect the dignity of human personality in everyone, and this attitude in me he must see for himself; but the essential thing is that there shall be a real feeling of brotherliness. How far this is to find complete expression in the sayings and doings of daily life must be settled by circumstances. The native is a child, and with children nothing can be done without the use of authority. We must, therefore, so arrange the circumstances of daily life that my natural authority can find expression. With regard to the natives, then, I have coined the formula: "I am your brother, it is true, but your older brother."—Albert Schweitzer

253

The Christian may hold none in contempt. To do so, said Jesus, to humiliate another, to rob him of self-respect, is to commit a sin against the soul no less serious than the murder of the body. "You have heard that it was said to the men of old, 'You shall not kill; and whoever kills shall be liable to judgment.' But I say to you that every one who is angry with his brother shall be liable to judgment; whoever insults his brother shall be liable to the council, and whoever says, 'You fool!' shall be liable to the hell of fire" (Matthew 5:21, 22, RSV). Rather must we stand in reverence before every human being, as in the presence of God. Each must be treated with respect and consideration.—R. B. Eleazer, "Christianity and Racial Adjustment"

254

Oliver Cromwell, the Lord Protector of England for several years in the seventeenth century, once received a letter from King Louis XIV of France addressed "To His Most Serene Highness, Oliver, Lord Protector of England"; but he refused to receive it, because this was not the phrase used by monarchs in communicating with their equals. He was next addressed as "Our Dear Cousin"; and again he refused to receive it. The king consulted his minister, Mazarin, who advised him to use the customary mode of address, namely, "Our Dear Brother." "What!" cried Louis, "Would you have me call this base fellow my brother?" The astute counselor replied, "Yes, Your Majesty; or you will presently have him beating at the gates of Paris!" For a like reason the address which a man uses in approaching Christ is important, since it determines the question whether or not he believes that Christ is the veritable Son of God.—David James Burrell

255

In the three areas of socio-economic, racial, and international relations, the spirit of brotherhood still has ample room for exercise. The crux of the problem, as an English political theorist has put it, is that "Men continue to maintain as citizens what they condemn as human beings." We must, therefore, draw our ideals and our lives closer together.

That is what brotherhood means. It is something not merely to believe; it is something to live.—Eldon L. Johnson

256

One day, Turgenev, the Russian writer, met a beggar who besought him for alms. "I felt in all my pockets," he says, "but there was nothing there. The beggar waited, and his outstretched hand twitched and trembled slightly. Embarrassed and confused, I seized his dirty hand and pressed it. 'Do not be angry with me, brother,' I said, 'I have nothing with me.' The beggar raised his bloodshot eyes and smiled. 'You called me brother,' he said, 'that was indeed a gift.' "—Archer Wallace

257

Help thy brother's boat across, and lo! thine own has reached the shore. —Old Hindu proverb

258

A Twentieth-Century Papyrus to the Most Reverend Paul:

I received your letter yesterday at the hand of Onesimus. In keeping with your request, I am accepting him as a Christian brother. I am glad that you converted him because he was always a source of ill will in my household. Maybe now he'll know how to keep his proper place and show a little more respect for his betters.

Of course, I really should not expect very much from him. These slaves simply do not have the abilities of cultured people like yourself and—if I may be pardoned—myself. I haven't seen one yet that could stand education.

I took Onesimus to his new quarters in the freed slave village just outside of town. I must admit that this section is a little run down, but there were once some elegant homes there. I can't see why they have to live packed so tightly in crowded quarters, but I guess they are satisfied. They don't take care of property anyway.

I'd invite Onesimus to our next Communion service, but I think that he will really be happier in the congregation the freed slaves have set up. It would be most embarrassing to have Onesimus commune with us. We are beginning to draw on the best people here in a new part of town.

I am sure you know how awkward it is for us to treat our ex-slaves as equals. It might drive some of the new prospects away. I think that just for once we might let Onesimus commune with us, particularly if he were to address us on "My Experiences with Paul in Rome." If he could leave just before the Communion service, it really would be better. If not, we can feature him as a foreign missionary.

Onesimus was very quiet when I told him where he would have to go. I think that you must have instilled a proper Christian attitude in him. He doesn't talk back as though he thought he were my equal any more. I don't think it's good for such people to get ideas. He might want to marry someone in the congregation, you know.

As I see it now, this was a test of my faith. I was so afraid that Onesimus might start talking and create a nasty situation. That could have upset things no end for me, and I like to think that our faith brings comfort. The times are upset enough without a lot of agitation. Now I can see that my fears were foolish. I simply cannot allow myself to do such negative thinking again.

Your servant,
Philemon

P.S. I really don't know what to suggest about getting Onesimus a job. He probably wouldn't stick to it anyway. My wife tells me that most of the ex-slaves are working in the quarries for Xenophon Anabasis. He's a hard man, and he hasn't any religious scruples such as I would have. He keeps them in line.—Wilson C. Egbert, *Lutheran Standard*

259

Brotherhood must have a religious basis if it is to have any real significance. Without faith in the Fatherhood of God, as Jesus and the prophets preached it, people have a pretty hard time being brotherly. They drift off into hate societies, or more often, into the society of the indifferent.—Edwin T. Dahlberg

260

We cannot hope to command brotherhood abroad unless we practice it at home.—Harry S. Truman

261

While the new order is destroying itself, a new relationship of men and nations is already beginning its slow but sure evolution, its name is "brotherhood," its method "cooperation."—William Mackenzie King

262

"Ye shall not see my face, except your brother be with you" (Genesis 43:3). These words from Joseph summarize teachings to be found in other parts of the Bible. For example, Jesus says that if we offer God a gift and have aught against a brother, we should first be reconciled to the brother before the gift is acceptable to God. We cannot come to God while pushing others aside. Except the others come with us, we shall not see God's face.—Harry V. Richardson

263

"When we understand each other, we find it difficult to cut one another's throats," wrote Van Wyck Brooks. This epitomizes the meaning of brotherhood.

264

Where brotherhood is practiced, men can live with a problem and still get along with each other with all their differences. At the same time, we know that brotherhood just doesn't happen. Brotherhood has got to be nourished and worked at. The danger is to over-sentimentalize brotherhood. It isn't something that just grows out of thin air—it is a dynamic skill, quite likely the greatest skill man will ever master. Our Christian teachings tell us it is good to love our neighbors as ourselves. We have wealth of experience and learning that points the way to putting this into practice.

First, we must believe that men are truly brothers, that we are all of one blood; that we have a common Father. Second, all men, regardless of race, creed, national or ethnic origin, have similar basic needs, aims, aspirations and sensitivities. Third, all Americans have some objectives in common; such as the Golden Rule, the right to worship as we wish, the right to be judged on our individual merits, the right to a job and a living wage, the opportunity to be educated, the right to decent housing, the right to vote, the right to life, liberty and the pursuit of happiness. Fourth, we know that in this highly complex civilization we cannot live unto ourselves; rather we must work together on common tasks and develop mutual endeavor.—Virgil L. Border, *The Christian Evangelist*

265

The world is my home and all the people of the earth are my brothers. As long as people and society continue to destroy the sacredness of personality, I must work to create abundant life. As long as people suffer from discrimination, poverty, and tyranny, I must live God's moral laws. As long as there are conflicts and tension, a world at war, I must give all diligence to promoting obedience to God's moral laws. In my hands are the instruments of peace and world order.

I am a Christian.—A young Christian's Charter

266

We do not want the men of another color for our brothers-in-law, but we do want them for our brothers.—Booker T. Washington

BUSY

267

Oddly enough—or perhaps naturally—the busiest people are apt to do the best job of giving-away. They are so busy that they have to obey their giving-impulses promptly, and get on with their affairs. Whereas people with plenty of time are likely to debate within themselves: "Shall I, or shan't I?" By the time the debate is over, the opportunity has passed.—David Dunn, "Try Giving Yourself Away"

268

No matter how busy you may think you are, you must find time for reading now, or else surrender yourself to self-chosen ignorance.—Atwood H. Townsend

269

A woman told me that she had thought she was too busy to take time to attend church. While in attendance one Sunday, however, she saw her doctor seated across the aisle and thought, "If one as busy as he is takes time to come, surely I ought to take the time—I'm not as busy as he is."—E. Paul Hovey

270

If we are:
  too busy to read a book that promises to widen our horizons;
  too busy to keep our friendships in good repair;
  too busy to maintain a consistent devotional life;
  too busy to keep the warm vital loves of our home burning;
  too busy to conserve our health in the interest of our highest efficiency;
  too busy to spend one hour during the week in church;
  too busy to cultivate our own souls;
then we are indeed
TOO BUSY!
—Pat Barlow, *Classmate*

CALVINISM

271

A Calvinist is one who "bends one knee before God and the other on the neck of a king."

272

Beginning with the absolute perfection of God and the absolute dependence of all His creatures on His will, John Calvin builds up a system of theology with the divine decree as its center. Predestination, election, total depravity, irresistible grace and everlasting perseverance of the elect, follow as necessary corollaries.—Andrew C. Zenos, *Compendium of Church History*

273

Calvinism is nothing more than theism.—Arthur A. Hays

274

Man's love of God, utterly unselfish and without thought of reward or punishment, is the greatest of all inducements to ethical conduct. This is too frequently forgotten in interpretations of Calvin's thought exclusively in terms of harsh legalism. Thus at the very beginning of the "Institutes" he is constrained to observe: "Besides, he restrains himself from sin, not merely from a dread of vengeance, but because he loves and reveres God as his Father, honors and worships him as his Lord, and, even though there were no hell, would shudder at the thought of offending him."

And later he puts it so strongly and so beautifully that it seems to come as close to revealing the real Calvin as anything in the entire "Institutes": ". . . when they say that there will be no concern about the proper regulation of life without a hope of reward being proposed, they altogether deceive themselves. . . . Can we be incited to charity by any stronger argument than that of John, 'If God so loved us, we ought also love one another'?" . . . no man can ever be captivated by the love of righteousness save as the spirit of God, which is the spirit of holiness, graciously grants him the power.—Robert D. Bulkley, *Presbyterian Tribune*

CHANCE

275

A man by chance meets an old friend in New York that he hasn't seen for ten years. They go to lunch together. Because of this, he is invited to participate in a new mining venture. It seems so important and profitable—he cancels the plane flight scheduled for that night. The plane crashes. Everyone aboard is killed. But that one man's life is spared. He is now president of a famous gold and copper mine in Canada.

276

An unnamed soldier on a battlefield of Gilead drew his bow "at a venture"

—without aim, by chance. The arrow happened to fall between the scale armor and the breastplate of an enemy warrior, pierced his vitals, and killed him. But the curious fact about this happenstance, as the ancient books of Kings and Chronicles relate it, is that it was announced beforehand by a prophet of the Lord named Micaiah (I Kings 22:1-28). And Ahab the king, to foil the prediction, disguised himself as a common soldier; the disguise was so successful that the enemy Syrians thought Jehoshaphat the king of Judah was Ahab and unsuccessfully tried to take his life. Meanwhile Ahab was slain —"at a venture!"

That incident spotlights the whole attitude of the Bible writers toward chance. Joseph's brothers were about to kill him when a band of traders happened over the horizon; his brothers changed their minds and sold him for a slave and he was taken to Egypt where he saved multitudes from starvation. "Be not grieved," he told his brothers when they met years later, "that ye sold me hither: for God did send me before you to preserve life." Peter, filled with the Spirit on the Day of Pentecost, denounced the "wicked hands" that crucified Christ—while at the same time he proclaimed Him "delivered by the determinate counsel and foreknowledge of God." Even the lot— is there any better symbol of what we call chance?—"is cast into the lap; but the whole disposing thereof is of the Lord" (Proverbs 16:33).

The Christian is assured with Paul that "in everything God works for good with those who love him" (Romans 8:28, RSV).—Andrew W. McDermott

CHANGE

277
These are days of change. Our customs, our ideals, our very civilization —all these are undergoing rapid change. We are not altogether sure in what direction some of these changes are taking us. Soon after the war, a biologist stood with a group of friends looking at the ruined and tortured strip of country that had been known as "no-man's-land." Someone asked the scientist this question: "Suppose a beautiful formal garden, like those at Versailles, were to be ruined as this area between the fighting lines has been; would anything grow on it afterward? If so, what?" The biologist considered for a moment, and then said: "Something would grow. I don't know what it would be, but I am sure of this: it would be something very different from what grew there before."

Perhaps a new civilization is growing up in our day. We do not know what it is to be, but there is one encouragement: since God is our refuge and strength we need not fear "though the earth do change" and though some of the mountains that we thought unchangeable should be "shaken into the heart of the seas."

278
From Exurbia come words of an alarming sequence. A housewife in a supermarket was overheard to wail: "They went from Episcopalians to Unitarians—and from Republicans to Democrats—all in one week."—John G. Fuller, *Saturday Review*

279
Changing conditions demand changing methods, and to hold to outgrown methods because of a loyalty to an irrelevancy destroys our integrity and encourages the lie.—Gerald Kennedy, *Who Speaks for God?*

280
A changed person cannot leave his community unchanged in a changing world.

CHARACTER

281

Character is what a man is in the dark.—Dwight L. Moody

282

Character is like a tree, and reputation like its shadow. The shadow is what we think of it: the tree is the real thing.—Abraham Lincoln

283

There is nothing so fatal to character as half-finished tasks.—David Lloyd George

284

Though goodness without knowledge is weak and feeble; yet knowledge without goodness is dangerous; both united form the noblest character and lay the surest foundation of usefulness to mankind.—John Phillips

285

Character is made by what you stand for; reputation by what you fall for.—Alexander Woollcott

286

Good, honest, hardheaded character is a function of the home. If the proper seed is sown there and properly nourished for a few years, it will not be easy for that plant to be uprooted.—George A. Dorsey, *Why We Behave Like Human Beings*

287

At the same time that the Rev. Arley Bragg of Minneapolis preached on the subject "Bad Hearts and Poor Eyes," the Rev. Richard Clearwaters spoke in the same city on "Hanging Hands and Weak Knees."

288

Someone once asked the great American statesman, Charles Sumner, what bribes had been offered him in the course of his political career. "No bribe has ever been offered me in all my political career. I have never been solicited with promise of payment to pursue any course, whatsoever." It might have been otherwise with Sumner. The fact is he was not a man to solicit temptation or dally with it, and people knowing that left him alone. Usually the people tempted are known as people who are in the market with principles to sell. Sumner was not that kind of man. No matter how men differed from him politically, they recognized his moral integrity.—Archer Wallace

289

When Edward Everett Hale brought his first report home from Boston Latin School, it showed that he stood only ninth in a class of fifteen. He was terribly downhearted, but home was his refuge and he had a good mother. She said, "Never mind, Edward, I notice in your report that you are first for good behavior and, Son, that means more to me than to have you head of the class and not behave well." What a sensible mother!

It is a striking thing that no one ever refers to Jesus as clever or brilliant. It is because all know that the supreme virtue is goodness.—Archer Wallace

290

Someone has declared that "in this emergency we must set aside our ideals and face facts realistically." Does this mean that Christians are to declare a moratorium upon their ideals during trying periods? To be patriotic and loyal must we for a time forget that we are Christians? Are we to assume that the gospel of love and good will is a garment to be put off and on at our convenience? If this is our opinion, then be sure it will be much easier to put off this garment of faith than it will be to put it on again. Ideals tarnish with disuse. Mental gifts and graces that are not refined and broadened by experience are likely to deteriorate. Skills that do not improve with use are often lost and forgotten. Character that does not greaten with the passing years is in grave danger of decay.

291

If we are to have an Age of Abundance, the businessman must be worthy of his great vocation. He must be worthy of this calling in two senses: first, in the sense of his own personal character; second, in the sense of the general character of the world-wide fraternity of businessmen. You are responsible for yourself; you are also your brother's keeper. Let me put the matter more bluntly. In my judgment we shall win or lose the Age of Abundance to the degree that the businessman exhibits two basic virtues. The first is honesty—downright, old-fashioned truth-telling. The second is that businessmen must have clear convictions about the kind of society, the kind of system they want, and they must be willing to stand up and fight for those convictions. The businessman must have courage—the courage of his convictions.—Henry R. Luce, "The Character of the Businessman," *Fortune*

292

A great society is a society in which its men of business think greatly of their functions.—Alfred North Whitehead

293

A political victory, a rise of rents, the recovery of your sick or the return of your absent friend, or some other favorable event, raises your spirits, and you think good days are preparing for you. Do not believe it. Nothing can bring you peace but yourself. Nothing can bring you peace but the triumph of principles.—Ralph Waldo Emerson

294

A ship-building company . . . has this sentence in its advertisement: "All of our timber comes from the north side of the mountain." Why the north side? What does that have to do with timber?

After investigation I found out that the best timber grows on the north side of the mountain because of the rigors of Mother Nature. The snow is deeper, the cold is colder, the winds are stiffer, and the warmth is not so warm as on the south side of the mountain. The very harshness of the weather is a contributing factor to the toughness of the timber.

Human character is not much different from timber. How often the best in personality grows on "the north side of the mountain"! We grumble about our hardships and difficulties, yet those very difficulties help us to grow and to become mature persons. Each can look at his own life and see that the time when he made the greatest personal progress was probably when life had him "on the north side of the mountain" and the going was not easy. . . . The harsh experiences of life draw out of us the brightest color and the richest flavor.—Edmond H. Babbitt

295

The inner braces of a man's heart must be equal to the outer pressure of life's circumstances.

296

When we develop character we acquire lovely personalities, for personality is character shining through everything we do and everything we say. —E. Maude Gardner

297

Personality has the power to open many doors, but character must keep them open.

CHARM

298
I think charm is the ability to be truly interested in other people.—Richard Avedon

299
Charm is a sort of bloom. . . . If you have it, you don't need to have anything else; if you don't have it, it doesn't much matter what else you have.—Sir James Barrie

300
I was discussing charm with my mother one time, and she talked of the great charm Robert Sherwood had. She said, "I don't know what it is. It isn't his looks, because he is not a handsome man. It isn't his eyes, because he never raises them from the floor. It isn't his hands, because they hang below his knees. It isn't his voice, because I'm slightly deaf and can't hear everything he says. And yet when he leaves the room, I always feel he is the most charming man I have ever known." I agree with mother; so does my wife, Lynn Fontanne. Charm is that extra quality that defies description.—Alfred Lunt

301
Charm seems to me to be the ability to captivate other people without doing anything about it. The "charm" of it is that one cannot define its ingredients.—Rudolf Bing

302
Being in the presence of a charming person is like being drawn into a magic circle where everything is fresher, cleaner. There is peace, warmth, comfort. Their smile is occasional, rather than constant, making one want to bring it back. The charming person puts one on trial in the sense that he produces the desire to be at one's best.—Alec Waugh

303
Zest is the secret of all beauty. There is no beauty that is attractive without zest.—Christian Dior

304
Charm is due to being pleased with where you are—pleased but not too pleased. Whatever it is, though, make bold to use it. Christina Rossetti's bidding is "Charm, O woman, be not afraid." Perhaps this needs the additional warning of Thomas Gray to men, as well as women: "Be with caution bold."—Robert Frost

305
Charm results from being truly alive. Inner aliveness, vitality in the spirit, projects the soul fascinatingly. No amount of sophistication, no emphasis upon dress can bring to life a person in whom is lacking an inner vibrancy. The Bible has the secret: "In him was life; and the life was light."—Norman Vincent Peale

CHEAPNESS

306
I do not prize the word cheap. It is not a badge of honor . . . it is a symbol of despair. *Cheap* prices make for *cheap* goods; *cheap* goods make for *cheap* men; and *cheap* men make for a *cheap* country!—William McKinley

307
For anything worth having one must pay the price; and the price is always work, patience, love, self-sacrifice—no currency, no promises to pay, but the gold of real service.—John Burroughs

308
Salvation is free to you because Somebody Else paid for it.

CHEATING

309

Did you know that cheaters actually outnumbered non-cheaters in most United States high schools and colleges? Spot surveys in Boston, New York and suburban Ridgewood, N. J., indicate that between 67 and 84 per cent of the high-school population has resorted to cheating at one time or another. A poll conducted by New Jersey's Fairleigh Dickinson College among 3500 students in 40 high schools and colleges showed that less than a third of the boys and girls regarded cheating as an act of delinquency. The tip-off on how the majority felt is to be found in scores of unsolicited comments like, "How else are you supposed to get ahead?" and, "It's okay if you get away with it," and, "It can't be so bad when everyone I know does it."—Elizabeth Pope, "Are We Teaching Our Children to Cheat?" *McCall's Magazine*

310

Let's not fool ourselves. Whether we like it or not, we parents play a major role in the cheating problem. In many cases we are actually teaching our children to cheat. What else does it amount to when we keep Mary home from school for a hair appointment and send her back next day with a phony sickness excuse? Or when we give thirteen-year-old Johnny only twenty-five cents for the movies because he's small enough to pass as ten? Or tell Anne to sit in the back of the car and look out for cops while we break the speed limit? Or brag at the dinner table about fixing a parking ticket? Or padding an expense account? Or dodging income taxes?

This sort of thing adds up to a lesson in dishonesty which only the dullest child could fail to learn. But parents' responsibility for cheating doesn't end there. How about the fuss we are always making about marks, so that our children come to see them as ends in themselves instead of means? Don't most of us vacillate between bribing and bullying in an endless campaign for better and better report cards? Psychologists have found that habitual cheaters are almost invariably youngsters who have been subjected to too much pressure. And in nine cases out of ten, the pressure comes from home, not school.—Elizabeth Pope, "Are We Teaching Our Children to Cheat?" *McCall's Magazine*

CHILDREN

311

Know you what it is to be a child? . . . It is to have a spirit yet streaming from the waters of baptism; it is to believe in love, to believe in loveliness, to believe in belief.—Percy Bysshe Shelley

312

He who helps a child helps humanity with a distinctness, with an immediateness which no other help given to human creatures in any other stage of their human life can possibly give again.—Phillips Brooks

313

A child educated only at school is an uneducated child.—George Santayana

314

The morning worship service had been unusually long and the small daughter of the Reverend Harry Johns was drawn into a conversation in the narthex following the benediction. "The more my daddy eats the longer he talks," she exclaimed, "and *this* morning he had *too* much breakfast."

315

Children are luckier than adults. They have no insulation, made up of familiarity, to deaden the electric surge of delight felt at discovering the many sweet, simple pleasures we take for granted.—Burton Hillis, *Better Homes & Gardens*

316

Children are a great comfort in your old age—and they help you reach it faster too.—Lionel M. Kauffman

317

Children in a family are like flowers in a bouquet: there's always one determined to face in an opposite direction from the way the arranger desires.—Marcelene Cox, *Ladies' Home Journal*

318

A child that is loved has many names.—Hungarian proverb

319

No man is really depraved who can spend half an hour by himself on the floor playing with his little boy's electric train.—Simeon Strunsky, *No Mean City*

320

You realize that your home is as you like it when you overhear a six-year-old hostess tell a little guest, "Don't worry about making noise. Our Mommie and Daddy like children. . . ."—Burton Hillis, *Better Homes & Gardens*

321

Around our neighborhood, we don't judge a fellow by the pictures of famous ancestors hanging on his walls, but by the happy kids hanging onto his pant legs.—Burton Hillis, *Better Homes & Gardens*

322

When grandchildren visit their grandparents, it is the happiest day in the grandparents' lives. The only day that is happier is when they go home.—Sir Frederick Messer

323

A happy childhood is one of the best gifts that parents have it in their power to bestow.—Mary Cholmondeley

324

Bill Norman agrees in part with the folks who say today's kids aren't responsible. "Not responsible, anyhow," he says, "for half the things they get blamed for."—Burton Hillis, *Better Homes & Gardens*

325

Children divine those who love them; it is a gift of nature which we lose as we grow up.—Paul de Kock

326

Some families can trace their ancestry back three hundred years, but can't tell you where their children were even last night. It is said that the reason so many children are found on the streets at night is that they don't want to be left at home by themselves. Many parents are finding that a pat on the back helps develop character . . . if given often, early, and low enough.

327

Booze or babies?

"Road Maps of Industry" for November 23, 1956, lists the business failures in the United States for the years 1929-1956. The report indicates that for the years 1953, 1954, 1955 the highest number of failures came in "Infants' and Children's Wear," while the lowest number of failures in those three years came in "Packaged Liquor."

328

What the best and wisest parent wants for his own child that must the community want for all its children.—John Dewey

329

If children are to be good, using the term good in its broadest sense, it is necessary for the parents to grow with the children.—Judge Jacob Panken

330

You cannot teach a child to take care of himself unless you will let him try to take care of himself. He will make mistakes; and out of these mistakes will come his wisdom.—Henry Ward Beecher

CHRIST

331

If I might comprehend Jesus Christ, I could not believe on Him. He would be no greater than myself. Such is my consciousness of sin and inability that I must have a superhuman Saviour. —Daniel Webster

332

The fact of Christ does not indeed show us everything, but it shows us the one thing we need to know—the character of God. God is the God who sent Jesus.—P. Carnegie Simpson

333

Had Jesus sprung fullgrown into life, we should always have felt that there were great areas of life's experience into which He had not entered.

334

The Christian faith is firmly rooted in the incarnation, in the conviction that "God was in Christ, reconciling the world unto himself." To believe in Christ is to believe that God has come to earth to dwell with men. . . . In Jesus, we meet the living. Jesus is more than a religious genius or a holy man or a spiritual pioneer. To believe in Christ is to believe that the living God has come.—Earle W. Crawford, "God Is With Us," *Pulpit Preaching*

335

He was allowed less than three years in which to do His work; little more than a year in His public ministry, and a year in retirement training His pathetic remnant. He was cut off in His young manhood, a little past the age of thirty. Socrates had taught for forty years, Plato for fifty, Aristotle had lived long and filled libraries with his learning, Buddha and Confucius had fulfilled their threescore years and ten. He was among a crushed people, under an oppressive legalism, zealously opposed and hated by scribes and Pharisees, betrayed by Jews and crucified by Gentiles. He left no book, no tract, or written page behind Him. He bequeathed no system, no philosophy, no theology, no legislation. He raised no armies, held no office, sought no influence, turned His back forever on might, magic and cheap miracle . . . [yet He was] to transform the bigoted Jew and universalize his religion; to show the philosophizing Greek the highest truth; to win the proud Roman to plant the cross on his standard instead of the eagle; to stretch out His hand to the great continents and transform them—to Asia, to savage Europe, to darkest Africa and to America.—Sherwood Eddy

336

Hold to Christ, and for the rest, be totally uncommitted.—Herbert Butterfield

337

Things Christ does which we cannot do for ourselves: (1) He forgives our sins. We can do nothing about that, but Christ can. (2) He gives us power to live as we ought to live. New Year's resolutions often make no difference. His power in our lives does make a difference. (3) He takes upon Himself the punishment due us. We do not force it on Him. He takes it.

338

Jesus did not spend His time guarding the customs; He was sent to His death by the men who did.—Kenneth J. Foreman, *The Presbyterian Outlook*

339

Like a group of men of varying height at the foot of Mt. Everest, differences of spiritual stature are practically unnoticeable when Christians . . . confront Christ.—John M. Gordon

340

If we wish to acquire the better beauty of a useful and influential character, our best example is that of Jesus. Toyohiko Kagawa, the Japanese Christian leader, describes Him in a poem as having "made a molten cast of God's portrait on His own flesh." Perhaps the best modern illustration of the value of the example of Jesus is the story of a boy whose father had died while the boy was a baby. He was curious to know something about his father and asked his older brother what he remembered about their father. Said the brother: "I can't tell you just how he looked, but some people who knew him say that I look like our father."

341

In enthusiasm for stewardship, we must not overlook evangelism. There is a connection between the two. When a man tries to give his heart to God, but not his treasure, he is alike shortchanging God and himself. The latter state of the man is likely to be worse than the first. But Jesus had God to give men in a sense in which it is not ours ever to give God. "If any one enters by me, he will be saved." There are many hirelings, and some of them conscientiously seek to bring men to a better life. But it takes Jesus to make men what they ought to be.—*Adult Student*

342

Great men have come and gone. He lives on.

343

The presentation of Jesus to another people is not international meddling, imposing on another people our religion. It is not "our" religion—it was not born with us—it will not die with us. It is God's gift to man and . . . the soul instinctively bows and says, This is it! We can no more confine this to ourselves than we can confine a truth in mathematics to ourselves. Truth by its very nature is universal. Two and two make four around the world.

If Christ is Truth, then that Truth belongs to every man as a man. You can no more confine Him than you can confine sunlight. As the sun is the only answer to the world's darkness, so Christ is the only answer to the moral, spiritual, economic, social and political darkness of the world. Put Him into any situation in the world and act in that situation on His mind and spirit and that will be the answer to that situation—and the only answer. To try to disprove that would ruin any situation in which it is tried.

For all the world Christ is the Answer. It is up to us to give that Answer without hesitation, without apology, without the stammering of the tongue—and with complete abandon! —E. Stanley Jones, *Adult Class*

344

Bishop F. W. Warne, who spent many years in India, told that once after conducting a service in northern India, a Mohammedan came to him and said, "We Mohammedans have something at least better than you. When we go to our Mecca we find at least a coffin, but when you Christians go to Jerusalem, where is your Mecca? There is not even a coffin, nothing but an empty grave." The missionary replied: "That is exactly where the difference lies. Mohammed is dead, he is in his coffin. But Jesus Christ, whose kingdom is to include all nations and kindreds and tribes, is not in a coffin,

He is risen."—Archer Wallace, *Classmate*

345

The dying Jesus is the evidence of God's anger toward sin; but the living Jesus is the proof of God's love and forgiveness.—Lorenz Eifert

346

Bishop Charles L. Slattery tells the following story: A new pastor had come to the village, and called at a certain cottage. When the husband came home from his work, the wife said, "The new pastor called today."

"And what did he say?" asked the man.

"Oh," she answered, "he asked, 'Does Christ live here?' and I didn't know what to say."

The man's face flushed. "Why didn't you tell him that we were respectable people?" he said.

"Well," she answered, "I might have said that; only that isn't what he asked me."

"Then why," continued the husband, "didn't you tell him that we say our prayers and read our Bible?"

The wife replied, "But he didn't ask me that."

The man grew more vexed. "Why," he continued, "didn't you say that we were always at church?"

The poor woman broke down. "He didn't ask that either; he asked only, 'Does Christ live here?'"

This man and woman pondered for many days what the pastor meant by his question. Little by little their lives were changed; little by little they grew to expect Christ, not dead, but gloriously alive. And some way, they knew not how, through great love and through a willingness to be surprised by the mystery of His radiance, they knew Him. He did indeed live there!

347

The exalted Lord is the remembered Jesus, the remembered Jesus is the exalted Lord! For those who had known Him, there could be only one interpretation, and understanding therefore caught up divinely into the fact itself: He was known to be the Son of God by "being raised from the dead." What "Son of God" meant to the first believers was also part of the divinely shaped fact. More than they could say they knew what it meant, they could feel its import—and they knew! In Him in whom God had become visible as Man, Man had become known as God—the God-Man. The total fact of Christ then is neither of the facts about which cluster the two universal Christian festivals, the Christmas fact and the Easter fact. It is the whole fact of the Word's incarnation. . . . What explains the cohesion of the church after Pentecost is exactly what explains the cohesion of the disciple band before the crucifixion—the Presence of the Lord! . . . This Man was the Resurrection before there was a resurrection, the Life before there was eternal life . . . the big question is not whether Jesus survived his execution. It is whether we are willing to undergo ours.—Willis E. Elliott, "The Risen Christ," *Baptist Leader*

348

From one point of view Jesus is painfully human. Painfully is the exact word—he shared our pains. At first blush He seems to be locked in our dilemma rather than sovereign over it. He went to the synagogue school like any neighbor's child. He worked at a bench, with weariness in His muscles like our weariness, with blood in His veins like our blood. Deceitful men gypped Him. Careless men forgot to pay Him for His work. He was caught in the crosscurrents of His time, for His land felt the impact of world affairs. He met traders from far lands . . . He lived in an "occupied" land; He had to decide, like any Jewish man of His generation, if He should join the open insurrection against Roman tyranny, or work with the underground, or walk some "idealistic" road. Nothing could be more mistaken than the phrase sometimes used of His life, "the Syrian Idyll"—his days were no idyll. . . . Life for Him was as hard as the nails in His shop, or the nails in His cross. . . . He ran afoul of the religious community, and would today, except for the saving heart of lowly devotion that always lives within the church; for He was branded a heretic, though worship was the flame of His life. He ran afoul of the empire, and would today; empire, together with the vested interests of the Temple traders and the Temple authorities, slew Him —not because He was a serious threat in their eyes, but because He was a troublemaker and because empires do not long tolerate troublemakers. He was strung up, and that was that. Could any story be more painfully human?—George A. Buttrick, *Presbyterian Life*

349

To regard the career of Jesus as something far removed from the situation in which we live is to lose the encouragement that comes from viewing our fate in the light of His. If Jesus faced life as we have to face it, not walking through life "on spiritual stilts" but "in every respect . . . tempted as we are," then we can take heart both from His faithfulness and also from God's vindication of that faithfulness. In the light of the crucifixion of Jesus—that greatest of all injustices—our grievances shrink small indeed. . . .

If Jesus lived out His life amid the realities of the same world in which we live, then we too can face anything. —Eliot Porter, *Forward*

350

Many and various are the ways in which persons enter into fellowship with Jesus. Some are kindled by the testimony of another disciple. Others will find Him in the pages of a book, in the mystic vision of worship, in quiet communion with nature, or in varied forms of human service. He will come to others when profound experiences of life have made clear their own helpless inadequacy and failure. And, again, He will be found of those who sought Him not.

351

A publishing concern ran the following advertisement: "You save $2.00 on The Life of the Lord Jesus Christ."

Which leads one to question what we mean when we use the words "save" and "salvation."

352

He never mobilized an army or drafted a soldier or fired a gun. Yet no military leader has ever enlisted as many volunteers as those who take orders from Him.

353

Jesus never wrote a book. Yet many libraries would be required to accommodate the books that have been written about Him. He never wrote a song. Yet He has furnished the theme of more songs than all the song writers combined. He never founded a college. Yet all the schools in the world put together cannot boast the number of students who studied under Him.

354

I feel that alike intellectual and moral honesty requires that I look Jesus full in the face and that I let Him look right into my life. And I find that when I do this, then I cannot, again with either intellectual or moral honesty, turn my back upon Him. Indeed, it is simply because I cannot turn my back upon Him that I am anything of a Christian at all. I am not in this judging others; I am only saying, not,

I hope, egotistically, how dealing fairly with the fact of Christ presents itself to me. I must leave it at that.—P. Carnegie Simpson

355

Within the framework of history has lived One in whom the divine mastery was so complete that He has become mankind's preëminent pattern, the true way of life. With such reverent sensitiveness to God's will did Jesus live, with such wholesomeness did he abandon Himself to its fulfillment, with such a torrent of holy, potent purpose did He feel His soul possessed and borne along from event to event, that His personality has laid hold not only upon the imagination of mankind and thrilled it to admiration, but also upon the reverent wills of men, and has drawn their feet toward the Godward path He trod.

Jesus "went about doing good"; went about being good. He banished the wall between the sacred and the secular, and made all of life—work and play—a sacrament. With love He overstepped the barriers between races, classes and faiths, feeling the common fraternity in which every man was at home. He filled life with an exhaustless jubilance and an enriching potency which caught in their contagion all who responded to His presence. With simplicity, with complete trust in His Father, with ardent love for men, Jesus gave to the world a pattern of life that lacks the elements of decay. He calls us to follow Him and to share His experience—to join in a constant search to know God and to do His will. Under the power of Jesus' life, our ability to hear the voice of God increases; our sensitiveness to His will is enhanced; our cooperation with His purpose grows. The clamor of the world is lessened, and the still, small voice of God grows more audible, for Jesus teaches our souls to hearken.

As the portrayal in human terms of the divine nature and redemptive purpose that dominated Him, Jesus is the Son of God. As the compassionate sharer of our human lot, He is the Son of Man, our Friend. As the guide of our minds in the discovery of eternal truth, He is our Teacher. As the possessor of the goodness and the love to which we aspire, He is our Master. As the protagonist of life, abundant and eternal, He is our Saviour.—Harold L. Bowman, *Monday Morning*

356

Jesus was the poorest man who ever walked the dirt roads of earth. Born in poverty and reared in obscurity, He yet lived to enrich mankind. A stable was His birthplace, a manger His cradle. For twenty years He worked as a carpenter in a poverty-stricken and despised village which bore the scorn of men as they asked, "Can any good thing come out of Nazareth?"

He began His ministry at the Jordan River, with no organization to support Him, no patrons to enrich Him. He publicly began a life of poverty that ended at the tomb. He preached without price, and wrought miracles without money. As far as we know, He never possessed the value of one dollar. How pathetic His words, "The foxes have holes and the birds of the air their nests, but the Son of Man hath not where to lay his head."

He was an itinerant preacher whose parish was the world. When invited, He entered men's homes for dinner. When unasked, He went hungry. He sought breakfast from the leafing fig tree, but found none. He ate grain from His hands as He walked through fields of corn. His support came from the gifts of a few women, and His treasurer stole part of the pittance put therein. He walked on over the hills of Judea and by the waters of Galilee enriching men, Himself the poorest of all. He slept often under the open sky, in the wilderness without food, by Jacob's well without water, in the crowded city without a home. Thus He lived and loved, toiled and died. His value was thirty pieces of silver when sold—the price of a slave, the lowest estimate of human life.

So poor was He that He needs must carry His own cross through the city until, fainting, he fell. In a potter's field, He was nailed to that cross between two thieves, stripped of His robe, the gift of love, for which inhuman soldiers gambled as He died. With no estate with which to endow His weeping and widowed mother, He bequeathed her to the love of the beloved John. Then He gave His peace to the disciples, His pardon to the thief, His life for the world, His body to the cross, and His spirit to God. His burial clothes were the gift of a friend. He was laid at last in a borrowed grave.

Truly, Jesus Christ was the poorest man that ever walked the dirt roads of earth. Though He was rich, yet for our sakes He became poor, that we, through His poverty, might become rich.—Author unknown

357

No name or word, no single discussion of who or what Jesus Christ was and is, can possibly express the whole truth about Him. Both He and His contemporaries employed many names and figures of speech to indicate some of the phases of His character and mission. For nineteen hundred years men have made Him the object of intensive study and have presented pictures and interpretations of Him to the world, but not one of them satisfies everybody. This very impossibility of capturing Him completely in a word or phrase, or in the experience or descriptive powers of any individual, is a tribute to His greatness. Rich and poor, learned and unlettered, men of all classes and all races—all have sought to pour Him into their own molds, because they saw in Him some excellence, some beauty and winsomeness not found elsewhere. Although Jesus Christ is too great for our small minds, yet He is available and adequate for our every need.

358

Bishop Arthur Moore has said that in every man's heart are a cross and a throne. "If he puts himself on the throne, he will put Jesus on the cross. If he puts himself on the cross, he will put Christ on the throne. With self on the throne, the immediate willful self will destroy the ultimate self. But if he puts Christ on the throne, Christ will raise the ultimate self to new glory, beauty, and power."

I am filled with a divine discontent when I do the things I ought not do. As the child said, "Sin is the me in me." I shall be stronger as Christ liveth in me.—Charles W. Brashares, *Christ and Myself*

359

Help us to have a treasured memory as contemporary of Jesus.—Branch Rickey

360

No one who has been divinely inspired by Christ lives in boredom.

361

Did you ever watch a little child take a lesson in model drawing? Never two strokes of the pencil without a glance at the model. And the first law and the last law of the imitation of Christ is just this—"looking unto Jesus."—George Jackson

362

Will-power does not change men; time does not change men, Christ does! Therefore let that mind be in you which is also in Christ Jesus.

363

We often wish that someone would be more Christlike—but do we do anything to help others acquire the teachings of Jesus?

364

Four-year-old Tommie cornered another four-year-old on the opening day of Vacation Church School and said firmly, "Richie, if you hear them say anything about Jesus, be sure to listen. That's what you are supposed to learn."—E. Paul Hovey

365

He comes to us as one unknown, without a name, as of old by the lakeside He came to those men who knew Him not. He speaks to us the same word, "Follow thou me," and sets us to the tasks which He has to fulfill for our time. He commands. And to those who obey, whether they be wise or simple, He will reveal Himself in the toils, the conflicts, the suffering which they shall pass through in His fellowship, and as an ineffable mystery, they shall learn in their own experience who He is.—Albert Schweitzer, *The Quest of the Historical Jesus*

CHRISTIANITY

366

Christianity is not a voice in the wilderness, but a life in the world. It is not an idea in the air, but feet on the ground, going God's way. It is not an exotic to be kept under glass, but a hardy plant to bear twelve months of fruits in all kinds of weather. Fidelity to duty is its root and branch. Nothing we can say to the Lord, no calling Him by great or dear names, can take the place of plain doing of His will. We may cry out about the beauty of eating bread with Him in His kingdom, but it is wasted breath and a rootless hope unless we plow and plant in His kingdom here and now. To remember Him at His table and to forget Him at ours, is to have invested in bad securities. There is no substitute for plain, everyday Christian living.—John E. Babcock

367

The early vigorous church was essentially a working, serving, and forward-looking church . . . the young church did not have much chance of becoming self-satisfied and complacent.—J. B. Phillips, *New Testament Christianity*

368

Christianity does not remove you from the world and its problems; it makes you fit to live in it, triumphantly and usefully.—Charles Templeton, *Life Looks Up*

369

We know that we would have a far happier world if all men were really Christian, but lots of us don't realize that any man who is a real Christian will be a far happier individual. It is just as true that the Christian religion is capable of increasing the happiness of anyone who believes in it, as it is true that nearly all the world's troubles would be solved if everyone believed in it. The unhappiness which comes with envy, the sorrow left by death, the fear that travels with insecurity, the misery that follows after mistakes—everyone is subject to these things. No one likes them. And anyone can learn how to deal with them better from the Christian religion. . . . Eternal peace is a large order. Internal peace is easier.—Drew Pearson

370

The Christian life is an enlistment for the whole man and for life. The call of Christ is a call to detach ourselves from many things that we may

attach ourselves to one person, Christ.
—Tyler

371

It is inaccurate to speak of "This year of our Lord." Probably it will be a year devoted largely to ourselves and the things of ourselves. One wonders whether we can spend one hour of this year in consecrated devotion to our Lord. The tragedy is not that a multitude of things demand our attention. The real tragedy is that a number of things demand our devotion. . . . In Jesus' time there were men busy changing money in the temple. Today the people in the temple are busy trading in excuses and self-deceptions. . . . Yet, suppose one comes upon a minute in which his whole being is consecrated to his God. One dare not hope for a year of our Lord. One is bold who dares hope for a single minute of our Lord. It will be a remarkable minute, for it will assume the dimensions of eternity. It will be an important minute, for it will make the difference between manhood and sainthood.—Robert H. Heinze, *Monday Morning*

372

Nowadays we realize more than ever in the past the immense need there is to redeem the world . . . to enter into its economic and social and political life and strive to being the principles of the gospel to bear on it, to enter into its intellectual life and try to make the influence of a Christian philosophy felt in the universities and in the arts and in the whole pattern of its culture. We live in a world which has become progressively alienated from Christianity.—Bede Griffiths, *Commonweal*

373

Christianity is in the blood of the races now in power.—William J. Tucker

374

I am a simple soldier with a simple mind. As I see it, the object of this conference is to find a Christian foundation for a new German army and a close cooperation for it with the foreign armies. I have listened to the all-too-able learned lectures; they have offered and laid open the problems, but I have not yet heard a solution. If we are going to be successful against the common threat of communism, we must find a greater means of cooperation to build a common foundation. . . . There is only one foundation on which all can hope to stand together: a sincere belief in Jesus Christ as the Lord of our life. This is what a soldier can understand.—Lt. Col. Hugh S. Freeth, *Time*

375

The statistical columns reveal a nation increasingly Christian. The news columns reveal a mounting paganism. —Charles Templeton

376

Christianity has taught us to care. Caring is the Christian thing. Caring is all that matters.—Friedrich von Hugel

377

Christians have been guilty of a kind of isolationism.—Charles Templeton

378

Driving in a rut can be dangerous— living in a rut is even more dangerous. And the deeper the rut, the harder it becomes to climb out. Have you become so "bogged down" that you've lost sight of your goals? The Christian way of life is not always easy, true, but it is never in a "rut"—it is joyous and challenging day by day. The best way to get out of a rut in life is to be an active Christian—participate wholeheartedly in your church's program.

379

The major issue confronting modern Protestantism in America is that of bridging the chasm between personal piety and the total social cultural life in which modern man lives. . . . Protestantism has been so successful in winning people, raising money, successfully publicizing the faith, doing needful works of charity . . . that it has not had to face up to the question of its obvious failure to relate its piety and beliefs to the day-to-day forms and decisions of modern living. . . . Both Puritans and Anglicans built well. We have been living off the capital of their solid instrument for several centuries, but we have long ceased to expend interest and appear to have depleted much of the capital.—Jerald Carl Brauer, *Newsweek*

380

An old sea captain was telling a story of days when men sailed in wooden ships. He related the tale of an inexperienced youth who went to a hiring hall in London to get a job as seaman.

"Have you ever gone around the Horn?" asked the hiring agent, well aware of the fact that shipping companies preferred seasoned sailors who had made a trip or two around Cape Horn. The young hopeful replied that he had never made this voyage. "Then," said the agent, "you will have to come with me into the next room."

The youth who wanted to become a sailor was led into another room where there lay a horn of a steer in the middle of the floor. "Now," said the agent, "just walk slowly around that horn lying on the floor." The startled would-be sailor did as he was ordered.

"You have now gone around the Horn," announced the agent in a businesslike tone, "and if you will

come over to the desk, you will get a contract to work as seaman on a trip to India." The youth had suddenly become a sailor—in name only.

Some people, in a somewhat similar manner, become Christians in name only, for they are accepted for membership in a church. They attend occasional services. And that is all.

The practicing Christian, like a real mariner, has sailed the heavy seas of life conscientiously. He has helped to bear the cross of Christ in every tempest. He has borne his brother's burden. He is a good neighbor, with love for the fallen, a friend to the sick and all the needy, a comfort to those who sorrow, a peace-maker; a seeker after the Kingdom of God.

The practicing Christian has, in truth, gone around the Horn.—Helmer O. Oleson

381

Everything good has a definite price. That is why certain articles are called fair price items. They are of certain value, and thus are not to be found on bargain counters. Today people are more price conscious, largely due to modern advertising. We see large signs, "Why pay more when you can buy for less?" Consequently, many who seek to find a bargain in sales find to their chagrin that you generally get what you pay for. . . . Religion is the same in principle. There is no bargain counter! There is a price to be paid to be a follower of Christ. Some may try to cut the cost of discipleship to Jesus, but they soon find they have a form without the power of God. . . . The ranks of Christendom would be full today if people could get away from humbling themselves before God.—Wilbur Morgan

382

In the early days of our republic, Patrick Henry inserted this closing paragraph in his will: "I have now disposed of all my property to my family; there is one thing more I wish I could give them, and that is the Christian religion. If they had this, and I had not given them one shilling, they would be rich; but if they had not that, and I had given them all the world, they would be poor."

CHRISTMAS

383

You can't escape Christmas; you can only escape yourself.—John Cogley

384

Families find themselves at Christmas. The true spirit of Christmas is much more perfectly expressed around the fireside than in the bustle of holiday commerce. Christmas is a time of ingathering, of the renewal of family ties, of the reappraisal of our several wearied personalities as we see each other anew and reaffirm our mutual esteem. It is also a time of thanks, not only for the gifts and remembrances of the moment, but for the kindnesses and benefactions of the year. It is a season of sparkle and keenness, and an occasion for joyous shout, ringing carol, and good cheer. It is an opportunity for fond recollections and a chance to rise outside our usual narrow selves. It is a time of general good will.—*Park College Record*

385

The most amazing thing of all about the Christmas story is its relevance. It is at home in every age and fits into every mood of life. It is not simply a lovely tale once told, but eternally contemporary. It is the voice crying in every wilderness. It is as meaningful in our time as in that long ago night when shepherds followed the light of the star to the manger of Bethlehem.

—Joseph R. Sizoo, *Presbyterian Tribune*

386

Christmas is a certain feeling. It is timeless, never quite absent any day of the year. But it quickens as the holly wreaths are hung and the gifts are prepared in the symbolism of love. At length it rises to the climax of the silent night, the holy night. Then men gather in sacred places, where their mood is tender with candlelight and prayers and gentle hymns about the One who came upon a midnight clear. And in this openhearted moment, He comes again, and men are flooded with a feeling He has always had about them. The feeling that no matter how imperfect men may be, deep inside their weaknesses and their errors is a yearning for perfection, an unquenchable brotherhood of goodness. What a hopeful, joyful, merry feeling it is! —*Saturday Evening Post*

387

How can you tell when it's Christmas time? Look into a child's shining eyes—you'll see Christmas there. See a neighbor's friendly wave, hear his cheerful greeting—you'll know Christmas is near.

388

What was it like that first Christmas? Haven't we all asked that question as, down through the years, the joy of Christmas comes ever fresh and new?

How many Christmases have there been? Over nineteen hundred? For the world, yes. But how many for you? There are some people who will have their first Christmas this year. That is right. There are people who, just within this past year, have been led to call Him Lord who came as a Babe in a manger. This is their first real Christmas.

For millions of others, Christmas has not come yet. They are still living B.C.

—Before Christ. Their roadway to Bethlehem is blocked by illiteracy. The Christmas Story will become really theirs when they can read it for themselves and receive it as their own.

389

While engaged in that seasonable occupation of standing in line at the Post Office, I heard a man exclaim, "Christmas comes but once a year!" After a brief pause, he muttered, "Thank God."

Parent's Magazine, on the other hand, ran an article entitled "Make It a Month-long Christmas."—E. Paul Hovey

390

People say that Christmas today is too commercialized. But I have never found it that way. If you spend money to give people joy, you are not being commercial. It is only when you feel obliged to do something about Christmas that the spirit is spoiled.—Eleanor Roosevelt, *Glamour*

391

God often seems to us to be so infinitely far that we think He is not concerned with our planet. It does in fact really seem as if He had left this earth to its own devices in order that mankind might at last destroy it completely. From this notion it is but a narrow step to the distrustful question, "How could God be concerned with me, a small, miserable, little man, in a time when hundreds of thousands and millions, perish dismally? Is that not utterly senseless and paradoxical?" The result of such thoughts, which actually force themselves upon us at this time, is that unconsciously we exclude the thought of God from what happens to us day by day, that we see only the human beings . . . and base on them, according to circumstances, either our hopes or our fears. This is the situation which I have in mind when I say "to live without God"; it prevents us from drawing from the Christmas story such comfort, joy and hope as our fathers did.

Precisely in this plight of the heart the glad tidings of Christmas will bring us help, if only we hear the message properly, and believe it as the word which the living God speaks unto us and which we shall meditate for a moment.—Martin Niemöller, *Dachau Sermons*

392

The essential spirit of that first celebration by the Magi—the simplicity, the wonder, the joy, the worship, the gifts—lives again each Christmas. From the beginning a strong, but by no means unique, appeal of Christianity has been what philosophers call its monistic embrace of the apparent dualism of the human and the divine, of the natural and the supernatural, of the mortal and the immortal, of heaven and earth, of body and soul, of knowledge and of faith and of the material and the spiritual.

Indeed, it did not take long for a symbolism to attach to the first Christmas gifts of the Magi. The gold was taken to represent the material things of this earth, and the frankincense and myrrh to signify those of the spirit. While idealists have on more than one occasion questioned the actual existence of perceptible material objects, few opposite philosophies confined to materialism alone have developed an enduring influence.

To men of all faiths, the Christian anniversary brings not only presents but also an opportunity quietly to replenish the human spirit—that immortal gift that distinguishes man. In an age of comfort and of pleasure and of wealth, it is important to give over a still time to the spirit. There is a phrase used to describe a primitive stage in the development of human maturity—naïve materialism. It refers to the trouble ancient, uncivilized people had in perceiving and appreciating the immaterial facts of life and to their belief that material things in themselves were the only or highest values.

We run a risk today at the very center of our civilization, in our homes where we seek to create and to gather things of beauty, of falling prey to a new sophisticated materialism. It may not altogether deny the spirit of man, but does indeed exalt the materials around him for their own sake or for an impression we wish to make on others. We may avoid that risk if the first gift we open this Christmas is that of the private and joyful world of the spirit—of the mind and of the heart and of the soul—without which mere things can have neither beauty, nor meaning, nor value.—William H. Lowe, Jr.

393

No wonder . . . Christmas is such a time of joy, for Christmas means that God is with us in Christ; that He is Christlike; that we live in a world governed and controlled by the Lord of love, the Father of our Lord Jesus Christ. Remember that when dark clouds of worry and fear threaten to hide the sun for you. Remember it when temptations and sins threaten your soul with disaster. "Where sin abounded, grace did much more abound" (Romans 5:20). A Christlike God is upon the throne of this universe.—A. Ian Burnett

394

Isaiah looked forward to the coming of a Messiah in these words: "For unto us a child is born, unto us a son is given." Genealogies are sometimes a source of discouragement. But the genealogies of Jesus, the son whom prophets predicted for the world, struck a true note when they described Jesus as "the son of David," the heart

of sound national life; as "the son of Abraham," the heart of true religious life; and as "the son of God," the perfect likeness of Him who created the world and all of us.

395

Christmas will be more than a time for counting blessings. It will be a happy season, as it should be, and a holy season, too. We shall be struck at least once with the wonder and the glory of it all, and be grateful for the miracle and mystery whereby the Word was made flesh and dwelt amongst us. At least once, amid the gift-giving and getting, the festive decorations, the countless hearings of "Silent Night" and "Jingle Bells," the quiet contentment of the Day, we shall think of the Child and be glad.—Editorial, *Commonweal*

396

When you ask in what respect is the Christmas story meaningful to our time, the answer is: it is the day when faith breaks through fear and frustration and despair. This is not simply the festival of one religion—it is humanity's day of jubilee. It shows what can happen to home when God shares it. The setting of that little family was stark and poor. . . . But because one day God shared this humble setting, we decorate it with holly and a new romance plays over it. So the humblest home can become radiant when the Christ Child is given an entrance. . . .

When God is given an entrance into family life and welcomed again at the fireside, there will come a new glow and peace to our home life.—Joseph R. Sizoo, *Presbyterian Tribune*

397

Christmas, when its true spirit and meaning dawn upon the world, lifts every man who struggles on this earth with a mighty tide of power. This inflow of . . . power . . . is due largely to the fact that men realize with sudden force that they do not fight their battles alone. It is remarkable what a change comes over us, no matter what our trials may be, when we become aware that someone is vitally concerned with what we do.—Carl Knudsen

398

The Christmas story shows what can happen to a community when Christ shares it. Bethlehem was not much of a town. It was no different from a thousand other villages in Palestine. It had a few narrow, smelly streets lined with drab houses of sun-baked clay and sod roofs. And what a strange commingling of people there was on the streets of that village! There were the shepherds whom the Jews hated; there were the Jews whom the Romans hated; . . . It was a community full of tension and intolerances. Class consciousness and racial antagonisms were rife. Then, suddenly, the heavens opened, choirs invisible sang their songs and Christ was born. At once contention ceased. . . . Rich and poor knelt side by side, and facing the new-born Christ, they *faced* one another. His coming brought to that community a new sense of oneness.

This has always been the message of this festival. It shows what can happen to a community when Christ shares it.

399

Christmas reminds us that we are inhabitants of a world in which Jesus has actually lived. He was really born in Bethlehem of Judea. The cradle and the Babe, the wise men and the shepherds, the angels and the star, are not just fragments of a beautiful dream, but solid historical facts. Men have seen Christ face to face. They have listened to Him teaching, have watched Him working, have touched Him with their hands, have witnessed Him die and rise again. Jesus Christ was a real man. His life is a fact of world history.—A. Ian Burnett, *Lord of All Life*

400

Let us seek, in the Babe of Bethlehem, the one who came to us in order to bear with us everything that weights heavily upon us. Then we will undoubtedly become aware of the great joy that is announced to us; and out of the brilliance that surrounded the shepherds, a shining ray will fall into our darkness. This child is called "Emmanuel, which being interpreted is, God with us." Yes, God Himself has built a bridge from Himself to us! A dawn from on high has visited us!—Martin Niemöller, *Dachau Sermons*

401

The Christmas story points to the divine possibilities of life. You see what happens to life when Christ shares it. Here is Mary, just a humble peasant girl from the uplands of Galilee. Her life was not unlike that of a thousand others, drab and commonplace. But suddenly, because Christ had come to her, she discovered the wonder of it all and sang her Magnificat . . . "he that is mighty hath magnified me. . . ." This is the meaning of the incarnation. What gladdened her was not simply how great was His glory, but how great was her glory now that He had come to her. Suddenly life is lifted out of insignificance and boredom. . . . Life is no longer so casual and commonplace as we had supposed. It suddenly becomes a sacred thing because of Him. It reveals the divine possibilities of the life which He shares. . . . If you think that life has no meaning, let the Christmas story walk into it and suddenly everything will become worth while.

402

Tinsel has become for many people the symbol of Christmas. Tinsel shining in candlelight is gay and pretty. Garish yellow gold and white shimmering silver can symbolize a happy holiday, but one that has little, if anything, to do with the birth of Jesus which we are supposed to be celebrating each December.

Hay is a much better Christmas symbol than tinsel. Hay is natural, it does not glitter but has a scent that sends one's thoughts and memories back to the real and simple things of life. Barns and cattle, the old farm in the country, the homestead, cosy and warm against the sparkling snow and cold of Christmas Eve without; and at least three generations, sometimes four, gathered in the parlor and decorating a fir tree, cut from the wood lot, with popcorn strings and homemade paper baubles, and hanging stockings of all sizes and shapes upon the mantelpiece in expectation of Santa's later visit when the children have gone to bed.

Hay, rather than tinsel, reminds us of homely joys of an earlier, simpler life now largely fictional for most Americans. . . . But hay sends us back even farther and deeper into the true Christmas celebration. It was in a manger filled with hay, in a shed or barn behind the crowded Inn of Bethlehem, that they laid the newborn Christ Child during the darkness before the first Christmas dawn. Unless our Christmas celebration begins at the hay-filled manger, it is sure to be a little hollow and somewhat artificial.

In a world filled with hate and hunger, cruelty and selfishness, how can we be gay at Christmas? Only as we recapture the faith that God did something so important on the first Christmas that all men can rejoice, however cold their night or dark their prospect.—Eugene Carson Blake

403

Matthew tells the story simply. The sight of a star brought extraordinary joy to three worldly members of the priestly class of Ancient Persia. Taking with them treasures, these Gentiles followed the star's light westward into the land of the Jews. It led to Bethlehem, where they knelt and worshipped a Child. Then, having presented their gifts, the wise men went home by a different route to avoid reporting the whereabouts of the newborn Christ to the curious King of Judea, who was already troubled by the portents of the mysterious birth.

Herod's concern was justified. In less than 350 years, that birth became the most meaningful single event in the history of western man; Christians were running the Roman Empire; their faith was dominant. No part of the world today is untouched by its influence.—William H. Lowe, Jr., *House & Garden*

404

Halfway through life (a matter of statistics), you look back upon all the Christmases you have known. Each one is a little different from the others. The Event remains changeless. You change though, and you either learn more of what Christmas means—which is growth—or the meaning of it begins to escape you—which, I take it, is retrogression. The child understands Christmas as a child; the . . . man . . . understands it as a man. It is better to be a man, unless you have lost the clarity of childhood—and then it may be better if you had never heard of Christmas because you have moved away from, not towards, the changeless Event.—John Cogley, *Commonweal*

405

There is another sense, however, in which the birth of Jesus means that God is with us. Frequently we speak of someone being "with us," when we really mean that we have their sympathy, their understanding, their support. And Christmas tells us that God is with us in sympathy and understanding, for through Christ He has had a share in our mortal life. "God was in Christ." That has always been the Christian faith about the man, Christ Jesus. Mary's Babe is none other than the only begotten Son of God . . . and what Jesus has experienced, God has also experienced.—A. Ian Burnett

406

A starlight night, a rude shelter, a lantern swinging from a beam, cattle chewing their cud, coarse shepherds standing at the entrance, a travel-weary young woman, an humble village carpenter, riders of the dawn, a song of angels, and a little Child wrapped in swaddling bands—that is all there is to the story. It is a simple, artless tale of which childhood never grows weary and for which age never loses its affection. What a difference that day has made. It brings the prodigal back home; it cushions the blows of adversity; it takes the sting out of defeat; it makes compassionate the calloused; it puts a song in the heart and gives life a new meaning.

407

The amazing thing about this ever, never, old story is its persistence. Age cannot affect it and time cannot dim its glory. Each recurring Yuletide, our reverence for it grows. It clings tenaciously, insistently and almost fanatically to the life of each generation. In darkest hours and in deepest desolateness, men have found in it their peace. Just when you think the world is through with it, it meets you around the corner. In the rough and tumble of history, it has elbowed its way into the present. Banish it in one place and it makes its appearance in another. The swirl of hate cannot bury it, the oceans of misunderstanding cannot drown it, and all the armies of the world cannot destroy it. It is the one

festival which will not be denied and refuses stubbornly to be rubbed out. —Joseph R. Sizoo, *Presbyterian Tribune*

408

When I was small, my mother read me a story about a little Dutch girl from a poor family. The little girl was told by her mother and father that they could not afford to get her any presents for Christmas, but the little girl laughed merrily and said that everyone receives something at Christmas.

On Christmas morning the little girl found in her wooden shoe, which she had set by the fireplace the night before, a baby bird with a broken wing. The bird had fallen down the chimney during the night.

"See?" exclaimed the little girl gaily to her parents. "I told you that I would get something for Christmas. I'll take care of this little bird so that he will get well."

This little girl had discovered the true spirit of Christmas. For her it was not a time for receiving lavish gifts. It was a time for helping those who were less fortunate than she was. —Sue H. Wollam, *The Hearthstone*

409

The wonder of Christmas is its simplicity. There is Mary, the mother; and there is Joseph, to whom she was betrothed. Plain and simple folks, these, even as you and I. There are the shepherds—the first Christmas congregation. Humble folks, these, folks who lived close to the things God made —the earth the carpet for their feet, the sun and stars their covering.

Yes, and the Child, too. Nothing here of the pomp and circumstances of life; only the simplicity of the divine. It is this simplicity which makes Christmas wonderful.

Here may we all come, suppliant. Not to a throne of human exaltation, but to a Throne of divine simplicity. Here may we worship, recognizing in the simplicity of the Child the meaning of God's redeeming love. Here may we bring our joys and our sorrows; our joys will be hallowed, our sorrows will be lighted. Here may we receive strength for the days to come, light for the time that shall be. And the Light that shines from a humble manger is strong enough to reach to the end of our days. Here, then, we come —the young, the old; the rich, the poor; the mighty, the servant—worshiping in the beauty of divine simplicity, marveling at its simple love. This is the wonder of Christmas.

410

What does Christmas mean? Can we say honestly, not from rote, without guile, without pretense, but from the depths of our being? And how can we say it?

Thornton Wilder found a way to say a part of it in his play *Our Town,* which many have seen. Many others have lived it. It is produced on a bare stage with the Stage Manager in plain sight. In the final scene, Emily Webb, a young woman in her grave, asks to relive just one day of her life.

The Stage Manager allows her to relive her twelfth birthday, beginning at dawn. It is a lovely day—how lovely she had forgotten—a sunny, snowy, anguished, heartbreakingly beautiful day. Each blissfully sad moment is an eternity. She cannot bear the blindness of those she loves. "Let's *look* at one another," she pleads. But they do not look, nor did she, then.

Through her tears, Emily asks the Stage Manager, "Do human beings ever realize life while they live it—every, every minute?"

"No," is his answer. "The saints and the poets, maybe—they do some."

Perhaps those of us who are neither saints nor poets cannot realize any moment of life to its fullest or tell what Christmas truly means, but we can, if we pause for a moment, say some of its meanings to ourselves.

We can say love—love in its widest sense, love that is the touch of young lips together and love that grows, love that is of human bondage and part courage to bear the burdens of love. We can say love, as the youngster carrying a crippled child said it: "He ain't heavy—he's my brother." Love has many faces but all are kind, from that of the Madonna to the love behind a smile for a friend or a smile of thanks or welcome to a stranger. A mother's love is largely working love, as is a father's, and their love for each other. All love is a part of what Christmas means.

411

One of the Christmas images calling for celebration is the image of the Babe of Bethlehem. The Christ Child, in the image of an innocent baby, symbolizes "new life." Nothing is so promising as a baby, for nothing is so new, so hopeful, as a baby. We all need new life—a new start anyway. For we have fears . . . and all of us are bothered by past failures, and so life itself sometimes seems fearful. What should make the Babe of Bethlehem a strong image is that, according to our faith, this Babe reveals the very heart of the Almighty God. The Holy One, the invisible One, the Creator, speaks in Christ, lives in Christ. He says that He loves all men . . . moved by the image of the Christ Child, we shall be able to tackle our problems as human beings, fearful probably, but free from the paralysis of fear.— Richard H. Rice, *Classmate*

412

Christmas waves a magic wand over this world, and behold, everything is softer and more beautiful. If only for one short day, ill will is set aside, and the effect upon our lives is miraculous.

What an astonishing contrast Christmas creates in the upsurging of love and kindliness in men's hearts! Everyone is happy.

The mental and spiritual health-giving quality of good will refreshes mankind like a tonic. Nothing during the year is so impressively convincing as the vision Christmas brings of what this world would be if love became the daily practice of human beings. What a world we will have when at last men heed His wise advice to "love one another"!—Norman Vincent Peale

413

God bless you all this Christmas Day;
May Bethlehem's star still light the way,
And guide thee to the perfect peace
When every fear and doubt shall cease,
And may thy home such glory know
As did the stable long ago.

414

Thoughts of Christmas suggest the difference between "presents" and "presence." In the long, long ago when the Creche was first enacted, the angel choir sang of the coming to earth of the Son of God that His "presence" should be known and felt by all men, and the presence of Him who later was to say: "Lo, I am with you always." And the second verse of the heavenly anthem, implicit if not then written in Holy Word, must have been of the Christmas time "present" of the great heavenly Father who "so loved the world that he gave his only begotten son." So, of course, it is fitting that we should all reflect the spirit of giving as we exchange Christmas time presents with kith and kin. And it is also wholly fitting and intensely meaningful that we should feel and know the presence of the Holy One in our very lives. But may there be a tendency to overemphasize the importance of the material presents, and minimize the so very real significance of the Holy Presence—Leslie A. White

415

A good many people with houses half empty on Christmas Eve have blamed the little innkeeper of Bethlehem because his place was full.—Roy L. Smith

416

Every little child in all the world has been a little safer since the coming of the Child of Bethlehem.—Roy L. Smith

417

He who has not Christmas in his heart will never find it under a tree.—Roy L. Smith

418

Identify yourself with the Christ life until the Christ of history becomes the Christ of experience. . . . Recall how Richard Wagner wrote some of his greatest operas. He had no theater. He had no orchestra. He had no chorus. He had to play the operas on his own piano. He could not hear them as they would really sound, orchestrated and rendered with many voices. He had to imagine how they would sound. So he wrote *Tristan and Isolde*. Years afterward he had not yet heard it. He could get no theater or opera house to produce it. He could listen to it only as he played it himself.

So it was with Christ. Long ago, in Palestine, He played the gospel on His own life. But you cannot adequately play the gospel even on His life. It takes an orchestra; it requires a chorus. It takes communities, cities, nations, the world. Jesus has never heard how His gospel would really sound. To enter into the problem, to catch His spirit, to reproduce His life in ourselves, our families, our nations, and our world until the Christ of history becomes the Christ of universal experience—that is Christianity.—Harry Emerson Fosdick, "A Christmas Message," *Family Circle*

419

Now the essence, the very spirit of Christmas, is this: that we first make believe a thing is so and lo! it presently turns out to be so.—Stephen Leacock

420

During the First World War there was a Christmas Day in Flanders which has been graphically described. As the dawn came, the soldiers swarmed out of the opposing trenches. Laughing and talking, they approached one another across no man's land. They exchanged small gifts and visited in a friendly fashion, and, for one brief, precious day, the fighting stopped. "Something had leaped across the intervening space like the leap of electricity between two overcharged spheres. The spirit of Christmas had been too much for war. We were soldiers who had to fight and had to continue fighting. To stop suddenly and be friendly seemed a preposterous thing, but there was a greater force than armies at the front that night."

In a burdened world, Christ and His church alone stand for the brotherhood and the unity of the human race. To that far ideal we resolutely turn our faces and on this Christmas take courage from the oldest and dearest story we know.—David Braun, *Social Progress*

421

If only the innkeeper of Bethlehem had known that the *King* was coming, he would never have been so curt or abrupt in his remarks; he would never have said: "There is no room in the inn!"

"If I had known. . . ." "Of course, if I had known who they were. . . ." But he did not. Shutting his door on Christ, taking his lantern and going

to bed, sleeping while the angels sang and the King appeared—here is a picture startlingly true of mankind's attitude today. We too have no time for stars. We too are often overbusy and too preoccupied to sing with angels, "Joy to the world! The Lord is come; Let earth receive her King." And yet, we dare not say: "If I had known!" Rather, in this Advent Season, we must exclaim: "I know. I know that He is come to seek and to save that which was lost."

There is something decisive about His coming. Beautiful as is the story of His lowly birth and sacrificial life, it is indeed more than an account of a good man who came to establish his kingdom of love. He is a King who makes demands upon our love and loyalty. The world has too often denied that Advent claim. It has tried to get along without Him too long . . . the better world for which we hope and pray and labor can come only when His will becomes our will, when we acknowledge sincerely with our "I know" that He is our newborn King.

422

It is one thing to be ready for Christmas and another thing to be prepared for it. . . . The Holy Family wasn't quite ready for Christmas but was, in fact, taken quite unaware. There was no room ready for Mary and Joseph at the inn, and all that Mary had was a bundle of swaddling clothes to wrap her baby in. According to the lovely old Christmas story, readiness wasn't too necessary for the role assigned by the wisdom of God to the chief characters. It was important, however, in the wisdom of God that Joseph and Mary be prepared for this great event. And so, the Gospels relate, Joseph learned in a dream of the significance of the child who was to be, and Mary was informed in a dream of the great gift and honor which was to be bestowed upon her. The early church pictures the Holy Family as being unready but well prepared!

About the only one who was ready for Christmas was Herod, but he was hardly prepared for it. He was ready with his legions. He was ready for any emergency. When the rumor came to him that a king was going to be born, who would someday ascend the throne, he was quite ready to prevent this. He passed the word along to his palace guard who sent out an order to the militia that every first-born boy in the Bethlehem district should be killed. Yes, Herod was ready but wholly unprepared. . . .

I think, in this connection, of the novel, *While the Angels Sang,* in which the heroine is a woman from Maine. She followed a custom, when family reunions took place, which illustrates the difference between being ready and being prepared. After working in the kitchen all Saturday, and as soon as the family was gathered for dinner and she had put things on the table, she would retire from the company for just a moment, saying: "Well, now everything is ready. I want to take a moment to be prepared." So, alone in her own room with God, she would . . . "catch her breath" . . . offering a silent . . . prayer of gratitude. "And so," explains the author, "she came down with a glow upon her face, saying to the company: 'Now, everything is ready, and I am prepared for it.' "—James Wills Lenhart, *Advance*

423

Nearly two thousand years ago there was born in Bethlehem of Judea a Babe, whose life was destined to affect countless millions. That Babe was Jesus Christ. The time was ripe for His birth. Roman roads had been built throughout the civilized world in preparation for the feet of His future messengers. The Greek language had become almost universal in readiness for the proclamation of His gospel. The people among whom He was born were poor and despised, having been conquered by the Roman power. In the heart of every man was a cry for deliverance.

The world knew not of His birth. Work went on as usual. There was no tremendous upheaval announcing a new order. Kings and potentates continued to rule as before. Nothing outwardly heralded His advent into the world.

Only heaven appeared to be interested. In fact, God had to arrange a welcome Himself, and so . . . angels circled the skies and heralded His birth. Wise men from the East, studying the stars . . . came with their gifts from afar. Shepherds bowed in adoration and worship. Rulers learned of His birth and became fearful . . . of losing their power; they sought His death by every possible means . . .

He did not come to a palace with marble halls and carpeted stairs. No luxurious bed chamber was prepared for His birth. Neither nurses nor doctors were in attendance. Cathedral bells failed to toll; bands were silent; no royal choruses burst forth in song. Only the music of heaven was heard. For He came to a stable, and He was laid in a manger. His mother had only the straw for a bed, and animals were her companions. There was no room in the inn.

Little did Caesar know that this Babe, through His teachings, would one day . . . be recognized by countless millions as the greatest of the prophets, the mightiest of all the mighty, the Saviour of the world, God incarnate.—Oswald J. Smith

424

The miracle of the manger is God getting a voice all men must understand. Henceforth, when men shall look upon that sacred scene in the City of David, they shall say, "God is like that."—Merton S. Rice, *Adult Student*

425

Many around us will enjoy themselves behind the many masks of Christmas. But they will relapse into joylessness, fear, and anxiety unless the One whose birthday we rightly celebrate becomes to them real, alive and contemporary. . . . By thought, by prayer, by every tried and untried means, let us do all that we possibly can to make known that astonishing mystery, which is also a historical fact, that God became one of us that we might become like Him.—J. B. Phillips, *God with Us*

426

Several Christmases ago, the ministers of three Albert Lea churches within a few blocks of each other posted these subjects for their Christmas Sunday sermons, in this order: "Where is He?" "He is here." "God changes His address."

427

A few days before Christmas, Mr. Falor drove up to his favorite gas station with his four-year-old son Bill. "Are you ready for Santa Claus?" the attendant asked Bill. The youngster gave the kind of answer one would expect. . . . "Do you like Santa Claus?" persisted the attendant. . . . "Yes," replied Bill. "But I like God better." The attendant was curious and so asked why. . . . "Because," said Bill, "you don't have to pay for the gifts God gives you."—*Rapid City* (South Dakota) *Journal*

428

An acquaintance of The Stroller, standing behind two teen-age girls at a Christmas window display in a Seattle store, heard one say: "Imagine that, mixing up religion with Christmas!"—*Seattle* (Washington) *Times*

429

You never realize how fortunate you are until you enter a gift shop and see how many things your friends haven't sent you.

430

There is always somebody that one is afraid not to give a Christmas present to.

431

Long ago, one glad night, a star beaming bright,
By its heavenly ray, led to where Jesus lay.
Blessed Babe, Hope of Earth, angels sang at Thy birth,
Blessed Babe, Hope of Earth, angels sang at Thy birth.
Child of God, Holy pure, may Thy love light endure;
'Til the people's acclaim, bless forever Thy name.
"Peace on Earth," let us sing, praise to Jesus our King.
"Peace on Earth," let us sing, praise to Jesus our King.
                    —Rose Jasper Nickell

432

Why is it that nothing makes you feel wickeder than disobeying a "Do Not Open Until Christmas" seal, and that you're always sorry afterward?—Katharine Brush

433

There is the glorious truth presented in the carol, "While Shepherds Watched." Picture the shepherds in the field, sitting quietly watching their flocks. Suddenly the angel came from heaven to tell of the Messiah's coming and saying, "And this shall be a sign unto you." What was the sign? A legion of angels? No. "Ye shall find the babe."

And how will the Kingdom of God come? By a process as normal as birth. It will come as men and women take

Him into their lives and into their daily living. The Kingdom will not come crashing in. It will come unobtrusively. By evolution, not by revolution. The sign? "Ye shall find a babe wrapped in swaddling clothes, lying in a manger," but The Babe will grow, and so will His Kingdom. It has grown to include today six hundred million people. Some day it will grow to the point of including everybody on the earth.—Charles L. Allen, *The Grace Pulpit*

434

There should be a great deal of joy at Christmas time for the Christian religion is a joyous thing. However, many of our Christmas customs are turning the day into a great birthday party, but forgetting the purpose of the One who was born.

A party is such a fragile thing—so easily ruined. A neglected invitation, a misplaced gift, the wrong choice of dress, a snubbed guest, and the party is a failure. When Christmas is only a party, the day and the season can be easily spoiled by little things and there is no joy in it.

But when the true purpose of our observance of the day is kept foremost, the little things which annoy are swept aside in the desire to keep the purpose alive. The true followers of the Christian Way find that hardships add the thrill that makes it worth following. One who is inspired by "a cause" strives to attain the joy that comes from serving that cause.

One can have joy at Christmas time but he must choose whether it be the joy that remains and becomes full, or the passing pleasurable joy of a social event.

He who lives for himself will have small troubles, but they will seem to him great. He who lives for others will have great troubles, but they will seem to him small. This is the spirit that is called Christmas.—E. Paul Hovey

CHURCH

435

How shall we evaluate the church? To some, the usefulness of a church is measured in terms of its numbers, the size and beauty of the building in which its people worship, the money it raises and spends for local support and benevolent causes. Others will measure the church in terms of changed lives, happy homes established, civic righteousness promoted.

Let us make no mistake. The church is a society of sinners. It is the only group in the world in which belonging is based on the single qualification that one shall be unworthy. Most Christian graces are like flowers, which blossom best in society. Where can a person learn patience, considerateness, forbearance, and brotherly kindness better than in the church?

We are asked to give to the fellowship of the church our strength; and from it we also receive of the strength of others, as we join forces in a common quest and a common task. It is simply not true that religion is a matter entirely of the relation of the soul to God. Jesus tells us that if we are going to worship, remembering that our brother has something against us, we are first to get right with him before we proceed with our worship.

No man can do his best work alone. Trifles can be done without assistance, but the world has never known a mighty work to be accomplished without cooperation. Men must work together when they wish to do great things. Combination is one of God's principles upon which the world is organizing its modern life.

436

The first task of the church, now as always, is to make known the gospel, and to assert the claim of Jesus Christ as the incarnate Word of God to the lordship of all human life.—Official Report of the Oxford Conference

437

The essential task of the church is to be the ambassador of Christ, proclaiming His Kingdom. While the church has no universally valid political or economic program, through its very existence within state and society it should serve as a waking and active conscience to emphasize Christian principles in social life. . . . Suffice it here to say that all the church's activities, whether social service, education, the spreading of Christian literature, the healing of body and mind, or any other work undertaken for man, follow from the essential task committed to it. They are signposts pointing to Christ as the Saviour of men and of human society. They are manifestations of His love in the hearts of His servants. They are the inevitable outcome of true and living faith in Him.

In its worship and witness the church is sustained by the assured hope of its final fulfillment in the eternal Kingdom of God.—The World Mission of the Church

438

What does the word "church" mean? We sometimes use it of a building in which we worship; sometimes of the group of people who meet to worship in that building; sometimes of the fellowship of Christians over a wide area . . . frequently of a denomination . . . sometimes of all the Christians now living in the world. The word "church" may be used and is used in all these senses. What gives these various senses their unity is that they all apply to *Christian* churches. Whatever reality these groups possess derives from the fact that Jesus Christ is the Lord of them all; that He is alive and at work in them, and that He calls all His followers to be like Himself. So

behind the question of the church lies the question as to the relationship between Jesus Christ and those who believe in Him.—Stephen C. Neill

439

In addition to the matters covered in the questionnaire, I would like to mention the fact that I feel that there are a good many ministers who feel rather lost. I'm among them. We simply cannot see where we are going in the church. Our churches are successful. We gain more members, we have more at church, we have bigger budgets, we have more activities, we have better Sunday school materials, and so on. But we can't see that we are making much of a difference in our communities or in the lives of the individual members of our communities. This disturbs me.—From a survey of 1,600 ministers, directed by Samuel Blizzard

440

The laity stand at the very outposts of the Kingdom of God. They are the missionaries of Christ in every secular sphere. Theirs is the task to carry the message of the church into every area of life, to be informed and courageous witnesses to the will of our Lord in the world. To this end they will need training and guidance. Such training involves instruction in the content of the Christian faith and in the significance of that faith for obedience and witness in the different contexts of lay life. This kind of training will require the services both of ministers and of experienced laymen.—*The Evangelizing Church*

441

America is a spiritual paradox: it is, at the same time, the most religious and the most secular nation in the world. From 1949 to 1953, U. S. distribution of the Scriptures jumped 140 per cent. In a recent survey of religious attitudes, more than four fifths of the U. S.

citizens said they believed the Bible was the "revealed word of God." But another survey shows 53 per cent unable to name even one of the Gospels. And a panel of 28 prominent Americans, asked to rate the 100 most significant happenings in history, ranked Christ's crucifixion fourth (tied with the Wright brothers' flight and the discovery of X rays).—*Time*

442

"How big is our church?" is a question people ask me every now and then. Of course, I have to answer them by saying, "That depends upon what you mean by big. . . ." A church is big when it provides opportunities for learning and becoming informed about the Christian way of life. . . . Any church is a big church if it has an outreach. A church that does not have an outreach is a dying church. . . . Last but not least, a church must have an upreach if it is to be a big church. If we don't point people to Christ, then we are not really a church but only a social club. We must point people to the Christ who can change lives. No church can give salvation to men, but it can hold high the Christ who saves men through His grace. . . . When a church keeps at its center the Christ who gives life abundant and life eternal, then we can know that it is a big church.—Merritt W. Faulkner

443

We can have a church dynamic with the power of God if we see the individual church, of which we are members, not as a burdensome responsibility or a conventional fellowship but as a divine opportunity to make our lives register unitedly for God, such as, when in the company of others in public worship we bear our collective testimony to the value of our faith before our friends and neighbors; when in the Sunday school and other organizations of the church in which our religion is taught, we take our places as students or teachers; when confronting our fellows, who may not have found Christ as Saviour and the peace and strength of Christian fellowship, we, under God, seek to do the work of an evangelist in introducing them to the Lord Jesus Christ; when in our recognition of the world meaning of our faith through the prayerful dedication of our substance, we make possible the world mission of the church; when in the presence of the narrowness, provincialism and prejudices of men, we assert in word and deed our firm belief in our human brotherhood in the sight of God and dedicate ourselves to the elimination of racial and class hatreds and factions which divide the body of Christ and menace the integrity of our souls as well as the unity of our world; and when we see our religion, not just as a matter of form or convenience, but as a living experience in which we reveal the same mind that is in Christ Jesus.—Spiritual Life Committee of the General Council, Presbyterian Church, U.S.A.

444

Jesus used the symbol of salt to describe the early Christian fellowship . . . "You are the salt of the earth." To understand what Jesus meant we remember that, in His day, salt was the only way known to preserve anything. There were no deepfreezers in those days! Jesus clearly meant by this symbol that the church is in the world to keep and preserve the best and finest values.

Surely this has been the experience of the Christian fellowship. Without a church in a community, the best and finest things somehow become corrupt. Unless there are men in places of responsibility in government who find their source of strength in religious values, any government soon becomes honeycombed with graft. It was the business of the early church, as it is the business of the church today, to preserve the true values of life.—Stuart L. Anderson, "Why the Community Needs the Church," *Advance*

445

The church through history simply cannot be explained, as other institutions may be, as a group of individuals entering into a "collectivism," banding themselves together to pool their common resources for what appears to be some common good. It always has existed, where it has existed, as a body of believers made one by the forgiveness and the forgiving that one receives from the indwelling presence of the same Jesus who sent out His disciples to tell "the lost sheep of the house of Israel" of their new Shepherd.—*Crossroads*

446

There is no gain for the angels when membership in [the church] becomes a matter of social convention or even—as with the man who notices that church affiliation seems to make one less of a security risk—of prudential calculation. It is, in fact, a real and present danger to religion. Where everybody is "religious" nobody is religious.—William Lee Miller, *The Reporter*

447

The founder of [the United Protestant Church in one suburb] began with this principle: "We try not to offend anybody. In the Navy I learned it was important so to conduct services that there wouldn't be any theological matter anyone could take exception to. The basic need is to belong to a group. You find this fellowship in a church better than anywhere else. What we're after is a sense of community. We pick out the more useful parts of the doctrine to that end."—George L. Hunt, *Rediscovering the Church*

448

Suburbia has introduced its concept of success into the very center of church life. Advancement, monetary and numerical extension of power—these are the criteria by which suburbia measures all things. Most church programs are now burdened with endless haphazard activity in the service of success so defined. The task of the churches as witnesses to Christ's Lordship and to the power of the cross has been submerged. Clergy and laity alike are infected with the advancement ideology out of which they have grown. The test of every parish enterprise is whether it will bring monetary and numerical progress.—Gibson Winter, *Christian Century*

449

The purpose of gathering together on Sunday morning is to praise God and to honor His name. This note is lacking in much contemporary worship. Church services are designed to "do us good," or give us a spiritual shot in the arm. The emphasis is all upon *us*, and what we "get out of it." Now worship that does not reach the participant can be very sterile indeed. But the center of attention in true worship is to be not us but God. Not our state of mind, but His glory, comes first. The significant thing is that God is honored through song, prayer, giving, and attentiveness to the hearing of His Word.—Robert McAfee Brown, *The Significance of the Church*

450

A person who is a member of the church is rightly termed a "communicant" because he has a part in the Holy Communion. Anyone who has been severed from the church is "excommunicate," that is, denied participation in the Holy Communion. Thus the very language we speak testifies to the central and decisive nature of worship and especially of Eucharistic worship.

—Scott Francis Brenner, *The Way of Worship*

451

The church also is, in its basic nature, a *redemptive* community. It is unfailingly true, and there is no need to flinch in saying so, that no "church" is there if nothing happens. There may be a splendid community institution, or even an institutional community; and it may even be a potent inspirational influence in the flow of the political and social stream. But unless it is redemptive, of itself, or of its own membership, and of the whole world which surrounds it, it is not the church. We should be careful not to miss the crucial point here. It is not simply that this is the mission of the church, or that this is its commission. It is rather that this is the nature of the church. Thus we have to say that where the "church" is not redemptive, reconciling men to God and to one another across the entire sweep of society, it is not the church.—Robert Clyde Johnson

452

In prayer also we are both individual and social. For a man to assert that he can be Christian without the church is as foolish as to pretend that an arm could live without its body. There is no hermit music, for even a solo implies a composer, just as he implies a long list of prior composers; and a soloist would die of sadness if there were no one to listen. How could Christ ever teach or live a hermit faith? The Lord's Prayer reminds us in its very first word that God is intent, not merely on individual perfection, but on the Beloved Community. It is true that corporate prayer would grow thin if each man did not pray in secret; but it is also true that lonely prayer would die of loneliness, and perhaps of lovelessness, if it knew no social bond.—George A. Buttrick, *So We Believe, So We Pray*

453

Our churches generally might well face the question: What does the church as church bring to the thought of its members apart from ethical advice with which in principle they agree? Can it give them a perspective from which to view the objective forces in our culture by which the minds of all of us are so easily formed, and our decisions so often determined?—John C. Bennett, *Christianity and Crisis*

454

A lot of what the church says is fine, but what's it doing about it? All my church does is give us a few parties and tell us to be good boys and think about God. Does this help solve the Negro problem? Will it prevent World War III? Will it save a single country from communism? Christianity has plenty of answers, good ones, but the people doing least about them are Christians. —*The New York Times*

455

An old tradition tells of the discovery of a church deep in the forests of southern Norway. The "Black Death" had completely wiped out the people of the community. Nature had taken over in her own way. Centuries later, a hunter discovered the ancient church. The church of Jesus Christ in our day is frequently lost in the forests of man-made institutions, human affairs, practical activities, religious philosophies, and spiritual nonessentials.

Let the church be the church, is an oft repeated slogan. The implication is that the church has been something else and must be rediscovered.

This requires that we remember: that the church is a spiritual house; that the living stones in the building are all believers; that it is built on one foundation, Jesus Christ; that the gates of hell shall not prevail against it; that Christ loved the church and gave Himself for it; that it is a glorious church, holy and without blemish; that its treasures are the Word and Sacraments; that its business is to preach the gospel; that it is commissioned to make disciples.

In the rediscovered church, the house of worship is the house of God, where His honor dwells, a house or prayer, where we call upon His Name, the place where God speaks His life-giving Word, where He bestows on us His grace and benediction.

456

The church admittedly has faults and failings and possesses a human side. However, it is not merely a voluntary association of those who happen to be interested in religion nor in accident of social evolution. Its roots lie not in the minds of men but in the heart of God, and its existence is a part of God's plan for the world. It is not an end in itself, but its commission is to proclaim the good news of the love of God in Christ to all the world. From Jerusalem the church has gone out into every land; and as Christianity continues to be propagated, it will be the church alone which will do it. Furthermore, the church strives to Christianize society and to bring peace to all nations. So much has the church transformed every environment in which it has been allowed to function that no one of us would want to live in a community without it.—Henry M. Shires

457

It may well be that the disease of many churches, denominations, and congregations is that they try to escape disease by cutting off what can produce disease. . . . Every minister who is proud of a smoothly running or quickly growing church should ask himself whether such a church is able to make its members aware of their sickness and to give them the courage to accept healing.—Paul Tillich, *Union Seminary Quarterly Review*

458

The church is the only organization in the world that has lower requirements than those for getting on a bus. —Harry R. Rudin

459

What Kind of a Member Are You?

Are you an active member, the kind that would be missed?
Or are you just contented that your name is on the list?
Do you attend the meetings, and mingle with the flock?
Or do you stay at home and criticize and knock?
Do you take an active part to help the work along?
Or are you just satisfied to be the kind that "just belong?"
Do you ever go to visit a member that is sick?
Or leave the work to just a few and talk about the clique?
There's quite a program scheduled that I'm sure you've heard about,
And we'll appreciate it if you will come and help us out.
So come to the meetings often and help with hand and heart,
Don't just be a member, but take an active part.
So roll up your sleeves and strike the gong,
You will be convinced, it will not take long,
To think this over, member; you know right from wrong,
Are you an active member, or do you just belong?

460

We need a doctrine of the church. Man did not build the church; man cannot destroy the church; but man can fail the church.

461

A sanctuary of the spirit; a friendly household; a training school for Christian character; a center of helpful service; a force for civic righteousness; a witness for God throughout the world; a spring of spiritual refreshment to all who come. Christ is its door, and through Him is the entrance to God's eternal Kingdom. You are invited to enter. It is the home of faith, where doubtings cease. Peace be with you.

462

While traveling last month, we Hillises stopped in a big city church. Though strangers, we were all welcomed with an invitation to dinner, my sixteen-year-old Rosemary got asked for a date, my twelve-year-old son, Burton, Jr. got invited to go swimming. "Isn't church membership wonderful!" said our impressed kids. For a fact, it is. —Burton Hillis, *Better Homes & Gardens*

463

Eleven out of every 100 of our Founding Fathers were members of a church.

464

Sometimes the church is unpopular because it understands our sin and righteousness too well, and because sometimes it points at us with the words, "Thou art the man."—Edward L. R. Elson, *America's Spiritual Recovery*

465

For me to go to church is a matter of course. My father set the example. And throughout the years too many for a still youthful spirit to count more than casually, I have been the beneficiary of such good counsel as comes to listening congregations from the pulpits—high and low—of at least a score of faiths. Orthodox and heterodox, and not at all improbably sometimes heretical, have been the sermons, but sincere and well intentioned virtually all of them.

All thinking minds are in quest of sometimes elusive truth, and virtually all clergymen, it seems to me, are tonics —in their discourses—good for our sometimes reluctant morality. But let me go to church always with an open and receptive mind.

As I entered a church some little time ago, a little girl, standing at the door, accosted me. "Mister," she said, "is God in there?" And I think I spoke truthfully when I answered "Yes."—*The New York Sun*

466

The real unity of the church must not be organized, but exercised.— Johannes Lilje

467

The church is not a company carrying a bunch of keys to unlock the doors to all our problems, but a people with a master key to the whole of life. —Edward L. R. Elson

468

Well, if trouble comes, it'll keep our religion from getting rusty. That's the great thing about persecution: it keeps you up to the mark. It's habit, not hatred, that is the real enemy of the church of God.—Bruce Marshall, *The World, the Flesh and Father Smith*

469

A high-school coach spoke at our church's Men's Club this week: "Some people refuse to go to church," he said, "because, they say, they're better than a lot of folks who do. Maybe they are. But a star basket-ball player can do a lot more for the game if he's on the team."—Burton Hillis, *Better Homes & Gardens*

470

A church was in debt. The officers were discouraged. Some feared that the minister might have to go and the church be closed. Money was needed badly. The church had no communion table. One Sunday the minister announced this fact from the pulpit, and asked each one to donate a part of a table. Each family was asked to furnish a piece of walnut lumber. The only specification was that the lumber be free from knots and other imperfections. The members worked together to build the table. This project resulted in uniting the members of that church. Money was raised. Debts were paid. Attendance increased. They were united by a table; so are Christians. Christ's people become one at this board.—J. D. Ryan

471

When the average church member finds himself in the church, he doesn't quite know where he is, how he got there, and what is expected of him.

472

The New York Times Magazine once had a cover on which was pictured a lovely church. The caption was: "Built with more than hands."

473

Some persons think they are doing the Lord's work simply by going to the church, but they should be thankful they are privileged to enter the doors of a church for there is a job to be done by every man, woman, and child in this nation; a job of Christian service.—Governor Frank C. Clement of Tennessee

474

A minister was talking with a small Sunday church school pupil when she asked: "Do you know why my daddy doesn't come to church?"

The minister said he did not.

"He doesn't like what you say," was the child's frank reply.—Robert Holmes

475

A little girl was taken to church for the first time. The minister that morning withheld no punches, and when the child was asked what she thought of church she said she didn't think that the man should have said all those bad things about the Christians, there might have been some of them there.

476

The church exists not as an option for the Christian but as the imperative in his life. . . . There is no other way to keep the faith, and there is no worthy way to transmit that faith except by and through the church . . . we are not connoisseurs, but crusaders. We are not passengers, but pilgrims.—Edward L. R. Elson

477

The church is not essentially a human institution but is the community of believers of which Jesus Christ is Lord and in which He works by His Holy Spirit. It is the gift of God for the salvation of the world through the proclamation of the evangel of good news to all men. It asserts the claim of Christ as the incarnate Word of God to the lordship of all human life.

It is universal in nature, standing greater than any group claiming exclusively to represent it, and above every nation and culture in which it finds its home. Belonging to all the ages, it defies the passing of the centuries and embraces within its visible and invisible membership both the living and the dead.

Though composed of both human and divine elements, its nature is not abridged by the frailties of those forgiven sinners who compose its membership. It is His body, the instrument of His active power, and the bond of fellowship between all those who accept His lordship.—Paul B. Kern, *What Methodists Believe*

478

Friends, you have come to this church; leave it not without a prayer. No man entering a house ignores him who dwells in it.

This is the House of God, and He is here.

Pray, then, to Him who loves you and bids you welcome and awaits your greeting.

Give thanks for those who in past ages built this place to His glory and for those who, dying that we might live, have preserved for us our heritage.

Praise God for His gifts of beauty in painting and architecture, handicraft and music.

Ask that we who now live may build the spiritual fabric of the nation in trust, beauty, and goodness and that as we draw near to the One Father through our Lord and Saviour Jesus Christ, we may draw nearer to one another in perfect brotherhood.

The Lord preserve thy going out and thy coming in.—Canterbury Cathedral, England

479

I am the church! In my sanctuary there is peace for tired minds, rest for weary bodies, compassion for suffering humanity, forgiveness for repentant sinners, communion for saints, Christ—for those who seek Him. I am the church! Without me civilization must crumble! With me is eternity.

480

In one sense, our church is a building. It was planned, erected, and paid for by those who had but one thought, that they were building an appropriate, dedicated place for the worship of God. Its architecture invites all who pass by to direct their thoughts from current earthly affairs to the higher values of our Christian religion.

Inside is a consecrated sanctuary where praise and prayer ascend to the throne of God and earnest sermons, based on the unfathomable depths of meaning in the Holy Bible, urge people to constant application of such truths to their daily life. Such services, week by week, help to lift burdens from those who are weary from their daily trials. Here hurt souls are comforted; childhood and youth acquire ideals that will be guiding lights along life's pathway; and those who face the sunset of life will put their trust in the Good Shepherd who will be with them as they draw nearer to the shadows of the valley of death.

Before the pulpit, lives have been consecrated to the work of the Lord; engaged couples have solemnized their troth in the vows that made them one; and the last rites have been said for those who have passed through the portal of death to receive a crown of glory.

Our church is more than stone or brick or lumber. Its influence spreads into homes where prayers are said and children are taught the Christian way of life; into office, shop, or field where the Golden Rule is applied to practical problems of industry and business; into schools where the quest for truth is guided by the Spirit of the Master of all truth; into quiet rooms with drawn shades where faith lights the way to realms beyond.

It is our church—and God's.

481

I am the best friend of mankind. To the man who prizes sanity, peacefulness, pure-mindedness, social standing and longevity, I am a necessity.

I am hung about with sweet memories—of brides, of mothers, of boys and girls, of the aged as they grope their way into the shadows.

I am decked with loving tears, crowned by loving hands and hearts. In the minds of the greatest men on earth I find a constant dwelling place.

I live in the lives of the young and in the dreams of the old.

I safeguard man through all his paths, from the first hour life's sun slants upon his footprints until the purple gathers in the west and the darkness falls.

I lift up the fallen. I strengthen the weak. I help the distressed. I show mercy, bestow kindness, and offer a friendly hand to the man in fine linen and the man in homespun. I am the essence of good fellowship, friendliness, and love. I give the gifts that gold cannot buy, nor kings take away. They are given freely to all who ask.

I bring back the freshness of life, the eagerness, the spirit of youth which feels that it has something to live for ahead. I meet you with outstretched arms and with songs of gladness. I am your comforter and best friend. I am calling you.

I am the Christian church.

482

I am the church. Through nineteen hundred years of vicissitudes I have stood. Under tyrants and dictators, oppressions and persecutions, the tragedies of war and the urgencies of peace —I have stood, and will stand.

I am the best friend to mankind. I am the friend of him who struggles and of him who aspires. I am to some, a quiet place . . . a turning of the crossroads . . . a candle in the dark. I am what you make me.

I am hung about with sweet memories of brides, memories of mothers and fathers, memories of boys and girls, memories of those who walk with brave hearts as the shadows lengthen. . . .

I have shared your tears, your heartaches, your joys! In the minds of the greatest men on earth I am a constant dwelling place. I live in the lives of the young and in the dreams of the old.

I am the essence of good fellowship, friendliness and love . . . I give gifts that gold cannot buy, nor rust corrupt, nor thieves take away. I bring back the freshness of life, the eagerness and the spirit of youth which feels it has something to give and something for which to live. . . . And to those who dread the dark, I hold up the light of His promise: "In my Father's house are many mansions. If it were not so, I would have told you. I go to prepare a place for you."

Some time, some day, some hour—in the near or far-off future—you will yearn for the touch of my friendly hand . . . I am your comforter . . . I am your best friend.

I am the church.

483

Deep in my heart I know that the church is of God. That in spite of human frailties she has brought blessings untold to all generations, including my own. That she has made my community and my country a better place in which to live, to work, to establish a home, and to rear my children. That I would not want to live or die in a land where no church spire points its people heavenward.

I also know that the church continues to live triumphantly even when men and nations reject her by indifference or open hostility.

In this knowledge I gladly give myself to my church and offer her my loyal support by intelligent membership, regular attendance, generous giving, ardent prayer, and devoted service.

484

Types of churchgoers:

Pillars—worship regularly, giving time and money.

Supporters—give time and money if they like the minister, the Chairman of the Council, the Chairman of the Board of Elders, and the Treasurer.

Leaners—use the church for funerals, baptisms, marriages only.

Working Leaners—work but do not give money.
Annuals—or Easter Birds—dress up, look serious, and go to church on Easter.
Hypocrites—Leaners who say they are better than the Pillars.
—St. Philip's Society

485

We are called to be members of a minority. We are already members of a minority by being merely members of the church. The church is a minority in the world, and we are members of that minority. But we are called more than that to be members of that other minority which is that of the true saints within the church of Christ. To the accusation involved in men's telling us scornfully that we are a poor minority, namely, that we are so few because we deserve it, our one sufficient answer is this, that throughout the centuries we are few because we are among those who take God's moral command seriously, and such persons are always few. Let our goodness and not our badness be found the reason for our being few. Let our high ideals and our lofty purposes be the reason for man's abandoning us; our being a minority be rooted in the selfish or craven unwillingness of most men to be bound by such uncompromising laws, such massive obligations as we recognize. . . . As in other centuries, we shall be Christ's epistles written in good deeds, written in flesh and blood and brawn, convincing and powerful evidence of the everlasting Lordship of the Head of the church, even Jesus Christ.—Rew Walz

486

At home, in my own house, there is no warmth in me, but in the church, when the multitude is gathered together, a fire is kindled in my heart, and it breaks its way through.—Martin Luther

487

Yes, the church exists because it was in the plan of God. So was life, but death came also. The church was given life because there was a purpose for it in the mind of God. Things die whenever they cease to function purposefully. No horticulturist would tolerate apple trees in his orchard which never bore fruit. The Scripture has a message for us on what should be done with things which are barren.

The local church will not live long if it is barren. What is a barren church, someone asks. A barren church is one where there is no soul-winning; where there is no sense of stewardship; where there is no purpose except in the doubtful joy of merely existing; where no young men or women are being called into active Christian service; where there is no vision except for the local organization.

The church of tomorrow has a great task. The church must strive for a return of the rule of the Spirit of God in a world which has wandered far from that ideal; where there will be real brotherhood among men.

488

I ought to belong to the church because I ought to be better than I am. Henry Ward Beecher once said, "The church is not a gallery for the exhibition of eminent Christians, but a school for the education of imperfect ones."

I ought to belong to the church because of what I can give to it and do through it, as well as because of what I may get out of it. The church is not a dormitory for sleepers; it is an institution for workers. It is not a rest camp; it is a front-line trench.

I ought to belong to the church because every man ought to pay his debts and do his share toward discharging the obligations of society. The church has not only been the bearer of good news of personal salvation; it has been and it is the supreme uplifting and conserving agency without which "civilization would lapse into barbarism and press its way to perdition."

I ought to belong to the church because of memories—memories of things I can never forget; memories of faces that will never fade; memories of vows that are the glory of youth.

I ought to belong to the church because of hope—hope that lives when promises are dead; hope that paves the way for progress; hope that visions peace and social justice; hope for time and hope for eternity—the great hope that casts its anchor behind Jesus Christ.

I ought to belong to the church because of the strong men in it who need reinforcing; the weak men in it who need encouraging; the rascals in it who need rebuking. If I say that I am not good enough, my humility recommends me. If I sit in the seat of the scornful, my inactivity condemns men.

I ought to belong to the church, but not until I am ready to join a going concern; not until I am willing to become an active partner with Jesus Christ.—Daniel A. Poling, *The Call of the Church*

489

The church is a revolutionary power, but the Christian revolution is not a revolt of violence; it is an inevitable and righteous revolution which demands that things be changed and man made free.—Charles T. Leber

490

Let us picture . . . this reborn church.

It would be the church of the Living God.

Its terms of admission would be love for God, as He is revealed in Christ and His living spirit, and the vital translation of that love into a Christlike life.

Its atmosphere would be one of warmth, freedom and joy, so sympathetically and distinctly manifest as to attract and win into its fellowship all those who are striving to live useful and worthy lives.

It would pronounce ordinance, ritual, creed, all nonessential for admission into the Kingdom of God or His church. A life, not a creed, would be the test.

Its object would be to promote applied religion, not theoretical religion.

As its first concern, it would encourage Christian living seven days a week, fifty-two weeks a year.

It would be the church of all the people, of everyone who is fighting sin and trying to establish righteousness; the church of the rich and the poor, the wise and the ignorant, the high and the low—a true democracy.

Its ministers would be trained not only in the seminaries, but in some form of work-a-day life, so that they might acquire a personal knowledge of practical problems. Thus they would live in closer touch with humanity, would better understand and sympathize with human difficulties, and would exert their influence as much in living as in preaching. . . .

I see all denominational emphasis set aside. I see cooperation, not competition . . . I see the church, through its members, molding the thought of the world and leading in all great movements. I see it literally establishing the Kingdom of God on earth. Shall some such vision as this be realized? Upon the answer to that depends in large measure the future of the Christian Church.—John D. Rockefeller, Jr., *The Christian Church*

491

Our sanctuary is the House of Prayer, the sacred place where God is worshipped, where His sacraments are administered, where His Word is preached, His will is made known, His grace is realized, and His people are refreshed.

On its altar are offered the sacrifices of adoration, praise, and thanksgiving; of supplication, intercession, and petition; of penitence, repentance, and confession; and of dedication, consecration and the renewal of our vows of loyalty.

From its chancel are radiated hope for the despondent, courage for the downcast, forgiveness for the sinner, comfort for the sorrowing, humility for the proud, mercy for the hardhearted, knowledge for the ignorant, light for those who sit in darkness, and inspiration for those who have been beaten down with misfortune and disappointment.

In its pews are those who, within the bonds of a blessed fellowship and in solemn covenant, have pledged themselves to attend its services, to obey its laws, to pray for those who minister and for fellow members of the congregation, to give generously to its support, and to work for the unity, peace, and prosperity of all who worship therein, secure, in a land of liberty. May our sanctuary ever witness to the sovereignty of God, the effectiveness of His redemption, and the ultimate triumph of His kingdom of righteousness, peace, and joy.—Norman E. Richardson

492

"I was glad when they said unto me, 'Let us go into the house of the Lord.'" Every cornerstone she lays, she lays for humanity; every temple she opens, she opens for the world; every altar she establishes, she erects for the salvation of souls. Her spires are fingers pointing heavenward; her ministers are messengers of good tidings, ambassadors of hope and angels of mercy.

493

I will love the church. I have gone over it all carefully and I will love the church. For that is the only honorable response I can make for all she has done for me. She has persistently held before me her lofty and divine compassion. She has made it live in my life every day, whether or not I draw upon what she has been and what she is.

I will not be content to be indifferent to her. I will not think of the church as just a pile of brick or stone. I will not think of her as a neatly articulated institution, impersonal and awesome. Nor will I think of her as a body of not too good people selfishly banded together. No, I cannot be happy in a remote indifference.

I will not be content simply to use the church. I will not selfishly accept the fact of her silent protection over the community where I live. I will not lightly accept her sacramental touch on the significant steps, the critical hours of my life. That is not enough. That leaves me with a cutting sense of the too utterly calculating and selfish.

I will not fight the church. She has made and she makes mistakes, some of them indeed serious. And since her high cause has to use workmen very inadequate for so challenging a task as hers, she appears now and then to fail. But she is still the church. Her mission is still holy. She has not failed. She will not fail. Though she is misunderstood so often and attacked, I will not consciously take my place with the misunderstanders and attack her.

I will love the church . . . I will give her my heart, my deep devotion, my passionate, if awkward, allegiance. I will love her the more because there are those who coldly disregard her, those who thoughtlessly use her, those who misunderstand her and make her way very hard. Truly she carries a load. It is a heavy load. Yet, she carries it. And she will carry it.

She is the one thing in this strangely baffled world that steadily holds aloft a cross on which one day a Holy One died. From that cross even I get hope, challenge, courage, freedom. Its light falls across every hour of my life. I will love the church.

She gets my vote. I will support her with my time and service generously, my money in honorable measure, my ardent love and my loyal devotion. I love Thy church, O God.—Louis W. Sherwin

494

This church attempts to present a religion as considerate of persons as the teachings of Jesus; as devoted to justice as the Old Testament prophets; as responsive to truth as science; as beautiful as art; as intimate as the home; and as indispensable as the air we breathe.

495

A church should be a power-house, where sluggish spirits can get recharged and reanimated.—Samuel A. Eliot

496

I am a real lover of America. There is something about its history that thrills me, but I love still more its religious freedom. I am worried about certain tendencies which seem to me to threaten a departure from that splendid heritage, and I am glad to contribute to what I regard the greatest institution in America for the preservation of those ideals for which our forefathers gave their lives—the Christian Church.

The older I become, the more clearly do I realize the value of character. I am glad to contribute to what I believe to be the greatest institution in the world for the building of character —the Christian Church.

A Christian spirit in a community is better protection than a police force. Nothing exceeds the joy of living in a real Christian environment, and I am willing to pay for the privilege. I am glad to contribute to the institution which more than any other insures safety and peace in a community— the Christian Church.

497

I believe in churches because Jesus believed in churches, and showed His regard for the church of His day, the synagogue, by attending it regularly. When He commissioned His disciples to carry on His work, He established the Christian Church, built, as He said, upon the "rock" of Peter's recognition of Him as the Christ, the Son of the Living God. Convinced as I am that Jesus is right, I must believe in churches.

I believe in churches because of what they have done for me. In them I have made my most intimate friends. In them again and again I have been brought into communion with God. In them I have been urged repeatedly to higher living. In them I have had fellowship with friends committed to the same faith. Without these friends, my light at times would have burned very low, if indeed it had not gone out.

I believe in churches because of what they have done for society. With all their weaknesses and faults, which I know so well, churches still remain the chief source of moral uplift and spiritual inspiration in any community. Practically all the great social reforms have had their birth in the churches and have received their chief support from the churches.

I not only believe in churches, but I believe also in The Church—the Christian Church—the fellowship of all those who honestly seek to serve God as He is revealed in Jesus Christ. The issue today is not between churches, but between The Church and paganism. The forces of evil which threaten civilization are so powerful that the united efforts of all Christendom are needed to meet their challenge. Christ prayed for the churches "that they all may be one." We must help to answer that prayer by making the church to which we belong a more effective member of The Church, which is the body of Christ in the world.—Harold V. Jensen

498

A church can give its members:

A sense of belonging to a worldwide unbroken succession of spiritual men and women, with its deep friendship.

A satisfaction in a common sharing of the high privilege of worship.

The assurance of God which comes from the association with those who experience relation to Him.

A sense of the continuity of life. Of Jesus Christ the same yesterday, today and forever, "O God, Our Help in Ages Past."

A working knowledge of the Book which has had a more profound influence on the destiny of men than any other.

The support and encouragement of many others who are following the highway of life.

Opportunities to find expression for one's self in spiritual activities, such as teaching, singing, serving.

Opportunities for sharing the racial heritage of ideas about God, man, and destiny. The really governing ideas of our race.

The emotional life of music in great hymns and compositions made possible by group participation.

A haven of peace for men and women distressed by the pain and struggle of the world.

A center for many social and fellowship activities, by which friendship and understanding are fostered.

An acknowledged sense of respectability because one is a member of a church.

499

My church is the place where the Word of God is preached, the power of God is felt, the Spirit of God is manifested, the love of God is revealed, and the unity of God is perceived.

It is the home of my soul, the altar of my devotions, the hearth of my faith, the center of my affections and the foretaste of heaven.

I have united with it in solemn covenant, pledging myself to attend its services, to pray for its members, to give to its support and to obey its laws.

It claims the first place in my heart, the highest place in my mind, the principal place in my activities, and its unity, peace and progress concern my life in this world and that which is to come.

I owe it my zeal, my benevolence and my prayers. When I neglect its services, I injure its good name, I lessen its power, I discourage its members and I chill my own soul.

I have solemnly promised, in the sight of God and men, to advance its interests by my faithful attendance, by reading the Holy Bible, by never neglecting its ordinances, by contributing to its support, by meeting with my fellow members, by watching over their welfare, and by joining with them in prayer and praise and service; and that promise I this day renew, before God my Father, Christ my Redeemer, and the Holy Spirit, my Sanctifier.

500

I am a part of the church; one among many, but I am one.

I need the church for the development of the buried life within me; the church in turn needs me.

The church may be human in its organization, but it is divine in its purpose. That purpose is to point me toward God.

Participating in the privilege of the church, I shall also share in its responsibilities, taking it upon myself to carry my fair share of the load, not grudgingly but joyfully.

To the extent that I fail in my responsibility, the church fails; to the extent that I succeed, the church succeeds.

I shall not wait to be drafted for service in my church; I shall volunteer, saying, "Here am I, send me!"

I shall be loyal in my attendance, generous in my gifts, kind in my criticisms, creative in my suggestions, loving in my attitudes.

I shall give to my church my interest, my enthusiasm, my devotion—most of all, myself.—Harold W. Ruopp

501

Friend, you enter this church, not as a stranger but as the guest of God. He is your Heavenly Father. Come then, with joy in your heart and thanks on your lips into His presence, offering to Him your love and service. Be grateful to the strong and loyal men and women who, in the name of Jesus Christ, builded this place of worship and to all who love this home of faith as the inspiration of their labor, rejoicing in the power of the Holy Spirit —and may that blessing rest on you, both on your going out and your coming in.

502

We frequently hear the injunction, "Let the church be the church" . . . unfortunately, many who say it actually mean, "Let the church be!" They would limit the church's task to verbalizing the gospel and administering the sacraments.—John D. Ickes

503

I am going to stay by the church.
I know that it has its faults and

that there are some people in it whom I do not like. But I am going to hold fast to it all the same.

When I get satisfied with the low and easy path, the church will be there to fix my eyes again upon the goal.

When the subtle temptations of life are brought close to me and the high-road of honor looks steep and hard, then I shall need some person and some place to hold me steady in the storm. And that person and that place I will find, I am sure, as nowhere else in the church.

Its minister will give me the friendly inspiration of his life.

Its prayers will steady me.

Its hymns will speak to my heart from the warm experience of the great souls of the past.

Its friendly companionship will surround me with a fellowship that in the dark and dangerous days of my daily life I shall need above all else.

In the church I can find Him who is "the way, the truth, and the life."

I intend to hold fast to the church.

504

Our Church—the House of God. We enter into its service reverently, for it is His dwelling place. We appreciate its power and beauty, remembering the sacrifice it cost in life, labor and love in its building. We ask for faith as we enter as its servants.

Our Church—the House of Prayer. The church is a sacred place where God is worshiped and where His will is revealed, and His people refreshed and sent on, in His way. At its altar prayers of adoration, praise, thanksgiving, supplication, intercession, petition, penitence, confession, dedication and consecration are offered by His followers. We ask for guidance as we enter as its servants.

Our Church—the Workshop of God. "Jesus answered them, 'My Father worketh even until now, and I work.' "

In the role of (teacher, missionary, or Director of Christian Education) we work for the unity, peace, and prosperity of our church that it may witness to the sovereignty of God, the effectiveness of His redemption, and the triumphal reign of His Kingdom.

We consecrate ourselves to perform the services of God unto His children through His church that they be led into His Kingdom.—E. Paul Hovey

505

God's Church

O that the world again might see
A church united, true to Thee!
A church for all, rich or oppressed
Whose every work by Thee is blessed.
A church beloved in every way
Where Christians work and praise and
    pray.
A church whose program is not bare—
The Holy Spirit's working there.
Upon whose altars gifts are poured
Lest Thy great Gift should be ignored.
A church that in all things would be
True to His call, "Come, follow me."
    —E. Paul Hovey

506

Man is a social being. He cannot live alone. The man or woman who chooses the solitary way of life, chooses a way of difficulty, loneliness and unhappiness. Man is a social being religiously, as in all else. We only realize fully the strength, the beauty and the usefulness of our life in God, and the joy of fellowship with one another when we lose ourselves in the great, corporate act of worship.

In that moment, our fears, our failures and our sense of isolation are forgotten as together, with friends and neighbors, with the Household of God on earth and with all the company of heaven, we come into His presence with love, with gratitude and. with great joy.

We turn again to life's daily round to find it touched with immortal grace and ourselves fortified with new courage, strength and joy. . . . "I was glad when they said unto me, let us go into the house of the Lord."—Norman S. Marshall

507

Our daughter Kathy often talks to God following her formal prayers. Usually, she asks for many things. But one night, after her list of requests, she paused and added, "And now, God, what can I *do for you?*"

The question jolted me. What *can* she—or I or anyone—do for God?

Certainly, I don't know if we can do anything *for* Him. But I've decided that one way to *serve* God is by taking a real and continuing part in church life. For me, there has been no one great inspirational moment. But, over a period of time, my family and I have discovered that church attendance and religious experiences have added new strength to our lives. It's a strength we all need . . . and you won't find it any other way.—Robert Young (star of the TV program "Father Knows Best")

508

I am for the churches because they have something for me, and something for civilization. Dr. Ernest Fremont Tittle, the late great minister of First Methodist Church of Evanston, Illinois, said: "Let God be thanked there is on earth an institution that has a high opinion of man, declaring that he is in some sense a son of God, who has within himself divine possibilities; an institution that transcends race, nation and class; an institution which is loyally undertaking to embody the Spirit of Christ, and in His name to relieve human suffering, promote human welfare and carry on a ministry of reconciliation among men."

I find myself unable any longer to answer that kind of platform with

"I'd rather go into the woods and worship alone. Many of the clergy are dull, concerned over trivial taboos. Sunday is my day for loafing."

Countless times I have found in church something which lifted my spirit. That, I now believe, was what I unconsciously sought. . . . When you go to church, you should actively seek something. You must not go like an empty bucket, waiting passively to be filled . . . take at least a hopeful, sympathetic attitude. That's the least you should bring to a church. . . . Whether or not we realize it, each of us has a personal spiritual quest. It is the most important thing we should be about, and it is only ourselves we cheat if we ignore it. In this, of all ages, it is time we pushed that quest. I have found the churches a good place to pursue it. If they offered nothing but that, they should now be upheld by all men of intelligence and good will. —Roger William Riis, "I Am for the Churches," *Reader's Digest*

509

The parents of America can strike a most effective blow against the forces which contribute to juvenile delinquency, if our mothers and fathers will take their children to Sunday school and church regularly.—J. Edgar Hoover

510

Have you ever stood next to your youngster in church? Then surely you've felt that surge of warm feeling spread over you . . . as I have. Perhaps it's the happy feeling I get at just being in church with my son. Faith has made life so much richer for my husband and me. That's why we want our son to grow up in its wisdom.— Rosalind Russell

511

In churches all over the world, I have made friends—people who have no use for pretense, for their faith makes them real—who don't need to escape, for they have the strength to stand fast. These people gather in church every Sunday, because they find here, each week, fresh strength and peace of mind.—Oveta Culp Hobby

512

Recently, an English friend remarked rather wonderingly to me, "I had no idea there were so many different kinds of churches in the States. You'd hardly recognize some of them as churches until you see the worshipers coming out."

"How do you recognize them as worshipers, then?" I asked.

"By the look on their faces," he answered simply.

Having traveled all over America, I know what he means by "different kinds" of churches. I know, too, what he means by "the look on their faces." Watch the faces of those around you next time you come from your church. . . . Peace and contentment . . . the inner joy and inspiration your fellow worshipers feel in their hearts are reflected in their faces. There's a shining, just-born look to their world. That look is on your face, too, that peace and contentment in your heart.—Will Rogers, Jr.

513

I do not believe it can be said of any church that it is "but the lengthened shadow of an individual." Rather, it is the composite shadow of many dedicated lives. While every leader has left some imprint of his presence on the character of the institution, and we are richer because of his work, not one stands out as the dominant personality of our history. Our church is the product of the devotion of a great variety of people, both past and present. It has grown out of their vision, their love, their prayer, their toil and their sacrifice.—Carl H. Lundquist

514

Into the hands of the church has been thrust the opportunity of changing the climate of the world.—Bishop Arthur J. Moore

515

Religious institutions need the stimulus of men who are in the thick of the battle for right, else their worship will become mere form.—William Green

516

The church can be creative only as it enters responsibly into all the ethical problems of our culture and our nation. Some of these problems involve technical details which must be taken into account by any person or organization that would speak with any degree of authority on moral problems. The most dominant characteristic of modern culture is the mastery of technics by the culture and over the culture. —Reinhold Niebuhr

517

Good churchmanship is consecrated and intelligent church membership. The good churchman accepts full responsibility for being a member of the Church of Christ and seeks to know the full scope of its program. The good churchman is acquainted with the history of the past in order that he may appreciate what the Church has done, and that he may assist in guiding it toward its further goals.

The good churchman fits himself to work effectively in local situations and enlarges his powers and the influence of his church through wider cooperation. The good churchman, if an office holder, studies his task and educates himself to perform it with efficiency. The good churchman, in the crises of

the world, believes that the church is divinely undergirded and humanly implemented to leaven the world with the Spirit of Christ. Through wise statesmanship he seeks to guide the Church in its world mission.—Earl F. Zeigler, *The Way of Adult Education*

518

The success of a Christian church is in proportion to its effectiveness in making Jesus Christ known to a perishing world.—John M. Gordon

519

A man without a country is not as bad off as a man without a church.

520

A canon of St. Paul's Cathedral, London, was startled with the information that the Cathedral was moving down Fleet Street at the rate of one inch every hundred years. "Dick" Shepherd thought the church should move faster than that! His life was spent in an effort to get the church to move faster in the service of human need. This is the effort of each Christian—to get the church to move faster!—Martin L. Goslin

521

An apostolic church is not necessarily one that is hoary with tradition, but one that is in mission to all the world and engaged in that mission with a compelling concern for the unity that belongs to the whole church. The church in mission exists that the world may know God as He is revealed in Jesus Christ. The church in mission represents part of God's agelong purpose in the world. The church in mission proclaims an unchanging gospel, but at the same time it is a church sensitive to the guidance of the Holy Spirit in the changed situations posed by each new day. . . .

The First Churches on Main Streets everywhere tend to think of themselves as fixed and settled largely within the boundaries of their own parishes. Such congregations need to be asked insistently, "To whom have you been sent?" It is only as a congregation in each generation recovers anew its apostolic nature that those responsible for leading its life may find themselves not pushing a program of missions, but guiding a congregation in mission.—*New Day Dawning*

522

Every Christian has been disturbed, at times, by the slow progress of the Christian faith. Often the church has seemed indifferent and stolid in the face of advancing wrong. We would that she would show her strength in all the social movements, from the sponsorship of a new social hall to taking sides in a war between nations. What churchman, perplexed of the aloftness of the church, has not been tempted to sing the parody:

> Like a mighty tortoise
> Moves the Church of God;
> Brothers we are treading
> Where we've always trod.

The church is a supranational institution. Its persistent finger, pointing to the Ten Commandments and the Sermon on the Mount, has been a mighty force in the elevation of the human race. Its members, stirred by the visions of righteousness, have participated in the social movements from the first year of our Christian era. And the church often has, itself, entered the ranks of the fighters when it has seen a righteous cause.

But history moves forward and individual crises pass. The institution which stakes its all on a temporary fight may compromise its eternal convictions. The fighting clergy of the great crusades darkened the cross as they moved to conquest. God can be cheapened by making Him a national-

istic figure. The psalmist is still right: "A thousand years in thy sight are but as yesterday when it is past, and as a watch in the night."—William H. Leach

523

The world is always in danger of permitting "time to crowd out eternity." Material things become so important that eternal values are forgotten or ignored. So persistent are the demands of the body that the longings and aspirations of the soul are stifled. The struggle for existence becomes so keen that the gift of eternal life through Christ Jesus is lost sight of.

In sharp contrast to all this the Christian Church proclaims, "One thing is needful," "Seek ye first the kingdom of God and his righteousness." Christ Himself places supreme emphasis on the importance of seeking His Kingdom first, but only the beginnings of that Kingdom are here in time; its consummation is in eternity.

In every part of our land, church spires continue to point heavenward, a visible testimony to the truth that man is not an earthbound creature with temporal success and happiness his supreme and only goal. They proclaim to all the world the undying faith of man that his ultimate destiny is eternal life in unrestricted fellowship with his Saviour.

524

The church to me is the on-going family of Christian people seeking to be God's ministers for His purpose in the world. You cannot belong to a family in any true sense without associating with its members continuously and regularly, and sharing in their calling to serve God. One can worship God alone, but it means more, much more, in the company of faithful men, women, and children—in church. —Charles P. Taft

525

My church stands as a beacon on the shoals of time. It is the lighthouse which points men, women, boys, and girls in the direction of the Christian way of life. Far and wide goes the beam of kindliness and love, the steady ray of hope, the sincere attitude of fellowship.

My church is the agency of God's salvation for mankind. It is the expression of the love of God as it is revealed in Jesus Christ our Lord.

My church is the only deathless institution. "The gates of hell shall not prevail against it." Its mission is eternal. Its work is divine.

My church seeks to build the Kingdom of God, beginning here and now, and continuing forever. It is not concerned primarily with the preservation of its own life. It seeks to do God's will "on earth as it is in heaven."

My church is composed of human beings, sinners saved by grace. It has no perfect people, but it seeks to make all men better. It offers no promise of easy living. Rather, it challenges persons to venture forth to live for God in the spirit of Christ.

My church needs me and I need my church. For this is the means God uses to carry forward His redemptive work —through human beings, who are His own creation.

My church needs my prayers, and I need its support in all experiences of life.

526

Some critics of the church may say that the church becomes more enlightened the greater the distance from the local situation. Local churches of the same denomination in some states would not be likely to say these things. Ministers in local pulpits would risk their chance of having any local influence if they were to say them with such forthrightness.

This . . . illustrates very clearly a fact about church life that needs to be understood; the local church is often less dependable in its ethical judgments than larger units of the church. In the local church there is a tendency for one social interest to be dominant, but in the larger units of the church there are several social interests present which can neutralize each other and prepare the way for a judgment which transcends them and has some claim to be Christian. Instead of being cynical about the fact that people often speak more clearly away from the local situation, we should recognize the sociological realities which underlie this tendency and emphasize the necessity of continued interaction between local congregations and the larger church. From this standpoint we can see how very much mistaken it is to put the major emphasis on the autonomy of the local church. The local church cannot afford to be autonomous, because it greatly needs correction from the experience and insight of other constituencies.—John C. Bennett, *Christianity and Crisis*

527

Truman Douglass has suggested that many churchmen spend so much time doing "church work" that they give little thought and effort to doing "the work of the church." What is the difference? The true work of the church is evangelism, bearing witness to Christ in the world. In a sense the "program" of the local church is preliminary and instrumental to the basic task of evangelism. Where work within the four walls of a church or on church projects is regarded as an end in itself, the church is failing to fulfill its basic responsibility. But where the Christian who is a business executive begins to interpret his responsibilities to his employees in pastoral terms; where the Christian who is an architect seeks to give honest and forthright expression to the needs of the day in concrete, glass and steel; where the Christian who is a labor leader insists upon fair play when his union meets with management; and where the Christian who is an attorney out of a deep concern for justice speaks the truth with love—there the church is doing that work in the world for which it was constituted. The church cannot be militant until its members are scattered as seeds of the Kingdom throughout the world.—Robert V. Moss, Jr.

CIRCUMSTANCES

528

It could be written, for most of us: due to circumstances *within* our control.—Marcelene Cox

529

Whether a man lives or dies in vain can be measured only by the way he faces his own problems, by the success or failure of the inner conflict within his own soul. And of this no one may know save God.—James Conant

530

Most people would succeed in small things, if they were not troubled by great ambitions.—Henry Wadsworth Longfellow

531

We feel that we are greater than we know.—William Wordsworth

532

I endeavor to subdue circumstances to myself, and not myself to circumstances.—Horace

533

Whatever happens in the world, let us sing and say, we will wait what God the Lord will do.—Martin Luther

534

At all times and under all circumstances, overcome evil with good. Know thyself, and God will supply the wisdom and the occasion for a victory over evil.—Mary Baker Eddy

535

He is happy whose circumstances suit his temper; but he is more excellent who can suit his temper to any circumstances.—David Hume

536

The height of human wisdom is to bring our tempers down to our circumstances and to make a calm within, under the weight of the greatest storm without.—Daniel Defoe

CITIZEN

537

Good citizenship is not enough. Every person is more than a citizen of a national state; he is more than a mere political animal. He is a human being, and a human being has more than a political nature. He has a social nature, an economic nature, an artistic nature, a moral nature. The objective of the social studies is more than to make good citizens; it is to make well-rounded, decent, and civilized human beings.—William G. Carleton, *Vital Speeches*

538

This country will not be a really good place for any of us to live in if it is not a really good place for all of us to live in.—Theodore Roosevelt

539

A citizen has a complex duty. He ought to learn to express his opinions and to make up his own mind on the principal public issues. He ought never to miss the ballot box. And when he casts his vote for somebody, he should weigh that somebody in the scale of morals—which includes intellectual integrity.—Herbert Hoover

540

Ten Marks of a Good Citizen

1. He is well-informed on local and world affairs. "Knowledge is the food of the soul" (Plato).
2. He is courteous, unselfish, friendly —gets along well with others—is a good neighbor. "All is well with him who is beloved of his neighbors" (George Herbert).
3. He is sincere, dependable, and takes an active part in the church or religious community of his choice. "Religion is the basis of civil society" (Edmund Burke).
4. He appreciates what others have done for him and accepts responsibility for the future betterment of his community. "A community is like a ship; everyone ought to be prepared to take the helm" (Henrik Ibsen).
5. He is fair and just in his relations with others. "Hear the other side" (Augustine).
6. He obeys the laws of his community and nation. "No man is above the law" (Theodore Roosevelt).
7. He votes regularly and intelligently at election time. "The greatest menace to freedom is an inert people" (Justice Brandeis).
8. He is interested in the freedom and welfare of all the world's peoples and does his part to secure them. "Slav, Teuton, Celt, I count them all my friends and brother souls" (Tennyson).
9. He is productive—renders a worthwhile service to his fellow man. "The highest of distinctions is service to others" (King George VI).
10. He sets a good example to the youth of his community. "A good example is the best sermon" (Thomas Fuller).—Herbert J. Taylor, *Rotarian*

541

My own deliberate opinion is that the more of pure moral principle is carried into the policy and conduct of a government, the wiser and more profound will that policy be.—John Quincy Adams

542

In the threat to free government in America, the religious people have more to lose than any other class. If the basic freedoms were to go, not only would the churches be closed, but the mouths of believers as well. If the church people will vote during the week as they vow on Sunday, representative government will gain a victory, whichever candidates win.

543

The humblest citizen of all the land, when clad in the armor of a righteous cause, is stronger than all the hosts of Error.—William Jennings Bryan

544

The very essence of a free government consists in considering offices as public trusts, bestowed for the good of the country, and not for the benefit of an individual or a party.—John C. Calhoun

545

Government is a trust, and the officers of the government are trustees; and both the trust and the trustees are created for the benefit of the people. —Henry Clay

546

"My country, right or wrong," may have a glorious ring in wartime, but how hollow it sounds in a civilized society, and what an invitation to chaos it would constitute if adopted universally.—Arthur Sweetser

547

If the nonvoters would only turn out and vote, they could, in most elections, decide the issue all by themselves. That's a measure of how little Americans really think of their boasted citizenship.—*Rapid City* (South Dakota) *Journal*

548

"Why don't they keep the streets a
    little cleaner?"
You ask with keen annoyance not un-
    due.
"Why don't they keep the parks a
    little greener?"
Did you ever stop to think that *they*
    means *you?*
"How long will they permit this graft
    and stealing?
Why don't they see that courts are
    clean and true?
Why will they wink at crooked public
    dealing?"
Did you ever stop to think that *they*
    means *you?*

549

We are apt to classify government in two categories: good and bad. It should be classified in three categories: aggressive government, indifferent government, and bad government. . . . Bad government cooperates in the violation of law. Indifferent government prosecutes whenever its attention is brought to a violation, but otherwise it does not act. Aggressive government does not wait to have violations brought to its attention but takes the initiative in cleaning up a community. . . . Too often a Christian citizen is satisfied with an indifferent government. So long as it does not cooperate in violation of the law he is content. . . . In one city a group of young people said that one cause of delinquency is community laws that are not strictly enforced. Their plea was, "Either do not pass a law or, if you pass it, enforce it impartially." It is important that your local government should not be guilty of lax enforcement, particularly of laws concerning children.—S. Edward Young, *Social Progress*

550

The best Christian is always the best citizen. He who is mindful of his eternal citizenship will most faithfully fulfill the obligations of his temporal citizenship. He who thinks most of heaven will do most for earth. To obey the highest law is to go beyond obedience to the lower.

551

Frequently, you hear this question: what good will one vote do? Well one vote had a lot to do with a lot of things in this country. Thomas Jefferson was elected president by one vote in the electoral college. So was John Quincy Adams. Rutherford B. Hayes was elected president by one vote. His election was contested, and it was referred to an electoral college. Again he won by a single vote.

The man who cast the deciding vote for President Hayes was a congressman from Indiana, a lawyer who was elected to congress by a margin of just one vote; and that one vote was cast by a client of his, who, though desperately ill, insisted upon being taken to the polls.

Just one vote gave statehood to California, Idaho, Oregon, Texas, and Washington.

Pause for a moment—by just one vote there came into the nation the states of California, Idaho, Oregon, Texas and Washington. That's a big chunk of territory and, today, all the millions living in those states are Americans by just one vote.

Now, you may say that the one vote situation applies to the past. Well, don't forget that the draft act of World War II passed the House by just one vote. You can carry this one-vote history on and on. For example, one more additional Democratic vote in each of Ohio's 8,800 precincts in 1944 would have defeated Mr. Taft. In 1948, one more additional Republican vote in each of the 8,800 precincts would have carried the state for Mr. Dewey instead of Mr. Truman.—*Ballot Battalion*

CIVILIZATION

552

Civilization is like a skin above bottomless waters.—Jacquetta Hawkes, *Man on Earth*

553

The true test of civilization is not the census, nor the size of cities, nor the crops, but the kind of man that the country turns out.—Ralph Waldo Emerson

554

When Albert Schweitzer revisited Europe after his long sojourn in Africa, one of his admirers asked him, "Well, what do you think of civilization?"

"It's a good idea," replied Schweitzer. "Somebody ought to start it."

CLEANLINESS

555

A missionary of the Congregational Christian Churches in Africa wrote: "One of our catechists prayed in a worship service, 'O God, be soap to wash our hearts!' We would make that the desire of our hearts. too."—*Christian World Facts*

556

There is an old proverb which says, "Cleanliness is next to godliness." Artemus Ward, the famous American humorist, said: "If you will show me a place where there ain't no meeting houses and where men don't pray, I will show you a place where people are slipshod and dirty, where gates are off the hinges, where old hats are stuffed in broken windows. . . ." That is a blunt way of saying that filth and ungodliness go together as often as cleanliness goes with godliness. We must be clean both inside and out, if we are to go into the presence of God. "Who shall ascend into the hill of the Lord? or who shall stand in his holy place? He that hath clean hands, and a pure heart . . ." (Psalm 24:3, 4). Merely washing our hands is not enough. Lady Macbeth found that repeated washing of her hands could not cleanse her heart.—E. Paul Hovey, *The Upper Room*

557

Many church members are neatly starched and ironed—but they've never been washed.

558

The story is told of a lad who was washed and ready to visit the park. When his father was about to start, he found his little son playing in the mud and said, "I can't take you to the park looking like that."

"Why, I'se clean; mamma scrubbed me," the child protested.

The wise father did not argue, but taking the boy in his arms carried him to a looking glass. It revealed an unclean face; yet they did not use the mirror to remove the dirt, for that is the function of soap and water.

Now the Bible presents the law of God as His moral looking glass. . . . As we look into it, our imperfections are revealed and our evil condemned. Shall we attempt to use it to wash away our guilt, or shall we retaliate by seeking to demolish the mirror? That would be worse than futile. The New Testament declares that "the law is holy . . . and just, and good." It is perfect as a mirror, but wholly useless as a cleansing solution. The mirror assists in determining the diagnosis; then the individual hastens to the Great Physician, who provides the gospel remedy.—R. F. Cottrell

CODE

559

No fairer or finer prospectus for any journey into our contemporary world could be formulated than that given by Zona Gale in the sentence which she calls her social code—"I am determined to increase the area of my awareness." That doesn't sound much like a creed. That's the beauty of it. Too many start out with a ringing, "I believe." Such an affirmation ought to be the end of a process of thought rather than the beginning. A really vital creed is nothing but the conclusion of a process of enlarged awareness. It begins with experience. To begin with a creed, religious, scientific, or economic, is merely to acquire a set of brittle dogmas which rattle around in the mind like marbles in a bag, with no growing roots to touch experience.—Halford E. Luccock

560

A Teen-Ager's Code

1. Don't let your parents down. They brought you up.
2. Stop and think before you drink.
3. Ditch dirty thoughts fast, or they'll ditch you.
4. Show-off driving is juvenile. Don't act your age.
5. Be smart; obey. You'll give orders yourself some day.
6. Choose your friends carefully. You are what they are.
7. Choose a date fit for a mate.
8. Don't go steady unless you're ready.
9. Go to church regularly. God gives you a week. Give Him back an hour.
10. Live carefully. The soul you save may be your own.—Virginia Chose, *Link*

561

Daniel had a funny kind of backbone. It could bow three times a day to God. But not once to the king in worship!

562

How much does a code ask? One's life?

563

As a soldier you failed. A new kind of war demands a new code.—*Time Limit*

564

I have broken my code and it feels good.—S. N. Behrman, *Jacobowsky and the Colonel*

565

The strength of a country or code lies in the true sense of loyalty it can arouse in the hearts of its people.—Louis C. Gerstein

566

In the scheme of democracy, as in the code of Christianity, all men are on a common level of dignity and importance.—Frank Murphy

COLLEGE

567

The freshman year is a little like a cold plunge. The students are impressed with the vastness and impersonality of the place. They often find the tempo faster and the standards higher. Back home they were the cream of the crop, but they come to Harvard to compete with lads who are just as bright.—Gaylord P. Coon, *The Harvard Crimson*

568

Robert Browning . . . started with a chemical laboratory, with chemical affinity, and from that he worked up to spiritual affinity which we call love, and from spiritual affinity he worked his sure-footed way up to the idea of spiritual reunion and heaven, but it seems to me that he did give us . . . in "Ferishtah's Fancies" . . . the definition of a liberal arts college. "Sure enough, we learned what was, imagined what might be."—Charles F. Wishart, *The Cultural College in a Troubled Age*

569

I am amazed by the number of Christian students who go to college counting on the church there to shelter and nurse them. They expect the Christian community to put them in contact with nice people, guide their feet on the straight and narrow path and keep them from losing their faith. The church is therefore expected to offer a program of activities which will achieve these ends. The more I live in this revolutionary world, the more disgusted I become with this idea. . . . When you go to college, God is calling you to carry on His work on one of the greatest and most important missionary frontiers in the modern world. As a Christian student in college, you have a mission—to make your whole life a witness to the new possibilities of life which are open to all in Jesus Christ. Think of some of the opportunities which you and other members of the Christian community on the campus have.—M. Richard Shaull, *Going to College Handbook*

570

No wonder colleges are reservoirs of knowledge. The freshman brings a little in, and the seniors take none away, and knowledge accumulates.—Abbott Lawrence Lowell

COMFORT

571

Einstein confessed, "To make a goal of comfort or happiness has never appealed to me." Some people take it that Einstein in essence was saying, "I prefer misery to comfort and I'd rather have trouble than happiness." Of course he meant no such thing.

Is there a game of words here? Could it be there are men who get comfort by going without comforts? Another little book could be written about how Einstein meant it that "comfort and happiness" are dangerous goals. Anyhow, we heard Rocky Marciano tell Ed Murrow that since he retired from the ring, quit being world champion, he had gained twenty pounds. And of the years when he fought forty-nine fights and never lost one, he said, "I was always hungry, always hungry."

So it seems that Einstein and Marciano had each his own way of guarding against the dangers of "comfort and happiness."—Carl Sandburg

572

Most of our comforts grow up between our crosses.—Edward Young

573

Of all created comforts, God is the leader; you are the borrower, not the owner.—Samuel Rutherford

574

Only he who himself turns to the other human and opens himself to him, receives the world in him.—Martin Buber

575

It is a comfort to the unhappy to have companions in misery.—Spinoza

COMMENCEMENT

576

Lament on Commencement Speakers

Our lids are heavy, our heads are bending:

Too much commencement—not enough ending!

—Richard Armour

577

We are acquainted with more facts than ever before, but these facts have turned upon us and become our masters, rather than our servants. . . . Knowledge, without proper moral and spiritual motivation which will insure a successful relationship to our problems and needs, may be filling the world with nothing more than clever devils. Although man has marvelously improved the tools of war over a period of 3000 years, the purposes for which they are used are still the same. . . . Our greatest need is moral and spiritual . . . the most logical procedure is to get into closer contact with the Source of such supply and to believe that that Source is more ready and able to give it to us than we are to receive it. If we are really desirous of meeting the needs of our day with our lives, we will start first of all with ourselves. We must change our questions in life. It is not, "How fast can I get there?" but rather, "Where am I going?" Not, "How much do I possess?" but, "How much am I worth?" And not only, "How shall I make a living?" but also, "How shall I make a life?" . . . become so wise that you will appear to be utterly foolish in the eyes of the world. . . . If you should dare to take that final leap and to catch something of that vision to which God calls you right now, then this may for you become the commencement of the most glorious and satisfying experience which life can offer.—Stuart M. Paterson, "Commencement—For What?"

578

Man's life may be compared to a tree —it must have deep, strong roots if there is to be fruit. The nature of these roots was defined at Harvard many years ago by Dr. Richard Cabot. In his practice he found countless people ailing, but the real cause of their illnesses was not physical. His pet prescription was "Real Life" . . . which came from the development of four areas: work, play, love and worship. I have seen hundreds of lives transformed from mediocrity to effective living through this simple approach. . . . The magic word is "growth." Proper roots plus daily nourishment gives us growth, out of which achievement emerges in line with the aptitudes of the individual. . . . When a man starts to grow he breaks fetters . . . one after another, and we find a new man emerging from the chaos of the past.—Melvin J. Evans, *The P. E. O. Record*

COMMITMENT

579

We feel satisfied—and we think others ought to be but they are not— they have not yet found the commitment of life in Jesus Christ. Neither have we or we would understand them and seek to minister to their needs. We diagnose and then treat for something different.

580

An Indian prince gave his Queen a valuable diamond. Later on a tour he stopped in England and during his audience he asked to see the diamond. It was brought and he held it in his hand and saw again its beauty and realized its value, but he said, "Again, I give it to you."

Committal is not a thing done once

and then all is over. It must be done again and again. It must be done each day.—Donald Lester

581

When a girl accepts a proposal of marriage she means she is willing to live in a daily relationship of love with the man she accepts. It is not mere mental assent, but complete committal.—Donald Lester

582

The typical servant in our time lacks a sense of belonging, a great attachment, a something beyond equality, an inner compulsion, a spiritual motivation, a joyous self-giving. . . . What is needed in our time, if the servant image is to become meaningful and potent, is an individual's sense of reverence and commitment to something bigger than himself. Let this something be one's brother man; let it be a human need, a great idea, a worthy cause. Above all, let it be a sense of God, and of one's indebtedness to Him and one's partnership in His divine, redemptive purpose.—John A. Mackay

583

In the *National Review* Willmoore Kendall had an article . . . "Do we want an open society? Does our Constitution oblige us to tolerate ideas and minorities which may destroy us?" . . . In the interests of freedom, Mr. Kendall would keep the door open as wide as possible but not all the way. Some beliefs are clearly incompatible with the American society's "way of life, with its deepest beliefs about God and man and society, and finally with the business it is at." Those who say everything may be discussed in the U. S. are simply wrong. Says Mr. Kendall: "A free society . . . has underlying commitments—to truth, reason, good manners, human dignity—that it cannot possibly pause to discuss, because in doing so it would deny its own foundations." . . . Indeed, properly read, the Constitution supplies the majority with the authority it needs to "proscribe" society's heretics.—John Cogley, "Open and Shut Case," *Commonweal*

COMMON

584

Nothing astonishes men so much as common sense and plain dealing.—Ralph Waldo Emerson

585

If a man can have only one kind of sense, let him have common sense—if he has that and uncommon sense too, he is not far from genius.—Henry Ward Beecher

586

If you haven't grace, the Lord can give it to you. If you haven't learning, I'll help you to get it. But if you haven't common sense, neither I, nor the Lord can give it to you.—John Brown of Haddington, to his students

587

The common man has an ego, highly developed, in a century of Democracy. He's got the idea that he doesn't have to be pushed around. . . . If you want to push him around you have to pretend he's a fellow member of a master race. . . . But the common man—and here's the rub—doesn't know by what processes of statesmanship and organization he can achieve . . . things. He's written the ticket, but he cannot write the program. For that he is looking to the uncommon men . . . uncommon men who, driven by a sense of their commonalty with common men, feel their responsibility to do something for the race to which they belong. They are possessed by the passion to preserve and improve society. . . . Such a man was Jesus . . . Jefferson,

Lincoln, Sun Yat Sen. . . . Sometimes they are crucified. But they are always recognized by the common man, sooner or later. Such an uncommon man is the alter ego of millions of common men. They know him to be of them, and eventually they make him their own, and lift him, hold him, and move forward through him.

588

We reject the idea that any American is a "common man." No man is "common" and no man is "average" in the sight of God. This is the faith on which we base our . . . mission for human freedom.—Arthur B. Langlie

COMMUNICATION

589

Communication is the life blood of all personal existence. It is as essential to one's whole being as breathing is to his body. Awareness of this basic human situation has prompted penal officers and outlaws alike to devise solitary confinement as the most rigorous kind of human punishment. All evidence points to the truth that the functional unit of a healthy humanity is not the lone individual but the community of two or more persons engaged in a variety of expressions of personal communication with each other.

By the same token, the "iron curtain" is a symptom of a most deadly disease. It threatens the very existence of mankind in every generation. . . . To be someone is to be in communication with someone else. To be alone, completely alone, is hell. The problem is fundamentally spiritual, and roots in the failure of communication between our spirits and the Spirit of God.—Allen O. Miller, *Theology and Life*

590

A man's power to connect his thought with its proper symbol, and so to utter it, depends on the simplicity of his character—that is, upon his love of truth and his desire to communicate it without loss. The corruption of man is followed by the corruption of language. When simplicity of character and the sovereignty of ideas is broken up by the prevalence of secondary desires, and duplicity and falsehood take the place of simplicity and truth, the power over nature as an interpreter of the will is in a degree lost; new imagery ceases to be created and old words are perverted to stand for things which are not. In like manner, the memorable words of history and the proverbs of nations consist usually of a natural fact, selected as a picture or parable of a moral truth. What is true of proverbs is true of all fables, parables and allegories.—Ralph Waldo Emerson

COMMUNION

591

If there be those who hunger and thirst, let them come. If any one knows that he has faults, that he has sinned and is discontented with himself, let him come to this table and be fed. Taking the broken bread, let him remember that Christ's body was broken for him. Taking the wine, let him accept the cup of salvation by faith and with thanksgiving.

May our hearts cherish every sacred memory and respond to the deep significance of the blessed bread and wine of the Lord's Supper. May a portion of the spirit which led our Saviour to the cross descend upon us and fill us with love to God and man. May every selfish passion and desire be overcome as we unite with our fellow men here and in all parts of the world in a common, universal prayer that the power of the life and death of Jesus may bring permanent peace and establish the Kingdom of God in all nations.

As I take the bread and the cup, I

find new strength and increased vigor coming into my life. With the bread, I look back in penitence and thank Him for His forgiveness. With the cup, I look forward and thank Him for His promise of strength for whatever comes. As I rise from this place, let me set out anew to follow Him wherever He leads.

592

Lord, this is Thy feast, prepared by Thy longing, spread at Thy command, attended at Thine invitation, blessed by Thine own word, distributed by Thine own hand, the undying memorial of Thy sacrifice upon the cross, the full gift of Thine everlasting love, and its perpetuation till time shall end.

Lord, this is Bread of heaven, bread of life, that whoso eateth never shall hunger more. And this the Cup of pardon, healing, gladness, strength, that, whoso drinketh, thirsteth not again. So may we come, O Lord, to Thy table; Lord Jesus, come to us.—Olive Wyon, *The Altar Fire*

593

The Lord's Supper is an ageless announcement of allegiance. It reaches across nineteen centuries to the apostolic age, when sufferings were endured with songs; when radiant faith survived persecutions; when Polycarp, tied to the stake and threatened with having his tongue torn out unless he recanted, cried, "Why should I speak ill of Him who has done only good to me?" It unites us with the cathedral age, when magnificent masses of chiseled masonry at Milan, Paris, Cologne, and Canterbury were erected to the living God by peasants, sculptors, masons, and wood carvers, and where entire communities knelt together. It carries us to Wesley's England, when Charles wrote immortal hymns, and John, whose heart was "strangely warmed," advised, "Never miss an opportunity to take the Holy Communion."—D. Finley Wood

594

"If I take the wings of the morning, and dwell in the uttermost parts of the sea . . ." (Psalm 139:9). "If you could keep a half degree ahead of sunup on the world's horizons, you'd see new light always breaking on some slope of ocean or some patch of land." Norman Corwin, radio playwright whom we have just quoted, and the psalmist both had the same idea. Both had wings and they use them. Both circled the world and did it in the same way, on wings of vivid imagination. Our modern writer had the advantage of a globe, and a timetable for the sun. But the author of the psalm was just as free. Neither of them was caged as he wrote his lines. Imagination had given wide cruising radius to their hearts. Pacing daybreak, they saw "new light always breaking on some slope of ocean or some patch of land."

The observance of World-wide Communion invites us to use our own wings. Let us imagine . . . what . . . we see as we circle the earth . . . rich earth yielding her fruit . . . a vast ocean . . . great forests . . . fertile valleys . . . streams . . . a rich world . . . which God made, and "saw that it was good."

We shall see a variety of people that are one humanity. They are black and brown, white and yellow . . . all are human, and all are grounded in God.

We shall see the world bound together with things visible and invisible . . . a network of lives tied in with one another. All . . . a preachment that no man lives unto himself or dies unto himself. . . .

We shall see trouble in the earth. Blood, desolation, and death . . . all that we have seen . . . are the materials of brotherhood, but not the brotherhood itself . . . the decision is ours. The eating of the Bread, the drinking of the Cup, these are high resolves. They are the surrender of ourselves, each for himself and each as part of the indivisible Body of Christ, unto God, that his will may be done on earth as it is in heaven.—Paul S. Wright, *Monday Morning*

595

No theory of the manner of Christ's presence in the bread on the Communion table is necessary in order to receive the benefit of the sacrament. . . . To be informed as to the precise manner of His presence in the bread, says the commentary of Robertson and Plummer on First Corinthians, "would not make us better Christians, any more than a knowledge of the chemical properties of bread would make us better able to digest it."

This, I think, is good news to those of us who are not quite sure we believe what we ought to about the bread and wine, and are not even sure what it is that we ought to believe.

Jesus also said that wherever two or three are gathered together in His name, He is there in the midst of them. The emphasis of His presence in the elements at Communion indicates He is there especially present. But . . . how this presence at Communion time differs from His presence with a few met less formally in His name is a subject for humble meditation.

This does not mean that it is either wrong or hopeless for us to ponder what Jesus meant by saying that the bread is His body. It might conceivably be simpler than we suppose, or, on the other hand, beyond our conceiving. . . . As Archbishop Temple wrote, when we isolate a few of Christ's words from the situation in which He spoke them, and "especially when we draw inferences from a great dramatic utterance as if it were a proposition in a textbook, we may no longer be sure we are true to His mind."

Roman Catholics hold that the bread and wine literally become Christ's body and blood. Luther seems to have held that they become Christ's body and blood and yet remain bread and wine. Others believe that the bread and wine are symbols—sacred symbols yet no more than that—of Christ's body and blood. . . .

Jesus said, "Do this," rather than, "Explain this." . . . We can be sure . . . that the bread and wine, in our hands and on our lips, silently reminds us of our Lord and His death on our behalf.—Eliot Porter, *Forward*

596

It was reported of the disciples at Emmaus that they knew Him in the breaking of bread. How did He break the bread?

He broke it reverently, thoughtfully and lovingly.

597

A starving man may be propped up, but to get real strength he must have food. At the Lord's table we are nourished. We are joined to a more than earthly source of power. Christ's qualities can enter into us. His burning love can make our hearts more warm and tender. His joy can make our drooping spirits soar. His ardor can renew our flagging wills.

We are hungry for so many things— for beauty, for righteousness, for security, for love. God put these hungers in us to bring us to that life in Christ by which they can be satisfied. . . .

Jesus loved table gatherings and used them to get very close to people. On the night before His crucifixion, He gave this memorial meal so that whenever it was repeated, those who loved Him could feel that He was there. As we bow at the table we can sense the blessed Presence; we can feel His hand reach out to us; we can hear Him answering our prayers.—George E. Sweazey

598

The Lord's Supper was not originated by any man or group of men. It was instituted by Jesus Christ Himself; hence it is of divine origin. As such it is supreme in range and power of influence among all the commemorative events of human history.

Our Lord broke the bread in order that it might be distributed. Each disciple received an equal part of the same loaf. This signified the *oneness* of their faith and their *equality* in His love. The broken bread and the shared wine betokened that His body would be wounded and His blood shed for the remission of the sins of erring men all over the world.

599

The Communion is primarily between Christ and the church. It is as members of the church, the Body of Christ, that we share in the benefits of the Lord's Supper.

The Apostle Paul rebuked those who failed to "discern the Lord's body" when they came together for this act of worship. That is, they did not recognize that individual blessing is made possible as each person is united in spirit with other souls in the church of Christ. Those who are concerned for personal spiritual growth alone, or who allow the artificial barriers of race and culture to separate them from their brethren in Christ, will not enter into the wonderful unity of the Christian community.

Nor can we share the Communion with our brethren in a condescending or patronizing spirit. The Lord has only one body, of which He makes us all partakers. By such participation we also are all made one body.

The Lord's Supper speaks of the living fellowship of Christ with His believing church. He is the Host at the table. His hands break the bread and offer the cup. His is the voice pledging the new covenant in His blood. He is present, as He was in the Upper Room, standing beside and dwelling in every believer personally and in the church corporately.

600

Communion is communion only when it is shared. It is this sacrament that binds us to all Christians everywhere. Here we see and feel and openly hail the fellowship that spans all centuries, all races; a fellowship that does not grow in upon itself, but is not less eager than God Himself to draw all men within its sweeping circle. This is the Communion of the Saints, or its foreshadowing. Beside us is the Holy Church Universal, past and present and to come. We commune not only with those who sit beside us in the silence, but with all those who once shared with us these still and solemn hours, but who now no longer in earthly token and symbol but in heavenly reality see their Lord face to face.— Kenneth J. Foreman

601

Here is a story of an early morning communion in a prison-camp . . . our company of inmates had already been held in detention for nearly two months, no communication with the outside had been possible. . . . Now Christmas was approaching. . . . Our thoughts and yearnings went leaping beyond the narrow confines of our quarters. We could not help wondering how long we were to be thus incarcerated without explanation. . . . Perhaps there might be release as sudden as our arrest! Would it be before Christmas?

Our intriguing little dream proved a vain hope. But we were not to be deprived of festal celebration—though in crude and cramped quarters, not too much unlike the circumstances of the manger. Sitting on the edges of our cots and piling up suitcases for a table, we spread our little feast and shared our delicacies. . . . Christmas morning was also Sunday morning. An early communion was arranged by the Anglican bishop, our fellow prisoner. Several of us, participating, got up silently ahead of the rising bugle, and assembled in the "common-room" for the spiritual feast and remembrance. Was it not to such a wretched world as ours that the Christ Child had come? To such helpless, needy ones was the Great Gift given! And what gifts had we to bring Him now? Ah, nothing but the burden of deep grief for our blind and selfish world, and the sense of shame for our too-unfaithful church. But yes, we had the simple offering of our contrite, yearning hearts.

About a score of us, British, American and Dutch, were seated upon the crude benches in the chill and silence of early morning . . . before us was the table with white cloth and sacramental emblems.

Now we were in the act of bringing our treasures to Jesus, the Lord of Life. It was no longer a "political" prison-camp; it had become the Holy of Holies. The bishop's voice was leading: "Because thou didst give Jesus Christ, thine only Son, to be born at this time for us . . . make us clean from all sin. . . . Hear what comfortable words our Saviour Christ saith . . . 'Come unto me all ye that travail and are heavy laden, and I will refresh you.' "

We stepped forth . . . and knelt . . . on the folded gray blanket . . . with reverential joy, we were partaking of the mystic sacrament which made us one with Him in suffering, in strength and hope. . . . "Do this, as often as you drink it, in remembrance of me. . . . The Peace of God which passeth understanding keep your hearts and minds. . . ."

After all, who shall rob the children of the Spirit of this blessed communion, and how? In this divine communion, our prison-camp somehow fits into the picture as having meaning in the great

purpose. It is not futile: "Be of good courage! Wait on the Lord!" Here we realize that peculiar sense of oneness with the Eternal Goodness; we have a feeling of closeness with loved ones though oceans apart; we are constrained to bear no thought of hatred toward those who are called our enemies; we are filled with the peaceful assurance of the coming victory of righteousness. "Who shall separate us from the love of Christ? shall tribulation, or distress, or persecution, or famine, or nakedness, or peril, or sword? . . . Nay, in all these things we are more than conquerors. . . ."—Roy S. Lautenschlager, *Ten More Stories of World Communion*

602

Be gentle when you touch bread. Let it not lie uncared for—unwanted. So often bread is taken for granted. There is so much beauty in bread— beauty of the sun and soil, beauty of patient toil. Winds and rains have caressed it, Christ often blessed it. Be gentle when you touch bread.

603

Whatever the language or the manner of performing this holy rite, there is always obedience to the Divine Master's words: ". . . this do in remembrance of me." Everywhere there is remembrance that the Host of that table in the Upper Room was the only-begotten Son of God, remembrance of His words, remembrance of His self-sacrificing life even unto death on the cross, remembrance of His assurance of glorious immortality to all who have accepted His gospel and put all their trust in Him.

In his mind's eye, the believer sees the Saviour at the center of the table, breaking the bread and passing the cup, declaring the new covenant, giving to the simple elements a meaning never limited by time, space, or any worldly condition. Paul wrote that, by means of the blessed bread and wine, all Christians experience communion of Christ. "For we being many are . . . one body: for we are all partakers of that one bread."

604

The whole gospel is dramatized in this ordinance of bread and wine. The Supper has been variously identified as the eucharist, the sacrament, Holy Communion, the memorial, the sacrifice, the offering, or, more simply, as the breaking of bread. These designations suggest the breadth of understanding attributed to the Supper and each in its way emphasizes particular aspects of an ordinance that speaks to human needs and yearnings as does no other act of faith and worship. Here is shown forth Christ's giving and our receiving. Here are His people made one in recollection, in worship and in commitment. Here we witness anew His incarnation, His life and ministry, His death and resurrection. Here we sense a Presence which time has not dimmed, and we rise on wings of faith to discern that hour when all men of faith shall share in the heavenly feast provided for those who love Him.—Charles L. Wallis

COMMUNISM

605

Is communism a religion? Some will say immediately that it is not; it is a political philosophy, not a religion. . . . However, from the beginning the Communists have recognized that faith and action cannot be separated, and they have been unceasing, therefore, in giving their people an interpretation of the meaning of life and have demanded the total response of their people to their new faith. Communism is religion and politics combined.

Herein lies the source of its terrific power. Other economists have developed similar doctrines and other political parties have been built upon them without rising to a place of such significance in our modern world. The power of Marx and his movement lies in the religious significance of their doctrine. . . . Marx established a competing religion. It has its own god, the party, and the workers are its chosen people, called to bring in a new age, to establish a perfect kingdom upon earth. Communism is thus a faith which answers all the basic problems of society, giving an intense meaning to life, and requiring absolute devotion to a cause. It has dogma, moral standards, rites, and ceremonies. He who enters it is thus provided with a faith, a cause for which to labor, and a mission to fulfill in life.—*The Society Kit*

606

In *Dawn*, a British publication, a Communist "missionary" tells why he believes in the eventual triumph of his "mission":

"The gospel is a much more powerful weapon for the renewal of society than is our Marxist philosophy, but all the same it is we who finally will beat you. We are only a handful and you Christians are numbered by the million. But if you remember the story of Gideon and his three hundred companions, you will understand why I am right.

"We Communists do not play with words. We are realists and, seeing that we are determined to achieve our object, we know how to obtain the means. Of our salaries and wages we keep only what is strictly necessary, and we give up the rest for propaganda purposes. To this propaganda we also 'consecrate' all our free time, and a part of our holidays. You, however, give only a little time and hardly any money for the spreading of the gospel of Christ.

"How can anyone believe in the supreme value of this gospel if you do not practice it, if you do not spread it, and if you sacrifice neither time nor money for it? Believe me, it is we who will win, for we believe in our Communist message and we are ready to sacrifice anything, even our life, in order that social justice shall triumph. But you people are afraid to soil your hands."

607

Communism believes that all evil is rooted in a system, not in man. Thus it must dedicate every effort to overthrowing that system by causing industrial warfare and strife. Over its ruins will be built the perfect Communist state, which can do no evil. From then on, life will be ideal.

Christianity continually reminds us that the root of evil lies in the heart of man, and that until man is changed, any system will lead to evils, exploitation, and oppression.

608

The cure for communism lies in a more effective Christianity. Communism is the devil's latest substitute for the Christian concept of the Kingdom of God. Christianity is based on love and is distinguished by stewardship. In the Christian context, we must provide for all mankind a better measure of security, without robbing them of their freedom. Clear thinking, forthright action, and sacrificial living will be required.—Frederick H. Olert

609

We have been talking anti-communism while the world at large was talking anti-famine, anti-disease, anti-misery. Let us talk anti-famine, anti-disease, anti-misery, and the rest of the world will talk anti-communism.— *United Nations World*

610

What is best in communism comes from Christian influence. It has often been called a Christian heresy, which could never have arisen except from Christian soil.

It borrowed its hope from Christianity. Like Christianity, and unlike the Orient and ancient Greece, communism thinks that history is going places, ending in a period of peace, righteousness, happiness and plenty. This dream is a secularized version of the idea of the Kingdom of God on earth.

It borrowed its faith from Christianity. . . . Marx couldn't do without the equivalent of God, so he transferred God's power to the Law of Change in history . . . the resultant Marxian creed: There is something in the world working for justice and righteousness; its triumph is sure; it should be co-operated with. What is this but a pallid and inadequate reflection of the Christian God who works in history to redeem, whose triumph is sure, and who calls for our service?

It borrowed its social passion from Christianity. . . . It borrowed its messianic consciousness from the Bible. The role of the working class as the vehicle of salvation is a secularized version of the messianic consciousness of the Jews as the Chosen People of God. . . .

"Salvation is of the Jews" says the New Testament. Yes, but which Jew— Karl Marx or Jesus Christ? Choose you, for Jesus said, "He that is not with me is against me." And choose Christ, for "there is no other name given among men by which we can be saved."— Culbert G. Rutenber, *Christ or Karl Marx*

611

Communism comes in the wake of . . . disillusionment and offers some kind of faith and some kind of discipline. To some extent it fills the vacuum. It succeeds in some measure in giving a content to man's life. But, in spite of its apparent success, it fails —partly because of its rigidity but even more so because it ignores certain essential needs of human nature. . . . Its supervision of individual freedom brings about powerful reactions. Its contempt for what might be called the moral and spiritual side of life not only ignores something that is basic in man, but also deprives human behavior of standards and values. Its unfortunate association with violence encourages a certain evil tendency in human beings. . . . Even if it does not indulge normally in physical violence, its language is that of violence, its thought is violent and it does not seek to change by persuasion or peaceful democratic pressures but by coercion and, indeed, by destruction and extermination. . . . Violence cannot possibly lead today to a solution of any major problem, because violence has become much too terrible and destructive.—Jawaharlal Nehru, *The New Leader*

COMMUNITY

612

I believe in the beloved community and in the spirit that makes it beloved, and in the communion of all who are, in will and deed, its members. I see no such community as yet, but none the less my rule in life is: act so as to hasten its coming.—Josiah Royce

613

The most important factor in the work of the church community clinic is the fomenting of lively interest in civic problems. It is fundamentally necessary to organize groups that will carry on constantly a fight for civic decency. Church people should become leaders in such groups, whether they be citizens' associations, parent-teacher associations, public welfare associations, prison associations, or associations of other character. One of the most important duties of the community clinic is to see that the capabilities for Chris-

tian leadership which exist in the church memberships are utilized in all the groups that are working for civic betterment. Too often we have looked upon the church as a thing apart—as a cloistered group specializing in the formalities of religion and divorced from the community. The time has come to prove that the church is an integral part of the community, actively at work in all its affairs, and not only upholding constantly the ideals of our Master but demonstrating that we have the capacity to roll up our sleeves and do our share of the hard work necessary to establish a community in which men are willing to strive together for the common good. —Wilbur La Roe, Jr., *Community Clinic*

614

Who are the children in your neighborhood? Who are your children? Flesh of your flesh, blood of your blood— this describes your own offspring. But they are more than this. They are through you, part of you; but these children you've conceived, borne, and nurtured are not you nor duplicates of you: they are themselves, and for this, in your reflective moments, you are ready to thank God. Thank him for creating them unique persons, with hope and promise that they can be better . . . than their parents. . . . Our children, then, are ours—but not wholly ours. They are their own persons, directly answerable also to God their Creator, with possibilities and rights that belong to themselves uniquely. And it is our business as Christian parents and "high priests of Almighty God" to teach them, to guide them, so that they shall perceive that they are not solely their own, but that they are God's sons and daughters. What is true of our blood kin is true also of our spiritual kin. And the children of our geographical neighborhood, our community, belong to our spiritual kin. For them also we have a responsibility.—Wesner Fallaw, *Crossroads*

615

In the years ahead, the churches face many difficult problems. Some of the practical are building membership, increasing personal loyalty, and financing the operation of the church itself. Other problems have to do with making Christian teachings effective—strengthening family life, giving leadership in the improvement and spiritual growth in the whole community. We have to realize that the church is no longer an effective influence in many communities, or in the lives of many people. Millions live as though God does not exist. Some thoughtful churchmen believe that organized religion has lost its force because it has not been concerned enough with crucial social issues or the daily problems that affect people. . . . As individuals, we don't live in a vacuum. Neither does the church. We're all part of the community we live in. In everything we do we have to take into account the attitudes and prejudices of other persons and organizations. A successful Christian program has to take these differences into account.—Samuel W. Blizzard, Jr., and Emory J. Brown, *The Church and the Community*

COMPASSION

616

I sought my soul—but my soul I could not see; I sought my God—but my God eluded me; I sought my brother—and found all three!

617

The only thing worse than hunger is to be able to look upon it and be unmoved.

618

You must look into people as well as at them.—Lord Chesterfield

619

The real solution of every problem can be found by those people who are hurt by it, if they will take hold of life where it hurts, and find out, not how they themselves can escape from that hurt, but how they can prevent that hurt from becoming a permanent factor in the lives of their brothers and sisters.—A. Maude Royden

620

Robert Browning . . . in commenting on the technique of realizing the most of life . . . speaks of the high necessity of "opening out a way whence the imprisoned splendor in us may escape."

The imprisoned splendor in us . . . and the necessity of finding a way to release it! It's one of those provocative phrases, with so elastic a quality that it may be applied to almost any area of our existence.—Clarence W. Hall, "Our Imprisoned Splendor"

COMPLAINTS

621

"Whenever you hear a motor knocking," I coached my beloved Christine in our car the other day, "you can be sure something is wrong with it." With sharp feminine insight she added, "I know—just like in people."—Burton Hillis, *Better Homes & Gardens*

622

Humans, like horses, cannot kick and go forward at the same time.—E. L. Benedict

CONCEALMENT

623

When men speak ill of thee, so live that nobody will believe them.

624

Something is wrong inside when Jesus is kept outside.

625

Keep clear of concealment, keep clear of the need of concealment. It is an awful hour when the first necessity of hiding anything comes. When there are eyes to be avoided and subjects which must not be touched, then the whole bloom of life is gone.—Phillips Brooks

CONCERN

626

If you have once planted a tree, you have always in it a peculiar interest. You care more for it than you care for all the forest of Norway or America. You have planted it, and that is sufficient to make it peculiar amongst the trees of the world.—Alexander Smith

627

Men will not make great intellectual readjustments for a gospel which does not greatly matter.—Reinhold Niebuhr, *Leaves from the Notebook of a Tamed Cynic*

628

Noblesse oblige . . . implies that the source of all behavior is an inner compulsion which makes it easy and essential that one be a disciple of the unenforceable. As a fountain is the end product of an unlimited source of water under pressure; as a spring has an unlimited supply of water from natural underground sources, so a nobleman has an unlimited source of power flowing from the idealism which has, from childhood, become the inner directing force. This inner force keeps alive the highest motivating forces of human behavior. . . . The nobleman is first a nobleman within before he is recognized as a nobleman by his fellows.

The noblemen who light candles are compelled to do so, for they must, because they belong to the order of noblesse oblige.—Charles L. Anspach, *Vital Speeches*

629

Christianity holds . . . that God is both Creator and Redeemer . . . that creation and redemption are different ways by which God works in history. . . . God participates in the push of the imperfect forces of human history, while at the same time He stands continually before it with the pull of His perfect purpose. . . . The push of progress resulting in the extension of man's modes of togetherness is due to God's creative activity. The pull of God's purpose, which draws men closer and closer to the Christian kind of community, is due to God's redemptive activity. . . . By God's purpose is meant His whole intention with history. . . . The push of progress is God's indirect work in history, His general foreknowledge of the circumstances which would condition men's moral and spiritual choices. In this sphere there is a givenness and a direction beyond the conscious planning of man. In the realm of the pull of God's purpose, however, lies man's freedom either to accept or to reject the persuasion of God's suffering love. Indirectly, God conditions man's experience to the extent, in the long run, of effectively guiding it as nature and human nature in constant interaction develop history; but directly, man's yielding to God, even though driven both by fear and by love, by need and by the positive experience of God's goodness, is a free choice, the willing surrender to God's grace. Thus purpose and progress . . . are two ways in which God works in history so that while ultimately He is its master, that very mastery entails the creation of a free fellowship based on love. . . . Man is free, but his experience as a whole is led by God and so conditioned as to point always to the only solution of his problems, namely the heeding of the pull of His purpose. Eventually God makes man's wrath to praise Him; but ultimately He receives no praise that does not come from a free and faithful fellowship with Him on the basis of His love.—Nels F. S. Ferre, *The Christian Faith*

CONFLICT

630
An age of conflicting goals. Conflicts are not new in history. Some are in pursuit of the dollar, others are striving for eternal life.

631
The leaders of the French Revolution, from the beginning, excited the poor against the rich; this has made the rich poor, but it will never make the poor rich.—Fisher Ames

CONFORMITY

632
We would rather live dangerously than conform—dangerously, but not recklessly or irresponsibly. We don't want to find ourselves again in the position of 1939 when, just to show what grand guys we were, we attacked Hitler's tanks with cavalry.—A Polish friend to Alexander Werth, *The Nation*

633
We must neither run with the crowd nor deride it, but seek sober counsel for it, and for ourselves.—Woodrow Wilson

634
It is not conformity in the outward signs which represents the danger; it is conformity in thought and in thinking. —Crawford H. Greenewalt

635
In this age, the mere example of nonconformity, the mere refusal to bend the knee to custom, is itself a service. —John Stuart Mill

636
Society requires some at least of its members to be free of it . . . free to go beyond it and make the ideal of civilization their own. . . . All of us know that we ought to go counter to the whole temper of our societies at times, since this temper in any but a perfect society makes impossible the realization of what ought to be.—Paul Weiss

637
In response to a survey, student editors expressed concern about the danger of conformity. One said, "People are too much alike and like it too much." That's not good: either for enduring freedom, or democracy.—Rae Noel

638
The tenor of the individual life was [to Jesus] of more importance than outward conformity, whether to a code of morals or a system of ceremonies. He looked to the thoughts and motives of men's acts and insisted that they be such as could bear scrutiny by a righteous God.—Kenneth Scott Latourette

CONSCIENCE

639
The church is the only conscience the government has. When a church is silent, the state can have no conscience. —Edward W. Grant

640
Nothing strengthens a man's conscience so much as witnesses.

641

Conscience is a still small voice that makes you feel still smaller.

642

If we can harness the moral conscience of the world, we shall have a force greater than armies.—Woodrow Wilson

CONSERVATION

643

As a city expands . . . a once proud river . . . becomes polluted . . . thus the very springs of the city's life are poisoned. The modern state of affairs suggests a report in Holy Writ, made thousands of years ago, about an ancient city. Jericho had every outward sign of prosperity. But there was a jarring discord spoiling its municipal music. Its water supply was tainted. That is a fatal blight to any city. Jericho's city fathers, alarmed at the situation which threatened the health of every man, woman and child in the town which seemed so fair and fortunate, came to the Prophet Elisha. "Behold," cried the members of the City Council, "behold, the situation of the city is pleasant but its waters are tainted!" That is the accusing consciousness now in America the beautiful, as we look out upon many of our broad streams . . . the waters are tainted.

The Biblical story declares that the prophet healed the poisoned waters by casting salt into the spring. In that incident is mirrored a fundamental service of salt. Were it not for the salty ocean, the pollution of our rivers would soon turn them into dead seas. One authority has declared: "If the sea were to lose its saltiness, the earth would soon become uninhabitable." The salt sea receives the tainted waters and, by its magic alchemy, they are sweetened and cleansed. That is not only a saving fact

regarding the earth. It is a parable about life on the earth.—Frederick Brown Harris

644

Soil is more than just dirt. It is a living organism. Like every living thing, it can be developed or it can be destroyed. Either it will benefit from man's wise and loving care, or it will suffer because of his ignorance or greed.

Today more is known about wise soil practices than in any previous period in history. Our concern is for a wider distribution of the know-how of good soil practices, a more complete acceptance of new methods of soil and water conservation, and a placing of soil conservation and community welfare ahead of selfish interests.

Basically, the problem of soil conservation is the selfishness of the human heart. The church, through its message and its ministry, can change the heart. It can curb selfishness. It can instill reverence and love of God. It can develop a genuine concern for others.

The church can make a contribution no other institution can make. It can put its finger on the sin of soil exploitation. It can give man a new motivation. The Christian farmer knows that good soil practices pay off in dollars and cents, but his motive will be higher. He will follow good soil practices because it is God's will. One way in which he responds to the love of God revealed to him in Christ Jesus is by being a good steward of the soil, by being a humble co-worker with the Creator, never defying His laws. The church can challenge him with the responsibility to improve his farming know-how, and to cooperate with his neighbors in conserving the soil of the community.

The church will support good soil programs that are being developed. But it will leave the doing of these programs to others and spend its energy in bringing its ministry to bear on the moral problems that are involved.— Soil Stewardship Advisory Committee

645

No one can live unto himself and be at peace with God or man. The word "neighbor" needs to be written large in our life. The Bible underlines this thought. Seven of the Ten Commandments deal with our relationship to our fellow man. . . . When a farmer follows poor soil practices, he hurts himself, but he also brings harm to his neighbor. . . . A Christian farmer will interpret the concept, "Love thy neighbor as thyself," so that it will include the fields of his fellow farmer. He'll make an honest effort to use the water that falls on his acres to the fullest, and control it so it does the least damage to the acres and brings the greatest benefit to the entire community. . . . Loving our neighbor also means for the tiller that he will have a concern for the man who will farm his acres when his task is done. We are on earth for a comparatively short time. Man departs but his acres remain to support unborn generations. The fields that the farmer tills today will be someone else's to till tomorrow. A Christian farmer will make every effort to increase productivity of his fields so that when his stewardship is over he can entrust to those who follow him an improved legacy.—Soil Stewardship Advisory Committee

646

We have come to realize that our present productivity and prosperity are not due to innate virtue of our own. They are not due to any superiority over other peoples. But rather they are due to our having been endowed with the great and varied resources we have. As we have recognized that fact, we have come to realize that unless we conserve those resources well, and unless we continue to have resources that are economically usable for decades to come, our prosperity will not go on unendingly. We know as we never knew before that it is our resources that have made our economy great.—Jean Lesage, Canada's Minister of Northern Affairs

647

Thou shalt inherit the holy earth as a faithful steward, conserving its resources and productivity from generation to generation. Thou shalt safe guard thy fields from soil erosion, thy living waters from drying up, thy forests from desolation, and protect thy hills from overgrazing by thy herds, that thy descendants may have abundance forever. If any shall fail in this stewardship of the land, thy fruitful fields shall become sterile, stony ground and wasting gullies, and thy descendants shall decrease and live in poverty or perish from off the face of the earth.—W. C. Lowdermilk

648

Conservation of the *soul* and conservation of the *soil* are inseparable. What is good for man is also good for the land. "The earth is the Lord's." Certainly this is true, for in the beginning God created the heavens and the earth and all things on the earth, including man, who is the image of God. And God alone, through the process of nature, can produce soil. His methods of preserving the soil were to cover it with grass and trees so the wind could not blow it away as dust, or the rains wash it away as silt in the rivers. . . .

Certainly, the ancient Hebrew psalmist knew what he was about when he cried out: "The Earth is the Lord's and the fulness thereof." But down through the ages, man had disputed God's ownership of the earth, using it for private and often selfish gains, rather than as God's steward. . . . Jesus once spoke of the rich man losing his own soul, saying; "What profiteth a man if he gains the whole world and loses his own soul?" We might draw a parallel here: "What has the tiller of the soil profited if he gains great temporary financial wealth, but loses the producing power of the soil for all generations to come?"—Bert T. Webb

649

Spiritual maturity begins when we realize that we are God's guests in this world. We are not householders, but pilgrims; not landlords, but tenants; not owners, but guests.—C. Willard Fetter

CONSTITUTION

650

The Constitution of the United States makes three negative references to religion. It forbids a religious test for holding federal office. It forbids federal laws "respecting the establishment of a religion." It forbids federal laws "prohibiting the free exercise" of religion. The meaning of the last two has been debated endlessly, but many would agree that at least they are "articles of peace."—*Information Service*

651

Our Constitution is an idea, and Americans must work toward making that idea a reality.—Leo Jung

652

The Constitution belongs to the people and not the people to the Constitution.—Theodore Roosevelt

653

The American Constitution—the most wonderful work ever struck off at a given time by the brain and purpose of man.—William Ewart Gladstone

654

Lovers of the Constitution have disputed who gave the most to it— whether Washington and Franklin, whose genius, patience and experience held in check the enthusiasms and excesses of others; Hamilton, whose brilliant theories of government were 145 years ahead of his time; Madison, who reduced Hamilton's theories to a workable, practical basis; Jefferson, whose insistence on the rights of man introduced so many saving clauses into the document; or Marshall, whose decisions created the nation and set upon its feet what finally became a strong, efficient government.—*Rapid City* (South Dakota) *Journal*

655

To many of us it doesn't seem that the teaching of the Constitution, American history and democratic principles rubs off on our children. It does not because they don't see the issue. We will attempt to show it is a real, vital issue by showing what the alternative is.—Charles Wesley Lowry

656

Because our Constitution was formed by men largely of educated English background, it, while aiming to provide equality for all, contained no federal provisions for public education.—J. W. Studebaker

CONTEMPORARY

657

It's a wonderful discovery when you realize that you can be contemporary with all times, crossing between the centuries and back and forth to your own with the same feeling of being at home that you have in your own neighborhood.

658

With respect to Him [Jesus] there is only one situation: that of contemporaneousness. The five, the seven, the fifteen, the eighteen hundred years are neither here nor there; they do not change Him.—Soren Kierkegaard

659

To be contemporaneous with Christ is to be contemporaneous with one who was present to Augustine as well as to Paul, and is in the presence of the least of his brothers.—H. Richard Niebuhr

660

The historical Jesus makes His influence felt in the contemporary impact of His eternal Spirit. . . . As the contemporary Christ, he confronts us with the challenge to undertake a creative venture in human relations, so that the ethical love of God's own making may be effectively expressed in current circumstances.—Donald R. Rowlingson

661

Some people are merely contemporary.—Harry Emerson Fosdick

CONTENTMENT

662

I am always content with that which happens, for I think that which God chooses is better than what I choose.—Epictetus

663

A man whose heart is not content is like a snake which tries to swallow an elephant.—Chinese proverb

664

A contented spirit is the sweetness of existence.

665

O God, teach us to love our country, not in word only, but in deed and in truth. Let us never rejoice in any pleasures which hurt others nor be content with a life of idleness while others toil for our comfort.—Pleasance Moore-Brown

666

Carlyle, in his "Heroes and Hero Worship," makes this striking observation: "The greatest of faults, I should say, is to be conscious of none." A minister once said he feels hopeless when a man tells him that he will not join the church because he is already good enough without it. Moral and spiritual conceit are always hard to contend with. . . . All of us would be in danger of this disastrous form of self-esteem were it not for the fact that one day in Bethlehem there was born into the world a babe who was to be called "Emmanuel—God with us."

667

The potentials that lie within mankind itself! The "imprisoned splendors" resident in human nature! The rich and untapped resources of man's mind and spirit!

Our imprisoned splendor. . . . Have we not all had moments when, with flashing clarity, we knew that there is within us a finer, nobler, richer self than has ever yet come to the surface?

Isn't it one of the major tragedies of life that so many of us go through life becoming so little of what we might become? Oliver Wendell Holmes, in a poem he called "The Voiceless," refers to people he terms the saddest who ever lived—the people "who die with all their best music still in them."—Clarence W. Hall, "Our Imprisoned Splendor"

CONVERSION

668

Conversion is a rich experience, but it does not produce spiritual maturity. That is something which must be achieved by a long process of education, effort, and self-discipline.

The sinner who is ignorant at the time of his conversion, remains ignorant after his conversion, except on the matter of his new-life experience. If he is ever to read, he must learn to read; if he is ever to make Christian decisions, he must have facts upon the basis of which he can judge. This calls for a growing intellectual life, and an increasing intellectual mastery. . . . Conversion means that we have taken a new way, a new direction, and that thereafter all decisions are to be made with reference to a new standard of value—the mind of Christ. The tragedy is that a great many Christians are suffering from retarded growth. Ten, twenty, forty, sixty years ago they were converted. For a little while they grew in their spiritual living, and then they became satisfied with their achievements and settled down. In all too many cases the word "down" is a perfectly accurate description of what happens.—Roy L. Smith, *The Christian Advocate*

669

When a piece of land is sold, it is said to have been converted from one owner to another. What then is conversion for us but the change of owners. From being Satan's, we become Christ's. Our affections, our desires, our longings go out to Him. The only difference between the two being that *we* submit to the Spirit and accept the offers of mercy from God. The word in its simplest interpretations means "being turned about." The traveler going in one direction finds that he has made a mistake in the way, so he turns squarely about; in a sense he has been converted. The old soldier gave a good definition of his conversion to Christ when he said that with him it was "right about face."—J. Wilbur Chapman

670

True conversion manifests itself in the life of the Christian. If the change has taken place, good works will follow. The first good work of the convert should be his own confession to others of Jesus Christ as Lord. This completes the cycle. He who has received the witness, repents, believes, and in turn becomes a witness to others. He is constrained by Christ's love to become His ambassador and so goes forth to beseech all men to be reconciled to God.—Franz Edward Oerth, *Baptist Leader*

671

Look . . . at this idea of the "split-second conversion." For many years it has been the "before and after" advertisement of Christianity. Before conversion, a sinner, an alcoholic, a prostitute, a wild-oat sower. . . . Then, in one supreme moment, God breaks through our fleshy barriers . . . and the after-product comes out a saint. The "split-second" conversion makes "instant Christians" with the same blinding speed we get instant coffee . . . men and women who have long been thorns in the flesh of God's will suddenly develop magnificent consciences. . . . All of us are familiar with its terrible beginning and its delightful ending, and all of us are familiar with the effects it has had upon many lives, perhaps our own. . . . What is . . . important, conversion to this type . . . is not a "one-shot" affair, but a continuing process. . . . The "split-second" conversion is meaningless unless it is followed by a lifetime of spiritual experiences that keep us close to God, seeking to do His will.—Ross M. Willis, *Front Rank*

672

I went to America to convert the Indians, now who will convert me?—John Wesley

673

"I think the church must preach a change of heart, a new life, and a new living." Who said it? Neither a preacher nor a missionary. It was a statement of Calvin Coolidge. In amplification, he said: "I sit at my desk day after day, worrying myself sick over our country, wondering what we are coming to as I observe wave after wave of lawlessness and crime. The only remedy I can see is through inward reformation, the renewal of men's hearts by the preaching of the gospel of the Lord Jesus Christ."—*Adult Class*

COOPERATION

674

I believe it a fallacy to assume that people can cooperate only if they understand each other . . . or if they like each other, or if they share certain preconceptions. The glory of modern large-scale democratically tending society is that it has developed the social inventions—such as the market, the practices and skills of negotiation, and the many other services which allow us to put forward in a given situation only part of ourselves—which allow us to get along and, usually, not to kill each other while retaining the privilege of private conscience and of veto over many requests made of us by our fellow men.—David Riesman, *Individualism Reconsidered*

675

No one can whistle a symphony. It takes an orchestra to play it.—Halford E. Luccock

COURAGE

676

Courage is not simply one of the virtues, but the form of every virtue

at the testing point, which means at the point of highest reality. A chastity or honesty or mercy which yields to danger will be chaste or honest or merciful only on conditions. Pilate was merciful till it became risky.—C. S. Lewis, *The Screwtape Letters*

677

To see what is right, and not to do it, is want of courage.—Confucius

678

To be courageous . . . requires no exceptional qualifications, no magic formula, no special combination of time, place and circumstance. It is an opportunity that sooner or later is presented to us all. Politics merely furnishes one arena which imposes special tests of courage. In whatever arena of life one may meet the challenge of courage, whatever may be the sacrifices he faces if he follows his conscience—the loss of his friends, his fortune, his contentment, even the esteem of his fellow men—each man must decide for himself the course he will follow. The stories of past courage can define that ingredient—they can teach, they can offer hope, they can provide inspiration. But they cannot supply courage itself. For this each man must look into his own soul.— John F. Kennedy, *Profiles in Courage*

679

In the moment of danger came the inspiration which is the theme of Stephen Crane's *Red Badge of Courage*. Of his hero he writes that "within him, as he hurled himself forward, was born a love, a despairing fondness for this flag which was near him. It was a creation of beauty and invulnerability."

This is the thing called courage, by which wars and battles are won. Wealth cannot buy it or command it. It comes to men who fight in lost causes, as to those who win victories. It is worth more than weapons in the final crisis of conflict. Without courage this nation could not have been built, nor defended; without courage, it has no future.

The late Sir James Barrie, in his most famous speech, told the students of St. Andrew's, in Scotland, that "courage is the thing. All goes if courage goes." . . . It is . . . courage that we honor, forged on the anvil of discipline or found in the storm of battle, humbly praying we may have as much to give when there is need. For when courage is gone . . . then all is gone.

680

Moral courage is great and admirable in itself; but it must be pointed out that it almost never appears except as part of that greater entity called character. A man without character may give fitful exhibitions of courage, as even Aaron Burr did when in the disputed election of 1800 he refused to bargain with the willing Federalists for the presidency. But no man without character is consistently courageous, just as no man of real character is lacking in consistent courage. In short, moral courage is allied with the other traits which make up character: honesty, deep seriousness, a firm sense of principle, candor, resolution.—Allan Nevins

681

It was said of Jesus that "He stirs up the people"; and it has been said of every prophet who ever appeared that he had the bad taste to speak of things which could have been kept covered. There is a kind of unity which can be attained if moral men will keep still, but it is a unity of sickness and not health. I still have my heart lifted high when now and again some man whom I least suspected, suddenly says, in effect, "This is wrong and I shall no longer accept it without vigorous protest."—Gerald Kennedy

682

Why do we blame those we love and not those we hate? We can't ask a man to be a hero forever. Don't judge a man for what he does under pressure.

683

Courage is rightly esteemed the first of human qualities, because . . . it is the quality which guarantees all others. —Winston Churchill

684

Never give in! Never give in! Never, never, never. Never—in nothing great or small, large or petty—never give in except to convictions of honor and good sense.—Winston Churchill

685

Faith and courage were the sources of the mighty power of the early Christians and their faith and courage were generated in fellowship with God, the living Christ and the brethren. Their ardent conviction that Jesus had risen from the grave and their eager expection of His bodily return transformed their attitudes toward life. They became possessed by religion and learned to be at home in the invisible world of the spirit.—Kirby Page, *Advance*

686

In my relationship to others, "When my brothers try to draw a circle to exclude me, I shall draw a larger circle to include them. Where they speak out for the privileges of a puny group, I shall shout for the rights of all mankind. I shall neither supplicate, threaten, nor cajole my country or her people. With humility but with pride I shall offer one small life, whether in foxhole or wheat field, for whatever it is worth, to fulfill the prophecy that all men are created equal."—Pauli Murray, *Common Ground*

687

Money lost? A little lost—
Bestir thee to get more.
A battle lost? Much lost—
Win the war, the past forgot.
Courage lost? All lost!
Better hadst thou ne'er been born.
—Goethe

688

This brings us to our final source of courage—a great faith that God is our Partner—without which the two previous aids to courage (keep your mind on what you have and are, and use to the full your powers of endurance) would be mighty grim. This is a faith, I say it candidly and frankly, but its proof is in the lives of countless men and women who testify, "No matter how unfavorable our situation, He cares!"—Howard Stone Anderson

689

"The bamboo for prosperity," a Japanese friend explained to me, "the pine for long life, the plum for courage—"
"Why the plum for courage?" I asked, picturing courage as a great oak.
"Yes, yes," answered my Japanese friend. "The plum for courage, because the plum puts forth blossoms while the snow is still on the ground."
—Anne Morrow Lindbergh, *North to the Orient*

690

It takes courage to give a small portion of yourself in lieu of some obviously valuable article. But a lively imagination made it possible for me to perceive a great many ways in which I might "spend myself," instead of the cash I lacked.—David Dunn, *Try Giving Yourself Away*

691

True courage is like a kite; a contrary wind raises it higher.—J. Petit-Senn

692

From imperfection's murkiest cloud,
Darts always forth one ray of perfect light,
One flash of heaven's glory.
—Walt Whitman
This is one thing I have found very true in life: that it is our duty, no matter how difficult things are, to find that "flash of heaven's glory."
It may be in the smile of children, in the expression of old women by the roadside, or any unexpected little event that gives one courage to go on.—Queen Frederika of Greece

693

Sheer courage to face life squarely and go ahead with less fear comes only after we begin to move forward. Until we actually begin to move toward the goal, we have little real courage to start. This psychological fact merely parallels the old like the problem of static friction that physics books discuss. You know how the wheels of a heavy train seem to stick so tightly to the spot before the straining locomotive can budge them into motion. . . . Real courage comes only after you begin to tackle the job. If you had just stood there waiting for sufficient courage to master the whole situation, you probably would still be standing and waiting.—John E. Crawford, *Classmate*

694

Keep your fears to yourself but share your courage with others.—R. L. Stevenson

CREED

695

A man's creed is not his religion, any more than his backbone is the man himself. But a good backbone is a very essential part of a man's body, and a good creed is a very essential part of a man's religion. We still hear it said occasionally that "it makes no difference what a man believes, so long as he is sincere. . . ."

A traveler takes the wrong train, going north, sincerely believing it to be the southbound train. Will it make no difference?

Jesus was so sure that a person's faith is of immediate importance to his salvation and to the welfare of the church that He challenged the faith of His disciples by asking, "Whom say ye that I am?" That is a personal question, as personal for us today as it was for the . . . disciples. . . . For Peter there was but one answer: "Thou art the Christ, the Son of the living God." For Thomas there was but one answer: "My Lord and my God." What is your answer?

696

The question, "What must I do to inherit eternal life?" is often answered in terms of creed alone. Why do we not listen to the answer given by our Lord? He said, "Sell what you have, and give it to the poor . . . and come, follow me" (Mark 10:21, RSV).

697

Whenever you tell another what you believe about anything, and particularly about God, you are stating a creed or confession. It may not be a statement of belief accepted by any church, but for you it is, or should be, an intelligent outline, in words, of the faith that is within you. It is what you believe. That word "creed," incidentally, comes from the Latin verb *credo,* which means, literally, "I believe."

Such a statement is vital to the faith of any man—and it is especially vital to the faith of a Christian. It is not enough to believe vaguely, without intelligent expression and action. People with a "faith" like that usually find the "faith" gone with the first wind. It just doesn't stick.—William M. Hunter, *God and You*

698

E. Stanley Jones once said, "Doctrines divide; Christ unites." . . . Two friends were literally at "swords' points" because of some theological difference. They were both unhappy about the division, and anxious to be reconciled. At length each took his hymnbook and chose his favorite hymn, and as they compared them they discovered that both were in adoration of Jesus. When they realized they were of one mind in their worship of Him, they became friends again. Their common creed really was, "Jesus is Lord." It is the great central creed of all Christians in all ages.—Thomas McDormand

699

The theory that history is working toward a religious synthesis is no more plausible in terms of religion than it is in terms of history. Of all possible outcomes, "syncretism" (to give it its technical name) is the most unlikely. It has never worked, as Constantine discovered to his cost. And the reason why it has never worked is so fundamental that we are justified in saying that it cannot work. It cannot work because it conflicts with man's fundamental religious impulse which leads him to worship the unique and the individual, not the common denominators Professor Toynbee so carefully disentangles for our edification. One has only to read Toynbee's elaboration of the "essential truths and essential counsels" of the seven "higher" religions to see what is missing. They leave us stone-cold. Unlike the essential tenets of Christianity or Judaism or Islam, focused on one decisive moment, his synthesis neither strikes the imagination nor warms the heart. Indeed, we may hesitate to call it religion at all. The reason men profess Christianity is not (as Toynbee seems to think) because it gives them a "deeper insight into the mystery of the universe" or "holds up a higher ideal" than other religions; it is because they accept and wish to follow Jesus Christ as Lord and Saviour. Between this and syncretism in any form an unbridgeable gulf is fixed.

The same applies, in their own contexts, to the other religions of the world: to Buddhism, to Mohammedanism, to Judaism, and the rest.—Geoffrey Barraclough, *The Nation*

700

Buckley came right out and claimed that there was a difference between Christianity and other religions; moreover, he added that the difference, as he saw it, was that Christianity was true and other religions were not. "I would not be a Christian if I did not believe that . . ." he added. . . . Why was Buckley's simple profession of belief in, first, the idea of religious truth, then in Christianity and finally in his own church so arresting? I think it was because so many people no longer think of religion in terms of truth or falsehood. Millions have stopped considering religion as something to engage the rational side of man. Religion is thought of as merely a form of cultural expression or laudable moral aspiration; to speak of its doctrines as being subject to such classifications as "true" or "false" sounds alien and downright impious.

The fear is that a man who believes in something so firmly that he says quite flatly it is true and its opposite false will be brutally intolerant of others. The feeling is that the only basis for tolerance is a kind of genteel skepticism. Firm belief leads to fanaticism. And fanaticism leads to community dissension and fearful intolerance. Admittedly, there is much historical if not intellectual justifica-tion for this claim. . . . Victor White once wrote . . . "Zeal for truth has too often been a cloak for the most evil and revolting of human passions." . . . White used the word "cloak," so the question is, is it really devotion to the truth or human frailty which has been responsible for wars of religion, bigotry, and crass intolerance?—John Cogley, *Commonweal*

CRIME

701

The cure of crime is not the electric chair, but the high chair.—J. Edgar Hoover

702

When a man of blameless respectability commits a crime and is sent to prison, we are far more horrified than when a dozen hardened criminals are convicted.—T. H. L. Parker, *Portrait of Calvin*

CRISIS

703

Our generation is doomed to live in a state of perpetual crisis. . . . Hence inner serenity must be cultivated if we are to safeguard our personal integrity, national freedom, and universal human values.—Haridas T. Muzemdar

704

In the crises of life . . . our words show where our souls have been feeding.—Harry Emerson Fosdick

705

Crises refine life. In them you discover what you are.—Allan Knight Chalmers

706

We need, in days of crisis, those who will make the daring choice.— Allan Knight Chalmers

CRITICISM

707

Criticism is the disapproval of people not for having faults but for having faults different from our own.

708

If I were to try to read, much less answer, all the attacks made on me, this shop might as well be closed for any other business. I do the very best I know how—the very best I can; and I mean to keep doing so until the end. If the end brings me out all right, what is said against me won't amount to anything. If the end brings me out wrong, ten angels swearing I was right would make no difference.—Abraham Lincoln

709

If we do nothing else, we are at least willing to put ourselves in the front ranks and take the criticism— and I know we will be criticized. I know this proposition will be lied about . . . I know that we may be misunderstood even by some friends, but I tell you that the world will never make a step forward unless there is a group of people who are willing to stand the brunt, and who, when their effort is successful, will not even be given the credit for what they did. . . .

But we men and women in the clothing industry have said to ourselves: we want to find out what is right, what is our duty, where our responsibility lies, and then go ahead and let the future justify our undertakings. If it had not been for a few people who had the courage of their convictions, we would today be living

in the jungle, if the beasts of prey had permitted us to live there. It was due to the rebellious spirit of a few that we made progress. . . . It is to the credit of our organization that we have always paid attention to what seemed right and we are willing to await the judgment of time.—Sidney Hillman

710

Some criticism, no doubt, is constructive, but too much is a subtle poison. A friend . . . told of a club . . . in undergraduate days at the University of Wisconsin. Members were . . . brilliant, some with real literary talent . . . they would read a story . . . and submit it to the criticism of the others. No punches were pulled; each manuscript was mercilessly dissected. The sessions were so brutal that the club members dubbed themselves "The Stranglers."

This . . . was a masculine affair, so . . . the co-eds formed . . . "The Wranglers." They too read their manuscripts aloud. But the criticism was much gentler. In fact, there was almost none at all; the Wranglers hunted for kind things to say. All efforts, however feeble, were encouraged.

The payoff came about twenty years later, when some alumnus made an analysis of his classmates' careers. Of all the bright young talents in the Stranglers, not one had made a literary reputation of any kind. Out of the Wranglers had come half a dozen successful writers, some of national prominence, led by Marjorie Kinnan Rawlings. . . . Coincidence? Hardly. The . . . basic talent in the two groups was much the same. But the Wranglers gave one another a lift. The Stranglers promoted self-criticism, self-disparagement, self-doubt. In choosing a name for themselves, they had been wiser than they knew.

Awareness of the power of affection to unlock human capabilities is at least 2000 years old: "A new command-ment I give unto you, that ye love one another. . . ." But affection is not much good unless it is expressed. What's more, I have a notion that unexpressed feelings have the tendency to shrink, wither, and ultimately die. Putting an emotion into words gives it a life and a reality that otherwise it doesn't have.—Arthur Gordon, "How Wonderful You Are," *Reader's Digest* and *Woman's Day*

CROSS

711

Some folk think they are bearing their cross when they are only putting up with themselves.

712

The physical structure of the cross symbolizes its essential significance as the meeting-point of the two dimen-sions of existence. That is its paradox. In it merge all the conflicts and con-tradictions of history, and these fuse into a new synthesis, a new resolution. In that suspended figure of the lonely, tortured Son of Man, God and Man, time and eternity melt into a unique unity. A theology that can see in the cross nothing more than a mere mar-tyrdom, however exalted, betrays its utter shallowness. It is as obtuse and vulgar as the materialism which can see in a Rembrandt canvas only so many yards of linen and so many ounces of paint. No death which was only a martyrdom could have involved the whole scale and dimension of time and eternity, which is what Christ's death did. In the cross is portrayed the final significance of our Lord for religion. "It was written in Hebrew . . . Jesus the King."

713

Christ's sacrificial ministry . . . means that when we indulge our physical appetites in the wrong way, when we neglect our duty, when we lose our tempers, when we are irritable and uncharitable, when we try to hurt other people by saying unkind things about them, when we have wrong attitudes toward our fellow men, when we misuse our powers and misdirect our energies, we are doing to God something similar to what they did to Christ in the garden of Gethsemane, in the court of the High Priest, in Pilate's judgment hall, on the way to Calvary, and upon the cross.—Walter L. Carson, *Interpretation*

714

In the biography of a great man who began life in the slums, there is this arresting sentence: "Some people are successful simply because they didn't have the advantages other peo-ple had." It is revealed in history that crosses are not conclusions. This is the Christian faith. It is also a cosmic fact. You may be defeated, but you can still win.—Virgil A. Kraft

715

During the "blackout" of the war, traffic lights were left with only an illuminated cross in the center of each light. If one asked why the sign of the cross was chosen, he was told that it had been discovered that the figure of the cross gives clearer guidance, with less danger of exposure, than any other design. So! We were guided through the blackout by a radiance streaming from the cross! Of course, this was a mere coincidence; but it was also prophecy.—Report of the Presbyterian Board of Christian Education

716

Man made of the cross a tree of shame. Christ changed the cross to a Tree of Glory. Man used it as a tree of death; Christ converted it to a Tree of Life. Man employed it for cruel oppression; Christ put it into the service of freedom. Man made it an agency of judgment and retribution; through Christ it became a means of forgiveness and mercy. In the hands of man the cross was an accursed tree; touched by the hands of the Son of God it became a tree of blessing. Before Calvary the cross instilled only fear; after Calvary it became a symbol of infinite love. Before Good Friday men turned their eyes from it in horror; after Good Friday men turn to it for comfort and reassurance. Before that day men shuddered at the mention of the cross; after that day men bow before the cross and are at peace. Once man disgraced this tree with crime and other sins; then Christ sanctified it with His holy and precious blood. Before Calvary it harshly enforced the Law; after Calvary it joyously proclaims the gospel. Before Good Friday it hastened man into outer darkness; after that it ushers men into Paradise and Glory. The shame of the cross was man, the Glory of the cross is Christ.

717

The Apostle Paul, in his writings, reverts to the cross again and again. He can look upon it only with awe; he can speak of it only with deep feeling. He sees the cross as a mystery, yet as one of the greatest of God's revelations to us. All religious thinking, if not done in the light of the cross, becomes superficial. It stops short with ethics, and for that reason proves ineffective. Yet the atonement, for which the cross is but the symbol, is wholly ethical in its implications; for in the cross . . . mercy and truth met together, righteousness and peace embraced each other. . . . The need is for a life transformed by the cross . . . only men with the cross in their hearts can withstand the pressure of these days; only such men can lead the world into the ways of peace and brotherhood.—Miles W. Smith, *Adult Class*

718

The greatest architectural construction consisted of two pieces of a tree nailed together to form the cross of Calvary.

719

There is no other way to a fuller life, there is no other way to a better social order, than Jesus' way. Not the way of making others serve you, but the way of giving yourself for others. The cross is rightfully the only symbol of redemption, because the giving of oneself is, by the very laws of human and divine nature, the only way of salvation. . . . It is not enough for you and me to know about the cross; you and I must know the cross.— William Thomson Hanzsche, *Presbyterian Life*

720

The cross had an appeal to Christ. He willingly went to the cross to die. He recognized that it was altogether right that the judgment of God should rest upon sin. He chose to go under that judgment which rested on man because of his rebellion against God. In His divine nature He absorbed the judgment in order that mankind might be saved from it. He chose to do that . . . He said, ". . . I lay down my life, that I might take it again. No man taketh it from me, but I lay it down of myself . . ." (John 10:17, 18).

The cross has an appeal for us. It lays bare the heart of God. It shows the Father as limitless Love, forgiveness beyond measure, tender compassion beyond all hope or imagination. . . .

The cross marks the Great Divide in human history. It also marks the Great Divide in any person's life. The world has been different since that hour when Jesus bore His cross. Human lives have been different from the hour when they began to bear their cross and live for Him.

721

I am the cross of Christ. I was a living tree. But I am dead. They killed me. Wicked hands fashioned me, and I was borne by Him who gave me life. The cruel nails that pierced His sinless hands I held. His everlasting arms were mine to hold. His broken body rested on my breast. The pressure of His weary head against my face drove ever deeper in the thorns that pierced His noble brow.

Yes, I am the cross of Christ, the accursed tree. I bore Him, but He bore the sin of the world. By me He was lifted up. But He draws all men unto Him. I held Him while He prayed forgiveness on His enemies and opened the gates of paradise to those who seek to be remembered. On me He was suspended while God forsook Him and man rejected and disowned Him. I trembled when He cried aloud, "My God, my God, why hast thou forsaken me?"

I am the cross of Christ. A dead tree. But He used me. He honored me, for have I not a part in His redemptive work? He sanctified me. On me flowed first the cleansing stream of His priceless blood. 'Twas I that first proclaimed to friend and foe alike that this despised and rejected One is "Jesus of Nazareth, King of the Jews."

I am the cross of Christ. On me He finished His redemptive work. Here He breathed His last, commending His Spirit into His Father's hands. In death His victory was won. I marked forever the spot where God and man were reconciled, where full atonement for sin was made. Through the earthquake and the long dark hours I kept the watch, until on Easter morn the trembling earth gave forth the triumphant Conqueror of all the minions of darkest hell.

I am the cross of Christ. I ought to be forgotten. He alone is to be remembered, exalted. I am only the dead tree that bore the Son of God, the Saviour of the world, the cross on which the King of Glory died.

722

Denial of God has passed beyond simple human defiance and has taken on the character of aggressively devilish hostility. In this situation God exercises His rule and works out the purpose for which He sent His Son. . . . In the cross the world meets God's refusal to answer the questions it asks, because they are not the real questions. In the cross the world finds an answer which it does not expect but which is the real answer to the fundamental questions of the world.—International Missionary Council Conference

723

There were three crosses on Calvary, each declaring its own message. The one proclaims the fate of an impenitent world. Refusing to recognize its own guilt and neglecting its day of salvation, the world goes to its doom without a word of comfort from the Saviour of mankind. It dies without hope.

A second cross demonstrates that "whosoever believeth in him shall not perish but have everlasting life." Even the criminal, the person who has lived his life away from God, shall find mercy when in penitence he turns to the Saviour who died also for him.

It is the third cross in which we glory. This supplies the answer to the question: "What shall I do to be saved?" Through the ages and to all peoples it declares: "Believe in the crucified Lord Jesus Christ and you shall be saved."

724

The sign of the cross is impressed upon the whole of nature. It forms a part of man himself, as may be seen when he raises himself in prayer.— Justin Martyr

725

The cross speaks of death. To all the world it proclaims the death of "Jesus of Nazareth, King of the Jews." Around the world the cross confronts men with the simple message, "The Son of God died on the accursed tree. The Lamb of God, bearing the sin of the world, died on the cross that He might bring 'life and immortality to light.' "

The cross speaks of life. To Christ it was the gateway to life in glory. Whoever in faith accepts for himself the atoning sacrifice of Christ on the cross "shall not perish, but have everlasting life."

Even as Christ died on the cross that in Him all men might have life, so the humble believer in Christ "dies daily to sin" but lives again in "newness of life." As all nature dies in the fall of the year only to break forth to new life in the spring, so he who puts away the old finds strength in the cross to live the new life in Christ.

726

It is often asked: Why did not God forgive us freely? Why was it necessary for Christ to die and thus to atone for our sins? The answer is that God *did* forgive us freely; He forgave us freely through the cross of Christ. The cross was God's way of expressing His free grace, for it was *God* who in Christ was "reconciling the world to *himself.*"

Christian thinkers have said that the cross satisfied the justice of God, or that it appeased His wrath. Such expressions . . . do not mean that God's love is not free. They impress upon us that our sin is a great injustice to God our Father and that it is a great dishonor to Him. The wonderful thing

about the cross is that, by the faith and obedience of Christ, it removed the injustice and dishonor of sin as well as bringing to us the forgiveness of God. But it was the love of God that satisfied the law and justice of God. When we remember that sin is a violation of God's law and of His Person, we see why, in forgiving us, His law did not remove but maintained it and established his claim to our reverence and worship. The end of God's forgiveness is that we love and obey Him as Father. To this end, God forgave us through the love and obedience of Jesus.—Joseph Haroutunian, *Counsel*

727

The call of the cross is to faith in the saving love of our God and Father in heaven. For who but a God of compassion and love would send His only begotten Son to die on the cross in order that "whosoever believeth in Him should not perish, but have everlasting life"?

The call of the cross is to pardon and forgiveness. It is the death of Christ on the cross that gives validity to the statement, "The blood of Jesus Christ, God's Son, cleanseth us from all sin. . . ."

The call of the cross is to sacrifice. The atoning sacrifice of Christ was unique, complete, once for all. It need not and never can be repeated in the lives of men. And still all who would follow the Christ must needs bring their own sacrifice. To walk the way of the cross means sacrifice. It means walking apart from the world and enduring its scorn, its jibes and its disdain. It also means assuming the obligation, sometimes at great cost and effort, to bring the message of God's saving love to those who do not know Him. He died also for them. His was the sacrifice, ours the benefit, ours the privilege of sharing it with others.

CRUCIFIXION

728

You may remember the reference to the crucifixion in Richard Jefferies' book, *Bevis: the Story of a Boy:* "The crucifixion hurt his feelings very much; the cruel nails; the unfeeling spear; he looked at the picture a long time and then turned the page saying, 'If God had been there, He would not have let them do it.'"

If God had been there! That artless comment discloses the whole glory and mystery of the Incarnation. Shakespeare himself could not have made dramatic irony more complete. For the whole of the Christian religion rests on the fact that God *was* there. It is a matter of historic experience that out of this lowest depth to which the race of men could go down, God made His highest revelation. God's mind and act are shown forth out of the very stuff of events which supremely illustrate man's mind and act.—J. S. Whale, *Christian Doctrine*

729

Christ's crucifixion did not change God's attitude toward us; it revealed what God's attitude already was. Christ's suffering did not induce God to let man go free; it rather illustrated what God has always been willing to endure in order that man might not have to endure for himself the full consequences of his wrongdoing.— Walter Lapsley Carson, "What It Costs God to Forgive Sin," *Interpretation*

730

A moment's serious reflection is enough to show that the bad elements of Jewish society, acting alone, could never have succeeded in bringing about the crucifixion of the Lord Jesus. Imagine a situation today in which only the conventionally bad people of any society were agitating for some obviously evil object. . . . What would happen? Of course, nothing, except the castigation of such a criminal agitation. But supposing the criminal elements were joined in their clamor by the good and the respectable, the moral, the most worthy, by the most responsible backbone elements of society, what then? . . . The wickedness and injustice, which would never be perpetrated at the insistence of the evil elements acting alone, becomes a reality when demanded by the good people. . . . Jesus' crucifixion was the result of the union of the good people with the worst people. The maintenance and commission of evil is mainly the work of good men. . . .

Evil and injustice are commissioned, and persist, only by the support of the best people in cooperation with the worst. This dreadful fact ought surely to inspire us with suspicion—at least suspicion—of the pretensions of this proud creature whom the scientists have classified as *homo sapiens*. It indicates a radical disease in the very vitals of humanity.—D. R. Davies, *The Art of Dodging Repentance*

731

It is the spirit of Jesus, giving of self, that has kept the flame of Christianity burning throughout the centuries. "The blood of the martyrs is the seed of the church. . . ." Milton Walter Meyer, son of Dr. and Mrs. Frederick W. Meyer, writes movingly of visiting Hopevale, in the Philippine Islands, where his father and mother, along with nine other missionaries and a twelve-year-old boy were captured and executed by the Japanese. Milton said: "I stood in the spot where my mother so often sang at the Sunday services, 'Were you there when they crucified my Lord?'" When he left Hopevale by plane to fly back to Manila, there kept ringing in his ears the lines from his mother's diary

". . . May the news soon to come be of tolerance and love, peace and happiness, for all nations and all peoples." That spirit of "lavishing one's life on others . . ." still lives!—Lawrence Fitzgerald, *Adult Class*

732

There were two people crucified on either side of Christ.

One was selfish, self-centered and egocentric in character. He cared little whether the central figure on the cross —Christ—was guilty or not. All that mattered to him was his own predicament. His feelings were quite similar to the sentiments of some people today.

The other malefactor on the cross was, however, quite different. He was repentant and fully aware of his guilt. His main concern was for his soul and for the establishment of Christ's innocence. No selfishness here, no personal aggrandizement—only consideration for justice, the welfare of others, and the magnifying of that which was good and pure!

Naturally enough, it was only the latter transgressor who received forgiveness and this comforting response from Christ: "This day shalt thou be with me in paradise." Only the unselfish repentant therefore received the assurance of forgiveness and the promise of the eternal life.

The world today has both kinds of people in it. Those who believe only because they think it benefits them— and those whose attitude, particularly when they stand next to the cross at Calvary, is one of beneficence, self-sacrifice, and goodness toward the work of Christ.—E. J. Meurer

DANGER

733

To be human is to be in danger.— Ashley Montague

734

From needing danger, to be good . . . Lord deliver us.—John Donne

735

One of the greatest dangers in a democracy is vulgarity; the danger that from the belief that no man is better than his neighbor before the law shall arise the feeling that no man should be better than his neighbor in culture, taste, refinement. This may seem a remote peril. But it is a very real one. —Edgar J. Goodspeed

DEATH

736

When death is imminent, we open our hearts quickly and wide. How much more Christian love there would be if we didn't wait for death to release our reserves!—Hazel Beck Andre, *Reader's Digest*

737

A fellow can't afford to die now, with all this excitement going on.—Will Rogers (a few months before his last flight)

738

When death comes to me it will find me busy, unless I am asleep. If I thought I was going to die tomorrow, I should nevertheless plant a tree today. —Stephen Girard

739

The greatest of men stand but a heartbeat from the grave.—Charles Templeton, *Life Looks Up*

740

Increasingly the use of the word death is causing resentment as applied to Christian people. We are beginning to use such terms as "passed on." A missionary once told a London audience that the people in the jungle of

Africa who have become Christians have such tremendous belief in the immortality of the soul that they refuse to refer to the departing of any one of them as a death. He said, "These people will tell you that the dead do not really die, that the body is but the cottage of the soul. They say, 'He has departed,' and again 'He has arrived.'" In Genesis we read of those who were "gathered unto their fathers," so even in the earliest times, men understood what Alexander McLaren called, "the social life of the hereafter." —Archer Wallace, *Classmate*

741

During these long months the king walked with death as if death were a companion, an acquaintance whom he did not fear. In the end death came as a friend. . . . After "good night" to those who loved him best, he fell asleep as every man and woman who strives to fear God and nothing else in this world may hope to do.— Winston Churchill, speaking of King George VI

742

Joseph Haroutunian has said, "But death can teach us wisdom." And not ever to give a fleeting thought to death is senseless, unchristian. In fact, when this is the attitude of our mind and heart, we reveal the impoverishment of our own soul. We say, in effect, that we don't know or don't believe the gospel of our Lord. This evasion of the fact of death reveals how secular we have become. . . . The greatness of the first century church was just this: that they challenged the pagan world's conception of death. The Christian Church has been doing that ever since. For the Christian has a faith which takes the sting out of death. You see, when one believes that this life is a part of a greater whole, then he lives differently, and dies differently. The Christian knows that the longest life is short, and he will live by faith that is suprascientific.—Leonard Odiorne, *Let's Talk About Death*

743

Our attitude toward death all hinges on our faith in God. It is horrible apart from faith in God. Paul's faith enabled him to say, "I have learned, in whatever state I am, therewith to be content."

We cannot expect to erase our fears of death easily. But we can draw this spectre out into the open, and we may be willing to see that, by an increase of our faith in God, in His promises, in the work of redemption of His Son, by the provisions for our welfare in this life and the next, we do not need to live in panic for fear of death. "Eye has not seen, nor has ear heard, neither has it entered into the heart of man, what God has prepared for them that love him." Death is not a frightful spectre but a rewarding reality.—William F. Knox, *The Christian Advocate*

744

No one wants to die unless he is already dead on the inside, and Jesus was more fully alive than anyone has ever been. This was no masochistic seeking of suffering. Jesus did not want to die . . . He did not want to lay down his life . . . *but He did it.*— Charles Templeton, *Life Looks Up*

745

I know of no other place more calculated to provide serious thought than a sunset viewed from the cemetery. The great orb of day, which seems so powerful in heat and light, gradually fades and sinks below the western horizon; darkness and the stillness that comes with it settle around you.

All is so mysterious; the human X ray (the mind), which has been able to penetrate every recess of the known world, has never cast a single ray of light into the open grave. Here all human resources fail—only faith remains; here also all human distinctions vanish. The great banker and janitor are put upon a common plane. . . . She who has led in society, and the poor woman who performed her most menial services, are treated alike. . . . Here differences between man and woman cease—all are on a common level.

Death is a grim reaper, and so unexplainable and unfair, viewed from the world's standpoint. The young, with all the fire and force of youth, may be taken, and the old, with nothing but the ashes of life, allowed to remain. Children who bring so much joy to parents who are well able to take care of them and educate them and make them a power for good in the world, are stricken; and others who are almost unwelcome to parents who can give them little, stay. The parent who is the mainstay of the family may be called, while others who apparently are not greatly needed are allowed to live on.

Apparently, how brittle is the cord and how shallow the feelings that bind in one case and how strong and enduring in others. As one lingers by the grave of his loved ones and observes the steady stream of the living passing and repassing, doing homage to the dead, he will see those whose hearts have only recently been crushed by the loss of a dear one, and he will see those who have been making pilgrimages to the grave for a quarter of a century. He will see the father standing by the grave with the tense muscles of self-control, and he will see the mother silently weeping as she kneels and "tidies up" the last resting place of her dear one, just as she had tucked the little one in bed in life. There is the grave that bears every evidence of being soon forgotten, and there are those that are kept green in fact and in memory.

But the sun has long since set, the living have returned to their homes, and the dead are left in the eternal sleep. The little bird has chirped the last goodnight to his mate. The chilly night air warns him who lives over in memory the life which he knows he can never again be on earth. Yet his heart so yearns for that human companionship by which they were united in life.

He looks upwards and sees myriads of worlds, millions of miles apart, representing so much in space and matter, yet so perfectly adjusted that they have moved thousands of years without the slightest variation in the regularity of the seasons. And he knows that such perfection can come only through a great Power, great Intelligence and great Love; and that Power, that Intelligence and that Love, which will cause the sun to rise in the morning in all His power and His glory, will also cause the spirit of his dear one to be restored to him.

So as we today cast flowers upon the grave of the lifeless body, may we realize that the spirit which inhabited that body at one time is eternal.

Busy, busy, here and there! It sums up almost all of our earthly life! And throughout it the Master comes along and puts not a few trusts into our hands. God helps us to hold them all firm and fast! May we never let slip what has been given us to keep, until this struggling, puzzling life be done, and that other life which we believe will end the struggles and clear the puzzles, has come with its reckonings, recompenses, and rewards.—H. L. Talkington

746

Death is not the enemy of life, but its friend, for it is the knowledge that our years are limited which makes them so precious. It is the truth that time is but lent to us which makes us, at our best, look upon our years as a trust handed into our temporary keeping.—Joshua Loth Liebman

747

Christ has made of death a narrow, starlit strip between the companionships of yesterday and the reunions of tomorrow.—William Jennings Bryan

748

William Henry Hudson tells in his autobiography, *Far Away and Long Ago,* of how as a boy he was thrown into consternation by the death of an old dog whom the family loved, and he realized for the first time that death must come to all. When his mother sensed the child's disturbance, she had a long talk with him during which she shared with him the Christian understanding of death. She put it in this way: the part of me that says "I" goes on living, but the part of me that was my body goes back to the ground. Writing as a mature man, he still remembered the sense of release which came to him with this interpretation.

This is not to say, of course, that the death of a dog may be equated with the death of a person. About this we do not know; our faith concerns relationships of men with God. But if the death of a pet leads a child to a realization of the death of persons, as in Hudson's experience, his questions should be met with a sharing of our Christian faith.—Helen and Lewis J. Sherrill, *Interpreting Death to Children*

749

In answer to the question, "Was Jesus really dead while in the sepulchre?" Dr. W. Douglas Chamberlain wrote: "Yes. The entire New Testament is based on the conviction that Jesus died on the cross, that He was buried, and that on the third day He rose again from the dead. This was the core of apostolic preaching. . . . It never occurred to the first century enemies of Christ to deny that He really died on the cross. Jewish unbelievers did not deny that Jesus died; they claimed that His disciples stole His body and announced His resurrection. The Gentile skeptics in Corinth did not deny that Jesus died or that He was raised again; they denied that His followers would be raised from the dead.

"The theory that Jesus swooned, being laid in a tomb where the coolness restored him to consciousness, is a rationalistic attempt to explain away the 'miracle' of the resurrection. This . . . creates more problems than it solves. No scholar treats it seriously today. It contradicts the whole of Scripture testimony."—*Presbyterian Life*

750

After one of the funerals, John came to Mother. "What is dying?" he asked. This time Mother said, "Dying is just opening a gate to a new world called heaven," and Father, coming into the room, smilingly agreed, then got on his thinking look. It wasn't long afterward that he preached a sermon called, "The Gate to Heaven."—Olive Knox, *Mrs. Minister*

751

What is the ultimate end of my life? It takes some time for the fact of death to have a personal meaning. Youth is a period of accepting mortality generally but never specifically. Yet, soon or late, there comes that momentous realization that we are no better than our fathers and death is our ultimate destiny. Stephen Vincent Benét, in a little poem entitled "Thirty-Five," indicated that this realization comes around that age.

Now, what is the real significance of all this? It means that life is essentially tragic, and that from the standpoint of this earth alone it has an unhappy ending. Paul could say that the last enemy to be overcome is death, but the man of this world only cannot say it. Death may be postponed by the use of our modern skill and wisdom, but it can never be eliminated. Some day I will die, and some day those I love the most will die. There is a parting at the end of the way and there is a cessation of my life at some rendezvous which I must keep.—Gerald Kennedy, *The Christian and His America*

752

We take our losses too personally. An animal loses its home by means of a flood, or fire, but the loss is not a personal loss. We look upon death as something being taken from us, as if we owned life. There is a stewardship of use; can we own what we do not use?

753

Death and hell hold no terror for the soul that is sheltered in the love of God. In one of the Gospels (Matthew 18:8, 9) Jesus depicts in awesome language the dread reality of judgment and future punishment. But, as always, He does not linger on this desolate theme. Swiftly He turns to words of compassion and forgiveness. He pictures a shepherd who, though he has ninety and nine sheep in the fold, goes out into the mountains in search of one that has gone astray. Having found it, he rejoices more for that one sheep than over the ninety and nine. "Even so," Jesus continues, "it is not the will of your Father which is in heaven, that one of these little ones should perish" (Matthew 18:14).

God's concern for the salvation of His children reached its climax in a cross on a Judean hill. "God was in Christ, reconciling the world unto himself . . ." (II Corinthians 5:19). There the divine Victim suffered for our sins. . . . He went to the cross for men who did not deserve His sacrifice. He prayed for the forgiveness of those who crucified Him, manifesting a redeeming love

that is stronger than death.—John Sutherland Bonnell, *Heaven and Hell*

754

Heaven and Hope: To a question asked by London's *Sunday Times*— "Do Men Survive Death?"—Bertrand Russell, the aging British mathematician and philosopher, gave a resounding "No." Earl Russell wrote: "When this question is viewed scientifically, and not through a fog of emotion, it is very difficult to see any reason for expecting survival. . . . The belief that we survive death seems to me . . . to have no scientific basis. I do not think it would ever have arisen except as an emotional reaction to the fear of death. . . . Undoubtedly, when those we love die, it is an immense comfort to believe that we shall meet them again in heaven. But I see no reason whatever to suppose that the universe takes any interest in our hopes and desires. . . . We have no right to expect the universe to adapt itself to our emotions, and I cannot think it right or wise to cherish beliefs for which there is no good evidence, merely on the ground that fairy tales are pleasant."—*Newsweek*

DECISION

755

Edward L. R. Elson said it was nothing but coincidence that his sermon topic was "Alternatives in High Decisions." And the previous week it had been "Decision and Discipleship" President Eisenhower heard both sermons and in between he made his own momentous decision—to seek a second term.

756

Most of a person's decisions are no longer individual decisions. Formerly, when a person made a decision, he saw the immediate effects of that decision;

he was rewarded or punished by that decision. Today, most decisions are chain decisions. Many people help make a decision. It is difficult to see what part of a decision was made by any one individual. Increasingly, a person does not know whether he has had any real part in a decision or not. He escapes responsibility for decisions. He is haunted by a sense of unimportance, of insecurity. Decision-making is based less and less on personal experiences and more and more on hearsay, on secondhand evidence, on the reports of others, on circumstances and conditions that are remote and impersonal.—William G. Carleton, *Vital Speeches*

DEEDS

757

A man of words but not of deeds is like a garden full of weeds.

758

The place you are in needs you today.—Katherine Logan

DEMOCRACY

759

In a democracy, the votes of the vicious and stupid count. On the other hand, in any other system, they might be running the show.—*Boston Globe*

760

Fisher Ames liked to compare democracy with a raft. The raft, he said, does not sink, but those who ride it are continually in danger of getting their feet wet. Among the many meanings which might be attached to this simile is the notion that every move in a democratic direction involves risk. Our founding fathers, for example, thought it might be dangerous to permit any but property owners to vote. This risk was finally taken, and we have now achieved universal suffrage. In the early days of the Republic, it was thought by many that education should remain a privilege of the élite. Nevertheless, this risk was also taken, and we now enjoy free public education for everyone.—Edouard C. Lindeman, *Saturday Review*

761

It is unfortunately one of the conditions of democracy that wisdom and its counterfeit go along together side by side.

There can be no tag or label to mark one from the other, nor would the people heed them if there were. But all this is well. It is better for men to choose the voice of wisdom for themselves rather than to have it infallibly pointed out by government. For the seat of wisdom is in the individual soul and it grows through individual effort.—David Starr Jordan, *The Voice of the Scholar*

762

Democracy demands more obedience to the moral law than any other form of government.—Louis D. Brandeis

763

A democracy cannot stay alive if the people in it do not urge change when change is necessary; it cannot grow unless the people have vision. Therefore, reformers, prophets, poets, and protest groups belong to the democratic way of life. If a man does not like them, he does not like democracy.—Lillian Smith, *Now Is the Time*

764

Democracy is based upon the conviction that there are extraordinary possibilities in ordinary people.—Harry Emerson Fosdick

765

Democracy is a complicated operation. Implicit in it is exercise of power with the consent of the governed—and, in turn, active participation by the governed in the making of important decisions, through freely and regularly chosen representatives. Democracy further implies separation of authority and delineation of competence among the executive, legislative and judicial functions and their respective institutions. A vital point is the recognition and legitimate functioning of an opposition and the right of institutional reform and change of government personnel and laws.—J. B. S. Hardman, "Legislating Union Democracy," *The New Leader*

766

In ancient times those who taught the children of a king were often the most powerful influence in shaping the destiny of even the most absolute monarchy. So it was with Anna in *The King and I,* and so it has been with countless nameless teachers who, over the centuries, for the most part worked to make the children of kings and other greats a little more worthy of their position and power.

The great unanswered American question is, "Can this be done for all the king's children of a democracy?" I can say only that it will not be done by all the king's horses and all the king's men. If it is done, it will be done by you and the likes of you. Don't forget to learn Anna's secret for being brave.—*John Sloan Dickey*

767

Democracy is nothing but an attempt to apply the principles of the Bible to a human society.—Wallace C. Speers

768

Democracy cannot be achieved or maintained merely by preferring it to other forms of government. It calls for high intelligence, tolerance, self-denial, personal responsibility—and without these, it cannot exist.—Robert Killam

DENIAL

769

Toward the end of his tragic, devoted life, General Robert E. Lee attended the christening of a friend's child. The mother asked him for a word that would guide the child along the long road to manhood.

Lee's answer summed up the creed that had borne him, through struggle and suffering, to a great place in the American legend. "Teach him," he said simply, "to deny himself."

770

The word "deny" is not a vague, foggy word, easy to evade. It is appallingly sharp and clear. . . . The denial of *self* . . . is making ourselves not an end, but a means, in the Kingdom of God.—Halford E. Luccock, *The Interpreter's Bible*

DESIRE

771

Do you suppose that through all eternity the price we will need to pay for keeping God will be that we must endlessly be giving Him away?—Frank Laubach, *Letters by a Modern Mystic*

772

It is less painful to avoid desire than to witness fruit on the tree of hope and fall after the frost of failure.— Douglas Meador

773

The greatest want of the world is the want of men—men who will not be bought or sold; men who in their inmost souls are true and honest; men who do not fear to call sin by its right name; men whose conscience is as true to duty as the needle to the pole; men who will stand for the right though the heavens fall.—E. G. White

774

A man travels the world over in search of what he needs and returns home to find it.—George Moore

775

Grandpa and John Gray are talking: John is setting off for war. Finally, Grandpa cleared his throat. "What you plannin' on doin' when you come back from, er, uh—Over There, son?". . . . "I've been thinking that maybe I'd like to write," I said. . . . Grandpa nodded at that, then he sighed deeply and turned in his chair. "Well, son," he said, "I guess you know I've always hoped that maybe you'd be a preacher?" "Yes," I said, "I know—but I don't think I was meant to be one." Grandpa looked at me closely. "You're not ashamed of religion, are you, son?" I shook my head. "No, sir," I said, truthfully, "I'd be proud to be a minister. When I was small I wanted to be one more than anything."—Joe David Brown, *Stars in My Crown*

776

We all desire inner peace, meaningful relationship to our fellows, a growing understanding. . . . Biographies of great people show many lives who were given what might be called misfortune, but who took the dark strands and so wove them into the cloth of life that it carried the sheen they wanted it to have. Beethoven and Edison were deaf. Milton was blind. Jesus, making the cross a symbol, not of defeat, but of victory, stands as our towering illustration. From the spiritual heights where He lives we can mold life after our dreams . . . "accept some tenet of faith and live with it as if it were true." Act as though you were engaged in an experiment to prove to yourself that your belief is valid. Throw uncertainty away, as you would an old garment that's worn out and of no use to anyone. Someone asked William Blake, "When the sun rises do you not see a round disc of fire, somewhat like a guinea?"

He replied, "Oh no! No! I see an innumerable company of the heavenly host, crying, 'Holy, Holy, Holy, is the Lord God Almighty.'" Such a faith, which looks out on life as if God were in every phase, will surely find Him there and will say, "I can and I will make it as I want it to be. . . ." The answer comes to use in the twentieth century as Jesus put it to a centurion in the first, "As thou hast believed, so be it done unto thee."—Lowell Russell Ditzen, *The P. E. O. Record*

DIET

777

A doctor said, "Just about every American would be better off physically if he ate less. . . . An economist said, "Every American would be better off financially if he ate less." And a pastor would say: "Every American will be better off spiritually if he conserves food to prevent starvation abroad." Thus there are three reasons—and mighty good ones—why all of us should give more than lip service to food distribution problems around the world. —*Sioux Falls* (South Dakota) *Argus Leader*

778

An overweight person is generally living beyond his seams.—Marcelene Cox

779

The Faculty Club are all going on a diet to see which one can win the no-belly prize.—Elwyn Schwartz

DIFFICULT

780

There are three things difficult: to keep a secret, to suffer an injury, to use leisure.—Voltaire

781

All great and honorable actions are accompanied with great difficulties, and must be both enterprised and overcome with answerable courage.—Gov. William Bradford

782

We must find our duties in what comes to us, not in what we imagine might have been.—George Eliot

783

I'll let you into the secret. It is nothing really difficult if you only begin. Some people contemplate a task until it looks so big it seems impossible, but I just begin and it gets done somehow. There would be no coral islands if the first bug sat down and began to wonder how the job was to be done. —Josh Billings

784

Difficulties are things that show what men are.—Epictetus

DISCIPLE

785

A. J. Cronin's novel *The Citadel* shows one doctor following the easy course of coddling wealthy hypochondriacs, and another devoting himself, with but little recompense in cash, to the needs of a Welsh mining town. Christ-love called one way, and self-love the other. Besides, the Welsh doctor had to plead for new sanitation, and so found himself in conflict with political-economic conservatism and greed. Following Christ is not easy.—George A. Buttrick, *The Interpreter's Bible*

786

There is no longer any room in the world for a merely external form of Christianity based upon custom. . . . The world is entering upon a period of catastrophe and crisis when we are being forced to take sides and in which a higher and more intense kind of spiritual life will be demanded from Christians.—Nicholas Berdyaev, *Freedom and the Spirit*

787

When Bishop Fulton Sheen registered at a hotel, he filled out a card at the desk. After the word "Representing" he wrote, "Good Lord and Co."

788

The people in this city have given up hope of reform in more places than the waterfront, and are cynical. Unless we can give them solid ground for Christian hope, we are in a tragic state. If it can't be done, I'd rather be somewhere in the South Pacific, where you can bring pagans to the Christian state —because you can't get Christians in this city to live up to Christianity.— John M. Corridan, *Newsweek*

789

Our lives are small and insignificant, not only in view of the vast world that the scientist opens to our minds, but also in respect to the great tides of world history that seem to dwarf our small human purposes. But when our purposes are by the imitation of Christ allied to those of God Himself, we can be sure that no matter what the world may do to us in this life, we shall be able to share with God and with Christ and with all His people in the ultimate joy and victory of the heavenly king.—John Marsh, *A Year with the Bible*

DISCIPLINE

790

Without dignity, discipline is impossible. Children need discipline as guidance; too often the family fails to provide it.—Ruth Alexander

791

Punishment is not revenge; it is a means of discipline. It must be used to instill fear of the consequences of criminal acts, in order to protect the law-abiding.—Ruth Alexander

792

Emotionalism is not good when you're flying these fast airplanes. Today's generation is growing up with a lack of discipline in the homes and schools and churches. When they get into this airplane business, they are plunged into an environment which demands discipline. They've got to be disciplined by the environment before it kills them.—*Time*

793

No horse gets anywhere till he is harnessed. No steam or gas ever drives anything until it is confined. No Niagara is ever turned into light and power until it is tunneled. No life ever grows great until it is focused, dedicated, disciplined.—Harry Emerson Fosdick

794

Youngsters don't rebel at discipline; they do rebel at inconsistency—overleniency now, strictness then. Many parents either do everything to keep their children occupied and then suddenly turn them loose on their own as teen-agers, or they encourage small children to "let off steam" but are shocked when as teen-agers they do this after sitting daily for hours in school.—*The Christian Science Monitor*

795

The word "discipline" has three distinct connotations. One is punishment—the penalty for disobedience. This idea has lost favor in the modern Western World to the point where maladjustment is often used to excuse the criminal rather than to explain the crime. Under such conditions, society's concept of right and wrong is weakened.

The second connotation sees discipline as a process of teaching and supervision—whose purpose is to correct, mold, strengthen, and perfect. It involves training a man to do a job, and imposing authority to see that the job is well done. Every successful organization requires the combination of training and authority—whether it is a football team, a business enterprise, or a military unit. . . .

The third and most fundamental connotation is that of individual self-discipline. This is the ultimate test of the worth of the free men or woman. Self-discipline does not rest on fear of punishment, nor on the dictates of superior authority, nor on the willingness to go along and be a good member of the team. It is a quality that evolves as the individual develops certain standards of conduct, which for him have sufficient value that to uphold them he will endure whatever comes.—Robert L. Garner, *Kiwanis Magazine*

DOOR

796

A door symbolizes the difference between barbarism and civilization . . . in the world of the savage there are no doors. . . . At every turn in life there is a door. We enter into experiences through a door, or we are barred from an experience because we cannot get through the door that leads to it.

Doors affect our religious life. Jesus made the door a symbol of the way into understanding and fellowship with God and also a symbol of the way out to sacrificial service. In fact, Jesus called Himself a door. He is the way out of narrow complacency into the more abundant and eternal life.—E. Paul Hovey, *Today*

797

E. Stanley Jones points out that during the days between Easter and Pentecost, the church was living behind closed doors (John 20:19). During that time the disciples had all the teachings which Jesus was to give them. But they lacked the spirit to go out and put those teachings into practice and pass them on to others. All too often, Christians find themselves like the church of those early days: for fear of something, they hide behind closed doors and the message which would heal the sin-sick world is shut up with them.

"Nothing," says Dr. Jones, "will be more tragic to the church and to the world than for the church to close itself up, encase itself in its own inner activities, while the great stream of the world's life flows past it and the church is not at its center."—E. Paul Hovey

798

Give me your tired, your poor,
Your huddled masses yearning to breathe free,
The wretched refuse of your teeming shore,
Send these, the homeless, tempest-tossed, to me:
I lift my lamp beside the golden door.
—Emma Lazarus, inscription for the Statue of Liberty, New York harbor

799

I am the front door of your church.
I want to be an easily opened and friendly church door. I have reasons other than pride for wanting to be conspicuous so that a hesitant visitor, a timid newcomer, or a doubtful stranger will sense my urgent invitation to "enter into his gates with thanksgiving and into his courts with praise."

I want people to pass through the doorway of God's house with a sense of privilege and high hopes. Incidentally, I do not want the church treasurer standing around, jealously eyeing my wide-open welcome and thinking of the coal bill. I like to be cut on generous proportions, as if I were saying: "Come one, come all. . . . My house shall be called a house of prayer for all peoples."

Am I boasting too much? Dare I tell of a secret ambition? It is a desire to have a sense of comradeship with One who said, "I am the door: by me, if any man enter in, he shall be saved, and shall go in and out. . . ."

My accessibility, my attractiveness, my friendliness, may mean giving Christ a chance to say, through me, to many hearts, "I am the door."—J. L. Johnson

800

Each sin has its door of entrance; keep that door closed.

801

Opportunity merely knocks—temptation kicks the door in!

802

The Christian is likened unto a key
Which unlocks the door,
That any may enter and find eternal life.

For the Christian is the key person,
Making that important personal contact
Which causes a change to be
Wrought in the life of a learner.

He is the key to the code
Which deciphers and interprets,
To those who would learn,
Those puzzling passages that
Make for Christian life.

These keys, held together
By the perfect circle

Of Christ,
Make the Christian disciple
A doorkeeper
To the Kingdom of Heaven.
                    —E. Paul Hovey, *Today*

DOUBT

803

Doubt may be one of the prices we pay for not reading our Bible.—Leonard G. Clough

804

I cannot rest in a Quest—for a Quest is often a Question Mark. I must meet certainty somewhere and make Question Marks into Interrogation Points.—E. Stanley Jones

805

When a man puts a limit on what he will do, he has put a limit on what he can do.—Theodore Roosevelt

806

All progress is made by men of faith who believe in what is right and, what is more important, actually do what is right in their own private affairs. You cannot add to the peace and good will of the world if you fail to create an atmosphere of harmony and love right where you live and work.—Thomas Dreier

807

This court is often in error, but never in doubt.—Justice Hitz

808

O Lord—if there is a Lord; save my soul—if I have a soul. Amen.—Ernest Renan, *Prayer of a Skeptic*

809

Among the great paintings of the world are those depicting the temptation of Jesus. Of the one by Cornelius, Dr. Albert Bailey has said: "The intensity of the struggle is indicated here in subtle ways; His eyes are red with lack of sleep, His hair has been blown into disorder by the wind —for days he has not thought of His personal appearance; His chin rests upon His right hand . . . and the problem? It was whether to trust without further proofs the new revelation that came to Him at His baptism. If thou art the Messiah—prove it on these stones. If thou art the Messiah— let all the people see it after the pattern of their expectations. Since thou art the Messiah—rule! It took Jesus forty days to think Himself clear of the entanglements involved in these suggestions; but He emerged with his future principles of action settled forever. They are these: I am the Messiah and my work is to establish the Kingdom of God; I will never use my Messianic power for my own gratification; I will never make a spectacle of myself to gain popularity; I will never rule, but only love and help and teach."

EASTER

810

An empty tomb, so says the cynic, is a poor foundation on which to establish a world religion. The Christian hope, however, is based not on an empty tomb, which is incidental, but on a Risen Lord. On that faith the Christian orders his life, his worship, his deportment. It is the source of his inspiration and action. For that faith men have gone through "peril, toil, and pain"; for it they have suffered death in the arena, have been burned at the stake, have endured torture and persecution. The opposition of twenty centuries has failed to dim the light of that faith or to crush its persistence. —*The United Church Observer*

811

It was through the resurrection that God demonstrated His power and achieved the victory over the dark forces which seemed to have won on Calvary. Through the resurrection the cross was proved to be not tragic defeat, but the great triumph of the ages. Not only was death vanquished but Christ was seen to have "despoiled the principalities and powers" and to have "made a show of them openly." Easter is both the symbol and the pledge of the new birth, that new birth which the Holy Spirit works in the believer, and which is the beginning of an eternal life of growth into the very likeness of God, until all of the ransomed sons of God had been saved to sin no more, and have been filled unto all the fullness of God.—Kenneth Scott Latourette, *Missions*

812

The Easter story is ever so simple, but means ever so much. As always, the simplest stories tell the most. This story tells about living forever, and everybody wants that if the forever life is good. We want our friends and dear ones to be with us in that life.

The events of that first Easter happened like this: A Man whom many people loved and who helped so many by acts of goodness, and who spoke with such great wisdom that He could tell the greatest truths with stories and words everybody could understand, was put to death by Roman soldiers on the false accusation of treason: that He had claimed to be Christ the King. He had said He was king, but that "my kingdom is not of this world."

His friends and followers thought Him too good to die; that He never would die, nor could! All of us think somewhat like that about those we love. But, after He had been nailed on a cross for a few hours, He did die, and the door of a tomb was closed on His body, many thought forever. His followers were confused. It seemed to them their greatest Friend had let them down.

On Sunday following that black Friday, some women took spices to the tomb to embalm Him. It was very early in the morning. To their amazement, the great stone door had been rolled aside, and a dazzling messenger of God sat upon it. They were terribly frightened. "Do not be afraid," said the angel. "He is not here. He is risen. Go and tell His followers. . . ." His sacrifice for us on Good Friday voices the sure hope that those we love can live, and we with them, and, that the forever life with Him is good.—John Evans, *Chicago Tribune*

813

It is the certainty, the direct and intuitive knowledge that comes from fellowship with the living Christ, that must be at the center of our witness to the resurrection today. Intellectual arguments about a 2000-year-old historic event, no matter how amazing the fact may be, will convince few; but practical evidence that He who then rose from the dead is still living, and that His Spirit is operative now in the lives of His people, cannot be resisted or denied.—*The Canadian Baptist*

814

We live in a time of crisis. . . . In an era of revolutionary change some rock of reality is needed on which to stand. Such was the experience of the first disciples. After the crucifixion they were discouraged and bewildered. They said, "We trusted that it had been he which should have redeemed Israel." Then came the impact of the fact of the resurrection. The stern task given them still remained. But now they understood as never before the meaning and purpose of God, of life, and their lives. They were given new insight, courage, spiritual power. For us also Easter may bring these great gifts as we realize the truth that Christ lives. The joyful news that He is risen does not change the contemporary world. Still before us lie work, discipline, sacrifice. But the fact of Easter gives us the spiritual power to do the work, accept the discipline, and make the sacrifice. —Henry Knox Sherrill, *Forth*

815

I can live forever with God. Trouble, illness, and death may come but my real self—my soul—will go on living in another existence with Almighty God. That is one of the plain meanings of Easter. Through Jesus it brought to visible expression the immortality of the human spirit whose life rests in God. With this in mind, one of the first-century Christians said, "For this corruptible shall put on incorruption, and this mortal shall put on immortality, and death itself be swallowed up in victory."

There are many reasons which support my belief in immortality. My simple desire for it is one reason. The world has provided the fulfillment for my every desire; I thirst, there is water; I hunger, there is food; I long for fellowship, behold my friends. It is reasonable to believe that there is an answer to my desire for immortality. —Clarence Seidenspinner

816

Resurrection and life are the day's promise, expressed in a manner more convincing than words by the Author of life. Easter is not a time for groping through dusty, musty tomes or tombs to disprove spontaneous generation or even to prove life eternal. It is a day to fan the ashes of dead hope, a day to banish doubts and seek the slopes where the sun is rising, to revel in the faith which transports us out of ourselves and the dead past into the vast and inviting unknown. Even the agnostic Ingersoll softened at the grave

of his brother and chanted the rarely beautiful words: "Hope can see the glistening of a star; love can hear the rustling of a wing." So it is that to those who have faith the story of the empty tomb gives assurance that all does not end with that which looks like death. "Such is the character of that morrow which mere lapse of time can never make to dawn. Only that day dawns to which we are awake. There is more day to dawn. The sun is but a morning star."—*Lewiston* (Idaho) *Tribune*

817

The message of Easter cannot be written in the past tense. It is a message for today and the days to come. It is God's message which must re-echo through your lives. . . .—Frank D. Getty, *Forward*

818

Easter can be different—if you want it to be. A greater *you* can be born—if you will deepen your consecration to Christ. And from your life a new radiance of happiness will shine into the lives of others.—Elizabeth Lee, *Adult Class*

819

Far be it from me to preach to you, but as a long-time usher and greeter, I suggest that if you begin attending church regularly about now, you won't feel like such a total stranger there on Easter.—Burton Hillis, *Better Homes & Gardens*

820

On that first Easter everybody was excited: The stunned high priest, surrounded by frightened guards, chattered incomprehensibly with startled Pharisees and scribes, none of them quite sure of the swiftly moving events. The disciples, downcast and in seclusion for two days and nights, suddenly sprang into action when the excited women brought them the electrifying news. In the words of the spiritual, "My Lord, what a morning!"—Thomas F. Chilcote, Jr., *Daily Bible Lessons*

821

A Roman magistrate greets a Christian prisoner . . . with these words: "I sentence you to death as a follower of the Nazarene." But the prisoner looks unflinchingly into the eyes of the magistrate and replies, "Sir, death is dead. It no longer has power to make me afraid. Our divine Master has conquered death and the grave. He said to us, 'Be not afraid of them that kill the body, and after that have no more that they can do.' "

So Rome lost the one instrument by which it had hoped to put fear into the hearts of these Christians. Little wonder that within three hundred years the cross of the despised Galilean took precedence over the Roman eagle.

To this day, the most convincing evidence for the resurrection of Christ is men and women whose lives bear witness to His living reality . . . — John S. Bonnell, *Heaven and Hell*

822

The resurrection of Christ from the dead is the source of the Christian message which has given hope to the hopeless and comfort to all in deep sorrow. The Christian fellowship in all the world attests to the strength that is gotten from that faith which commends the souls of our beloved dead to the keeping of Christ. And so we lift up our hearts as we repeat the ancient creed so familiar to many of you: "I believe in the resurrection of the body, and the life everlasting, Amen."—Winfield Burggraaff, "Easter for You"

823

Easter Day sheds its light on the church of Jesus Christ, revealing it in its full, its deathless dimensions. When you and I, like the first disciples after the first Easter, hear the voice of the risen and majestic Christ, we know that the church must be something more than our group of neighbors who gather for worship every Sunday morning. . . . To be in touch with Christ is to have the mind expanded. The boundaries of selfhood are razed. To know Him is to know that His concern is not limited to any self-concerned group. It goes out to the ends of the earth. When you enjoy His compassion you do not undergauge the extent of it. You realize that the number of those who consciously accept it—which is the church—cannot easily be counted.

But that is only one aspect of the church. On Easter Day the veil between time and eternity thins to gossamer. Jesus Christ declares Himself the Lord and Friend not only of us who live here but of those who live there. He is the bond between us and those whom we have loved and lost—and yet not lost, because in the power and love of God they cannot be lost. "O blest communion, fellowship divine—we feebly struggle: they in glory shine." Easter discloses the church as a divine as well as an earthly society. Easter shows the church to be what the old Cambridge Platform of 1648 says it is, "the whole company of those that are . . . called . . . unto . . . grace . . . in Jesus Christ."—Douglas Horton

824

A minister, visiting a church one summer, found a banner used the previous Easter. It read, "He is Risen," and was tucked away behind the coal bin. How tragic for a life if Easter is but a brief experience each spring! To Paul in the stress of life the Risen Christ said, "I am with thee." Easter was a continuing experience for Paul. The Easter radiance abides. Whatever else the future holds for me, it holds Christ. Wonderful indeed are His

words, "I am with thee."—D. Hobart
Evans, *Forward*

825

The resurrection of Jesus Christ separates Christianity from the other religious systems of the world. Buddhism, Confucianism, and many other religions are based on moral codes. Certainly these systems have benefited their believers in many ways. But their fault lies in their limitation. They have never mastered death and never will.

Take the resurrection of Jesus Christ from Christianity, and you have only another moral code—one higher than the others, but still just a way of life based largely on the precept, "do unto others as you will have them do unto you."

Paul wrote to the Corinthians, "And if Christ hath not been raised, then is our preaching vain; your faith also is vain."

The resurrection of Jesus Christ is our hope today. It is our assurance that we have a living Saviour to help us live as we should now, and that when, in the end, we set forth on that last great journey, we shall not travel an uncharted course, but rather we shall go on a planned voyage—life to death to eternal living.—Raymond Mac-Kendree, *Queens' Gardens*

ECONOMICS

826

Like theology, and unlike mathematics, economics deals with matters which men consider very close to their lives.—Kenneth Galbraith

827

On the moral side, the church should make it plain that no mere man-made economic system can succeed unless it has sound character behind it.—Eddy Asirvatham

EDUCATION

828

The defense against a bad idea is a better idea; the defense against propaganda is education; and it is in education that democracies must put their trust.—William F. Russell

829

Do you remember in Robert Sherwood's play *The Petrified Forest,* the character of Alan Squier and his philosophical discourse on "the vanishing race of the intellectuals"? Alan Squier carried in his rucksack Jung's *Modern Man in Search of a Soul,* but he never learned how to search for—and find—his soul. And so he became a "vanishing intellectual." And worst of all—an intellectual sorry for himself.

We cannot afford, these dire days, either to coddle ourselves in the phoney martyrdoms of philosophic despair or to allow our intellectuals to become a "vanishing race." In our time, educated men and women come close to being our one indispensable.

You've heard about the old man in New England sitting on his porch, recovering from a stroke? A neighbor came along, asked him how he was getting along. "Well," drawled the old fellow, "I eats purty good. I sleeps purty good—and I gets around to doing the chores some. . . . Of course, my mind's gone . . . but it seems somehow I don't miss that much!"

The one thing we can't afford to miss is the educated mind, the mind trained to find its way between the confusing and conflicting issues of our confused and conflicting times. Never before in history has the world so needed what someone has called "the glory of the lighted mind!"—Clarence W. Hall

830

Education's real challenge is to produce men and women who know how to think; and knowing how, do it; and having done it, voice their opinions. —Henry T. Heald, *The New York Times Magazine*

831

Christian education is the process by which persons are confronted with and controlled by the Christian gospel.— Paul H. Vieth, *The Church and Christian Education*

832

The first thing education teaches you is to walk alone.—*Trader Horn*

833

The home, the barn, the river, and the school made this Willie White. The school only taught him superficial things—to read, write, and figure, and to take care of himself on the playground. But those other ancient institutions of learning taught him wisdom, the rules of life, and the skills which had survival value in the world of boyhood.—William Allen White, *Autobiography*

834

The business of the teacher is to ring the rising bell in the dormitory of the soul.

835

Education means teaching people to behave as they do not behave.—John Ruskin

836

Don Bosco prepared a way for the good that lies in every soul to come to the surface, instead of neglecting and then assaulting the seeds of evil. His method was to keep the boy's mind filled to the overflow with the legitimate interest and pleasures of boyhood. There was no space for any other influence. There was no mansion of the soul to let.—Shane Leslie

837

The person who determines your way of living and your chance of salvation is not the man who pays your wages, nor your president, nor your doctor or policeman, nor yet even your spouse, but the one who looks you in the face when you are young, calls you by your true name, and says, "Go forth!"—Agnes de Mille, "The Valor of Teaching," *Atlantic Monthly*

838

Somebody once said that the supreme purpose of education was to enable a man to ask the right questions. We may expand and adapt that wise saying and state that the essential purpose of Christian education is to enable men to ask fundamental questions. One of the saddest features of our age is the widespread mentality which asks only trivial questions, the answers to which are utterly insignificant either way.—D. R. Davies, *The Art of Dodging Repentance*

839

Christian education would encourage and direct us in that greatest adventure of the human spirit, the discovery of God. It would raise a temple for the mind, build an altar for the heart. It would provide that depth of peace and joy which come to a pure heart in love with God and man.

Christians believe education should never end. Do not use your diploma as a padlock on your mind. Do not regard graduation from any educational institution as graduation from the task of getting an education. Responsibility for nurture and growth of the mind is a life-long assignment to every human being by the Author of wisdom.— Everett W. Palmer

840

There is danger in judging mass media chiefly by entertainment standards. The test of entertainment is immediate pleasure. The test of education may come today, tomorrow, or ten years from now. Entertainment helps us forget; education helps us remember. Entertainment aims to relax . . . education should keep us awake and alive . . . it thrives on disciplined thinking and aims to make the learner independent. Entertainment makes us less able to "entertain" ourselves. However, we need entertainment. But we can have too much of it. The sauce that adds flavor . . . becomes the whole meal. Education is in a race with catastrophe, but it is also in a race with entertainment.

All mass media are "formers." They use our time, shape our tastes, muddy our ideas, or make them clear. We are being changed and are instruments in changing others. . . . Rome never lacked entertainment, but it was not able to assimilate the cultures which it engulfed or created.—Edgar Dale, *The Church Woman*

841

People have to be, so to speak, "introduced" to Jesus before yielding to Him. Here is the justification of all that we have come to include under the general term of "religious education." There have been, of course, those who supposed that religious education was a substitute for conversion. It is clear that they were wrong. But it would be foolish to regard the alternative as being the giving up of religious education. If that were done, there could never be any conversions. Our task is to lead people to definite and genuine Christian decision, but that can be done only as there are certain preliminary steps.—Edwin Lewis

842

The highest goal of liberal education is to implant in the pupil the desire for freedom of mind and spirit. It is the foe of deterministic explanations of human behavior.—Hollington K. Tong

843

The outcome of a college training ought to be a sound body, a disciplined mind, a liberal education, a right character.

He who carries the torchlight into the recesses of science and shows the gems that are sparkling there, must not be a mere hired conductor, who is to bow in one company, and bow out another, and show what is to be seen with a heartless indifference, but must have an everliving fountain of emotion that will flow afresh as he contemplates anew the words of God and the great principles of truth and duty.—Mark Hopkins

844

The things most people want to know about are usually none of their business.—George Bernard Shaw

845

Exclude religion from education and you have no foundation upon which to build moral character.—Charles W. Eliot

846

To educate a man in mind and not in morals is to educate a menace to society.—Theodore Roosevelt

847

The first business of education is to make sure that the discovery of one's self is reasonably complete. . . . A second result to be expected from modern education is that it can give him contact with the mind of his time. . . . The third result which education ought to be expected to give . . . is the clear and sure access to truth. Not possession of it in any large degree—that is the work of a lifetime—but access to it. —William J. Tucker, *The Making and the Unmaking of the Preacher*

848

The aim of education is not to add to the sum of human knowledge. Its purpose is to open the mind and not fill it, as we would an ash can or even a golden bowl.—Christian Gauss

849

Your education begins when what is called your education is over.—Justice Oliver Wendell Holmes

850

Education makes a people easy to lead, but difficult to drive; easy to govern, but impossible to enslave.—Lord Brougham

851

Every time you pray, if your prayer is sincere, there will be new feeling and new meaning in it which will give you fresh courage, and you will understand that prayer is an education.—Dostoevski, *The Brothers Karamazov*

852

The mixing of learning and teaching in the same person is especially important. Indeed, it is probably at just the moments of mixing that the touch of magic enters into the hard work of education.—John Sloan Dickey

853

The profession of learning watches over its own integrity. We must reject the assumption that its integrity can be preserved only if legislators or self-appointed bodies can periodically call upon the universities to justify themselves.—Louis M. Hacker

854

There is nothing so stupid as the educated man, if you get off the subject he was educated in.—Will Rogers

855

Education is an ornament in prosperity and a refuge in adversity.—Aristotle

856

What greater or better gift can we offer the republic than to teach and instruct our youth?—Cicero

857

We live in a world where our power gives us the chance of doing unlimited harm; and we need an education which teaches us not merely how to use that power but how to use it well. To build up in every man and woman a solid core of spiritual life, which will resist the attrition of everyday existence in our mechanized world—that is the most difficult and important task of school and university. Barbarian tribes destroyed the Roman Empire. There are no such tribes to destroy modern civilization from outside. The barbarians are ourselves. The real problem is to humanize man, to show him the spiritual ideals without which neither happiness nor success is genuine or permanent, to produce beings who will know not merely how to split atoms but how to use their powers for good. Such knowledge is not to be had from the social or physical sciences.—Sir Richard Livingstone, *Some Tasks for Education*

858

Education is for all, and there can be no compromise with the proposition. . . . We teach our entire youth, but we do not teach them enough. What was once for the few must now be for the many. There is no escape from this—least of all through any sacrifice of quality to quantity.

An ancient sentence about liberal education says it is the education worthy of a free man, and the converse is equally ancient: the free man is the one who is worthy of a liberal education. Both sentences remain true, the only difficulty being to know how many men are capable of freedom. . . . Liberal education in the modern world must aim at the generosity of nature, must work to make the aristocrat, the man of grace, the person, as numerous as fate allows. No society can succeed henceforth unless its last citizen is as free to become a prince and a philosopher as his powers permit. The greatest number of these is none too many for democracy, nor is the expense of producing them exorbitant. "A new degree of intellectual power," said Emerson, "is cheap at any price," and this is true no less for a country than for one of its citizens.—Mark Van Doren, *Liberal Education*

859

More people than ever before are graduated but not educated.—Robert G. Gunderson, *Vital Speeches*

860

Christian education would teach us to think. It would require of us a mind disciplined for concentration, clarity, accuracy, and hard work; a mind open and alert, responsive to new ideas, unafraid to follow truth; a mind trained to be discriminating in judgment, not given to generalization without facts, not slothful in knowing the meaning and proper use of words. Christian education would make us aware of standards, sensitive to excellence. This is the essence of good taste, the measure of manners and morals, the index of character.—Everett W. Palmer

861

Christian education would convert the mind from the knowledge and love of what is cheap and mediocre to the knowledge and love of what is worthy and noble.—Chalmers

862

What sculpture is to a block of marble, education is to the soul.

863

Last fall a youngster who had done pre-nursery and nursery school went to real school for the first time. He came home downcast and said glumly, "I'm tired of being taught to play. I want to be taught to learn."—Robert Sylvester, *Chicago Tribune*

864

The child who is not taught to see some connection between his play and religion will grow up into the person who sees no connection between his vocation and religion.—E. Paul Hovey

865

Education is a kind of continuing dialogue, and a dialogue assumes, in the nature of the case, different points of view.—Robert M. Hutchins

866

If education pushes back a man's horizons, enabling him to see further than his fellows, it thereby imposes on him an obligation to point the way for them, to serve as a social engineer.—R. E. Womack

867

An educated man is one who can entertain a new idea, entertain another person and entertain himself.—Sydney Herbert Wood

868

Though goodness without knowledge is weak and feeble; yet knowledge without goodness is dangerous; both united form the noblest character and lay the surest foundation of usefulness to mankind.—John Phillips

869

The chief value of education is not the accumulation and possession of an extraordinary amount of factual information, but the development of a distinctive sense of values and an appreciative awareness of conditions and opportunities which the untutored mind never recognizes. The educated person is one who has an awareness of conditions and opportunities, coupled with the ability to turn these two assets into practical ends. A person sees in everything just what his mind has been trained to see. One person looks at a field and sees it covered with wild vegetation which he determines to plow up before planting the next crop. Another person looks at the same field, and in that same vegetation he sees a valuable soil builder, with roots rich in nitrogen, which if left as a cover crop for a season will enrich the soil and contribute toward a much greater yield in future harvests. One person hears in a knock on an office door an interruption which will delay the completion of the day's work; another person hears in the same knock an opportunity to serve someone in need.—Virginia S. Ely, *The Church Secretary*

870

There is nothing more pitiable than the person who is always answering questions no one has asked. He may be a master at articulation, he may be forceful and dogmatic, he may know all the answers, but he is not the sort of person who makes a good religious educator. The person who really counts in the religious field is the one who can listen. Unless one listens, he cannot hear the voice of God, nor can he hear the questions of his neighbor. Unless he listens, he cannot aid others in finding the answers they really want and God has to give. . . . In terms of religious experience God takes the initiative, but He does not force Himself. . . . A person might be convinced through logical proofs that there is a God, but unless his belief becomes a transforming experience, he is still

without God. . . . If one listens to what others are saying, then he may find the truth of God revealed through them. If he listens to the questions they are asking, he may find the truth maintained in his religion. If he listens and his religion does not point to the answers, then his God is too small. Then it is time for him to re-examine his own beliefs.—Lee A. Belford, *Information Service*

871

Education is dynamic and is tested by what the educated man does in the world. It was the tragedy of the Middle Ages that the scholar, the man with the cultivated mind, found the world intolerable and withdrew from it.

The obligation of the educated man is quite the contrary. The characteristic of a free society is that there is no privilege that is not to be counterbalanced by an appropriate responsibility. Unhappily there are men who all their lives plow the fields and take the crops from the soil of freedom and make no effort to restore the fertility . . . education is a privilege . . . it involves the responsibility of leadership.—Clarence B. Randall, *Rotarian*

872

Young gentlemen, you have come here in the hope of furthering your education. . . . An educated man is a man who, by the time he is twenty-five years old, has a clear theory, formed in the light of human experience down the ages, of what constitutes a satisfying life, a significant life, and who, by the age of thirty, has a moral philosophy consonant with human experience. If a man reaches these ages without having arrived at such a theory, such a philosophy, then no matter how many facts he has learned or how many processes he has mastered, that man is an ignoramus and a fool, unhappy, probably dangerous.—William Harper, when President of University of Chicago

873

Intelligence is derived from two words—*inter* and *legere*—*inter* meaning "between" and *legere* meaning "to choose." An intelligent person, therefore, is one who has learned "to choose between." He knows that good is better than evil, that confidence should supersede fear, that love is superior to hate, that gentleness is better than cruelty, forbearance than intolerance, compassion than arrogance and that truth has more virtue than ignorance. —J. Martin Klotsche, "On Being an Educated Person," *Vital Speeches*

874

Money enables a man to get along without education, and education enables him to get along without money. —Marcelene Cox, *Ladies' Home Journal*

875

Whereas education "leads out," to think out something, religion "binds in," to believe in something. Education is a process of the laboratory; religion is the purpose of the sanctuary. The key word in education is "experiment"; in religion, "experience." In education man validates experiment; man *does* something. In religion man enshrines experience; man *becomes* something. —Martin M. Weitz

876

True education makes for inequality; the inequality of individuality, the inequality of success, the glorious inequality of talent, of genius; for inequality, not mediocrity, individual superiority, not standardization, is the measure of the progress of the world. —Felix E. Schelling

877

American education is dedicated to equality of opportunity. This is as it should be. The phrase, however, must be amplified before it can become a safe guide to action. Equality, after all, can be achieved by diminishing as well as by increasing the value of what is given. Unfortunately, there is such a thing as equal denial of opportunity. . . . Children of average or less than average ability are not the only ones who deserve consideration in a democracy. The child of high intellectual capacity has his democratic rights, too. He is entitled to receive, in an American public school, an education equal in seriousness, intensity, and comprehensiveness to the education that a child of similar capacity would receive in the best school systems of any other country. —Arthur Bestor, "Educating the Gifted Child," *New Republic*

878

Your work . . . has interested me more than any other achievement in modern education. You not only imparted language to Helen Keller but you unfolded her personality; and such work has in it an element of the superhuman.—Albert Einstein, speaking to Anne Sullivan Macy

EFFORT

879

Keep the faculty of effort alive in you by a little gratuitous exercise every day. That is, be systematically ascetic or heroic in little unnecessary points; do every day or two something for no other reason than that you would rather not do it, so that when the hour of dire need draws nigh, it may find you not unnerved and untrained to stand the test. So, with the man who has daily inured himself to the habits of concentrated attention, energetic volition and self-denial in unnecessary things, he will stand like a tower when everything rocks around him, and when his softer fellow mortals are winnowed like chaff in the blast.—William James, *Principles of Psychology*

880
About the only thing that comes to us without effort is old age.

881
Training for an articulate democracy, as John W. Studebaker, former Commissioner of Education, said of teaching, is not "a task for timorous or feeble souls; nor for the complacent and uncertain. It requires Americans whose faith in democracy does not waver or falter because they know whereof they speak and are convinced that the values they defend are eternally right and true."—*Congressional Record*

882
It's easier for you to learn to play than to work, so we'll teach you to work.

EMOTION

883
For some strange reason . . . man, although proud of the thinking that has led to systems of philosophy and to scientific invention, proud also of the achievements of the human will, is ashamed of his emotions.—Leslie D. Weatherhead

884
Emotion is not something shameful, subordinate, second-rate; it is a supremely valid phase of humanity at its noblest and most mature.—Joshua Loth Liebman

885
To be stirred out of comfortable self-interest by emotion directed toward higher powers gives evidence that man —even primitive man—does not live by bread alone.—Georgia Harkness

886
Emotion is the chief source of all becoming-conscious. There can be no transforming of darkness into light and of apathy into movement without emotion.—C. G. Jung

ENCOURAGEMENT

887
When Victor Herbert was the conductor of an orchestra, an aspiring composer brought him a march and asked him to play it.
Herbert saw that the score lacked merit and turned it down. Miffed, the composer cracked, "I thought you said you encouraged home talent."
"I do," retorted Herbert, "I encourage it—to stay at home."

888
Many learned volumes have been written on the subject of preaching, but no analysis has ever approached the Apostle Paul's: ". . . he who prophesies speaks to men for their upbuilding and encouragement and consolation" (I Corinthians 14:3, RSV). That word "encouragement" is a touchstone as to whether one who speaks for God succeeds or fails.—Andrew W. McDermott

ENEMIES

889
Perhaps the funmaker who said, "Speak well of your enemies—remember you made them," had it about right. At least most of the differences in life result from our getting offended, not the other fellow.

890

Sympathy is extended to good neighbors Jack and Elisabeth McInnes. Their Jeannie, having been naughty and duly scolded, was invited to ask the blessing at lunch. She prayed, "Thank thee, Lord, for preparing a table for me in the presence of mine enemies."—Burton Hillis, *Better Homes & Gardens*

ENERGY

891

If I were a heathen, I would rear a statue to Energy, and fall down and worship it.—Mark Twain

892

Prayer . . . the very highest energy of which the mind is capable.—Samuel Taylor Coleridge

893

We seldom have enough energy for our human needs. You might say that most of us consciously or unconsciously hunger for energy night and day.—Conrad Richter

ENTHUSIASM

894

The capital of the orator is in the bank of the highest sentimentalities and purest enthusiasms.—Edwin G. Parker

895

Nothing ever succeeds which exuberant spirits have not helped to produce.—Nietzsche

896

You cannot kindle a fire in any other heart until it is burning within your own.

897

Enthusiasm for work may not last but the memory of enthusiasm will. All the best things in the world started with somebody's enthusiasm. And they were passed on because there was somebody enthusiastic waiting to receive them.

898

The prudent man may direct a state; but it is the enthusiast who regenerates or runs it.—Edward Bulwer-Lytton

899

In order to do great things, one must be enthusiastic.—De Rouvroy

900

Enthusiasm is a wonderful word. But more—it is a wonderful feeling. It is a way of life. It is a magic spark that transforms "being" into "living." It makes hard work easy—and enjoyable. There is no better tonic for depression, no greater elixir for whatever happens to be wrong at the moment, than enthusiasm. No person who is enthusiastic about his work has anything to fear from life. . . . I have found enthusiasm for work and life to be the most precious ingredient in any recipe for successful living. And the greatest feature of this ingredient is that it is available to everyone—within himself.—Samuel Goldwyn

901

Nothing great was ever achieved without enthusiasm.—Ralph Waldo Emerson

ENVIRONMENT

902

The Book of Numbers contains the sad story of a people who were able to get out of Egypt in a few days but who were unable to get Egypt out of their lives for many years. . . . It took time to train a nation to keep the covenant.—Ray Freeman Jenny, *Bible Primer*

903

Why should we think upon things that are lovely? Because thinking determines life. It is a common habit to blame life upon environment. Environment modifies life but does not govern life. The soul is stronger than its surroundings.—William James, *Principles of Psychology*

904

H. A. Taine believed that if one understood the climate of England, he would know something of the forms which English literature must inevitably take. Writers untouched by higher tradition are likely to write of human life as completely submerged in circumstances. It is one of the deepest lessons of history that men do not need to be the slaves of their surroundings. They can master them. Every exodus in the history of mankind has been led by a Moses who was stronger than his environment.—Lynn Harold Hough, *The Interpreter's Bible*

905

Civilizations come to birth in environments that are unusually difficult and not unusually easy.—Arnold J. Toynbee

EQUALITY

906

Real equality is not something to be decreed by law. It cannot be given and it cannot be forced. It must be earned. Those who have won this decision must realize this and will labor to that end.—Raymond Moley, *Newsweek*

907

The idea of bringing all men on an equality with each other has always been a pleasant dream; the law cannot equalize men in spite of nature.—Varvenargues

908

Equality is the share of every one at their advent upon earth; and equality is also theirs when placed beneath it.—Enclos

909

I will attribute to those who differ from me the same degree of sincerity that I claim for myself.—Walter W. VanKirk

910

The world is my home and all the people of the earth are my brothers. As long as people and society continue to destroy the sacredness of personality, I must work to create abundant life. So long as people suffer from discrimination, poverty, and tyranny, I must live God's moral laws. So long as there are conflicts and tension, a world at war, I must give all diligence to promoting obedience to God's moral laws. In my hands are the instruments of peace and world order. I am a Christian.—A Young Christian's Charter for World Order

ERROR

911

Nothing is more harmful to a new truth than an old error.—Goethe

912

In my youth I once worked in a steel mill as a day laborer. One day I was given the job of wheeling a heavy wheelbarrow, loaded with bricks, over a narrow plank, underneath which were continuously passing white-hot lengths of steel. Wheeling the barrow along the ground was comparatively easy. A mistake was neither here nor there, nothing more than an overturned barrow, which had to be refilled. But a mistake on the plank might mean death. So I exercised very great care on the narrow plank. I concentrated like grim death. On that plank, my first mistake would also have been my last. Our Western civilization has, in its journey, arrived at the narrow plank, on which the repetition of the old errors will end in disaster.—D. R. Davies, *The Art of Dodging Repentance*

913

Men in high places in industry, government, radio, press, etc., can often spread enough error in a day to keep the forces of enlightenment busy for a year.—Glenn D. Hoover, *Vital Speeches*

ETERNITY

914

The late Lorado Taft, one of America's great artists and lovable souls, often said that a work of real art must have in it "a hint of eternity." Perhaps every piece of work should have in it some suggestion of permanent values beyond so many pieces of silver. The writer of Ecclesiastes says that God has not only "made everything beautiful," but He has set eternity in the heart of man. When we do a good piece of work, whether it is part of our vocational task or not, we may find in it a hint of eternity, the abiding value that outlasts silver or gold.—*Studies for Youth*

915

In the day of Columbus, maps were marked "here be demons," "here are dragons," and "here the end of the world," because so little was known about what existed on the other side

of the world. The explorations of Columbus brought a revelation of the world.

In the time of Christ, men did not know what existed on the other side of death. But after the crucifixion and the ascension, Christ brought back the word that there is eternal life.—Robert Chamness

EVANGELISM

916

When I began to understand what the Christian faith is and what it could mean to me, I concluded it was *not mine to keep.* It was something I had to share. I became interested in evangelism. To me, this is both natural and necessary to living a full Christian life, for evangelism means sharing one's faith.

You need not have had a startling, dramatic religious experience in your life in order to share your faith. God calls each one to witness for Him in a special way. . . . God is seeking to fulfill His purpose through you. To fail to share one's faith is to stand in the way of God's purposes. Realizing this, you will come to say of your faith, "It is not mine to keep."

917

The most wonderful story a person can tell is the difference that Christ has made in his life. The most gratifying satisfaction a person can experience is to share that difference with one who has lost his way.

The sharpest dividing line cutting across our world today is the one separating those who believe that there is such a God as Christ revealed, and those who do not. To bring a person across that line to faith in Jesus Christ is the basic Christian responsibility. It is the surest service to Him who said, "Ye are my witnesses."

This is evangelism.

918

No man on earth is getting along "pretty well" without Jesus Christ.— William Fraser McDowell

919

The American mind to which the church must address itself is a complex structure. It is all cluttered up with snippets and patches of information, a veritable hodgepodge of bits of half-understood science, magazine morality, pseudo-Christianity and humanistic idealism. Americans are enchanted by the glamor of a "success culture" but are haunted by the memory of their puritanical antecedents. Daily we are brainwashed with ideas born on Broadway at 42nd Street and Hollywood at Vine. Raised in a climate of freedom of speech, we are given to self-expression, but seldom stop to inquire whether we have a self worthy to be expressed.—Charles B. Templeton, *Evangelism for Tomorrow*

920

The greatest sin of the church is that it holds the gospel from itself and from the world.—Emil Brunner

921

The minister lives behind a "stained glass curtain." The layman has opportunities for evangelism which a minister will never have.—James McCord

922

Everyone's portrait of Jesus is incomplete. Did someone see Jesus in you today? Did they see enough?—J. Willis Hamblin

923

In order to live, we have to breathe both in and out. Evangelism is needed as the outgo in the Christian faith.— David Read

924

The church that does not reach out will fold up.—Halford E. Luccock

925

When it comes to speaking about their faith, some folks are like rivers running into the North Sea—frozen up at the mouth.—Dick Ferrell

926

If a person is a socialist or a communist, I will know it in twenty-four hours; if he is a member of a labor union, I will know it within a few days; but if he is a member of a Christian church, it may be years before I will ever learn of it.—Hughes Wagner, *The Presbyterian Record*

927

We ought not to encourage people to lower their standards. We ought to convert them.—John Sutherland Bonnell

928

No man can bring another man closer to Christ than he is himself.— Dwight L. Moody

929

Do you have any non-Christian friends? Do you ever feel sad about it? Do you really care that they are not Christians?—David Read

930

Philip . . . was not prepared single-handed to lay [the request of the Greeks] before the Master—evidently being dubious how it might be received. And after all, he had probably heard Christ saying to another Gentile claimant, and she in sore straits, "I am not sent but unto the lost sheep of the house of Israel." Happily he bethought himself of Andrew, and consulted one who seems to have been the kind of man that people in difficulties can and do consult; and apparently on Andrew's advice, they went together and told Jesus of the request.

Seldom was our Lord so deeply moved. . . . Christ sees past them to the dim Gentile peoples, masses of them down the centuries. . . . It had begun! His lifework had not been in vain. "The hour has come for the Son of Man to be glorified."—Arthur John Gossip, *The Interpreter's Bible*

EVIL

931

It is but rarely in history that the hierarchy takes a prophetic view of a prophetic initiative against evil. Perhaps that is because its chief function is to guard the truth rather than to proclaim it. . . . Yet when evil appears, and especially when evil shows itself in an attack upon personal freedom, surely then, if ever, the Christian conscience should awake and should see to it that the church not only speaks but acts! Nothing of the kind has happened in South Africa. We like to think it has. We like to think that "the voice of the church," uttering through official channels its condemnation of the different acts or measures, is a proof of its vigor and its life. Yet we know very well that these utterances have been totally ineffective in preventing inroads upon personal freedom and that when particular persons have been attacked and shackled in this way, no united effort has been made by the church to aid them. The blunt truth is that the church, the ordinary Christian man and woman, is not prepared to regard the state as an aggressor in South Africa. . . . The church is in the deadly grip of fear . . . it sits patiently, like the rabbit before the cobra, awaiting the next move and hoping (perhaps even praying) for a diversion which will allow it to scuttle to its den unharmed.—

Trevor Huddleston, *Naught for Your Comfort*

932

We are our own devils; we drive ourselves out of our Edens.—Goethe

933

All that is necessary for the triumph of evil is that good men do nothing.—Edmund Burke

934

We have learned the doctrine that evil means pain, and the revolt against pain in all its forms has grown more and more marked. From societies for the prevention of cruelty to animals up to socialism, we express in numberless ways the notion that suffering is a wrong which can and ought to be prevented, and a whole literature of sympathy has sprung into being which points out in story and in verse how hard it is to be wounded in the battle of life, how terrible, how unjust it is that anyone could fail.—Oliver Wendell Holmes

935

It is among the profound convictions of a free society that the last word is never left with evil, that God never gets in a blind alley, and that even from the conspiracies of malevolence some good may be drawn, because importunity wins its consent even against the most reluctant.—James H. Robinson, *Tomorrow Is Today*

936

The causes of good and evil are so various and uncertain, so often entangled with each other, so diversified by various relations, and so much subject to accidents which cannot be foreseen, that he who would fix his condition upon incontestable reasons of preference, must live and die inquiring and deliberating. . . . Every man is placed in his present condition by causes which acted without his foresight, and with which he did not always willingly cooperate; and therefore you will rarely meet one who does not think the lot of his neighbor better than his own.—Samuel Johnson, *Rasselas*

937

Evil has already demonstrated its ability to do terrible things. No man can be blamed for fearing. In fact, there are no people who "fear nothing." All of us are afraid of something, and well we may be, for evil is a matter of desperate seriousness. But evil has its limitations. In the first place, it is temporary in any world in which God reigns. Anything evil is doomed; its death sentence has already been passed. Any man . . . allied . . . with the right may be sure that he will see the victory if he persists in his stand. Jesus said, "Heaven and earth may pass away, but my word will not pass away."

EXAMPLE

938

Example is not the main thing in life—it is the only thing.—Albert Schweitzer

939

Of all commentaries upon the Scriptures, good examples are the best and the liveliest.—John Donne

940

We may make these times better if we bestir ourselves.—Benjamin Franklin

941

In Catamarca, Argentina, townspeople set their watches by a four-sided clock that rests high atop a pedestal in the business section. As they note the time, they are also reminded of a perhaps more important fact. . . . "This Is the Hour to Do Good" is lettered across each clock face. Somehow, the constant reminder seems to make a difference in the life of the city.

EXPERIENCE

942

Experience is remolding us every moment, and our mental reaction on any given thing is really a resultant of our experience of the whole world up to that date.—William James

943

Experience has ways of "boiling over" and making us correct our present formulae.—Lloyd Morris

944

The best of truths is of no use . . . unless it has become the individual's most personal inner experience.—C. G. Jung

945

Children are like grown people; the experience of others is never of any use to them.—Alphonse Daudet

946

Experience does not allow a gross lie to have a long life; it challenges it with constant contradictions.—M. C. D'Arcy

FACTS

947

The brightest flashes in the world of thought are incomplete until they have been proved to have their counterparts in the world of fact.—John Tyndall, *Fragments of Science*

948

"Don't confuse me with the facts. My mind already is made up."— quoted by Dorothy Fosdick, *Common Sense and World Affairs*

949

The modern intelligent mind, which has had its horizons widened in dozens of different ways, has got to be shocked afresh by the audacious central fact that as a sober matter of history, God became one of us.—J. B. Phillips, *New Testament Christianity*

950

No progress is made by running in advance of facts.—William J. Tucker, *The Making and the Unmaking of the Preacher*

951

Facts are to the mind what food is to the body. On the due digestion of the former depend the strength and wisdom of the one, just as vigor and health depend on the other. The wisest in council, the ablest in debate, and the most agreeable companion in the commerce of human life, is that man who has assimilated to his understanding the greatest number of facts. —Edmund Burke

FAILURE

952

History's records have carried its symptoms [coolness] before. The preacher in Ecclesiastes knew that marvels and failures totaled up only to vanity. The wisdom which resulted had an utter simplicity: stay cool. This sentiment runs through the centuries because human existence must contain defeats and accomplishments short of intentions. Yet men before us, beaten once, hoped and tried again. They did not cut their goals in the desperate hope of cutting their losses. Nothing ventured, nothing gained, they said, and so they ventured. Nothing ventured, nothing can be lost, we say, so stay cool.—Richard L. Schoenwald, "The Cool Approach," *The New Leader*

953

Never give a man up until he has failed at something he likes.—Lewis E. Lawes

954

You must have long-range goals to keep from being frustrated by short-range failures.—Charles C. Noble

955

When I was a young man I observed that nine out of every ten things I did were failures. I didn't want to be a failure. So I did ten times more work.—George Bernard Shaw

956

No man is a failure until he gives up.—Bishop of London

957

It happens very often that one tries to do something and fails. He feels discouraged, and yet he may discover years afterward that the very effort he made was the reason why somebody else took it up and succeeded. I really believe that whatever use I have been to progressive civilization has been accomplished in the things I failed to do rather than in the things I actually did do.—Senator George W. Norris

FAITH

958

Faith is not a human dream or illusion. Faith is God's work within us. It transmutes us and makes for our rebirth in God. It kills the old Adam and makes us different, recreating our heart, courage, understanding, and all other forces, and it carries with it the holy spirit. There is a power and life about faith that makes it impossible not to do the good. Faith does not inquire whether there are good works to be done, but even before asking questions, faith has done these works already.—Martin Luther

959

Faith enables us to rise above many things that would otherwise defeat us. It does not guarantee our prosperity. In a world as closely related as is ours, financial failure can come to any of us through no fault of ours. If religion were such a guaranty, our churches would be crowded . . . everyone would claim to believe in God. But we know that God is not so much interested in our prosperity as in the quality of our lives. . . .

To give up faith in times of misfortune is a sign of immaturity. . . . The most influential people in the world have been those who have suffered. . . . We sing "Faith of Our Fathers, Living Still"—and mention the cost in prison and dungeon; or tell the story of the cross, the very center of our Christian religion. This is the victory of faith—to live so as to encourage those who may come after us.—Gilbert S. Cox, *Adult Student*

960

Faith is the pencil of the soul that pictures heavenly things.—T. Burbridge

961

This life has all come out of a single, simple faith. God "has shone in our hearts to give the light," "the light of the knowledge of the glory of God in the face of Christ." There lies our faith. That is the way it all began, with the light of the living God in Christ. By that light we live

. . . we cannot stop here. "The faith" is not something out there which the church sets up and simply asks us to believe. "The faith" is lifeless and impotent without "faith." In "the faith" we try to set forth what God has said to us. In "faith" we make the living answer to this living God who comes to us in Christ. The living answer means a personal surrender and a life that is changed and made to serve.—H. F. Rall, *The Christian Advocate*

962

There is nothing passive about faith. It insists that we do more than have a care for the spiritual welfare of others. We are obliged to bring them to Jesus by whatever means may be at our disposal. It requires decision. It demands action.

963

Holy Carelessness: "If we cannot sleep at night, it means we cannot let go . . . cannot trust God," declared the Very Rev. James A. Pike. . . . Pike advised the congregation to set aside a quiet hour each day to meditate and resolve problems, then trust in God to "carry on" through the night while they sleep. This "holy carelessness," he insists, will fend off worries that "assail you in the dark and keep you awake."—*Newsweek*

964

A youngster, whose garden was growing well, told his mother, whose garden was not doing so well, "I just put my seeds in the ground, cover them, and say to God, 'It's up to you to make them grow.'"

965

Faith is a kind of winged intellect. The great workmen of history have been men who believed like giants.—Charles H. Parkhurst

966

I couldn't quit. I didn't think God would like it.—Glenn Cunningham

967

Whenever I've been tempted to quit, either in business, or in bridge, or in my writing, I call on myself for a little more effort, another try.—Ely Culbertson

968

When you think you can't do a thing, you are apt to be right. It's a confession that you don't trust God, don't have enough faith in Him. And so how can you have the faith that you can win?—James A. Farley

969

We who stand on religion's side, beckoning to those on the opposite shores, know they could make it across. Only *they* cannot be certain. Therefore we implore you to trust *us* and *not* your doubts. Be creative. Take the plunge.—James W. Fifield, Jr., *The Single Path*

970

A man of great faith can afford a little skepticism.—Nietzsche

971

Fear knocked at the door. Faith answered. No one was there.—Mantel of the Hind's Head Hotel, England

972

Communist leaders know that they must somehow put out the lights of religious faith if they are to triumph over the people and finally make them accept slavery. But they have faced in the power of faith more resistance than they had anticipated. Not believing in God themselves, they find it impossible to understand what makes people so determined in their reaching out for God.

After thirty years of communism in Russia, the leaders dare not trust even 5 per cent of the Russian people to be members of the Communist party. None who cling to religious faith in any form may qualify.

Perhaps one day the divine spark, which free men believe resides in every human soul, will burst everywhere into flame. It will consume the arrogant dictators who have rashly made war on all faiths. For faith, like fine steel, has always been tempered in the fires of persecution.—*Senior Scholastic*

973

Man is not master of the universe because he can split the atom. He has split the atom because he believed in his own unique mastery. Faith led to the material achievement, not the achievement to the faith.—Barbara Ward, *Faith and Freedom*

974

It is no easy task to build up the faith of one generation and not destroy the supports of the religion of the other.—Reinhold Niebuhr, *Leaves from the Notebook of a Tamed Cynic*

975

I have never known a worthwhile man who has not had . . . doubts and . . . spiritual lapses. But I am not disturbed because I know this: sooner or later every man needs God. The stronger and more male the man, the surer he is to need Him, and to need Him is to find Him.—Mary Roberts Rinehart

976

An empty, meaningless faith may be worse than none.—Elton Trueblood

977

Let us by conscious and deliberate effort begin to exercise the long-discussed faith-faculty.—J. B. Phillips, *New Testament Christianity*

978

Faith is love taking the form of aspiration.—William E. Channing

979

The principal part of faith is patience.—George Macdonald

980

Knowledge of things divine escapes us through want of faith.

981

If it weren't for faith, there would be no living in this world; we couldn't even eat hash.—Josh Billings

982

Mine is a scientific faith. I believe in Christ and His teachings because to me they seem the only way to successful living. I have come to believe in these valuations—that truth is worth more than popularity, love more than power, duty more than pleasure.

Happiness is the goal of most people. Some expect to get it through freedom to do as they please, and others through power or wealth. I believe it is the by-product of Christian living. It is scientific to prospect for gold or oil in certain places. It is also scientific to look for honest men, faithful wives and trustworthy leaders in Christian homes.

Steel is the modern symbol of strength. Yet rubber tires outlast steel wheels. This fact is also true in human values: wealth and power are most sought after, yet in the test of living, forgiveness, charity and love will be coveted long after wealth and power have ceased to be. Name all the things most valued in life—trustworthy friends, honest businessmen, good government, charitable giving, help in time of trouble, sympathy in sorrow, respect and understanding for children, a good community. All are synonymous with Christian living.—Lester H. Harsh, *The Christian Advocate*

983

Faith is not belief in spite of evidence. It is life in scorn of consequence.—Kirsopp Lake

984

Contemporary man begins to realize that his faith will stand the test of our age nowhere but in the questions and decisions of everyday life. He seeks practical directives to meet the requirements of the day.—Reinold von Thadden

985

The architect builds a great cathedral with the chancel toward the east so that the worshiping congregation faces the dawn. It is a beautiful symbol of our Christian faith. The church must always keep mankind facing the morning light.—Elmer L. Hobbs

986

Man cannot live without faith because his relationship with the future is an affair not alone of thought but also of action; life is a continuous adventure into the unknown.—Harry Emerson Fosdick

987

I respect faith, but doubt is what gets you an education.—Wilson Mizner

988

We live in an age of flux, of challenge to cherished ideals, of bleak iconoclasm, and of cynical disbelief. But we live also in an age of faith.—Ben Hibbs

989

The widow of Zarephath and her son were faced with starvation, but through her trust in God and devotion to the prophet Elijah, they were provided with oil and flour. She lived in a Gentile country and had been a heathen, but in some way had come to faith in the God of Israel later in life. Most of us have been believers since childhood. In spite of this advantage we too frequently fail to trust our Lord in the manner of this widow. Her trust in the Lord's care leaves us without any excuse for our own lack of trust and faith and should serve to inspire in us a similar confidence. Actually, is the experience of the widow so unusual? Isn't it rather the daily occurrence of our lives? Maybe we aren't at the point of eating our last crumb . . . and haven't been granted a special vision, but aren't we guilty of taking for granted every day the very thing that happened to this widow? . . . Every day, in every way we experience the care of our Lord. . . . However, let come the slightest crisis and we doubt whether God is equal to helping us.—Paul E. Daneker

990

"It is the half-faith," said Henry Hitt Crane, "that always lights the fagot." Repeatedly we attempt to legislate, to hedge conduct about with restrictions, to trust to rules, when we ought always to rely on our basic belief in conscience. We should have enough faith in the power of God to transform man.—*The Christian Advocate*

991

The fundamental contribution that Christendom can make to the world is still what it was in the beginning, its faith.—Richard T. Baker, *Let's Act Now!*

992

Faith is no more a virtue than an ear for music; you either have it or you don't.—Beverly Nichols

993

Nothing in life is more wonderful than faith—the one great moving force which we can neither weigh in the balance nor test in the crucible.—Sir William Osler

994

Christianity never began as a religion men were to build by keeping a set of ethical rules. Rather, it started as a movement in which, as men were transformed by their right relationship with God, they would live in right relationships with their fellow men. It is a religion in which men are saved by faith, rather than ethical rules. There are many people today searching for such a religion in which "faith is the force of life."—Thomas S. Kepler

995

It is now obvious that for a number of generations we have been attempting to hold on to Christian practices without possessing Christian beliefs. But Christian behavior, which is not supported by Christian faith, is a wasting asset, as we have discovered to our great dismay.—Arnold J. Toynbee

996

The question which we cannot evade is, having heard the word of Jesus, do we do it? He says, "Love your enemy." He says, "Do not lay up for yourselves treasures on earth." He says, "Do not be anxious. . . ." If we even *want* to find a way of escape from these words, there is no faith in us. No amount of enthusiasm for Jesus and for His church is a substitute for the unconditional obedience of faith.—James D. Smart, *This Generation*

997

Once a business friend of mine explained why an associate of his never rose to the top ranks of management in his office. "Mr. Blank," he explained, "keeps us out of trouble, but he also keeps us out of business. He never wants to go ahead unless he is absolutely sure. He is so cautious that he can't be creative." But the Christian doesn't want to live that way. He will go out before all the answers are in. He will dare in spite of the consequences, because he knows what it means to live by faith. Faith in Christ leads the Christian to venture into life on the basis of things he hopes for, even when all the evidence of the right course is not in.—Leonard Odiorne, *Crossroads*

998

History is not in vain and we do not start each generation all over again. . . . There is a God. He is a living person. He created heaven and earth and has authentically revealed Himself in history. His essence is love and therefore He both suffers and has suffered for our sins and always forgives. . . . The intellectual and spiritual principles in man are supreme over any other principle.—Charles Malik, "Crisis of Faith"

999

A little girl was distressed by the discovery that her brother had set traps to catch birds. Asked what she had done about the matter, she replied, "I prayed that the traps might not catch the birds." "Anything else?" "Yes," she said, "I prayed that God would prevent the birds from getting into the traps." "Anything further?" "Yes, I went out and kicked the traps all to pieces." That child seems to have mastered the doctrine of the futility of faith without works. Real faith is not static. It is dynamic. It does not seem too much concerned with security. It even risks danger. It is bold to invade the unknown.

1000

Although I never met General William Dean personally, he has enriched my life by teaching me two things: (1)

Don't sell faith short; (2) a man's example lives beyond his presence.—Hal Boyle

1001

It is easy to achieve emancipation from false and little faiths. It is quite another thing to come to a large and life-giving faith. Yet this is what we all need.—Nathan M. Pusey

1002

Here comes an attractive chap, evidently well-to-do and well-bred. Jesus loves him upon sight, for he is graceful and wistful and young. He asks about inheriting eternal life. Why does Christ make it so hard for him? Can't He see that He is demanding too much in asking the young lawyer to sell all that he has? Isn't some reasonable compromise possible? The disciples need money, and this young man needs to be a disciple. Surely halfway is better than no way at all! Couldn't he be allowed some benefits of this world, while generously helping the other? Yet Christ lets him go. It is so hard to die utterly that in consequence one may live wholly. The needle's eye is so impossible—yet inevitable for the Christian; otherwise God would not be necessary absolutely. "With God all things are possible. . . ." Heaven is not a matter of proved fact, but of faith. He who lives by demonstrable proofs must always speak of it conditionally. Only the Christian who lives by faith may speak of it absolutely; and, even so, he posits this affirmation on a prior act of faith, upon his faith in God.—Paul S. Wright, *Monday Morning*

1003

When Florence Nightingale was asked the secret of her rich and useful life, she replied: "I had faith; that was all."

FAMILY

1004

The concept of the family of God widens in concentric circles as the Biblical account unfolds. As it widens, it deepens. In the Old Testament, we read of a covenant people who stand in a peculiar relation to God: first a man, then a family, a clan, and a nation. Participation in the common privileges was determined by blood and sealed by the rite of circumcision. In the New Testament, the horizon widens to include all mankind, and the more intimate figure of the family is used to describe the relations of the members to one another and to God the Father.—William Douglas Chamberlain

1005

Older people's participation in our lives gives our children a sense of continuity—a sense of generations, of the flow and ebb of life. This perspective is one that children absorb: A realization that age means experience, that age need not be feared; a dim recognition that parents, too, were once children. Today we have suburban developments where children of young families are growing up without seeing old people as part of their day-to-day living. It seems to me that children need the natural balance of both young and old—and contact with their grandparents helps to provide this.— Mrs. Jonas E. Salk, *Family Circle*

1006

Christian character is nurtured, not in the fleeting moments of glorious experience, but in the common activity of everyday affairs, in a continuous, often undramatic, obligation. What counts in the long run is neither the few high points nor the blundering mistakes, but the general average of training over the years. Perhaps those daily times of worship have seemed prosaic to the family, yet in the long run they have been a powerful force for good.—John Charles Wynn, *How Christian Parents Face Family Problems*

1007

The richest tributes a child can lay at his parent's feet are the little troubles he brings them to share.— Burton Hillis, *Better Homes & Gardens*

1008

This family is achieving something! Within this home are gaiety, laughter, cooperation, understanding, neighborliness, community-mindedness and world concern . . . as you enter you are conscious, not of architecture or an interior decorator's art. This home has . . . atmosphere. It is a mingling of hospitality, refinement, and good cheer. . . . Do you see that map . . . on the wall? This family likes to find places they hear about in school and church . . . the dining room . . . is not just a place where people eat. God is thanked before every meal . . . father and mother have managed to put into each of the children's rooms a lovely picture, a Hofmann's head of Christ. . . . Christ with boys and girls of all colors around him. . . . No race prejudice enters this home. . . . In dad's and mother's room is a quotation from the *Odyssey* . . . "There is nothing mightier or nobler than where man and wife are one heart and one mind in a house . . . to their friends' great joy, but their own hearts know it best." . . . One has the feeling that in this place a devoted husband and wife, together with their children, are achieving the finest of all institutions— a Christian home!—Ruth McAfee Brown

1009

How shall we expect charity toward others when we are uncharitable to ourselves? Charity begins at home, is the voice of the world. Yet is every man his greatest enemy, and, as it were, his own executioner.—Sir Thomas Browne

FANATIC

1010

A fanatic is one who, having lost sight of his aim, redoubles his effort. —George Santayana

1011

What is fanaticism today is the fashionable creed tomorrow, and trite as the multiplication table a week after.—Wendell Phillips

1012

The weakness of human nature has always appeared in times of great revivals of religion, by a disposition to run into extremes, especially in these three things: enthusiasm, superstition, and intemperate zeal.—Jonathan Edwards

1013

Fanatic faith, once wedded fast to some dear falsehood, hugs it to the last.—Moore

FATHER

1014

Build me a son, O God, who will be strong enough to know when he is weak and brave enough to face himself when he is afraid; one who will be proud and unbending in honest defeat, but humble and gentle in victory. Build me a son whose wishes will not replace his actions—a son who will know Thee, and that to know himself is the foundation stone of knowledge.

Send him, I pray, not in the path of ease and comfort but the stress and spur of difficulties and challenge; here let him learn to stand up in the storm, here let him learn compassion for those who fail.

Build me a son whose heart will be clear, whose goal will be high; a son who will master himself before he seeks to master others; one who will learn to laugh, yet never forget how to weep; one who will reach into the future, yet never forget the past, and after all these things are his, this I pray, enough sense of humor that he may always be serious yet never take himself too seriously. Give him humility so that he may always remember the simplicity of true greatness, the open mind of true wisdom, the meekness of true strength; then I, his father, will dare to whisper, "I have not lived in vain."—General MacArthur, "Father's Prayer"

1015

Father is one of the most wonderful of all words in our language. We give thanks for our earthly father; for the father of our country, George Washington; for our spiritual father, Abraham, the man of faith; and for our Heavenly Father.—Merritt W. Faulkner

1016

A little boy asked his father for assistance in repairing his broken wagon. When the job was done, he looked up and said, "Daddy, when I try to do things by myself, they go wrong. But when you and I work together, they turn out just fine." There is just no substitute for dad.

1017

Every father can teach Christian principles.

He teaches kindness—by being thoughtful and gracious even at home.

He teaches patience—by being gentle and understanding over and over.

He teaches honesty—by keeping his promises to his family even when it costs.

He teaches courage—by living unafraid, with faith, in all circumstances.

He teaches justice—by being fair and dealing equally with everyone.

FEAR

1018

Strangely enough, it seems to be fear of each other which makes people brave enough to fight.—*Boston Globe*

1019

Men hate each other because they fear each other; they fear each other because they don't know each other; they don't know each other because they are separated from each other.—Martin Luther King, Jr., *Newsweek*

1020

I am frightened of well-meaning men who are ignorant, but I am frightened to death of clever men who are unconverted. Why is it that today we are sick and beside ourselves with the fever of disillusionment? The reason is this: we have tried to believe in man without believing in God and now we can believe in neither. With the loss of our faith in the living God and His purpose for mankind, the world has gone to pieces. Men have no courage for the fray, little hope for the future and little belief in their fellows.—H. R. L. Sheppard

1021

Men fight because they are afraid. Men fight because they feel insecure. Greater insecurity and greater fear will not contribute to a climate for peace.

Peace cannot be built on fear, but its opposite—trust; peace is not a negative quality but a positive aspect of human living. Peace is the end result and product of love, security and trust.—Israel Mowshowitz

1022

Don't try to stop being afraid; some fear is a good thing. But just try to keep facing up to what your logical mind tells you is back of your fears. Don't make excuses for, or ignore, the basic causes.—*Newsweek*

1023

Fear is a basic emotion, part of our native equipment, and like all normal emotions has a positive function to perform. Comforting formulas for getting rid of anxiety may be just the wrong thing. Books about "peace of mind" can be bad medicine. To be afraid when one should be afraid is good sense.—Dorothy Fosdick, *Common Sense and World Affairs*

1024

We have no fear of what has happened. Our fear is of what might happen. Our fear, therefore, is merely opinion. What will happen is entirely unknown to us. Why give life, then, to something that does not exist? Fear never need enter your life if you decline to accept it. Life is growth in things that do exist. Life is rich with the good and noble, if we make it so. Life is a concrete fact, filled with abundance. Fill your mind with the blessings of life and there will be no room for fear.—John Glossinger

1025

The child's verses by James Whitcomb Riley warn you that the "gobble-uns" will get you "ef you don't watch out," but the verses don't tell you just where to watch, or how, and this is a serious oversight. The "gobble-uns" of Riley's day came only in the night, but nowadays they come both night and day . . . for the gobble-uns have the bomb; we know it, and they know that we know it; also, they know that we have it. One side or the other might be willing to use it, but what would be the good if it couldn't keep the other side from using it? . . . In all our talk about freedom, and in our efforts to defend it, we labor under one heavy handicap. We are going out to do battle for the minds of all the more backward peoples of the earth; we have to win that battle, or see the gobble-uns win it and shut us off . . . from . . . products needed by our economy. . . . We are in the midst of a war, a life-and-death struggle for the minds and consciences of mankind; and we fight that war with handcuffs on our wrists and a ball and chain on our ankles. If we lose, what we lose is America.—Upton Sinclair, *The New Leader*

1026

Saul was afraid of David for two reasons: the Lord was with David, and the Lord had departed from Saul (I Samuel 18:12). Actually, there was no real cause for fear in the first reason. Saul should have been thankful for this demonstration of divine love. But Saul viewed this development with fear because, by his unbelief, he had caused God to depart from him. And therein was real cause for fear. There is nothing more dreadful and hopeless than to be rejected of God. . . . On the other hand, there is no greater joy and comfort than to be assured that God is with us.—Lorenz Eifert, *Portals of Prayer*

1027

Fear isn't cowardice; neither is the tension arising from pressure and irritation. Cowardice is failure to fight fear. Yet, temporary failure to overcome fear or tension is not cowardice. Put it this way. There are two kinds of men. One feels fear and fights it. The other feels fear and quits to it. —George Tebbetts, "All Ball Players Are Afraid," *Look*

1028

Without fear, there would be little occasion for foresight, little stimulus for planning, little need for sharpening the wits—and, as a consequence, little progress. . . . Instead of fearing probable things, we seem most inclined to fear the improbable. . . . Fears resting upon small probabilities run counter to the very necessities involved in living. Such fears can and should be eliminated.—E. Winston Jones, *The Christian Advocate*

1029

The man who has lost his sense of awe and reverence before God, who imagines himself to be "as God, knowing good and evil," is already delivered over to presumptuous sins. Almost at once he succumbs to that form of idolatry which transfers to another the fear which should be for God alone. How quickly he provokes the jealousy of God because he is afraid of offending someone! The commandments of God are forgotten because of the urgent necessity of pleasing husband or wife, employer or servant. The young person becomes afraid of the crowd. The politician becomes afraid of the people. The minister becomes afraid of the congregation. A white man ought to be afraid to discriminate against a Negro. If he isn't afraid, it is an indication that he has no fear of God before his eyes. A man or a nation ought to fear God and be afraid to follow the leading of self-interest to a place of special privilege that denies justice and a fair field for all. A person ought to be afraid to give way to wrath, to seek vengeance, to bear a grudge against his neighbor. He ought to be afraid to indulge in obscenity, impurity, profanity. Fear ought to restrain him from spitefulness and malicious gossip. He ought to be afraid to speak anything but the truth in love. He ought to be afraid to vex the stranger sojourning in the land. He ought to be afraid to turn a deaf ear to cries of need, or to shirk his proper place of leadership in church and community. Fear alone ought to prompt him to bring his tithes and offerings to the storehouse of God. . . . —Barnett S. Eby, *Westminster Adult Bible Class*

1030

If we fear long enough, we hate. If we hate long enough, we fight.—Henry Gonzalez

1031

Our anxieties could disintegrate us, cause us to lose our heads and to act impulsively. But they need not have that effect. Rightly handled fear can stimulate, arouse, and impel us to wise achievement—by waking us up to the consequences if America does not pass the test. "Fear," said Ralph Waldo Emerson, "is an instructor of great sagacity."—Dorothy Fosdick, *Common Sense and World Affairs*

FEELINGS

1032

Blessed is the man who has a skin of the right thickness. He can work happily in spite of enemies and friends. —Henry T. Bailey

1033

In Emil Ludwig's *Life of Lincoln* there is an incident I have never found elsewhere. It tells of how an old friend of Lincoln visited him at the White House. After they had talked awhile, the President asked his friend what he wanted of him. "Nothing," was the answer. "I just came to say that I love you and believe in you." Lincoln sprang up, grasped his friend's hand and said, "You don't know how much good that does me. You are about the only man who has come to see me here that hasn't wanted something from me." As I read, I thought of God, and

of how often we come to Him, seeking something for ourselves. May it not be that He is pleased when we come as friends just to tell Him that we love Him and believe in Him?—William P. Merrill, *The Presbyterian Banner*

1034

When happiness or sorrow becomes chronic, then it becomes dangerous. Permanent sorrow is produced by the exaggerated pictures of our imagination; the longer we allow ourselves to dwell in that state, the further we drift from reality. Permanent happiness tends to make most people selfish, oblivious of reality, uninterested in anything outside their own happiness.— Rom Landau, *God Is My Adventure*

1035

To bear up under loss; to fight the bitterness of defeat and the weakness of grief; to be victor over anger, to smile when tears are close; to resist disease and evil men and base instincts; to hate hate, and to love love; to go on when it would seem good to die; to look up with unquenchable faith in something ever more about to be—that is what any man can do, and be great.—Zane Grey

1036

The secret of charm is emotional directness. It consists in direct emotional communication with others . . . with total honesty, with sincerity, with deep concern, and without guile.— William James

1037

Sin is anything that separates us from God. If we are so good that we don't feel any need for God's mercy, then our goodness is sin.—Alexander Purdy

1038

What has for centuries raised man above the beast is not the cudgel but an inward music; the irresistible power of unarmed truth, the powerful attraction of its example. It has always been assumed that the most important things in the Gospels are the ethical maxims and commandments. But for me the most important thing is that Christ speaks in parables taken from life, that He explains the truth in terms of everyday reality. The idea that underlies this is that communion between mortals is immortal, and that the whole of life is symbolic because it is meaningful.—Boris Pasternak, *Doctor Zhivago*

FIGHTER

1039
We often are relieved of the necessity to strain ourselves when our apparent opportunities seem beyond our powers. We can relax and stay put in good conscience.

Our experience often is a reflection of the mood of Hans Castorp, in *The Magic Mountain* . . . when he learned he had a slight touch of tuberculosis. . . . He felt as he had in school as a boy when he had been told "he would not be promoted; therefore, no further effort had to be made the remainder of the term. . . ."

Our willingness to relax in the face of challenge is a serious hazard in our time, as Czeslaw Milosz notes in his book *The Captive Mind*. He observes pointedly that the rise of communism has been in exact proportion to man's loss of faith in himself and in God.

More and more people everywhere are haunted by the feeling that they are victims of social forces and therefore can do nothing to change anything. The result is that man becomes nothing because he has persuaded himself he is exactly that. Unfortunately, once we have persuaded ourselves we are nothing, we are likely to accept anything even though it may be bad. We are defeated, however, not by external conditions, but rather by our own self-doubt. Nine times out of ten, we can deal with difficulties on the roads we travel and with tangled human relations if we venture with faith in ourselves and God.—Harold Blake Walker

1040
When you have a fight with your conscience and get licked, you win.

1041
Weak characters may go out on their own feet, but for a fighter who never quits, being thrown out is the only fitting and proper end.—Gerald W. Johnson, "The Superficial Aspect," *New Republic*

FINISHED

1042
There is a vast difference between saying "it is finished" and "he is finished." The latter may mean "washed out" while the former may mean completed, brought to triumphant finality.

1043
A latecomer asked the usher how much of the service was finished. The usher responded, "The sermon is through, but it ain't been done yet."

1044
Many people want Jesus to do something for them and not with them! "What a friend we have in Jesus," but He wants us to be His friends also. The most perfect way to misery is to be a halfway Christian—incomplete.—Joseph Fort Newton

1045
No generation looks at history from the same perspective as its predecessor, and this is why no final history is ever written and why every generation must rewrite history. Because Christianity is an historical faith, there can never be a

final theology of the New Testament. Even the attitudes of purely literary criticism change from one generation to another. It is a mistake to suppose that it is the accumulation of scientific data which is chiefly responsible for the constant need of the restatement of man's apprehensions of ultimate truth. From the point of view of the committed Christian, New Testament theology involves the unrelenting effort at restatement of the faith of the church of Jesus Christ in the light of changing attitudes and of new knowledge.—Alan Richardson, *An Introduction to the Theology of the New Testament*

FLAG

1046

Born during the nation's infancy, I have grown with it, my stars increasing in number as the country has grown in size; the domain over which I wave expanding until the sun on my flying folds now never sets. Filled with significance are my colors of red, white and blue into which have been woven the strength and courage of American manhood, the love and loyalty of American womanhood. Stirring are the stories of my stars and stripes. I symbolize the soul of America, typifying her ideals and aspirations, her institutions and traditions. I have faith in the value of the common man and believe his possibilities are infinite. I reflect the wealth and grandeur of this great land of opportunity. I represent the Declaration of Independence. I stand for the Constitution of the United States. I signify the law of the land. I tell the achievements and progress of the American people in art and science, culture and literature, invention and commerce, transportation and industry. I control the strong, protect the weak, relieve the suffering, and do all I can for the betterment of mankind. I stand for peace and good will among the nations of the world. I believe in tolerance. I stand for a big and broad patriotism and a rational nationalism. I wave exultantly over the schoolhouses of the land, for education is the keystone of the nation and the schoolroom is my citadel. I am the badge of the nation's greatness and the emblem of its destiny. Threaten me, and millions will spring to my protection. I am the American Flag!

1047

The question has been raised in a recent news story . . . as to how big is a big flag. There is no standard-size American flag. The main criterion is that the flag's width be two-thirds of the length. We think that there are certain general dimensions, however, that should be observed.

A flag is a symbol, of course, and as such it should represent the qualities for which it stands. Consequently it can be large or small. It should be large enough to deserve respect and allegiance wherever it is flown. But it should not be so big that it can serve as a ready shield for scoundrels, the intemperate or the ignoble. It must not be so small that it is easily forgotten in the times or places where liberty is a dim and distant thing. It must be large enough to win a place dear to hearts of its sons and daughters. But it should not be so big that its sight strikes terror and fear where it is shown.

It should be large enough to cover all its people, not just the few. It should not be so small that it is easily waved in moments of wild, careless enthusiasm for causes that in a more sober, reflective moment would be rejected as unworthy. It matters little if a flag's history is long or short, its colors bright or pale, its design simple or complex. What matters is that where the banner waves, those who live under it dwell in peace, in liberty and in justice.—*The New York Times*

1048

The flag is intended to wave over a free, responsible people—not to be a screen for the schemes of superpatriots who would fatten their purses by undermining the reputations and rights of our citizens.—Woodrow Geier

1049

The flag pictures the vision of a people whose eyes were turned to the rising sun. It represents the hope of a father for his posterity. It was never flaunted for the glory of royalty; but to be born under it is to be the child of a king, and to establish a home under it is to be the founder of a royal house. Alone of all flags, it expresses the sovereignty of a people, which endures when all else passes away. He who lives under it and is loyal to it is loyal to truth and justice everywhere. He who lives under it and is disloyal to it is a traitor to the human race everywhere. —Calvin Coolidge

1050

We take the star from heaven, the red from our mother country, separating it by white stripes, thus showing that we have separated from her, and the white stripes shall go down to posterity representing liberty.—George Washington

1051

Wherever the American Flag has gone, it has been a herald of a better day—it has been the pledge of freedom, of justice, of order, of civilization, and of Christianity.—A. P. Putman

FORCE

1052

We have reached the point, in any event, when force cannot unite the world; it can merely destroy it.—Robert M. Hutchins, *Commonweal*

1053

When one subdues men by force, they do not submit to him in heart, but because not strong enough to resist. When one subdues men by virtue, they are pleased to the heart's core, and sincerely submit.—Mencius

FORGIVENESS

1054

Forgiveness isn't easy. Nothing is harder in all the world. And one reason why forgiveness is so hard is that often we try in all sincerity to forgive others because we have been told that we should do so, but we don't really have any very clear understanding of exactly why we should be forgiving. Under such circumstances, forgiveness doesn't give us much satisfaction because it doesn't go deep enough. We go through the motions of forgiving the injury in question, but we don't *forget it*. "We dutifully bury the hatchet," as someone once put it, "but we don't forget where we buried it."

1055

Forgiveness is necessary because we aren't Robinson Crusoes. A person who lives all by himself on a desert island can afford to do as he pleases. But . . . we live in a world where we rub shoulders with thousands of other human beings, in school, on the job, in our social life, and every single one of those human beings is in some way different from all the others. . . . Since we are all different, there are bound to be times when we come into conflict with the wishes of others. And in such a crowded world, we can well imagine what would happen if on such occasions every single one of us "stuck to his own guns" and refused to give an inch to the other fellow . . . a person who, while holding fast to his own principles, when those principles really matter, realizes that in his daily life, having his own way is not nearly so rewarding as getting along with his fellows—he is a person who has mastered the secret of successful living. He forgives, and he forgets as well.

1056

William Makepeace Thackeray and Charles Dickens, toward the middle of the nineteenth century, became rivals and estranged. Just before Christmas, 1863, they met in London, and frigidly failed to recognize each other. Thackeray turned back, seized the hand of Dickens and said he could no longer bear the coldness that existed between them. Dickens was touched; they parted with smiles. The old jealousy was destroyed. Almost immediately afterward Thackeray suddenly died. Sir Thomas Martin later wrote, "The next time I saw Dickens he was looking down into the grave of his great rival. He must have rejoiced, I thought, that they had shaken hands so warmly a day or so before." Is it not always well to seek forgiveness now? Are we sure that another opportunity will be afforded? —*The United Presbyterian*

FOURTH OF JULY

1057

The United States is the only country with a known birthday. All the rest began, they know not when, and grew into power, they know not how. If there had been no Independence Day, England and America combined would not be so great as each actually is. There is no Republican, no Democrat, on the Fourth of July—all are Americans.—James G. Blaine

1058

As we come to this Fourth of July, we are again reminded of the fact that our nation is great because it has had a center—God. Just as the universe must have the sun at its center to keep it from flying off in space, so every nation and every individual must have a center.

Before our forefathers landed at Plymouth Rock, they had a business meeting in the cabin of the ship and drew up the Mayflower Compact. That compact put God at the center of their lives and the life of the nation they were to found.

When our forefathers signed the Declaration of Independence, they had great hope for the little nation called America, for they knew that it was founded upon a solid rock—belief in the guiding hand of God. . . . We became a great nation under God, a nation full of hope.—Merritt W. Faulkner

FREEDOM

1059

Only free peoples can hold their purpose and their honor steady to a common end and prefer the interests of mankind to any narrow interests of their own.—Woodrow Wilson

1060

It is the claims that man and men make on the basis of their religious loyalties, or on the basis of other loyalties, that represent the real threat to the idea and fact of freedom. Man is always behaving as the child who, in his play, says in the words of an old English nursery rhyme, "I am the king of the castle; get down, you dirty old rascal." Sometimes the castle of which man claims to be king is his view about race, the Aryan race, for example; or a theory about his nation or group. Thus today we have seen or heard self-appointed high priests of "Americanism," men who claim to be, if not the creators of Americanism, at least its valid or final incarnation. From the point of view of this particular king of the castle, everyone else is by definition, "a dirty old rascal." Sometimes, again, the castle may stand for a religious community, a particular "Holy hill," a particular church with special and exclusive rights.—Ursula W. Niebuhr, "Man's Freedom Under God"

1061

It would seem that the present danger to civil liberties lies not so much in public apathy as in a fundamental blindness. There is something provincial in our pluralistic society which produces a tendency among us to identify liberty with "liberties" which we approve, and "license" with the activities of our nonconformist neighbors. We look upon our particular exercise of free speech, freedom of religion, freedom of association, and the like, a somehow definitive of the whole class of freedoms, and inalienable because legitimized by the authority of a certain church, or social class, or by the prevailing mood of popular opinion. We do not see any connection between the need for tolerating ideas which we loathe and the free exercise of our own civil liberties.

Shortsightedness, excusable in society at large, is hard to account for when found in the educated minority whose function it is to inform public opinion. —Thomas E. Kennelly, *Commonweal*

1062

Freedom—no word was ever spoken that has held out greater hope, demanded greater sacrifice, needed more to be nurtured, blessed more the giver . . . or came closer to being God's will on earth.—Omar N. Bradley

1063

Students should discover that they are free—not just at large.

1064

If the cross is the measure of God's respect for man's freedom, then we can take new hope that freedom will survive all man's attempts to destroy it. God's permission of the crucifixion is a sure sign that man's capacity for freedom is rooted in what God wills for man. Since that is so, then it is surely indestructible.

In defending human liberty, both the spiritual substance and its political reflection, we are defending nothing less than God's purpose. Whoever seeks to destroy that liberty is setting himself against the will and purpose of God. If the evil represented in the crucifixion of our Lord was powerless to destroy freedom, then nothing can. We can, therefore, strive and labor for the preservation of man's freedom without anxiety or fear or panic, because God wills that man shall remain a free and responsible being.—D. R. Davies, *The Art of Dodging Repentance*

1065

The final contribution of religious faith to the whole problem of freedom is the freedom to confess our sins; the freedom to admit that we all stand under the ultimate judgment of God. —Ursula W. Niebuhr, "Man's Freedom Under God"

1066

Name any road and it is still one of two roads. That is why the adjective "selfish" is so elusive. A saint is selfish in the sense that he is doing what he pleases, yet he has willed to seek his pleasure by the high road. Thus we rightly keep the word "selfish" to describe the low road; it is the road of self rather than of God. The high road is the road of "my sake" rather than of self.

This choice, this fork in the road, is the sign and occasion of our freedom. If there were no choice, we would not be free; if there were a million equally good choices, we would not be free. —George A. Buttrick, *The Interpreter's Bible*

1067

God has laid upon man the duty of being free, of safeguarding freedom of spirit, no matter how difficult that may be, or how much sacrifice and suffering it may require.—Nicholas Berdyaev

1068

Is it possible to control man's mental evolution so as to make him proof against the psychoses of hate and destructiveness? Here I am thinking by no means only of the so-called uncultured masses. Experience proves that it is rather the so-called "Intelligentsia" that is most apt to yield to these disastrous collective suggestions, since the intellectual has no direct contact with life in the raw, but encounters it in its easiest, synthetic form—upon the printed page.—Albert Einstein

1069

Our Declaration of Independence said that "all men are created equal." Its author, Thomas Jefferson, believed that "all eyes are opening to the thoughts of man . . . the mass of mankind was not born with saddles on their backs, nor a favored few, booted and spurred, ready to ride them by the grace of God."

Tom Paine spoke of the "small spark kindled in America" that would never be extinguished. Washington was certain that democracy throughout the world was "finally staked on the experiment attributed to the American people," and remarked that he felt "irresistibly excited when in any country I see an oppressed people unfurl the banner of freedom."

His successor, John Adams, said that the development of American democracy was the "opening of a grand scene and design of Providence for the emancipation of the slavish part of mankind all over the earth."

"The right of revolution," said Lincoln, "is a most sacred right; a right which we believe is to liberate the world." Our revolution, he thought, would ease the lot of peoples "over a great portion of the globe."

A few years later, General Ulysses Grant spoke of the sympathy of the American people for all whose "who struggle for liberty and self-government."

What the peoples of Asia, Africa and South America expect from us today is not a departure from this tradition but a bold reaffirmation of it.—Chester Bowles

1070

No man has a right to all of his rights.—Phillips Brooks

1071

Freedom is a costly thing. And since it is a costly thing, it entails a responsibility which limits our rights to do as we please. How costly freedom is—and how valuable—we have learned anew. . . . It costs the sacrifice and the blood of men. Indeed, all the benefits we enjoy, this vast continent with its wealth and its measure of security, has cost a long and continuing price of the generations that have gone before us, and whose labor has given us all that we possess. And while it would be ridiculous to sentimentalize it, the fact remains that the very receiving of these benefits lays upon us a responsibility for our fellow man and his rights, and the rights of future generations. We, therefore, do not have the right by our carelessness to let slip these liberties which cost so much. We do not have the right by a selfish attitude to make mockery of liberties for which our betters have suffered. We do not have the right to plunder the resources our predecessors have given us as if we were to be the last generation to inhabit this continent. We have, on the contrary, the responsibility to protect our liberties for future generations—to protect them by exhibiting them.—John Bright

1072

Man is really free only in God, the source of his freedom. . . . Freedom was first achieved among the Hebrews and the Greeks, therefore we find it expressed in the religion of the Bible and in the writings of the Greeks, for the whole story of Greece was one long struggle for liberty. . . . Hegel concludes his *Philosophy of History* with his oft-quoted statement that "the History of the World is nothing but the development of the Idea of Freedom." —Sherwood Eddy

1073

Liberty is always dangerous, but it is the safest thing we have.—Harry Emerson Fosdick

1074

Freedom means mastery of our world. Fear and greed are common sources of bondage. We are afraid, beset by anxiety. We do not know what tomorrow will bring. We seem so helpless over against the forces that move on without apparent thought for men. And our inner freedom is destroyed by greed. We think that if we only had enough goods we should be free, happy, without care. And so there comes the lust for money, and slavery to the world of things. The world can enslave; it can never make us free.—H. F. Rall, *The Christian Advocate*

1075

In the tenth century before Christ there lived an Edomite named Hadad. Son of a king, he was brought up in Egypt, where he enjoyed every privilege and was married to the sister of the queen. Pharaoh lavished everything upon Hadad. But one thing Hadad wanted above all else—his freedom.

"What lackest thou?" asked Pharaoh. "Nothing," replied Hadad. "Only let me go."

Freedom of his own soul was more important to Hadad than all the kingdom Egypt. . . . Hadad asked freedom . . . that he might return to his own country and help his people rebuild their kingdom and achieve liberty. . . . Hadad went forth from luxury to spend himself for his fellows.—Frank Curtis Williams

1076

To say that it is "fun to be free" comes close to a repudiation of real freedom. Freedom is not fun. . . . It is responsible choice. Freedom is not so much a right as a duty. Real freedom is not freedom from something; that would be license. It is freedom to choose between doing and not doing something, to act one way or another, to hold one belief or the opposite. It is never a release and always a responsibility. It is not fun, but the heaviest burden laid on man, to decide his own individual conduct as well as the conduct of society and to be responsible for both decisions. The only basis of freedom is the Christian conception of a man's nature; imperfect, weak, a sinner . . . yet made in God's image and responsible for his actions.—Peter Drucker, *Virginia Quarterly Review*

1077

Jesus offers to every man, not success, but salvation; not prestige, but peace; not popularity, but self-respect; not freedom from persecution, but fervor of spirit; not carnal joys, but character; not an easy life on earth, but an eternal life in heaven; not fortune, but freedom. "If the Son therefore shall make you free, ye shall be free indeed."— Clarence W. Cranford, *Adult Class*

1078

The escape from the Ten Commandments through violating them has never kept its promise of giving a new freedom. The experience is like the attempt to escape from the law of gravitation by defying it. The result is likely to be at least a bad fall. The philosophy of license is really a network of clever lies. The apostles of license are all the while promising that which they cannot give. You cannot become free physically by defying the laws of nature. And you cannot become free morally by defying the laws of ethics.—Lynn Harold Hough

1079

We find freedom when we find God; we lose it when we lose Him.—Paul Scherer

FRIEND

1080

Friendship is almost always the union of a part of one mind with a part of another; people are friends in spots.—George Santayana

1081

You can soon wipe out friendship by sponging on it.—George M. Ray

1082

A friend is one who knows all about you, and likes you anyway.

1083

No man is the whole of himself; his friends are the rest of him.—Harry Emerson Fosdick

1084

In the field of human relations, no place is more important than the little plot of ground that is your neighborhood. To grow something besides old on it, enrich it with a full measure of genuine friendliness.—Burton Hillis, *Better Homes & Gardens*

1085

I never considered a difference of opinion in politics, in religion, in philosophy, as cause for withdrawing from a friend.—Thomas Jefferson

1086

You can make more friends in two months by becoming interested in other people than you can in two years by trying to get other people interested in you.—Dale Carnegie

1087

Friendship is a sacred name, a holy thing; it never occurs but between virtuous people and springs from a mutual esteem; it is not so much kept going by gifts as by a good life. . . . There can be no friendship where there is cruelty, disloyalty, or injustice; and when the wicked get together, it is a plot, not company; they are not friends, they are accomplices.—La Boetie

1088

The duties of friendship are not focused on material but on ideal ends; friends do not become friends so as to maintain each other, but to sustain each other by spiritual means. If, over and beyond that, one is able to succor his mate with material help, that is indeed a great privilege for both. Practical benefits thus may result, but they do not influence great friendships. What sets it aside from any other relationship is just this spiritual freedom that accords at any given moment to both parties of the mutual compact the same amount of importance, value, and advantage. In a great friendship there can be no questions of weak and strong, of poor and rich. Equality is the basis, and friends are equal because they choose to be so.—Elizabeth Selden, *Book of Friendship*

1089

Three men are my friends—he that loves me, he that hates me and he that is indifferent to me. Who loves me, teaches me tenderness; who hates me, teaches me caution; who is indifferent to me, teaches me self-reliance.—J. E. Dinger

1090

We have not won our victory until our foe becomes our friend.

1091

Friendship is the only cement that will ever hold the world together.—Woodrow Wilson

1092

The Christian should never complain of his hard fortune while he knows that Christ is his friend.

1093

The greatest thing in the world is friendship. It is all that is claimed for it. It alone provides the surroundings in which minds can come to expansive fullness of health: the loyalty that grows out of it is a business asset beyond compute: it alone provides the subtle defense needed by the human spirit. . . . The church is the great medium. . . . It is built upon friendship. It believes that God is the friend of all men. It is a powerhouse of friendship: it will extend the hand of friendship to you and give you a chance to extend yours to others.—Douglas Horton, *The Art of Living Today*

1094

When he was in his seventies, the late Charles M. Schwab was the victim of a nuisance suit. The sum for which he was sued was extremely large. Mr. Schwab, who could have settled for a fraction of the amount named, refused to do so. He let the case run its legal gamut, won it in a walk, and, before leaving the stand, asked the court's permission to say a few words not concerned with the matter at hand.

"I'd like to say, here, in a court of law, and speaking as an old man, that nine-tenths of my troubles are traceable to my being kind to others. Look, you young people; if you want to steer away from trouble, be hard-boiled. Be quick with a good loud *no* to anyone and everyone. If you follow this rule, you'll be seldom molested as you tread life's pathway. Except," and the great man paused, a grand smile lighting his kindly features, "Except—you'll have no friends, you'll be lonely—and you won't have any fun!"—Mary Alkus

1095

There's an arithmetic of the spirit you don't find in schoolbooks. It has to do not with the sum of one apple added to another but with the sum of two people who understand each other.

The sum total includes what each becomes in an atmosphere of emotional warmth that neither one could become in a cold or neutral atmosphere. Freed and stimulated by understanding, each becomes human being unlimited, and their unity becomes a new, unlimited part of the universe. This is the miracle of togetherness.—Harry and Bonaro Overstreet, *McCall's Magazine*

1096

The friendship between Ray Lyman Wilbur and Herbert Hoover began at the door of a college dormitory . . . both were struggling young students, each working for the funds to secure an education.

Young Hoover was acting as salesman for a laundry service, and he called on Wilbur, who was working as a laboratory employee at fifteen cents an hour. Through the prosaic task of collecting laundry, this famous friendship began. . . . Both developed lives rich in usefulness, influencing citizens of many different races. At the time of his death,

Wilbur had twenty honorary degrees from world-famous universities. The work of Hoover had made him an international figure. Yet these men formed their valuable friendship when they were students. . . . In taking time to establish friendships with others of like ideals and Christian purposes affords an opportunity for growth and development of leadership.—Ruth C. Ikerman

1097

In *Martin Chuzzlewit* Charles Dickens penned some lines which could well become a motto for any public relations department. "What we've got to do," he wrote, "is to keep up our spirits, and be neighborly. We shall come all right in the end, never fear." —J. Carlisle MacDonald

1098

A man, sir, should keep his friendship in constant repair.—Samuel Johnson

FUTURE

1099

A primitive people speaks of "backing into the future." The future is full of unknowns to them, but they have seen that which is past.

1100

The major events that determine the future have already happened, and irrevocably.—Peter Drucker

1101

The best thing about the future is that it comes only one day at a time.

GENIUS

1102

Genius is the unlearned, the unborrowed, the unlearnable, the un-

borrowable, the intimately individual, the inimitable. As such it is known among all nations, and as such it will be known so long as men think, feel and speak.—Lavater

1103

When a man of genius appears in the world, it is immediately recognized by the fact that all the blockheads join forces against him.—Jonathan Swift

1104

Unless one is a genius, it is best to aim at being intelligible.

1105

Doing easily what others find difficult is talent; doing what is impossible is genius.—Amiel

1106

Common sense is instinct, and enough of it is genius.—George Bernard Shaw

1107

Genius is not a quality with which a few lucky mortals are endowed and which others entirely lack. It is only a quantitative difference in a certain combination of attitudes present in all human beings; in some it is more prominent, and thus more dominant, than in others.—Ernest Jones, *Newsweek*

GIVING

1108

Everything we have is really loaned to us; we can't take anything with us when we depart. If we have no use for a thing, we should pass it on to someone else who can use it—now.—Norma S. Scholl

1109

You do not have to be rich to be generous. If he has the spirit of true generosity, a pauper can give like a prince.—Corinne U. Wells

1110

To believe you are more generous than you really are is hazardous.—Dorothy Fosdick

1111

God loves a cheerful giver, but we settle for a grudging one.—Mildred McAfee Horton

1112

Giving is the secret of a healthy life. Not necessarily money, but whatever a man has of encouragement and sympathy and understanding.—John D. Rockefeller, Jr.

1113

What do we hope to accomplish when giving a gift? To pay a debt? Perhaps to encourage an exchange? Or to let someone know they are in our thoughts and affections, that we find real pleasure in their happiness and hope to enlarge it by this expression of our regard? That is Christian giving, rich because mutual, satisfying because disinterested, seeking no reward.

Jesus has made giving a joy, not a duty. He gives to build community, not to buy credit. He gives to enrich, not pauperize. In giving Himself, He shows how we may give without being obnoxious "benefactors" or selfish alms-givers. By His giving, we are convinced that God does love us; there in we find security and peace.

1114

The writer of the Epistle to the Hebrews saw in Christ's coming something tremendous in the happenings of the world. He calls Jesus the Pioneer of our salvation. To him the world was wild, uncivilized, uncontrolled, but at least this much had happened—the trail blazer had come. Is not that the way everything worth while starts? Once there was no scientific medicine —but then, Pasteur; once there was no competent nursing for the sick—but then, Florence Nightingale; once there was no religious liberty free from the State's regimentation—but then, Roger Williams. We do not see all things brought under control. Far from it! But we do see the Pioneer. But at least He has come; a start has been made; much has happened. Such is involved in the gift of Christ to the world.

1115

A little girl in a migrant camp fell in love with one of the dolls in the toy box, but she had to put it back when play time was over.

At Christmas time the camp staff arranged to give toys and agreed to let the child with perfect attendance have first choice. A beautiful doll was placed in the center of the gifts and the little girl having had perfect attendance was permitted to choose first. Her eyes nearly popped as she stood rigid before the doll. She stared in wonder, then she turned and walked down and took a tricycle.

When asked why, she said her little brother had wanted a bike and now she could give him one.—Dean Collins

1116

The giving of gifts is a great art. Not only their selection but the impelling motive and the manner in which conferred are significant.

"The gift without the giver is bare." Just how does one give himself with his gift? It may be that he does it somewhat when he so identifies himself with the recipient that the thing selected meets the other's secret hope or need. Perhaps that sense of mutuality suggests something the other really needs but is not conscious of lacking.

1117

Unselfish giving is the mark of a civilized man or woman. This impulse is a true measuring rod of the development of America and of civilization itself.—Arnaud C. Marts, *Christian Herald*

1118

The supreme meaning of Christmas is that God gave Himself to us. The supreme challenge of Christmas is that we give ourselves to God and help others to see Him as He is. It is very likely that none of us realize how desperately men long for revealing assurance that God is with them and cares what happens to them in these days. A boy in an orphanage received a present. Other boys received the same present, a basket of fruit, which they promptly proceeded to devour. But this boy set the basket in his window. When asked for a reason, he said wistfully: "I want to keep my present so people can see that someone cared for me on Christmas."—Carl Knudsen, *Pulpit*

1119

Give what you have. To someone it may be better than you dare to think. —Henry Wadsworth Longfellow

1120

We give not just to make the church go, but that it may grow.

GOAL

1121

Steadfastly setting one's face means that one is in position to overcome discouragement, to conquer self-pity and to direct ourself toward the objective or goal. Being human we tire easily, we become confused by issues, we get hopelessly entangled in our own reasoning and faltering methods of communication, to the end that our vision becomes clouded and our objective blurred. And then a leader lights a candle and we see again.—Charles L. Anspach, *Vital Speeches*

1122

The important thing is not where we are but where we are going.

1123

A man may have the finest automobile, be the best driver, have perfect vision and a heart of gold. But if he tries to find his way around Paris with a map of Chicago, and around Hanoi with a map of Oakland, California, he just will not arrive where he set out to go.—Walter Lippmann

GOD

1124

It is as difficult for an American as it was for a loyal Jew to believe that God might use a most hated and dangerous enemy to hammer His truth into their souls. And there are not many Americans today who would agree that God may be using Russia . . . to teach us the humility that we have lacked so long. Isaiah said that Assyria was God's hammer which crushed a nation, but brought them to their knees where they could find true religion.—*The Churchman*

1125

If God has spoken, why is the universe not convinced?—Percy Bysshe Shelley

1126

God leaves no room for doubts and ambiguities. His way is clear. Remember that He, in His loving kindness, imposes responsibilities, tasks and duties on you.—James Fifield, Jr.

1127

God has tried again and again to speak to me, but I wouldn't listen.— Oliver Wendell Holmes

1128

I never once felt that I was alone. I always felt that God was there. And because of His presence, I felt in contact with all other men and women, everywhere.—Martin Niemoller, when asked about his solitary confinement

1129

John Milton once said, "The great majority of us must be content to be in the register of God rather than in the record of man." Only a dozen or so people in each century achieve immortal fame upon the earth. We must look beyond our immediate friends and beyond our immediate environment for adequate encouragement for unselfish living. To grasp the significance of "Emmanuel—God with us" is to find a lasting incentive to live for the imperishable values of life.

1130

If Christ does not mean "God with us," the singing of "O Little Town of Bethlehem" becomes not a hymn of praise but a poem of mere pretensions. If God is not with us, then from the hymn we would need to delete the "hopes" and doubly emphasize the "fears." Then what would there be to sing about? Absolutely nothing; for men do not sing of fears. A fearful heart, a hopeless heart is not a singing heart. Only when we are assured that the hopes are of sufficient reality and strength to subdue our fears do we venture to sing of our fears.—Waights G. Henry, Jr., *Upper Room Pulpit*

1131

Those who have not taken God for their ruler will eventually take a ruler for their God.—George Sweazey

1132

The coming of God to share man's life on earth forever settles the question whether He is indifferent to man and his destiny. The incarnation convinces us that God is tremendously concerned about men and their affairs. He is not a God who sits apart as a spectator, merely observing the actions of men. He has come to participate actively in the affairs of this earth. The incarnation also convinces us that God has taken the initiative in delivering men from evil. He did not wait for man to seek Him. God made the first approach. He came in Jesus as the Good Shepherd, coming into the wilderness to seek and to save the lost sheep.—Earle W. Crawford, *Pulpit Preaching*

1133

While I was setting up my camera, loaded with color film, to look deeply into the azure depths of one of the great hot springs of Yellowstone National Park, one of the Park Rangers happened along. We became engaged in conversation about its possible depth. His comment was significant to a student of the Bible: "No man living has ever plumbed the depths of this pool or of the geysers in the Park." It humbles one to know that there are some things a man cannot know in the physical realm as well as in the unsearcheable and penetrating depths of God and His word.—John L. Sawyer

1134

We relate to God in the same manner that we have known relationships with men, that our relationships on both human and divine level are part of the same parcel. We approach God in the context of our everyday life. Our total impression about life has a great deal to say to our total feeling about God.—Robert C. Leslie

1135

When one thinks of God, he sees some picture of God. The danger lies in the fact that it can be the wrong picture, which can be tragic. One becomes like his image of God, and if it is the wrong image, the man becomes wrong.—Charles L. Allen, *God's Psychiatry*

1136

The first commandment is somewhat surprising. We would think that it would be, "Thou shalt believe in a God," a law against atheism. There is no such law. God took care of that in our creation. We do not teach a baby to hunger or to thirst; nature does that. However, we must train our children to satisfy their hungers and thirsts with the right things.—Charles L. Allen, *God's Psychiatry*

1137

The astronomers have shown us a universe so immense that we feel lost in it. And so we think God is lost too. And then the mighty torrent of history, sweeping human beings and civilizations along, and all the vast upheaval of our time have shaken our faith because, quite simply, we have believed in a God too much like ourselves, a little God. *We* feel overwhelmed and we think God must be overwhelmed. But this only means that we have confused the great God with frail and mortal man. And when we stop believing in a great God, we try to play God. Trying to make ourselves masters . . . we become fanatics, intolerant, ruthless. O man, remember! You are a creature, not the Creator, a servant, not the Master. Our times are in His hand!—Herman F. Reissig, "The Greatness and Nearness of God"

1138

God does not love only those who seem deserving, He loves *all* men—good and bad, saint and sinner. . . . "God so loved the world"—not part of it, not the people in it, but *the world*. . . . God loves us, *all* of us, no matter who we are or how grievously we may have sinned; He loves us and He has faith in us! —Charles Templeton, *Life Looks Up*

1139

Balaam was right when he said of Israel: "Israel has no need of diviner or soothsayer: it is enough to say in Israel, what hath God wrought." The men of our time must be made to see and to know their place in the long plan of God.—William J. Tucker, *The Making and the Unmaking of the Preacher*

1140

God needs no protectors. For God lives in the open mind, in the power of its thought, in the voice of its truth, the inner impulse of its honesty. He needs no protection. . . . Just give Him room.—A. Powell Davies

1141

Man has discovered that to kneel before God at least is more dignified than to lie down before a psychiatrist.— William A. Donaghy

1142

The honor that God offers us is this —that He will condescend to use us, lean upon us, call for our poor help, give us a real share in His own agony and saving of the sinful world. Christ expects that that will not scare us away, but thrill us, win us . . . draw us irresistibly. Such faith has He in you and me.—Arthur J. Gossip, *Expository Times*

1143

"If you aren't as close to God as you once were," said a wise mother, "you can be very certain as to which one of you has moved."—Burton Hillis, *Better Homes & Gardens*

1144

Sometimes a nation abolishes God, but fortunately God is more tolerant. —Herbert V. Prochnow

1145

If you believe in the Lord, He will do half the work—but the last half. He helps those who help themselves. —Cyrus K. Curtis

1146

A pathetic ad appeared in an intellectual magazine: "Having lost God, wanted: a substitute." Through the labyrinths of science and philosophy, the advertiser has lost his faith in the Eternal, and now finds a void in his soul and hunger in his heart. "Wanted: a substitute." But what can fill the place of God?

It is a question that the whole world, and especially the communist portion of it, might well ponder. Machinery and electronics, technology and controlled government—in the end they give but poor satisfaction to the hungering soul, and but faltering leadership to society. Having lost God, we have no substitute.—Grace Helen Davis

1147

When David came home from school one day to find his puppy had disappeared, he was heartbroken. A search failed to turn up the dog, and we decided we'd better consult with God.

"Now if we believe that God is everywhere, then your pet can't possibly be out of God's sight," I explained.

David pondered this and agreed. "Then he *is* all right," he said, with conviction, "wherever he is. But, gee, I want him back."

"All right," I told him, "let's take another look. But let's remember, God *knows* where he is. So let's ask Him for guidance." David was completely calm when we began our second search. We found the dog, unharmed, under an overturned box several blocks away. You say we would eventually have looked under that box whether we had consulted God or not?

Perhaps. But the point is, we went about our search in the knowledge that David's dog was in God's hands. This knowledge guaranteed a peaceful solution before we ever began to look for the pup. And so it is with other family problems to which we must seek answers. We begin in the full knowledge that a happy solution is certain because we've already consulted with God and are following His guidance.—Joseph N. Bell, *Family Weekly*

1148

I love that little boy who told his parents he didn't want to leave church because "I haven't seen God yet." Too many do, before they do.—Burton Hillis, *Better Homes & Gardens*

1149

The world is not drifting. God's hand is still at the helm. We are moving into new regions of thought and life and God knows the way we take.—Stuart Nye Hutchison, *The Presbyterian*

1150

When the Egyptians set out to find the Jewish Holy of Holies, they expected to find an idol. But when they came upon the tabernacle of the Hidden God they found nothing, only emptiness. The man who seeks for the American holy of holies may also expect to find some thing, an ideology, a philosophy. But when he gets there, the man will make a surprising discovery. If he unveils the American holy of holies, he too will find emptiness, but the void will be filled with voices engaged in argument and debate.— John Cogley, *Commonweal*

1151

Intellectually puzzling, the doctrine of the Trinity was developed out of plain human experience. If it is hard to understand, it is even harder to avoid in day-by-day living. God in His heaven, to us earth-bound mortals, often seems incomprehensibly vast, and too far away. We might believe in Him, we might adore Him at a distance. But in the hurly-burly of trying to wring a little time for living out of our lives, He is easy to forget, and hard to get into the focus of human vision even when we remember Him.

But our Lord is memorable to us, because he dwelt in the world of touch and sight and sound that we know. Still, Jesus knew that we would need more than historical records of His career to serve and save us in our specific struggles centuries after His life on earth. The problems of a married man rearing a family in a Northern climate, for example, may not find a ready solution in the glib question, "What would Jesus do?"

So He sent us a "Comforter"—the Holy Spirit. This Person of the Trinity is nearer to us than our brain or heart, knows us better than we know ourselves, even loves us more than we love ourselves. And the three—Father, Son, and Holy Spirit—are somehow One, and evermore shall be.

1152

It is at once a breath-taking and a breath-giving experience to be both captivated and liberated by Him who is called our "Servant Lord." On the one hand, it takes away the breath not only of our body, but also of our soul; not only of our heart, but also of our mind, as we stand there in His meek yet luminous presence, overwhelmed and awe-stricken, so much so that "we do not (even) know how to pray as we ought." On the other hand, it also breathes into our very core the breath of a new beginning, of a new life and obedience, until we all become, spontaneously and joyfully, members of "His servant people."

The Servant Lord and His servant people—are there any words that could more appropriately describe God's redemptive design and man's ultimate destiny?—Bela Vassady

1153

D. T. Niles tells of a service being held in a cathedral in Norway. Bishop Bergraav was preaching. Worshipers had noticed that the ceiling was low in proportion to the rest of the building. During the sermon Bishop Bergraav told the congregation that the ceiling which they saw was not the true ceiling. It was the working floor for artists who were painting the life of our Lord on the true ceiling. Some day the working floor would be taken down and then they would see what the artists had been doing.

As we look up and try to see what God is doing in our world, we are tempted to feel disappointed. We look for soaring arches, delicate stone work, and a height that reminds us of infinity. But one day our working floor will be taken away, and then we will see what the Great Artist has been doing.

1154

It is the task of religion to give meaning to life; to describe goals worth working for, worth achieving; to give vision and the far view—perspective. When we do not have a far view of the world—our world— it goes to pieces and falls in upon us. As Edna St. Vincent Millay has said: "And he whose soul is flat—the sky will cave in on him by and by. . . ." We may feel that God and man have deserted us, and that only the depths of hell itself are left to us. Then we must, as Edna St. Vincent Millay has said, "split the sky in two, and let the face of God shine through." That face is there, but it is we who must look.—Russell L. Dicks, *God and Health*

1155

Matthew Arnold defined God as "the power not ourselves that makes for righteousness."

1156

A Christian has been defined as "one who makes it easier to believe in God." I like that. . . . It rings true . . . when I read the New Testament . . . I do not find it hard to believe in God.—Harry C. Meserve, *Atlantic Monthly*

1157

In one of his letters, Paul refers to God as "the God of all comfort." It is interesting to explore this comforting power of God in reference to the infinite powers attributed to Him. They are commonly described as Omniscience—God knows everything; Omnipotence—God can do everything; Omnipresence—God is everywhere.

One notes immediately that these three attributes fill out and correct three states of chronic need and ardent desire in man. We certainly do not know everything—yet normally long to do so. We cannot do all we would like to do. We cannot be everywhere we desire to be. Thus God becomes the promise, indeed the guarantee, of our achieving these things if it be true that we are the children of His love.—Albert D. Belden, *Classmate*

1158

God can become small—not little—but man-sized, so that a human being can have some idea of God.—Arthur L. Miller

1159

During our years on the bench, we have found no simple formula for wiping out juvenile delinquency. If we were to compress into a capsule what we have learned from working with boys and girls in trouble, we would surely never sum up our findings in the two-word panacea, "Get tough." The answers to juvenile delinquency are elusive, and cases vary. We who believe in the great possibilities of today's youth believe in firmness and in discipline, but we also cherish each young person as an individual worthy of respect, love, and training.

King Edward VI used a striking quotation as he accepted the crown of England: "I said to the Man of the Year, 'Give me a light that I may travel into the unknown.' He answered, 'Go out into the world and put your hand in God's. It is better than a light and safer than a known way.'"

We do not know the answer to the problems of delinquency, but we do respect each young person brought before us as a child of God, and we firmly believe getting tough is not enough. A child wants to trust and to be trusted. Putting a child's hand in God's may be the answer.—Judge Elizabeth McCain, *National Parent-Teacher*

1160

What does a man think about when he is flat on his back on a hospital bed, hanging precariously between life and death because of a serious heart attack? He opens the files of memory and reads thoroughly the history of every recallable experience he has had. Then, with sober thought, he begins to philosophize about life in quest of the purpose for living. It is soon easy to determine if he has been a friend to God or if his Christian faith has been a pretense.

The man who has found God to be the Shepherd of his soul in all of life's experiences—through the good and the bad—sees even the prospect of death one in which God will guard his soul against all evil. He has no fear, only trust. He's an easy patient to treat because his problem is not complicated by emotional tension. . . . He has been honest with God so he and God are on good terms.—James E. Smith, *The Christian Evangelist*

1161

In Fulton Sheen's book *Peace of Soul,* there is a chapter entitled, "Is God Hard to Find?" He says . . . there are three false fears that keep us away from God. First, we want to be saved, but not from our sins. Second, we want to be saved, but not at too great a cost. Third, we want to be saved in our way, not God's. . . . My instinctive answer . . . is, "Yes, God is hard to find." Then . . . I remember . . . the psalmist who found it impossible to get away from God . . . "Whither shall I go from thy Spirit, or whither shall I flee from thy presence?" . . . Not only is the psalmist saying that God is not hard to find; he is actually saying that it is impossible to lose God . . . but . . . we hear the cry, "O that I knew where I might find Him." . . . There is no question about it in Job's mind—God is hard to find . . . we have the opposite poles a God . . . seeking us whose presence we cannot escape . . . a God who veils Himself and cannot be found. . . . The fact is that both these seemingly contradictory views are true, and each demands the other for its completion. Neither one alone can reveal the full and complete reality of God. Certainly there are experiences in which we cannot escape from God, and certainly there are other experiences in which we cannot find Him. . . . Life consists of opposing forces, and the pull of these opposing forces can either make us or break us. It is God's plan that the pull of these opposite forces shall make us, and not break us. Browning caught the truth of this, and revealed it in this way: "When the fight begins within himself, a man's worth something." Without temptation there is no character, without sorrow there is no joy, without pain there is no pleasure, without fear there is no courage, with-

out doubt there is no faith, and without adversity there is no struggle.—Clinton E. Ostrander

1162

It is no secret that most people do not feel at home in the universe. Made in God's image, with His purpose that we shall be His sons, still we are beset by the incongruities of our situation. Given a faith in the creative God who is never less than His creation, nor lost in it, we may handle the vast expansion of knowledge concerning it and "dream it for a greater God." . . . To accept God's gift of Himself to us is to come to be at home in God's universe. Acceptance means obedience and to be in stride with His will.— Paul Covey Johnston, *Presbyterian Life*

GOLDEN RULE

1163

No man can break God's law; he breaks only himself. Very important is the order in which God stated His laws. The first four deal with man's relationship with God, the last six with man's relationship with man. Before man can live rightly with others, he must first get right with God. Someone has said, "The Golden Rule is my religion," but the Golden Rule is nobody's religion, because it is not a religion. It is merely the expression of religion. As H. G. Wells put it, "Until a man has found God, he begins at no beginning; he works to no end."—Charles L. Allen, *God's Psychiatry*

1164

The great thing about the Golden Rule as a program is that it is simple and always ready for use. All that is required is just to begin dealing with people as one would like them to deal with him, especially if he were in their places and they in his.—Clarence E. Flynn, *Adult Leader*

1165

One must recognize that the Golden Rule alone is powerless without that great reverence for human personality which is born of the conviction that every soul is of eternal value. Just as a simple rule for social behavior, the Golden Rule loses its power. But, when it is an expression of a noble conviction about life's eternal meaning and consequences, it is filled with dynamite. The larger setting in which the Golden Rule becomes meaningful is that of Christian faith—a faith in the victory of goodness, the significance of man and the purpose of God.—Russell A. Huffman

GOODNESS

1166

Let us not underestimate the value of a simply good life. Just to be good! To keep life from degrading elements, to make it constantly helpful in little ways to those who are touched by it, to keep one's spirit always sweet.—E. H. Griggs

1167

He who would do good to another must do it in minute particulars.—William Blake

1168

Better do a good deed near at home than go far away to burn incense.—Chinese proverb

1169

A precinct committeewoman called the secretary of a ministerial association during a pre-election period and asked for a list of the local ministers. During her conversation she remarked, "You know, we have been neglecting the ministers and they are the ones who can do us the most good."

Unfortunately she was unmindful of the "greatest good" to which the ministers might direct *her*.

1170

The only way to compel men to speak good of us is to do it.—Voltaire

1171

We are all ready to be savage in some cause. The difference between a good man and a bad one is the choice of the cause.—William James

GRATITUDE

1172

He knew how to receive so graciously that the gift was enhanced by its reception. It was the rarest pleasure to bring things to him. . . . Warmed by his welcome, how beautiful became the things one brought to him.—Anne Morrow Lindbergh

1173

To receive a present handsomely and in the right spirit, even when you have none to return, is to give one in return.—Leigh Hunt

1174

Gratitude is not a virtue that comes easy to the human race.—W. Somerset Maugham

HABIT

1175

William James, in his famous study entitled "Habit," pointed out that the only certain way to break a bad habit is to substitute a good habit for it, one both easy and pleasant to form.

1176

Habit is a cable; we weave a thread of it every day, and at last we cannot break it.—H. Mann

1177

The moral virtues are habits, and habits are formed by acts.—Robert M. Hutchins, *Commonweal*

1178

When everyone has the same amount of time, how is it that some people manage to do so many things, while others appear unable to get anything done?

HAND

1179

I have lived, seen God's hand through a lifetime, and all was for the best.—Robert Browning

1180

God warms His hands at man's heart when he prays.—John Masefield

1181

We entrust our legal matters to the hands of the lawyer, our health to the hands of the doctor; we need to place the spiritual in the hands of God.

1182

Jesus' faith was trust. He put His life trustingly into God's hands. The words recorded as spoken from the cross, "Father, into thy hands I commit my spirit," had not been reserved for that moment at the end. They expressed the spirit of His whole life, at the very beginning and through all His days.—E. Paul Hovey

1183

One of the most tremendous sermons in English is by John Donne on the text: "It is a fearful thing to fall into the hands of the living God." Yes, but what must it be to fall out of His hands, he asks; to be ignored and let alone as past hope of amendment, as no longer worth bothering about, "to be secluded eternally . . . from the sight of God"?

1184

The work of man's hands alone is neither great nor enduring. Bricks and stones soon crumble—or are destroyed by man himself. But to build with love in our hearts, and with a small vision of the Master's plan, is to build what can never be destroyed.—Don Romero, *Christian Herald*

1185

However supple the wrist,
    However closely one stands,
So long as each clinches his fist,
    Two cannot contrive to shake hands.
        —Richard Armour

1186

People who throw mud always have dirty hands.

1187

Anxious parents came to the rural church reporting that their frail little daughter was lost. Her health was such that she could not survive the exposure of the night in the open. A search party was gathered and they tramped the nearby fields in vain. Then someone suggested that they join hands and like a giant comb make their way up and down the field. In a short time they found the little girl's body; the exposure had been too much for her. One of the group lamented, "Oh, if we had only joined hands sooner."—Robert Satterfield

1188

Hands that guide are praying hands. They pray, "Let the little children come to me." Hands that prepare food are praying hands. They pray, "Give us this day our daily bread." Then they join with God in bringing the answer to that prayer. Hands that build are praying hands. They pray for a city that hath foundations, whose builder and maker is God. Hands that heal are praying hands. Clasped in the hand of the Great Physician, they pray for life and health and well-being. Hands that teach are praying hands. They echo the prayer of the great teacher, "Go ye, therefore, and teach all nations." Hands that make music are praying hands. They continue the prayer of thanksgiving that began when the morning stars sang together and all the sons of God shouted for joy. "They maintain the fabric of the world, and in the handywork of their craft is their prayer" (Ecclesiasticus 38:34).

HAPPENINGS

1189

There are three kinds of people: a few who make things happen, many who watch things happen, and an overwhelming majority that have no idea what has happened.

1190

Jesus was what may be called "a small-town man." He was called by the name of the small town where he grew up: "Jesus of Nazareth." The novelist, Mary Austin, wrote a book about Jesus which she called *A Small Town Man.*

One great danger of living in a small town is that some have a tendency to think it unimportant and the life there dull. They put in a lot of effort trying to get away. Thus they miss the opportunities and privileges that life in a small town offers, if a person is not too dull and dumb himself to see them. Often people say: "Nothing ever happens here," when the truth is that they are too dull to see it.—Robert E. Luccock

1191

For the one hundredth anniversary of the birth of Abraham Lincoln . . . John T. McCutcheon . . . drew a cartoon showing two men standing on the edge of a snow-covered forest in Kentucky. One is asking the other: "Anything new?" The other answers: "Nothing much. Oh, there's a new baby over at Tom Lincoln's. That's all. Nothing ever happens around here."

HAPPINESS

1192

Happiness is a by-product; it is never directly acquired. You cannot be grateful unless there is something to be grateful for, nor happy unless there is that to be happy about.—Douglas Horton

1193

If it seems that the poor in spirit are not blessed, then ask yourself whether it is the arrogant in spirit who are really blessed. Do you say that those who mourn are not blessed? Well, ask yourself whether that man is truly happy who knows none of the sorrow of the world. Is he the man whose life is richest who has never known sorrow, who has never had the sorrow of the world pressed upon him, who has never known the suffering of little children or the distress of the afflicted? You say it does not sound right to declare that the meek are the happy ones. As a matter of fact, are the proud the happy ones? Is the man who is necessarily always on the lookout for his own rights, seeking to assert his will against everything, is he the happy man? Will you say that the man with a passion for righteousness is not happy? Then who is? Is it the man who does not care for righteousness at all, is he the happy one? Merciful— let us say that he is not the happy one; then is the unmerciful the happy one? Is Scrooge in his cold office on Christmas Eve happy, unmerciful and bitter, or is Scrooge, flying about London on Christmas morning with his arms full of packages, the happy one? —Cleland Boyd McAfee, *Studies in the Sermon on the Mount*

1194

A personnel expert . . . made an informal survey. He interviewed two hundred people, asking them whether they were happy at their work and whether religion played a meaningful part in their lives. His results: almost 100 per cent of those who were unhappy in their work life had no positive connection with a religious belief. And the opposite was true too; those who claimed to be religious also stated that they were content in their work life. —James Fifield, Jr., *The Single Path*

1195

Unhappiness lies in not knowing what we want out of life, and killing ourselves trying to get it.

1196

Happiness is not a destination. It is a method of life.—Burton Hillis, *Better Homes & Gardens*

1197

No person can tell another just how to make the joy of life. Some find it in one field, some in another, and some find it all over the place. I am certain only that it is a learned dimension of life, that its learning is the prime business of any lifetime, and that Robert Louis Stevenson was eternally right when he told us, in "The Lantern Bearers," that those who miss the joy miss all.—John Sloan Dickey

1198

It is not in life's chances but in its choices that happiness lies.

1199

In our frantic search for happiness we assume it resides in something that we can possess or manipulate: a spacious home, smart clothes, powerful automobiles or a huge bank account; we think of expensive vacations or costly amusements. We are sorely mistaken. If we have material comforts and at the same time possess happiness, it means that our happiness stems from within ourselves. It resides in something we *are,* not in what we *have.*—Kenneth Hildebrand, *Achieving Real Happiness*

1200

Human affairs are not so happily arranged that the best things please the most men.—S. R. Crockett

1201

The profession one chooses to follow for a livelihood seldom brings fame and fortune, but a life lived within the dictates of one's conscience can bring happiness and a satisfaction of living far beyond worldly acclaim. I expect to pass through this world but once, and any good therefore that I can do, or any kindness that I can show to any fellow creature, let me do it now. Let me not defer or neglect it, for I shall not pass this way again. Happiness must be sipped, not drained from life in great gulps—nor does it flow in a steady stream like water from a faucet. "A portion of thyself" is a sip of happiness as satisfying as it is costless.

1202

Let the divine mind flow through your own mind, and you will be happier. I have found the greatest power in the world is the power of prayer. There is no shadow of doubt of that. I speak from my own experience.—Cecil B. DeMille

1203

Many persons have a wrong idea about what constitutes true happiness. It is not attained through self-gratification, but through fidelity to a worthy purpose.—Helen Keller

1204

The essence of human happiness is found in a quality of life uniquely characteristic of human beings. It is born of the mind's probing and of the soul's hunger. It pertains to that in man which tends a bed of roses, kneels before an altar, stakes all for the right, and lays down life for his brothers. It is fashioned from the discovery that the best in us does not hammer against closed doors, that reality responds with redemptive reinforcement and liberating fulfillment. The essence of happiness is found in knowledge of and obedience to the wisdom and mission of Jesus Christ.—Everett W. Palmer, *Together*

1205

Sour godliness is the devil's religion. —John Wesley

1206

How is happiness defined? Separate the word into three parts and the search is ended, for "happiness" becomes "happen in us." We are born again; new life has come. That is where and how happiness is found— through the things that "happen in us." And when people learn to write "happiness" as "happen in us," their quest is ended.—E. Paul Hovey, "Why Isn't It Fun?," *Upper Room Pulpit*

1207

Actually, we must lose ourselves in order to find true and enduring happiness. This means that we must rise above self-consciousness. After all, self-consciousness is just another term for self-centeredness. It means that we are putting ourselves first in our thoughts and feelings, and letting everyone else come second. This is not practicing good will, but working for a reward. —David Dunn, *Try Giving Yourself Away*

1208

Edna Ferber makes a character in one of her novels say, "I like people with a splash of splendor in their make-up." There is no splendor about a person whose sole interest in his own happiness . . . if you want to cultivate a little splendor about your life, begin distributing your happiness. If you can stand up and say from the heart, "I want no security for myself apart from the security of the rest of mankind, and covet no destiny to the exclusion of others," then yours is the joy of team loyalty, for which no other joy can be substituted; then life becomes, in a subtle and truly exhilarating way, worth living.—Douglas Horton, *The Art of Living Today*

1209

Man is always searching for happiness; he is not content for the happiness of the moment alone, but wants a happiness that endures not only for tomorrow but one that will comfort his memory also.—Lionel Crocker

1210

It's pretty hard to tell what does bring happiness. Poverty and wealth have both failed.—Kin Hubbard

1211

Happiness is a hard thing because it is achieved only by making others happy.—Stuart Cloete, *The Third Way*

1212

Where Is Happiness?

Not in unbelief—Voltaire was an infidel of the most pronounced type. He wrote: "I wish I had never been born."

Not in pleasure—Lord Byron lived a life of pleasure and ease. He wrote:

"The worm, the canker and grief are mine alone."

Not in money—Jay Gould, the American millionaire, had an enormous fortune. When dying, he said: "I suppose I am the most miserable man on earth."

Not in position and fame—Lord Beaconsfield enjoyed more than his share of both. He wrote: "Youth is a mistake, manhood a struggle, old age a regret."

Not in military glory—Alexander the Great conquered the known world in his day. Then he wept because, "There are no more worlds to conquer."

Not in earthly achievement—Solomon had about everything this world has to offer. But he said: "Vanity of vanities; all is vanity."

Where, then, is happiness found? The answer is simple: In Christ alone. He said: "Your heart shall rejoice, and your joy no man taketh from you."

1213

Happiness itself cannot be guaranteed, only the right and assistance to the pursuit of happiness. Our founding fathers recognized this. They could guarantee life and liberty, but not happiness, only the freedom to pursue it. Man must have confidence in self, in other people and in Christianity. Don't merely do the things you like, but like the things you do.—J. Howard Kramer

1214

Happiness is a state of mind secured by one's own endeavor.—S. Parkes Cadman

1215

Grief can take care of itself; but to get the full value of joy you must have somebody to divide it with.—Mark Twain

1216

We have no more right to consume happiness without producing it than to consume wealth without producing it.—Bernard Shaw, *Candida*

1217

Happiness is the sense that one matters. Happiness is an abiding enthusiasm. Happiness is single-mindedness. Happiness is whole-heartedness. Happiness is a by-product. Happiness is faith.—S. M. Shoemaker, *How You Can Find Happiness*

1218

Happiness does certainly not depend immediately on external things at all, but upon our inward mode of dealing with them.—William E. Hocking, *The Meaning of God in Human Experience*

1219

The opposite of joy is not sorrow. It is unbelief.—Leslie D. Weatherhead, *This Is the Victory*

1220

Those whose happiness is founded on a rock will experience the same blows and sufferings as come to others, for faith does not provide exemption from suffering but only from defeat at its hands; but underneath will still run the current of a deeper happiness which nothing can shake nor take away. There is a "joy that seeketh us through pain."—S. M. Shoemaker, *How You Can Find Happiness*

1221

The happiest people I know are genuine Christians, but there are entirely too many unhappy persons in the church today. Happiness is characteristic of childhood; when children are unhappy, we know something is wrong. It is likewise a mark of Christianity, and we should be concerned that so many professing Christians, who are supposed to have found the secret of joyous living, are anxious about the present and fearful of the future.—Henry Blackburn, *Upper Room Pulpit*

1222

Happiness is not an end in itself. Why be humble of spirit? Why hunger and thirst after righteousness? Why be merciful and pure in heart? Just to be happy? Not at all. We are happy as we do these things because the doing of them brings us into a true and active fellowship with God.—Charles M. Crowe, *Sermons from the Mount*

1223

The days that make us happy make us wise.—John Masefield

1224

"Why does the church make faith so it is not fun?" Ruth Seabury once asked. Then she told of a young native of India confiding to her that "Christians in America are grim." She advised us to let go, and feel the joy of the Lord, the thrill of the love of God. She said: "We have not got the good news unless we give it with joy."

1225

"Children of joy" was the name which Barnabas, a first-century writer, gave to his Christian friends—and not because they had an easy time of it either! The book of The Acts relates how they were always getting into trouble. Constantly persecuted and in imminent danger of death, "they were the most essentially happy people of the day. . . . They faced the world and astonished it by more than their stubbornness."—J. Carter Swaim, *Forward*

1226

Happiness sneaks in through a door you didn't know you left open.—John Barrymore

1227

Religion is only a caricature of itself until it becomes exhilarating good news.—Harry Emerson Fosdick, *Ladies' Home Journal*

1228

When a family learned from their dying grandfather how lonely he had been because none of them had been interested enough to go with him on his sketching trips, they determined to change their way of life. They knew that they "couldn't make it up to Grandpa," but it wasn't too late for the rest to "start sharin' our enjoyin'."

HARM

1229

Nothing can work me damage except myself; the harm that I sustain I carry with me, and I am the real sufferer by my own fault.—St. Bernard

1230

Give me a newborn child, and in ten years I can have him so scared he'll never dare to lift his voice above a whisper, or so brave that he'll fear nothing.—George A. Dorsey

1231

Civilization ceases when we no longer respect and no longer put into their correct places the fundamental values, such as work, family and country; such as the individual, honor and religion. —R. P. Lebret

1232

If our world is to survive in any sense that makes survival worth while, it must learn to love, not to hate; to create, not to destroy.—King George VI

HEART

1233

No matter how widely you have traveled, you haven't seen the world if you have failed to look into the human hearts that inhabit it.—Donald Culross Peattie

1234

Hatred toward any human being cannot exist in the same heart as love to God.—Dean Inge

1235

If it isn't heart-keeping, it isn't housekeeping.—Marcelene Cox

HELP

1236

No man can sincerely try to help another without helping himself.—J. B. Webster

1237

A writer of the Middle Ages used this quaint illustration to bring home to the people of his day the love of God. Supposing, he argued, that a king were sitting with his council, deliberating on the high affairs of state in his own country and in the surrounding nations, and suddenly he heard within his home the sorrowful cry of a little child who had fallen down or been frightened by a wasp. He would immediately leave the council, said the preacher, and hasten to help the child. Why, then, do we think it dishonorable that the King of kings, who is our Heavenly Father, should consider the affairs of his children?—Archer Wallace, *Classmate*

1238

If anybody were to ask me how to find God, I should say at once: Hunt out the deepest need you can find and forget all about your own comfort while you try to meet that need. Talk to God about it and—He will be there. You will know it.—Frank C. Laubach

1239

I can still see the examiner who said: "You think you have done good and helped the Koreans by running high schools for thirty years?" "I do." "You are wrong, you have done nothing but harm. You have just put a crook into those boys in thirty years that it will take the Japanese Government 300 years to cure." I do not know how he meant it. I know he went on beating me after he had said it—but as I get perspective, I am inclined to take it as his apology for what he did to me, and a covert appreciation of missionary work. In any case, God grant it may be true, and that the "crook" may be a "closed curve" leading to God and to the Kingdom of Heaven.—E. W. Koons, *Looking Back on Internment*

1240

One who cannot himself do great things may be the cause of other people doing them.

1241

Empty years, like used and discarded paper cups, are scattered beneath the fountain of life. Some are crushed and soiled from the careless tread of impetuous feet. A few have been drained slowly and placed on the ledge of progress with consideration for others who may thirst.—Douglas Meador

HEREDITY

1242

It is a common practice to mulch the family tree with gold instead of gumption to the extent that it will bear delicate and frequently worthless fruit in future seasons.—Douglas Meador

1243

What you have inherited from your fathers you must earn for yourself before you can really call it yours.— Goethe

1244

On the body of a Jugoslavian guerrilla was found the following letter, addressed to his unborn son:

"My child, sleeping now in the dark and gathering strength for the struggle of birth, I wish you well. At present you have no proper shape, and you do not breathe, and you are blind. Yet, when your time comes, your time and the time of your mother, whom I deeply love, there will be something in you that will give you power to fight for air and light. Such is your heritage, such is your destiny as a child born of woman—to fight for light and hold on without knowing why.

"May the flame that tempers the bright steel of your youth never die, but burn always; so that when your work is done and your long day ended, you may still be like a watchman's fire at the end of a lonely road—loved and cherished for your gracious glow by all good wayfarers who need light in their darkness and warmth for their comfort.

"The spirit of wonder and adventure, the token of immortality, will be given to you as a child. May you keep it forever, with that in your heart which always seeks the gold beyond the rainbow, the pastures beyond the desert, the dawn beyond the sea, the light beyond the dark.

"May you seek always and strive always in good faith and high courage, in this world where men grow so tired.

"Keep your capacity for faith and belief, but let your judgment watch what you believe.

"Keep your power to receive everything; only learn to select what your instinct tells you is right. Keep your love of life, but throw away your fear of death. Life must be loved or it is lost; but it should never be loved too well. Keep your delight in friendship; only learn to know your friends. Keep your intolerance—only save it for what your heart tells you is bad. Keep your wonder at great and noble things like sunlight and thunder, the rain and the stars, the wind and the sea, the growth of trees and the return of harvests, and the greatness of heroes. Keep your heart hungry for new knowledge; keep your hatred of a lie; and keep your power of indignation. Now I know I must die, and you must be born to stand upon the rubbish heap of my errors. Forgive me for this. I am ashamed to leave you an untidy, uncomfortable world. But so it must be.

"In thought, as a last benediction, I kiss your forehead. Good night to you —and good morning and a clear dawn." Here the letter ends. . . .

The day the avenging partisans swept back into the village they found the widow had been murdered a few days before her child would have been born. The letter that his comrades could not deliver has become instead a letter to all the unborn children in the great, mad world.

1245

A Sunday school teacher suddenly stopped reading a passage in the Bible and asked the youngsters: "Why do you believe in God?"

She got a variety of answers, some full of simple faith, others obviously insincere. The one that stunned her came from the son of a padre. He answered apologetically: "I guess it just runs in our family."—*Illustrated Weekly of India*

1246

We have come from somewhere and are going somewhere. The great architect of the universe never built a stairway that leads to nowhere.—Robert A. Millikan

1247

My best wish for you is that your future can include assurance that the Lord has built the universe, that there is a living, loving God into whose hand you can commit your future.—Mildred McAfee Horton

1248

Heredity is an omnibus in which all our ancestors ride, and every now and then one of them puts his head out and embarrasses us.—Oliver Wendell Holmes

HERO

1249

To live well in the quiet routine of life; to fill a little space because God wills it; to go on cheerfully with a petty round of little duties, little avocations; to smile for the joy of others when the heart is aching—who does this, his works will follow him. He may not be hero to the world, but he is one of God's heroes.

1250

If we cannot have heroism for the masses without war, we must do without heroism.—Sir Llewellyn Woodward

HISTORY

1251

History is full of surprises and nothing in history is inevitable until it has happened, and passed into history. The possibility of overcoming a feeling of fatalism exists. So long as a nuclear war has not been precipitated, there is still the chance that it may not be. Even if such a war seems probable, it is not a foregone conclusion. "That is why Dr. Edward Teller, 'father of the

H-bomb,' suggests this definition of a wise optimist: 'An optimist,' he says, 'is someone who believes the future is *still* uncertain.' "—Dorothy Fosdick

1252

History fortunately has a way of developing beyond the intentions of the agents of its actions.—Reinhold Niebuhr, *Christianity and Crisis*

HOLY SPIRIT

1253

One wonders whether Paul might ask the same question if he came to us today. If he saw a civilization supposed to be basically Christian, which after centuries has not been able to outlaw war, would Paul say, "Did ye receive the Holy Spirit when ye believed?" If he came to a great free Christian nation with untold resources and found religion left out of the councils of government, education completely secularized, and a great church growing rather meagerly, would he say, "Did ye receive the Holy Spirit when ye believed?" If he came to one of our congregations and found less than half of our people worshiping on Sunday, many of us doing little or nothing to bring the thousands about us into a knowledge of Christ . . . would he repeat his question?—W. Sherman Skinner, *New Life Through the Holy Spirit*

1254

The real horror of idols is not merely that they give us nothing, but that they take away from us even that which we have. By the act of imagining power in the fetish we rob ourselves, and the Holy Spirit within us, of that much power. . . . The more we look to material objects for help, the less we can help ourselves or ask help from the grace of God. If we are to be saved, it will not be by wood, however well carved and polished; nor by machines, however efficient; nor by social planning, however ingenious. If we are to be saved, it must be by the one power that is built into a man at his beginning and that he does not have to make with his hands—the power of the Holy Spirit, which is God.—Joy Davidman, *Smoke on the Mountain*

1255

"In that day ye shall know." When Jesus referred to "that day," He meant that on *any* day, when *any* men, *any*where, turn from self-will and yield themselves completely to the everpresent Spirit, such men *shall know.* But what shall men then know? The answer . . . what the early disciples came to know. . . . Scripture clearly sets forth . . . their experience. . . . They knew the Way. There came a new sense of direction. They saw . . . the King's Highway was not a military road of might and power . . . but the lowly path of ministry to others. They knew the Truth. Not all at once . . . but . . . an illumination . . . pierced the bandages of tradition covering their eyes. . . . They knew Life. Not by the testimony of others, but by personal experience they came to realize . . . that "eternal life" did not mean a future life in another world, but a higher life in this. . . . They knew Power; spiritual resources within themselves; the invincible might of the indwelling God; the ability to achieve the impossible. They knew Fellowship . . . with God and one another. They knew their Task . . . the high calling wherewith they were called. So they began and continued to manifest the new life, to use their enhanced powers . . . received from the life and light of the indwelling Holy Spirit.—James E. Clarke, "When the Paraclete Comes"

1256

The word "Comforter" as applied to the Holy Spirit needs to be translated by some vigorous term. Literally, it means "with strength." Jesus promised His followers that "The Strengthener" would be with them forever. This promise is no lullaby for the faint-hearted. It is a blood transfusion for courageous living.

HOME

1257

The most influential of all educational factors is the conversation in a child's home.—William Temple

1258

He is as free as smoke, and as homeless.

1259

By profession I am a soldier and take pride in that fact. But I am prouder to be a father. My hope is that my son, when I am gone, will remember me not from battle, but in the home, repeating with him one simple prayer, "Our Father which art in heaven."—General Douglas MacArthur

1260

The only religion that is any good is home-made religion.—Paul Calvin Payne, *Presbyterian Life*

1261

There is no substitute for Christian parents. Before the church can make itself strong in the nation and the world, it must make itself significant in the home. Many see the vital need of the church in their house when they have children of their own. Even those adults who feel that they have outgrown the need of religion for themselves feel the need of it for their children. One such parent came to her pastor recently. She had had some religious training, but she felt no particular need of the church now. It was the same, she said, with most all her friends and companions.

"But," she sighed, "our children are little pagans. I cannot endure the prospect. I cannot face the consequences. I must have some religion to give them."—Lawrence O. Lineberger, *Adult Student*

1262

What is home? A roof to keep out the rain. Four walls to keep out the wind. Floors to keep out the cold. Yes, but home is more than that. It is the laugh of a baby, the song of a mother, the strength of a father. Warmth of loving hearts, light from happy eyes, kindness, loyalty, comradeship. Home is first school and first church for young ones, where they learn what is right, what is good and what is kind. Where they go for comfort when they are hurt or sick. Where joy is shared and sorrow eased. Where fathers and mothers are respected and loved. Where children are wanted. Where the simplest food is good enough for kings because it is earned. Where money is not so important as loving-kindness. Where even the tea-kettle sings from happiness. That is home. God bless it.—Ernestine Schuman-Heink

1263

We must strive to overcome the apathy, ignorance and guile which nourish the twin enemies of our freedom—crime and communism. Let us never forget that strength and good character, like charity, begins at home. So long as the American home is nurtured by the spirit of our Father in heaven and is a center of learning and living, America will remain secure.—J. Edgar Hoover, *Vital Speeches*

1264

Homes are the nation's chief teachers of religion. To be sure, the church schools aid the homes signifi-

cantly, but in the last analysis, the day-by-day living of parents with their children can scarcely be overestimated in its teaching influence. . . . In a real sense, therefore, the nation's homes are schools of religion and the nation's parents are teachers for or against religious living.—Nathaniel F. Forsyth

1265

Children will outgrow their need of affection and demonstrativeness, but husbands won't.—Paul Popenoe

1266

Modern version: If at first you don't succeed, blame your parents.—Marcelene Cox

1267

Marriage is not altogether an easy proposition, joining as it does two different personalities. Togetherness is the creative, cohesive mechanism which fuses the man and woman into a team, and later draws their children into the same warm circle of unity. Togetherness is shared work, shared play, shared faith . . . in the church and the community as well as in the home. But togetherness must and should begin with the family . . . with love and understanding and religion woven into the fabric of daily life.—Norman Vincent Peale, *McCall's Magazine*

1268

Life is lived more outside the home, in both work and recreation, so the harder to keep it together, the more cherished is family intimacy, and the more disturbing the introduction of another generation.—Dorothy Thompson, *Ladies' Home Journal*

1269

A little boy was once heard to remark: "We haven't got any God at our house." His parents never read the Bible nor worshiped together. His remark reveals an alarming condition that exists in too many homes across our country. The innocent victims of this neglect are the children. The secret of security and happiness in family life is the abiding presence of Christ. For when He is invited into the home, anger, bitterness, envy, and discontent move out. With Him comes love, contentment, joy and peace.

We have failed in our Christian duty when a child in our community can say, "We haven't any God in our house." It is our privilege and joy to witness for God and to share with others the blessings that come to those who know Him through prayer and daily worship.

1270

Good family life is never an accident but always an achievement by those who share it.—James H. S. Bossard, *The Large Family System*

1271

We get our parents so late in life that it is impossible to do anything with them.—From a child's essay in Nottingham, England

1272

Folks used to pity that little girl the Browns adopted years ago, because they couldn't afford a car and she didn't get to go many places. Now grown, she finally told us how she always felt about it. "Didn't take me anywhere?" she exclaimed. "Why, my folks took me to their hearts!"—Burton Hillis, *Better Homes & Gardens*

1273

If Christ dwells in the family circle, parents are held in honor and children practice obedience.—E. C. Peters

1274

Brothers fight; parents and children clash frequently. Living in intimate relationships, ego desires come into conflict with the rights or desires of other members of the family. Yes, there is tension and conflict within the family. They get on one another's nerves. But having learned to love the others as himself, they forgive. They learn to balance justice and mercy— the strong and the tender responses of love. They learn to work together, play together and worship together, while holding different opinions and having occasional clashes of interest. . . . Peace, happiness, and family solidarity become theirs. The capacities thus developed within the family become operative in the wider circles of social, economic and international relationships. Peace and stable society will be the result.—Guy L. Roberts, *The Way of Life*

1275

Man is like a child in a family. He can tolerate much deprivation, much sickness, even much pain, if only he be securely at home, sure of belonging, confident of being loved. But if these central assurances are lacking, then food and shelter and toys in abundance can leave him empty and insecure in the center of his life. So it is with man in his world.—Angus Dun, *The Saving Person*

1276

Philip T. Hartung in reviewing the movie "The Bachelor Party," says the saddest of all is the final shot—of perennial bachelor Warden. "What's there to go home for? I've read all the papers." And he sits at one end of a long bar starting a conversation with a frowsy woman at the other end.— *Commonweal*

HUNGER

1277

Much of the world has never been free, and a large part of mankind has always been hungry. Once this was inevitable, but now hunger is not necessary, and freedom is possible. Men who have never known freedom are today willing to die for it. Men who have seldom known what they would eat tomorrow have learned the truth, that there can be enough for all. These men will not rest until they have emerged into the light, and the world will know no peace until their just demands have been met.—*Commonweal*

1278

The first illusion is that communism is the greatest problem which we confront. It is *not* the basic disease. The greatest illness on earth today is the hunger and distress which gave birth to communism! There never was any communism in Russia or China or Guatemala or India or South Africa or France or Italy without something rotten for communism to feed on—hunger, hopeless debt, sick bodies and sick minds, and the sullen resentment caused by oppression. *Hunger* is the world's chief problem—not alone hunger of the stomach, but hunger for all those things which relieve poverty of body, mind, and soul.—Frank C. Laubach, *The World Is Learning Compassion*

1279

The sermon is an effort to help and encourage and to feed the hunger of hearts of those who have come seeking and expecting help.—Charles L. Allen, *When the Heart Is Hungry*

HYPOCRITE

1280

Why put a soul on trial and then rule out its own testimony?—Willis King

1281

Our political life is predicated on openness. We know that the only way to avoid error is to detect it; that the only way to detect it is to be free to inquire.—J. Robert Oppenheimer

1282

No man is a hypocrite in his pleasures.—Samuel Johnson

1283

The old-style hypocrite was a person who tried to appear better than he actually was; the new-style hypocrite tries to appear worse than he or she is.—Charles Templeton

IDEALS

1284

Ideals are the greatest power in the world and are able to make, move, and mold all forms of mechanical power. When a man realizes that this power is within himself and in his apprehension of real ideals, then his power for service and the power of his personality are increased enormously.

1285

One trait derives more than any other from our past as a nation of immigrants. Without underrating the material motives that helped bring the Old World to the New, we can believe that idealistic impulses counted for much more. The Puritans were a people as religiously dedicated as any in history. On their heels came colonists athirst for liberty, toleration and social equality.

The spirit of Penn, Roger Williams and Nathaniel Bacon went into the American soul when it was still young. Thereafter, generation by generation, countless people came because they hated oppression, injustice and violence, and hoped to help create peace, brotherhood and freedom. No growing nation had such numerous and powerful contributions to its idealism. It would have been strange if, in the world's tremendous . . . crises, the American people had not made an exhibition of idealism unprecedented in strength and scope.—Allan Nevins, *The New York Times Magazine*

IDEAS

1286

New ideas can be good or bad, just the same as old ones.—Franklin D. Roosevelt

1287

A single idea of a single brain is mightier than Niagara, for we can chain and use it.—J. Brierly

1288

If you want to get across an idea, wrap it up in a person.—Ralph Bunche

1289

At Koenigsberg, "just one of the teachers," Emmanuel Kant, wrote very abstrusely that the important thing is to have a good will, to obey authorities. This sounded like a good, even pious idea, popular, of course, with authorities. However, it needed an equally learned critical evaluation in the light of the whole Truth, which it did not receive, for those who might have done so were busy with other things. The idea spread and grew ultimately into a nation of Nazis, goose-stepping obediently behind Hitler to destruction. That idea killed the people who thought it, destroyed the very buildings in which it was taught; but the idea lives on in the modern mind. . . . If . . . ideas in the modern mind are not corrected soon by true ideas, then our age is a dream that is dying.—Williams L. Rossner, "Today's Need: American Scholarship," *Vital Speeches*

1290

Ideas cannot be destroyed by military force. It is possible to destroy the cities.

. . . But an ideology cannot be . . . demolished by atomic bombs. Ideas are conquered by better ideas, whose truth has been revealed in practices that enrich personality.—G. Bromley Oxnam, *Adult Student*

IMMORTALITY

1291

Many of the Biblical incidents fit into the structure of the three-act play which uses the first act to introduce the players; the second act gets them hopelessly snarled in conflicts; and at the end of the third act, almost everybody has arranged to live happily. They put a sunrise in the third act.

1292

He hath changed sunset into sunrise.—Clement of Alexandria

1293

The scene was etched forever on my mind—Peter lying on the stretcher where the two orderlies had put him down for a moment, while the ambulance waited just outside the front door. Peter had looked up at me and smiled through his pain, his eyes full of tenderness, and I had leaned close to him and said, "Darling, I'll see you in the morning."

As I stood looking out toward that far horizon, I knew that those words would go singing in my heart down all the years . . . "See you, Darling, see you in the morning. . . ."—Catherine Marshall, *A Man Called Peter*

1294

A generation ago a famous novelist named Guy Thorne wrote a book of fiction entitled *When It Was Dark*, in which it was supposed that the body of Jesus had been found, and, as a result, millions of believers were suddenly plunged into spiritual darkness. The book created something of a sensation and it was answered by another who wrote a book entitled *When It Was Light.*—Archer Wallace

1295

Experience teaches us that it is much easier to believe in immortality when we are living the kind of life that is worthy of being immortal. Trivial living, selfish living, invariably causes the fires of immortal hope to burn low in the heart. Living under the domination of great motives brings to the soul the conviction that eternal life may indeed begin here and now, even as Jesus said. No life was so pure, so lofty as His, and He lived in the very atmosphere of eternity.—Francis L. Strickland, *Foundations of Christian Belief*

1296

There is only one way to get ready for immortality, and that is to love this life and live it as bravely and faithfully and cheerfully as we can.—Henry van Dyke

1297

What a man believes about immortality will color his thinking in every area of life.—John Sutherland Bonnell, *Heaven and Hell*

1298

Alfred Sadd as a boy was the despair of all the decent people of the English village in which he lived. He was an example of what every good mother did not want her son to be. He was . . . vulgar, profane. Then one day the Spirit of Christ entered his heart and he became different. He offered himself for missionary service in the South Seas. After proper training, he was sent to the Solomon Islands. When he reported at the office of the British Governor of the Island, he greeted the governor by saying, "Good morning, sir, I'm Sadd." To which the governor replied, "That's too bad, but you certainly don't look it."

Through years of loving, unselfish service, Alfred Sadd became greatly loved by the natives of the Solomon Islands; and, what is more important, he led them to love and serve his Master who had saved him from a life of recklessness and sin. Then war came . . . the Japanese seized the Solomons. All white people were thrown into concentration camps. One night, American bombers blasted several towns on the islands. In anger the Japanese seized a group of prisoners and shot them . . . Alfred Sadd was one of them. Word went to England, and a casualty list was announced over the radio. In the list was this brief word, "Alfred Sadd, missing—believed dead." But a Christian announcer read it, "Alfred Sadd, missing—believed immortal!"—Thomas McDormand, *Intermediate-Senior Class*

IMPOSSIBLE

1299

Nothing is impossible. God meant it that way.—Queen Wilhelmina, Netherlands

1300

Jimmy learned that Ohio has no state motto. The eleven-year-old figured this gap should be filled. When he learned he needed petitions to get state legislators to introduce a motto proposal, he went into action. Most of his spare time went for gathering signatures, mostly door-to-door. He got aunts in other towns to help. He wangled a spot on a radio show to ask for signers, and set up a booth at a food show. It was hard work. "You'd be surprised how many people just don't want to sign their names to anything," he said. "And a lot of them are afraid it would cost them something." When he tried to get an introduction to Gov. C. William O'Neill, State Senator William Deddens came to his aid. . . . When the governor arrived, Jimmy explained his petitions and asked, "Will you sign?" The governor signed.

Deddens also promised to invite Jimmy to the state capital to speak for his proposal. . . . The next step is easy. Jimmy has already figured out what he thinks will be the right motto: "With God all things are possible." —Associated Press

1301

"Impossible!" That is not good French.—Napoleon

1302

Nothing is impossible; there are ways that lead to everything, and if we had sufficient will, we should always have sufficient means. It is often merely for an excuse that we say things are impossible.—La Rochefoucauld

INFLUENCE

1303

A few folk were ready to welcome Christ when He came, and they have changed the climate of our world. Denis de Rougemont has somewhere a figure of a few reeds growing in a river, and gathering enough other reeds so that after a while they change the river's course. The Christian . . . may be such a reed. What other faith makes sense? What other faith has not suffered eclipses? It would seem that now history must take a Christian turn or end. You will see God either in the fires of judgment or in the gentleness of a new obedience. You will see Him so, and perhaps all that matters is that we see God.—George A. Buttrick, *Motive*

1304

There was a dachshund, once, so long
He hadn't any notion
How long it took to notify
His tail of his emotion;
And so it happened, while his eyes

Were filled with woe and sadness,
His little tail went wagging on
Because of previous gladness.

1305

The great conquerors, from Alexander to Caesar, and from Caesar to Napoleon, influenced profoundly the lives of subsequent generations. But the total effect of this influence shrinks to insignificance if compared to the entire transformation of human habits and human mentality produced by the long line of men of thought, from Thales to the present day, men individually powerless, but ultimately the rulers of the world.—Alfred N. Whitehead, *Science and the Modern World*

1306

Lincoln once said at a rough time during the Civil War: "This is a time for heroes to live in!"

We're not heroes, but let's be more than bumps on logs. . . . Let's try to act like Christians and influence the tide of history in our time!—Emrys Thomas

INTEGRITY

1307

The keystone of professional conduct is integrity. And integrity is not a divisible entity. It does not exist now and then in the same person. It cannot be separated into personal and professional compartments.—Henry T. Heald, *The New York Times Magazine*

1308

The American people have a right to bitter complaint over . . . disclosures of dishonor in high places. . . . Dishonor in public life has a double poison. When people are dishonorable in private business, they injure only those with whom they deal or their own chances in the next world. But when there is a lack of honor in government, the morals of the whole people are poisoned.

The drip of such poisons may have nothing to do with dishonor in some college athletics or the occasional policemen on the beat. But the rules of the game have been loosened somewhere. . . . No public man can be just a little crooked. There is no such thing as a no-man's-land between honesty and dishonesty. Our strength is not in politics, prices or production. . . . Our strength lies in spiritual concepts. It lies in public sensitiveness to evil. . . .

Our greatest danger is not from invasion by foreign armies. Our dangers are that we may commit suicide from within by complaisance with evil. Or by public tolerance of scandalous behavior. Or by cynical acceptance of dishonor. These evils have defeated nations many times in human history. The redemption of mankind by America will depend upon our ability to cope with these evils right here at home. — Herbert Hoover, *Vital Speeches*

1309

Long years ago my father taught me the significance of sincerity. We were coming home from church after listening to a visiting preacher who had spoken with great eloquence. I liked him. "Let's go back and hear him again tonight," I suggested. "No, I don't think I will," my father replied. I was astonished, because my father always went to the evening service. "Why not?" I asked. "Well," he answered, "do you remember that story he told about the farmer he met on the road?" I remembered. "The preacher said that episode happened to him. It didn't. I heard that story twenty years ago." Then he added words I never have forgotten. "If I can't trust a man to be honest in the little things, I can't trust him to be honest about the most important things in my life."—Harold Blake Walker, *Specialty Salesman*

1310

It was an exciting basketball game. The home crowd was partisan, as one would expect. They were giving the visitors and referee a hard time. At one point, a player on the visiting team made a pass to his teammate that wound up in the crowd. What the crowd didn't see was that one of the home team made a lunge for the ball and just ticked it as it went out of bounds. But the referee saw and called "out of bounds" in favor of the visitors. Then the entire roof fell in. . . . All the bad manners that we display when we go to an athletic contest were brought into play—the crowd booed and jeered and called the referee a lot of names. . . . One old grad . . . ran onto the floor . . . about to punch him. The referee got so mad at that point that he pushed the old boy off . . . and said, "Wait a minute." He looked at the players, found the boy who had touched the ball, called him over and said, "Son, did you or did you not touch that ball?" The boy looked him squarely in the eye without hesitation and said, "Sir, I touched it." Then the crowd gave the boy and the referee a tremendous cheer.

Athletics at that school, where such honesty is displayed, are worth all they cost. It's all a matter of a sense of values —integrity.—*Kiwanis Magazine*

1311

"Oh, what a terrible thing it must be to have to tell the truth." This was the lament of one of the characters in James Montgomery's comedy *Nothing But the Truth*. The play deals with the difficulties that face a man who has agreed to tell the exact truth about any matter that arises.

"Did you like my sermon?" asked Bishop Doran, another of the characters. "I was asleep," confessed Robert Bennett, the man who had agreed to tell "nothing but the truth."

Would you answer with such frankness? . . . Few of us would feel any uneasiness about meeting such a question with a little "blarney." We give such answers as a matter of common courtesy. In so doing, we do not feel that we compromise our integrity.—*Honesty and Integrity*

1312

There is no neutral ground in the battle of life, where great issues are at stake. One way of life is to enlist on the Lord's side: to live for God, for duty, for personal integrity, for love, for the world-wide dominion of Jesus Christ; to "let this mind be in you, which was also in Christ." The other way of life is to give allegiance to our own will: to set out in life with the idea that we may do what we like, living only for our poor and perishing selves.

We can have no real grounds for doubt whether we have made the right choice. Not to choose God's way is still to make the choice of our own way. Our Lord drew the line plainly when He said, "He that is not with me is against me."

1313

The man of honesty and integrity must make as many daily choices in his conduct as his less honest fellow. Again we could not satisfy our requirements for the title if each choice were an easy one. We say anyone can do right when it is easy to do so. No, we want to test the individual when the choice is a hard one. When we are in school, we measure the integrity of the student by his refusal to cheat when to do so would be easy and when his refusal means to fail. In a child we recognize the quality when he tells the truth in the face of almost certain punishment. Because of the nature of their occupation, members of the Armed Forces are obliged to rely upon the integrity of their fellows, and in turn each must

himself be reliable. . . . Faced with great inconvenience or personal loss, we often are tempted to compromise our integrity. . . . The nation . . . will live because of the integrity of its people, or it will die because its people have lost their integrity.—*Honesty and Integrity*

1314

One of the greatest mysteries in the world is the success that lies in conscientious work.—Calvin Coolidge

1315

I. Q. could mean internal quality. —Elmaar Bakken

INTERRUPTION

1316

"I am hampered in my work by a thousand interruptions. Nearly every hour comes a letter from some scholar and if I undertook to reply to them all, I should be obliged to devote day and night to scribbling. Then through the day come calls from all kinds of visitors. . . . These interruptions are now becoming too serious for me. . . ." Does this sound like the confession of a twentieth-century businessman? It could be. This, however, was written by a Venetian printer to his friend—in A.D. 1514!

JOKE

1317

I have always noticed that deeply and truly religious persons are fond of a joke, and I am suspicious of those who aren't.—Alfred North Whitehead

1318

It is a great thing to have a sense of humor. To go through life with no sense of the humorous and ridiculous is

like riding a wagon without springs.
—Henry Ward Beecher

1319

Men show their characters in nothing more clearly than in what they think laughable.—Goethe

1320

While there is infection in disease and sorrow, there is nothing in the world quite so irresistibly contagious as laughter and good humor.—Charles Dickens

JOY

1321

Joy is one of the great Christian virtues. An uplifting part of the joy Jesus brought to His disciples was the joy of sharing. And sharing is of the essence of the Christian gospel. Let us enter into this joy . . . the more we share the richer is our own cooperation with God in His work.—Lucius C. Porter

1322

Joy is an elation of spirit—of a spirit which trusts in goodness and truth of its own possessions.—Seneca

JUSTICE

1323

He who decides a case without hearing the other side . . . though he decide justly, cannot be considered just. —Seneca

1324

He that will not hear cannot judge. —William Penn

1325

There's one thing you can justify. You can justify begging God for guidance.—Governor Frank G. Clement

1326

Justice has nothing to do with expediency. Justice has nothing to do with any temporary standard whatever. It is rooted and grounded in the fundamental instincts of humanity.—Woodrow Wilson

1327

If there is one thing which I have learned as a result of four years at the United Nations, it is that the sense of justice is very much the same in every man. Regardless of whether he comes from Asia, Africa, Europe, or America, he has very much the same idea of fair play as his fellow man who may come from a country 10,000 miles away. That sense of justice is expressed in one way or another in almost all governments— except the Communist government which knows not the meaning of the word. Yet even the individual Russian appears to be born with a sense of fair play, however much his government may suppress it. The future of the world depends on the extent to which we can base international relations on that sense of justice and fair play which is in every human heart. On it alone can we build a durable peace.—Henry Cabot Lodge

1328

At one point in *The Crucible,* John Proctor is called upon to justify his failure to attend the church of the Reverend Mr. Parris and to have his children baptized by that divine. He replies that he disapproves of the clergyman. "I see no light of God in that man," he says. "That is not for you to decide," he is told. "The man is ordained, therefore the light of God is in him." And this, of course, is the way the world is. In a free society, any one of us may arrive at and freely express a judgment about the competence of duly constituted authority. But in an orderly society, no one of us can expect the protection of the law whenever we decide that a particular authority is unworthy of our cooperation. We may stand by the decision, and we may seek the law's protection, but we cannot expect it as a matter of right. There are many courses of action that may have a sanction in morality and none whatever in law.—Richard H. Rovere, "Arthur Miller's Conscience," *New Republic*

1329
Ladies and gentlemen of the jury, you now approach the performance of one of the most sacred duties of citizenship, the meting out of justice. Just after you were sworn in as jurors, I took occasion to make a few remarks which I shall now repeat in somewhat different form, as the thoughts I then expressed are peculiarly applicable to the period of your deliberations in order to reach a just and true verdict.

I then told you to be patient and said that there are few qualities in life so important. I said that if you once get yourself in the frame of mind where you know that you have a task ahead and it has to be done carefully and it has to be done just right and you know that it will be wrong to let little things disturb you, then there comes a certain calm and peace of mind which are of the essence in the administration of justice.

When you get yourself in that frame of mind, you find not only that the task ahead becomes much easier, but, in addition, that the quality of your work in the administration of justice is of the quality that it should be. Justice does not flourish amidst emotional excitement and stress. . . . —Judge Harold Medina, *Vital Speeches*

KINDNESS

1330
In this world, one must be a little too kind to be kind enough.—Marivaux

1331
You cannot do a kindness too soon, because you never know how soon it will be too late.—*Highways of Happiness*

1332
Act with kindness, but do not expect gratitude.—Confucius

KING

1333
Once a king's son sinned against his father, the king. His father expelled him from his house. As long as he was near his home, people knew he was a king's son and befriended him and gave him food and drink. But as the days passed, and he got farther into his father's realm, no one knew him and he had nothing to eat. He began to sell his clothing to buy food. When he had nothing left to sell, he hired out as a shepherd and no longer was in need because he needed nothing. He would sit on the hills tending his flocks and singing like the other shepherds, and he forgot that he was a king's son and all the pleasures that he had been used to.

Now it is the custom of the shepherds to make themselves small roofs of straw to keep out the rain. The king's son wanted to make such a roof, too, but he could not afford one, so he was deeply grieved.

Once the king happened to be passing through that province. Now it was common practice in the kingdom for those who had petitions to the king to write out their petitions and throw them into the king's chariot. The king's son came with the other petitioners and threw his note in which he petitioned for a small straw roof such as shepherd's have. The king recognized his son's handwriting and was saddened to think how low his son had fallen, that he had forgotten that he was a king's son and felt only the lack of a straw roof.

It is the same way with our people. They have already forgotten that they are each of them king's sons and what they really lack. One cries that he is in want of a living and another cries for children, but the truth that we lack all the treasure we had of old—that is something they forget to pray for.— Hasidic Rabbi Halverstan of Zans

1334
One of the characters in Lloyd C. Douglas' story, *The Robe,* talks with a Roman soldier who had seen the crucifixion of Jesus. He asks the soldier about Jesus—"Was he a king?" Slowly the soldier shook his head and muttered, "Something greater than a king."

1335
In an old church in England, there is a striking epitaph, honoring a Cavalier soldier who had sold much of his property and given a great deal of his money to the Royalist cause. When he was killed in a battle against the Roundheads, his friends paid him tribute in these words: "He served King Charles with a constant, dangerous, and expensive loyalty."

It is to the same kind of service that we are called in this place, in these days of dread and opportunity. But we are called for a cause and by a King greater by far.—Arthur R. McKay, "The Seed and the Spirit"

1336
A story is told of the children of the King of England getting lost and going to a cottage to ask directions. When asked who they were they responded, "We are just nobody, but our father is the King!"

KNOWLEDGE

1337
It's what you learn after you know it all that really counts.

1338
Knowledge begins with wondering. Set a child to wondering and you have put him on the road to understanding. —Samuel Langley

1339
William Temple, Archbishop of Canterbury, used to say that his mother once remarked: "William, you know more than I do, but I know so much better."

LABOR

1340
Labor Day is the only national holiday dedicated to plain people, rather than heroes and historic events. It provides an opportunity for all of us to recognize and honor the working men and women who have built America to its present stature and keep it going with such steady efficiency. We need this annual reminder because during the rest of the year the contributions made to our well-being by the unsung workers of our country are taken for granted. Only when some dramatic interruption takes place, do we begin to realize how dependent we are in our daily lives upon the continuous miracle of production and service rendered by the great army of free American workers. — George Meany, *Vital Speeches*

1341
Frequently we hear people ask: "What does labor want? What is labor looking for?" The most direct answer to such questions can be summed up in one word: "More." But let me make it clear that we want more not only for ourselves, but for all Americans—for the farmers and the businessmen as well as for wage-earners.

When we fight for a higher standard of living, we are helping all workers, not only union members. We are also helping employers and farmers, who must depend upon the high purchasing power of city workers to buy their products. When we campaign for legislation to build better schools, to erase slums, to broaden and improve social security and to provide national health insurance, every American family, not only the families of union members, stands to benefit.—George Meany, *Vital Speeches*

1342

With six days of hard labor we buy one day of happiness. But whoever does not know the six will never have the seventh.—Auguste Rodin

1343

Small boy to mother: "Please don't ask me to work, mommy, I feel unbusy today."—Marcelene Cox

1344

Keep this union clean. Keep it free, free for all of you to express yourselves decently and proudly. You never can be too radical against evil nor too conservative for good.—Allan Haywood

1345

We can't talk pious on Sunday, and then treat our employes or our boss like objects and obstacles during the week. —Samuel M. Shoemaker

1346

Some years ago I heard the labor expert, Whiting Williams, tell of a squad of day laborers who were hired one morning and put to work. . . . The foreman . . . set them to digging holes some three feet deep. When a hole was finished, it was inspected and the workman was ordered to fill it up and to come to another point and to dig another hole of the same depth. This went on for most of the morning and finally the foreman noted the group talking in a huddle and then their spokesman came over and said

. . . "We're gonna quit . . . give us our money. You ain't gonna make . . . fools out of us!" The foreman's eyes narrowed, and then understanding broke over him, and he said quietly, "Can't you see, we're trying to find where the broken pipe is?" "Oh," said the man, and after a hurried word with the others . . . returned and said, "Where you want us to dig next?"— Douglas Steere, *Work and Contemplation*

1347

Advocates of the union shop would compare it to our American system of government—all members of the community are taxed for the common welfare. To institute a system of voluntary taxation would mean the collapse of our national defense, our public safety, our education system. We do not compel a man to vote, to hold office, to serve on community committees, but we do compel all to pay taxes to support the benefits he gets from our American way of life. Union shop advocates believe that every worker covered by the benefits of a contract has a moral obligation to support the system which has brought these benefits on-the-job just as he must support the system which has brought so many benefits off-the-job.—Marshal L. Scott

1348

If equitable solutions to the common problems of employers and their employees are mutually sought in good faith, they can be found. Thousands of labor contracts are negotiated by union and management representatives each year without bitterness or strikes, and with regard to the public interest. Unfortunately, these settlements are rarely featured in the newspapers, while strikes are headlined. . . . Leaders of labor and management know that the progress of American industry depends largely upon their ability to cooperate for the common good. This is the road for free men of enlightened consciences to follow. Christianity may ask for more, but can ask for no less. Since God is our Father, we must ever strive to work together as brothers.—National Council of the Churches of Christ in the U.S.A.

LAW

1349

There is wisdom in common people which a government cannot get along without; it is not a good government which does not keep alive and active the principle of consent among the people.

The God of the Hebrews is not the God of war and power nor the God of the fertility cults. He is a God who is a covenant-making, covenant-keeping God, who expects men to enter into covenant with Him. The will and purpose of this God finds not one but many expressions. It is something to make people conscientious; it is more important to make them conscientious about the great issues of life. The prophetic contribution to social thinking was significant because the prophets wrote into the conscience platforms of the Hebrews planks that were fundamental. Their codified list of virtues was a significant and not a petty one. They were of the kind which would make people have a concern about the simple, fundamental issues of life. They had more of a regard for common men than they did for kings and princes and the great of the earth. The Hebrew stories rejoice in the times when the common people rose up and took control of their affairs. You could never build a doctrine of the divine right of kings on the basis of what is told in the books of Judges and Kings in the Old Testament.—Arthur E. Holt, *Christian Roots of Democracy in America*

1350

Where there is lawlessness, there is no hope. When you have law, you tend to have order, and a predictable society. When you have no law, society is unpredictable. And, to a lawyer, things that are unpredictable always are puzzling.—Joseph Welch

1351

We say the time has not yet come in these United States when an order of a Federal Court must be whittled away, watered down or shamefully withdrawn in the face of violent and unlawful acts of individual citizens in opposition thereto.—Opinion of the 8th Circuit Court of Appeals

1352

Laws reflect reform; they never induce reform. Laws that violate or go contrary to the mores of a community never bring about social peace and harmony.—Congressman Noah M. Mason, *Vital Speeches*

1353

They must obey the law. I do not refer to the civil law that protects one man against another. I refer to the spiritual law that protects a man against himself. For all men are tempted to slip down from their best standards. We have to watch—and pray.—J. C. Penney, *Rotarian*

1354

The laws of England failed to stop people from practicing their own forms of faith. King James I said: "I will make them conform or else harry them out of the land." He did succeed in the latter. The leaders of the sorely tried sects sought a haven in America. There some of them borrowed the very same methods of force to impose their views of the "true faith."

Conspicuous exceptions in America were Roger Williams, a Baptist; Lord

Baltimore, a Roman Catholic; and William Penn, a Quaker. They paved the way for religious liberty.—*Senior Scholastic*

1355

The life of the law has not been logic; it has been experience.—Oliver Wendell Holmes

1356

Is not education better than legislation? Both are necessary. Neither will work alone. . . . In a democracy they are mutually dependent. Laws do not *make* people good. They *protect* the people from those who try to harm them. Most of us can be taught to observe the rights of others, but there are the few who do not learn their lessons. The law is to protect us from these few and to remind us of our own obligations as citizens. No reasonable person would suggest that we not have traffic laws but instead "leave it to education." The word education is a bit ambiguous, too, for we can educate children to break traffic laws or observe them, to steal another's rights or to protect them. Which we do depends finally on our values, our sense of right and wrong. In a democracy we need not only laws and education, but a clear moral sense of our obligations to others.—Lillian Smith, *Now Is the Time*

LEADER

1357

Why we lack leaders: "Maybe we're educating too many just pretty well." —Grayson L. Kirk, President of Columbia University

1358

When high-level leadership commits itself to a closed program, it inevitably admits that organization is not a way of life but an expedient to attain cer-

tain ends which, once attained, will render organization superfluous. It is a view much more restricted than the British concept that, once the ends are attained, then organization will be free to proceed to the enrichment of life which is its final and limitless program. —Gerald W. Johnson, on labor unions, *The New Republic*

1359

Our purpose in this campaign is not to "give 'em hell," but to give them leadership.—Governor Arthur B. Langlie

1360

It is essential that the leader shall not follow or be pushed on from behind. He must heed the voice of the people, but he must inform and direct the people also. Having weighed these factors, he must decide what, according to his lights, is the right course and follow that course regardless of what the polls may reveal or what the commentators may cry.—Lester Markel, "The Future of the Printed Word," *Vital Speeches*

1361

There go the people. I must hurry and catch them, for I am their leader.

1362

The other day I saw a small boy begin his first journey, just a few tottering steps between the outstretched hands of his father and his mother. Each time he reached this goal, he shouted with glee over his achievement. Here in miniature was the whole drama of life, the drama of opposed voices. One voice coming, as it were, from the millions of years of animal ancestry was saying, "You're only a little animal. Crawl on all fours." The other voice, rising from the few thousand years of civilized effort, was saying, "Stand on your feet and walk. You are destined to be a man." This higher impulse wins.

Millions of parents are learning today that their children require discipline just as much as they need love. Neither by itself will suffice. Love alone leads to indulgence and a pampered child. Discipline without love begets resentment which later grows into bitter hate. It is the devoted and skillful blending of the two that develops adults of self-reliance, self-mastery and courage.

Leadership capable of meeting the crisis . . . will be born of our moral and spiritual strength. These forces make dictators tremble and eventually put tyranny to flight. We must "stand up to life."—Charles Haven Myers, *P. E. O. Record*

1363

Men like to be led. That is why Dr. Thorndike mentions "satisfyingness of submission to the right kind of leadership." I do not mean to imply that men want to be ordered around by a martinet. But we all know it is a mighty comforting thing, when one is in a tight spot, to have somebody's shoulder one can put his head down on and receive guidance and help. I remember the strange feeling I had when I was made president of my company . . . after twenty-seven years of service and discovered that there was no longer any shoulder left for me to lean on. In whatever post a man labors, he never ceases to crave sources from which to seek help and assistance. Everybody likes leadership of the right kind.— H. W. Prentis, Jr.

1364

It's the price of leadership to do the thing you believe has to be done at the time it must be done.—Senator Lyndon B. Johnson

1365

We have heard of a community that has been crying for leadership for the past five years, but when a leader appeared the other day, they crucified

him.—Roy L. Smith, *The Christian Advocate*

1366

What is a leader good for? Obviously, to tell his followers which way to go, and if he has no followers it is clear that he is good for nothing. A leader begins to function only after he has acquired a following; Napoleon without an army is only one small Corsican, of no great significance to anyone; his genius begins to flame as the battalions begin to form, and not before. Hence a man trained magnificently for leadership, but with nobody to lead, or only an undisciplined mob to lead, is a man as completely wasted as would be the top honor graduate of the Johns Hopkins Medical School set down to practice on Robinson Crusoe's isle. . . . Our purpose is . . . the ultimate consumption of leadership. While only a few men exercise it, we all make use of it, and whatever a man uses he can abuse.—Gerald W. Johnson, *Saturday Review*

1367

A leader is never a movement, but a leader may determine whether an army, an institution, a nation or a church marches or marks time. . . . Spiritual leaders, like military commanders, know there are three factors essential to advance: objective, mass, impulsion. Every move must have an objective and every objective of every unit be in harmony with the Supreme Command. Mass signifies all that the leader commands in men, material and moral. Impulsion is the key word. It means the multiplication of mass by concentrating it upon a particular section of the line so that, even when outnumbered, the leader has more men at the point of attack than the enemy. . . . Leadership . . . characterized by reverence, relevance, and radiance . . . knows that the Eternal who keeps the stars in their courses also notes the sparrow's fall . . . believes that God's love is not our impersonal love for mankind in general but a personal love for each . . . in particular.—G. Bromley Oxnam

1368

What makes a leader—intelligence, integrity, imagination, skill: in brief, statecraft? Not at all. It is the fact that the man has a following.—Gerald W. Johnson

1369

He can inspire a group only if he himself is filled with confidence and hope of success.—Floyd Filson, *Pioneers of the Primitive Church*

1370

The leader is necessarily one who breaks new paths into unfamiliar territory. The man who directs us along the old familiar ways is not a leader; he is a traffic cop—a useful and worthy functionary, but not inspiring.—Gerald W. Johnson

LEISURE

1371

If you are losing your leisure, look out; you may be losing your soul.—Logan Pearsall Smith

1372

Leisure and I have parted company. I am resolved to be busy till I die.—John Wesley

1373

A normal man who never rests (John Wesley was not a normal man) gets taut, overwrought, strained and ultimately breaks down. Leisure has its place in life. There is a rhythmic law underlying all existence, an ebb and flow; a movement of periodicity. And in that ebb and flow, work and leisure both have a place.—W. E. Sangster, *Christianity Today*

1374

One of the differences between work and leisure is that work must be done whether you like it or not, but leisure ought to allow room for the expression of preferences and the satisfaction of wholesome desires.—W. E. Sangster, *Christianity Today*

1375

Leisure has its place in the pattern of life, not as something to be wasted and forgotten, but as something to be cherished and guarded.

1376

Leisure is a beautiful garment, but it will not do for constant wear.

1377

Leisure is an empty cup. It all depends upon what we put into it.—Raphael Demos

LIBERTY

1378

No man can speak on religious liberty and walk the earth realistically without understanding that religious liberty eventually includes all of the liberties.—Reuben E. Nelson

1379

When one's belief collides with the power of the State, the latter is supreme within its sphere, and submission or punishment follows. But in the forum of conscience, duty to a moral power higher than the State has always been maintained. The essence of religion is belief in a relation to God involving duties superior to those arising from any human relation. One cannot speak of religious liberty, with proper appreciation of its essential and historical significance, without assuming the existence of a belief in supreme allegiance to the will of God.—Dissenting opinion of Justices Hughes, Holmes, Brandeis and Stone in the Douglas Clyde Mac-Intosh case.

1380

The struggle for freedom is never ending. We need that same spirit of dedication, that same faith in God and in our country which brought America to where it is today. If we can be true to this faith, then America can face the future with unshakeable strength, sure of itself and of its destiny to help in building a better world.—General Matthew B. Ridgway

1381

The mastery of Jesus leads us into the God-controlled life; Christian discipleship makes us righteous, heroic, loving, reverent children of God, engaged in helping to make the Kingdom of God a reality on earth. We have surrendered ourselves to that love of God that possessed Jesus and shone through Him, and we are free.

One of the great minds of our age, Albert Einstein, declared . . . "I am enthralled by the radiant figure of Jesus. If Jesus' teachings and example would really be followed, there would be a finer and a happier world." Are we enthralled by the radiant figure of Jesus? Has He captured us and brought us into the liberating fellowship of the will of God? That is liberty.—Harold L. Bowman, *Monday Morning*

1382

Real freedom is positive. It is not mere freedom *from* something—from interference or restraint or fear. It is freedom *for* something—freedom to be and to do what we judge to be best. —Luther A. Weigle, *The Methodist Layman*

1383

Liberty is not the right to insult with impunity. . . . It is not to incite hatred and violence, nor is it to stimulate negative instincts to make them

sources of power. Liberty requires conscience and vigor to keep it alive and defend it. If order based solely on force cannot create liberty, it is truer that disorder always destroys it. The strength of a people lies in intelligent conduct and the use of power for the common good.—Jimenez of Venezuela

1384

If man has no individuality of his own—no spiritual existence, if he is no different from every other in any essential characteristic—then we are bound to concede that no case can be made out for individual freedom, for the dignity of man, for the human institutions which give expression to them, or for any spiritual life either within ourselves or the community in which we live.

It is on this that I would wish you to ponder—for here to be found is the future of the human race—its progress to a higher human existence, or its decline and fall to the level of organized robots. . . .

We have the right and the glorious opportunity to develop our own separate individualities, in the pursuit of happiness not only for ourselves but for those we love, for our fellow men, for mankind in general.—Sir Percy Spender, "Liberty and the Individual," *Vital Speeches*

1385

Liberty is the most contagious force in the world.—Justice Earl Warren

1386

Democracy and liberty are not identical. Democracy is mass participation in community decisions—in the modern age, operating through groups and group pressures. Liberty is the opportunity to make personal choices in significant life situations. Groups help educate individuals as to their interests and help them fight for those interests —hence they are democratic. Groups also force other groups to respect the individual choices of their members—hence they are libertarian. This is the general tendency.—William G. Carleton, "Citizenship and the Social Studies," *Vital Speeches*

1387

Perfect conformity to God's will is the sole and complete liberty.—Jean Henri M. D'Aubigne

1388

The history of liberty is a history of limitations of government power, not the increase of it.—Woodrow Wilson

1389

Liberty does not consist . . . in mere general declarations of the rights of men. It consists in the translation of those declarations into definite action. —Woodrow Wilson

1390

A long view will require courage. It is easier to deal quickly with the little things than it is to take a slower, sounder approach to the big things. And freedom is a big thing. The freedom referred to here is not that described by the words "individual liberty." It refers rather to that collective freedom of the spirit which conditions a society to be "fit for free men without fear or hatred or inward slavery."—Lucy Mazine Lee, *The National Voter*

1391

It seems to me liberty is given to man like a piece of land. It is entrusted to him for faithful cultivation and safekeeping. Man can nourish it and provide it the necessary safeguards; but only if he is self-reliant enough—and if his dedication to free principles is great enough.—Admiral Arthur Radford, *Vital Speeches*

LIFE

1392

A man who protects and hoards his life may lose it anyhow. Perhaps to protect it is to lose it in the most real sense of the word, for cowardice means spiritual death.—Sherman E. Johnson, *Interpreter's Bible*

1393

We come into this world crying while all around us are smiling. May we so live that we go out of this world smiling while everybody round us is weeping.—Persian Proverb

1394

Live your life so that whenever you lose, you're ahead.—Will Rogers

1395

Life is a grindstone and whether it grinds a man down or polishes him up depends on the stuff he is made of.— *Weekly Spoke,* Weburn, Canada

1396

There was a man one day who had a lot of pearls . . . all good pearls, fine pearls. He had spent his life collecting them. And then he saw a Pearl of Great Price, and for joy he sold all he had, all his pearls, that he might get the Pearl of Great Price. Did he say, "No I can't give up these yet. It costs too much." No, he didn't. He concentrated on the Pearl of Great Price and forgot about the other pearls, on what he was getting, not on what he was losing. That is what the cross is.

Why does God demand these things of us? Because He wants to give us abundant life; and we insist on keeping less than abundant life. He wants to give us gold; and we insist on keeping our brass. He wants us to see the angel vision over our heads; and we won't take our eyes off the muck heap.—

Walter H. Judd, *A Philosophy of Life That Works*

1397

In his book *The Dignity of Man,* Russell W. Davenport refers to an ancestor of his, Col. Abraham Davenport, as a "Candle-in-the-Dark." On May 19, 1780, the sun scarcely appeared and as the darkness increased, many people becoming alarmed, concluded the world was about to come to an end. Many members of the Connecticut Assembly being of the same opinion, proposed to adjourn the assembly. Col. Davenport . . . said to his fellow legislators, "The Day of Judgment is either approaching, or it is not. If it is not, there is no cause for adjournment; if it is, I choose to be found doing my duty. I wish therefore that candles may be brought." The assembly did not adjourn, for the wisdom and calmness of one man allayed the fears and restored the confidence of his associates.—Charles L. Anspach, "Candles-in-the-Dark," *Vital Speeches*

1398

So live that your proud differences may be apparent to all and respected by all. "Behold how you are numbered among the children of God, and your lot is among the saints." It was not that you might be the mediocre, moral equals of the spiritually underprivileged who have faint faith, scant hope, and frigid charity, that so much was devised by heaven and sacrificed on earth in your behalf. . . . You are the sons of prayers and spiritual yearnings, of divine hopes as well as of human blood, sweat, and tears. Our children are not born of the will of the flesh alone, not only of the will of men; they are born of God. Christ did not become incarnate, His apostles did not preach and His saints suffer, His people did not withstand the slings and arrows of outrageous fortune through all the history of the Caesars and the Vandals, the Huns and the feudal princes, the national kings and the modern dictators, in order that, after all these aspirations, you might add the final outrage of annulling their sacrifices by accepting mere equality of dogmatic faith and moral worth with their detractors and their persecutors.—John J. Wright, *Vital Speeches*

1399

Our chief want in life is somebody who shall make us do what we can.—Ralph Waldo Emerson

1400

The world is moving into a happier era than it has ever known. Mankind cannot long continue to preserve any degree of sanity or balance unless it can find a way to diminish nervous stress. The world has begun to go rather slowly and rather tentatively toward life, as opposed to death.—Bertrand Russell, *Newsweek*

1401

Religion is fitted to make us better in every situation in life.—Mary Lyon, founder of Mt. Holyoke College

1402

"If we live in a great spirit we shall be ready for a great occasion." When Saint Gaudens was asked why he worked all day and every day, regardless of inspiration, his reply was, "If I do, and inspiration comes at any time, I am sure of its finding me at home."

1403

Life is the gift of God but it is capital that must be spent or it dissipates.—Charles Templeton, *Life Looks Up*

1404

No human life, however seemingly full, is ever complete in this world. But there is a vast difference between a life which is unfinished because it has not reached its end, and a life which is unfinished because it is left at loose ends.—Ralph W. Sockman

1405

There is always hope for an individual who stops to do some serious thinking about life.—Katherine Logan

1406

Willy Loman, in *Death of a Salesman,* with his pitiful goal in life of becoming merely a salesman with a better sales record, and ending finally in suicide when things have gone wrong, indicates why "unluckily the sinners stay" within the breasts of many of us; we lack a great goal for living, and we have no great religion to help us achieve that goal. John Mason Brown, dramatic critic, carefully analyzes the trouble with Willy (and many of us): "The play shows the futility of life without character or spiritual resources. Poor Willy is desperate for the lack of any spiritual guidance in his life, and can only cling desperately to the empty ideas of hail-fellow-well-met success, measured in terms of sales volume." "Sales volume" as a life motive is not enough, and "the longer thread of life we spin, the more occasion still to sin." Man ultimately must admit that he needs the gospel.

1407

There is no power on earth that can neutralize the influence of a high, pure, simple and useful life.—Booker T. Washington, *Up from Slavery*

1408

What a pitiful sight it is to see men well past middle age, with ample means to enjoy life, still insisting on going on in their businesses and professions. These men are afraid to stop. They are afraid of life because the ends of life have dried up within them. Very often we hear Americans say: "It is better to wear out than to rust out." What a horrible conception of man, torn between wearing and rusting out. As if that were the alternative! The alternative is not whether to wear out or to rust out but whether to give more time to the beauties and mysteries of living.—William G. Carleton, "The Goal Is Man: Individual Man," *Vital Speeches*

1409

The life of every man is a diary in which he means to write one story and writes another; and his humblest hour is when he compares the volume as it is with what he vowed to make. —J. M. Barrie

1410

The greatest discovery of my generation is that human beings can alter their lives by altering their attitudes of mind.—William James

1411

We too have always liked, as John Mason Brown recalls it in one of his books, the place in *Mrs. Wiggs of the Cabbage Patch* where Lovey Mary starts off on her famous trip to Niagara Falls. Mrs. Wiggs gives her a bottle and asks her, as a special favor, if she will please bring it back full of water dipped from the falls so that right in her own sitting room she can enjoy the splendor of Niagara!

1412

It's not important for a man to be superior to somebody else. The big achievement, in sports or character, is being superior to your previous self. —Burton Hillis, *Better Homes & Gardens*

1413

We must Christianize life—all of life—and we must mean business by it.—Bishop Ralph S. Cushman

1414

As a plane leaves the runway, it strains as it rises, but when it has attained a cruising altitude it levels off and the strain ceases. We need to reach a cruising altitude in our living and stop the strain in life.—Arthur L. Miller

1415

A boy from the American Middle West, who had never before seen the ocean, made a trip to the West Coast. As he looked out across the vast Pacific, he stood quiet. "Well," asked a friend, "what do you think of it?"

"It's wonderful," replied the boy, "but I hate to see all that water out there doing nothing."

So it is with scores of people in every community. People who can and won't. People who should and don't. People who take from life and never give.—Wallace Fridy, *The Rotarian*

LIGHT

1416

The word "light" is one of the most expressive words in the Gospel of John. It invites figurative use and is so used everywhere and in practically all religions. . . .

Light is a necessity of daily existence. In the ancient world especially, the dark could be cold, dreary, and full of danger. Artificial light was very scarce until modern times.

Light was considered a symbol of divinity. In kinship to the stars it was heavenly. In the temples it was an effective symbol of the divine presence.

Light was, at least to the more educated, a symbol of truth or reason. It signified the achievement of the highest faculty men possessed. Light is more than knowledge or logic; it is the insight that is a guide to man's deepest fulfillment. It frees man from slavery to ignorance.

Light was symbolic also of the good, as the dark was of evil . . . varied and rich meanings of . . . "light" were well known . . . to the Jews to whom Jesus spoke.—Ward Redus, *Adult Student*

1417

The crew at a certain lighthouse kept the place in show-window order. It was spick and span down to the littlest detail. They enjoyed keeping the lighthouse in that fashion. But they had one disagreeable task, namely, that of going out in the dark on stormy nights to rescue men from floundering ships.

Finally one man said, "We are rescuing too many people; they are messing up our lighthouse. Every time we bring someone in, the place gets all dirty and we have to work hard to get it back in order."

And another, who had lost the real purpose of the lighthouse, said, "Yes, and we have to be careful that they don't take our jobs."—George Skaret

1418

There is a strange nonmetallic substance in chemistry known as selenium. When placed in the dark, it serves as an insulator and electricity cannot pass through it. But as soon as light is flashed upon it, it becomes a conductor and an electric current can flow through it.

In God's world, you and I are just like a piece of selenium. If we stay in the dark and do not allow the light of Christ to shine upon us, we become insulators. No current of love can flow through us. Through us the world will learn nothing of the Christ. But as soon as we subject ourselves to His light, we become Christian conductors, and love and happiness and service can flow through us into the world.—John M. Younginer

1419

She lets her light shine without turning the spot on herself.

1420

A window does two things. In daytime it lets the light in. At night it lets the light out. A vital Christian is like that. In the day when God's light is shining, he lets God's light into his spirit. . . . But at night when the lights have gone out . . . the Christian's light shines through to give courage and inspiration to others around him.—Edward DeWeese, Jr., *Classmate*

1421

Light may disclose a jewel, but it takes darkness to disclose a star.— *Ohio State Sundial*

1422

Light has the characteristic that, once let loose, it cannot be confined. Strike a match in the darkness, and it can be seen in all directions. . . . Jesus Christ, once let loose upon the world, cannot be confined.—Lawrence Mac-Coll Horton, *Presbyterian Life*

1423

Truth never need fear the light. Sunlight falling on a dead log may hasten the process of decay, but sunlight falling on a living tree makes it grow and become luxuriant.—Joseph R. Sizoo, *The Way Out of the Dark*

1424

A young Burmese came to our Ashram group and, when he went away, he said so simply and sincerely, "I came here a flickering torch, but I go away a flaming torch." This must happen to people as they come to our churches.—E. Stanley Jones

LITTLE THINGS

1425

The star of the TV show, "Private Secretary," was being taken to task by her boss for having left the word "not" out of a letter.

"After all," she pouted prettily, "it was just one little three-letter word."

"So one little three-letter word isn't important, eh?" roared the boss. "Well, where do you think we'd be today if Moses had left out the word 'not' when he wrote the Ten Commandments?"

1426

Make no little plans. They have no magic to stir men's blood. Make big plans: aim high in hope and work.— D. H. Burnham

1427

A thread will tie an honest man better than a rope will do a rogue. —Chinese proverb

LOVE

1428

God's love is not a conditional love; it is an openhearted, generous self-giving which God offers to men. Those who would carefully limit the operation of God's love . . . have missed the point.—J. B. Phillips, *New Testament Christianity*

1429

Children need love, especially when they do not deserve it.—Harold S. Hulbert

1430

There is no one so small but that he cannot achieve greatness in loving service.

1431

Genuine love must be narrow in a sense. The person who truly loves deeply and beautifully, and through that love can love the whole world, is the man or woman who also deeply loves individuals. Intense love of a man for his wife . . . means that the soul is attuned to all that is beautiful in love. Herein is the secret of God's great love. We sometimes think that the universe itself is so immense that God cannot give peculiar care to the individual. But Jesus says that God did not build man for the universe but the universe for man. . . . God could not love the world without loving the individual. It is idle to speak of loving humanity but refusing to love men as individuals. We must first choose the narrow way.—Fred R. Chenault, *Christian Herald*

1432

Some years ago, the *New Yorker* presented a cartoon which shows two young theological students walking within the cloistered walls of the seminary. One of the students has a baffled expression on his countenance, and is remarking to the other: "What gets me about this place is that they want you to love people you don't even like!"—Robert E. Fitch, *The New Leader*

1433

Faith has to do with the basis, the ground on which we stand. Hope is reaching out for something to come. Love is just being there and acting.— Emil Brunner, *Faith, Hope, and Love*

1434

The Christian is faced by a dilemma; he would like to love his neighbors without intermediary, as man to man; it is characteristic of love that it is addressed to one irreplaceable person, whom Jesus defined as follows (in the words of Pascal): "It was for thee that I shed this drop of my blood." An administration does not speak like that. In order to do something for a certain person, the administration has to cease regarding him as a person and turn him into a "case" with a Social Welfare number, entitled to a priority file, etc. . . .

Moreover, the driving power behind this social therapy no longer seems to have any connection with the proclamation of God's Kingdom. All these bodies tend to become mere machinery for correcting the imperfect functioning of the social structure. . . . This situation presents a real problem to the militant Christian who wonders if he can introduce a Christian gesture in the world. Whatever he does runs the risk of becoming more and more impersonal, more and more emptied of its prophetic substance.—P. Ricoeur, *The Ecumenical Review*

1435

[God] loves because He wants to give not to get, He wants to share, to give of His own to those who lack, who have need of what He gives. His love is entirely unmotivated by any value outside Himself. His love, therefore, is entirely spontaneous, motivated only by His will to give, to share, to communicate His own, an expression solely of His free will. He loves for no other reason than that He wants to love.—Emil Brunner

1436

Against persistent love there is nothing that can be done; it blunts all weapons.—Stuart Morris

1437

There is no love which does not become help.—Paul Tillich

1438

Love does not die easily. It is a living thing. It thrives in the face of all life's hazards, save one—neglect. —James D. Bryden, *Presbyterian Life*

1439

"It is a mystery to me what she sees in him!" You have heard this comment with variations many times . . . the father of our most troublesome youngster in school said, "Our kid has his faults but we love him and he still looks good to us." . . . Actually, love does see more in the beloved than others ever can see. We do look good to those who love us. We are more tolerant of the behavior of persons we like. . . . Love sees more for it sees the beloved when surrounded by love. —Richard E. Lentz, *The Christian Evangelist*

1440

The purpose of the gospel is not simply that we should believe in the love of God; it is that we should love Him and neighbor. Faith in God's love toward man is perfected in man's love to God and neighbor. We love in incompleteness, not as redeemed but in the time of redemption, not in attainment but in hope. Through Jesus Christ we receive enough faith in God's love toward us to see at least the need for and the possibility of a responsive love on our part. We know enough of the possibility of love to God on our part to long for its perfection; we see enough of the reality of God's love toward us and neighbor to hope for its full revelation and so for our full response.—H. Richard Niebuhr, *The Purpose of the Church and Its Ministry*

1441

Infantile love follows the principle: "I love because I am love." Mature love follows the principle: "I am loved because I love." Immature love says: "I love you because I need you." Mature love says: "I need you because I love

you."—Erich Fromm, *The Art of Loving*

1442

Persons are to be loved; things are to be used.—Reuel Howe

1443

We must never be bitter—if we indulge in hate, the new order will only be the old order. . . . We must meet hate with love, physical force with soul force.—Martin Luther King, Jr.

1444

Archibald MacLeish has said: "A man who lives not by what he loves but what he hates is a sick man."

Anger can be a source of strength when properly motivated and worthily channeled. Some situations in this world should move us to provocation, but the individual who gets mad only at people is the victim of a temper he cannot control.

If you have ever learned to like another person through genuine effort on your part, you have grown personally thereby. Everyone has a best side, even the most difficult. . . . Man is made for fellowship. No man was ever born a hermit. When life moves out to life in terms of understanding and mutuality, we are moving on a positive plane. "God is love." We speak of the love "of" God, but may forget the love which "is" God creatively at work in human relationships. Feuding is no substitute for fellowship. —*New Christian Advocate*

1445

It is not those who work for us that we love most. The friends who need us count more than those we need. . . . Thus love for God will have reached its climax when it no longer expresses need; when we are so at one with ultimate Reality as not to be believing, but *"living* God."—Aelred Graham, *Commonweal*

1446

Doctors say that infants need love —without it they die. We are all children of God—without His love we die spiritually. God's love is there—reach out for it with your own love, and you will become one with God!—James W. Fifield, Jr., *The Single Path*

1447

If you have to tell your children that you love them, then you certainly do not.

1448

To love anyone is nothing else than to wish that person good.—Thomas Aquinas

MAN

1449

We've done precious little about man himself. Man is still the Great Unknown. Man is still our unexplored frontier . . . we realize that it's on this frontier—not the geographic one, not the scientific one—that our civilization is going to stand or fall. The horizon of our hope is no longer in things; it's in Man himself. The plain fact is that Man's skills have outstripped his morals. His engineering has leapt ahead of his wisdom. And though scientifically we've moved into the Atomic Age, morally we're only a step or so past the Stone Age.—Clarence W. Hall

1450

Man's conquest of nature has been astonishing. His failure to conquer human nature has been tragic.—Julius Mark

1451

A machine cannot be guilty. Nor can it love. Whether man is conceived of as a set of nerve cells, or society as a combination of many interacting nerve cells, does not make much difference. The main thing is that in such a world we need no Redeemer. What we need, at best, is a repairman.—Karl Stern, *Commonweal*

1452

We all know that man has advanced to a very creditable stage from a low beginning, but to hear sentimentalists talk, one would think man began as an angel, and ended up as a savage.—E. W. Howe

1453

The sense of being lost does not make a man a Christian. It only proves that he is a man.—Arthur E. Holt

1454

Nothing brings out the best in men like trouble.—Hal Boyle

1455

There is something wrong with men —all men, common and uncommon. The whole of human history and the entire body of human experience stand behind that verdict. Man himself is the worm in the apple! Ignorant or enlightened, illiterate or cultured, behind an ox-drawn plow or behind a panel of electronic knobs and switches —man has always been (and unless redeemed by a power higher than his own, will always be) the world's and his own worst enemy.—Herman W. Gockel

1456

We need no more expansion of the Science of Subnormality. We do need . . . a Science of Normal Man . . . normal man contains in his nature quite as much "imprisoned splendor" as he does inhibited deviltry. To limit the study of Man only to sub-normal man makes about as much sense as if the College of Music studied only discords . . . the Engineering classrooms devoted themselves only to stripped gears . . . Forestry studied only stunted and fruitless trees . . . Home Economics dabbled only in the ingredients of fallen cakes . . . Business Administration was bemused only with cock-eyed accounting . . . and the Dramatics Department put on only bad plays!—Clarence W. Hall

MARTYR

1457

If one would be great he must possess the spirit of the martyr. . . . Iris Gabriel . . . dreamed of a career as an actress . . . won beauty contests . . . was invited to Hollywood . . . had fame and wealth . . . then contracted tuberculosis . . . left the hospital discouraged but . . . registered in the University of Chicago. . . . One day, President Hutchins asked . . . "What has been the greatest force in the history of society . . ." The students answered, "Religion, democracy, the printing press, the wheel—fire." After the answers were all in, Hutchins wrote . . . one word, "Martyrdom," . . . saying, "Men who die for what they believe give immortality to their ideas and inspire the rest of us to greatness. If you want to become important in this world, be a martyr; give yourself away." This inspired Iris . . . to found the Silent Guide Foundation . . . she found the secret of life which Tagore called, "We earn life by giving it away." Each individual must learn the importance of this essential to worthy living . . . which we see exemplified in mother love . . . and in the words "Greater love hath no man than this, that a man lay down his life for his friends."—Charles L. Anspach, *Vital Speeches*

1458

The Greek word for a witness was *martyros* and the early Christians staged many a tragi-triumphant scene for the Roman spectators in their stadia. Victorious living and, where needful, victorious dying—these were what converted the pagan world rather than potent homiletical utterances or moving worship experiences. . . . It seems to be God's intention that the main impression on a pagan world should be made not by words from the lips of an orator, but by power in the lives of God's alerted people.—John M. Gordon

1459

There have been more martyrs in our generation than in any previous generation: in Korea, China, Europe and other places.—Bishop R. S. Hubbard

1460

He who risks his life and hands it over to God will share in the life of the world to come, whether martyrdom is his lot or not; but cowardice is certain death for the soul.—Sherman E. Johnson

MATURITY

1461

Maturity is an attitude, and an attitude is a prepared way of acting. It is an attitude that enables a person to handle an adult situation . . . in a way that benefits everyone concerned. —Dr. John A. Schindler, *National Parent-Teacher*

1462

A church member who has never developed into a committed Christian is like a child whose mind has never matured.—Robert Beach Cunningham

1463

What is going to happen to the children when there are not more grown-ups?—Noel Coward

1464

Security means inner harmony of the personality with the environment. Man must learn how to balance emotional stress against his own emotional supports. And he must be mature.— William C. Menninger

1465

The last lesson learned in childhood is that adults don't know everything, either, or even very much.—*Boston Globe*

1466

So far in the history of the world, there have never been enough mature people in the right places.—G. B. Chisholm

1467

One lesson of life which our culture seems unwilling to accept graciously is that "to err is human." . . . There was a time . . . when men at the top passed on the responsibility for the mistake to their subordinates, and they in turn passed them on down . . . this was far from a sensible way of facing human limitations. . . . Somebody must take the blame. Today, it often happens that when somebody makes a mistake, an all-out effort of management is made not only to hide the mistake but also to keep the man who made it from taking responsibility for it. . . . The mature man knows that he is likely to make mistakes. He wants to take responsibility for them. Only by facing his mistakes does he learn to act more responsibly.— Richard H. Rice, *Classmate*

1468

A mistake is evidence that somebody has tried to accomplish something.— John E. Babcock

MIND

1469

I am uncurably convinced that the object of opening the mind, as of opening the mouth, is to shut it again on something solid.—G. K. Chesterton

1470

The narrower a man's mind, the broader his statements.—Burton Hillis, *Better Homes & Gardens*

1471

You may feel that no one has captured your mind. But think for a moment, how original are you? Who decided what you are wearing? You all alone? Who sets the pattern in music? We are victims. You can buy, says the ad, a soap that will get you engaged. Is the design of the car you drive your idea? Who gave us the idea that one party can save democracy? Who gave us the idea that other races are inferior? The Apostle Paul wrote: "Let that mind be in you which is in Christ Jesus." Jesus said "Seek first the kingdom" and the rest of our needs would be added. Has Christ captured your mind or is your mind the victim of something else?—Martin Goslin

1472

Every now and then a man's mind is stretched by a new idea and never shrinks back to its original proportions. —Oliver Wendell Holmes

MISSIONS

1473

God's love for the world is the motive of missions. God's love is what we have to tell, and God's love is why we have to tell it.—Ben L. Rose, *Christian World Facts*

1474

The great gulf between the Christian and the non-Christian is in their experience of God. . . . The strength of the Christian witness today lies in its witnesses. . . . The strategy of the new era of the world mission is that of penetration from within, through the witness of the men and women who compose the churches established during the pioneer age of missions. . . . The faith of men must be respected and guided to enable them to discover Christ as the guide of life.— Willis Church Lamott, *The Chaplain*

MONEY

1475

"It's an old and much ridiculed bromide that money can't buy happiness, but there's a great deal of truth in those words," was the statement of J. Paul Getty, whom *Fortune* Magazine called the richest man in America, following surgery on his twelve-year-old son, Timothy.

1476

Money spent in bringing children up to be strong, intelligent, and resourceful is the best saving, both for the individual and for civilization.— Margaret Culkin Banning

1477

The theory of the automatic, unearned allowance for children is one of the greatest disservices ever perpetrated on education and the American people.—Henry C. Link, *The Way to Security*

1478

References to money popped up all over Jimmy's small world, and slowly but surely he collected an odd and unrelated set of facts and fancies. He learned that money doesn't grow on trees. . . . He heard that a ten-dollar bill simply melts away and that money has a way of slipping through fingers or burning holes in pockets. He wasn't willing to accept the fact that money talks, however, because he had spent many odd moments questioning both the paper and silver variety without getting so much as one word in response. . . . Suddenly he wondered whether anyone would object to his taking money which they had poured down ratholes. But where was a rathole?

The shadow of money hung over Jimmy's very playmates. Alice, Grandmother said, had been born with a silver spoon in her mouth. . . . Maryanne, whose mother was poor as a church mouse, was considered a darling, and Billy was pitied because his family lived "over their heads." Jimmy spent every minute he could spare from playing to watch for penny-pinchers, spendthrifts, and squanderlusts. Whenever he happened to have a penny of his own, he would clutch it very tightly, remembering the words Aunt Emma was forever saying so darkly, "A fool and his money are soon parted."— "Money Management: Children's Spending"

1479

It's good to have money and the things money can buy. It's good, too, to check up once in a while and make sure you haven't lost the things money can't buy.—George Horace Lorimer

1480

Something better is needed than the system of the young bride who summarized one month as, "March 1, Jim gave me $100"; then, on the opposite page, "March 31, spent it all."—John Charles Wynn

1481

"Eternal life" was James Bernard Schafer's stock in trade. To hear him tell it, he could also materialize money and dematerialize people. The fantastic cult he set up in the late 1930's, The Royal Fraternity of Master Metaphysicians, took care of the money part. . . . Schafer gathered some 4,000 followers and accepted contributions estimated at $150,000 for his cult . . . bought a . . . Vanderbilt estate and hung up a big sign which read "LIDGTTFATIM." This meant: "Lord, I do give Thee thanks for the abundance that is mine." Schafer lived royally on the financial "love offerings" . . . until 1942 when he went to prison for cheating a cultist out of $9,000. . . . When . . . he got out . . . he still had enough money to buy an $80,000 . . . estate . . . and set up a thriving correspondence school . . . which brought his students Schafer's version of the secrets of peace, life, and wealth.

"There is no single problem that money will not solve," Schafer taught. In 1955, he proved that neither his money nor his mumbo jumbo was of any real avail against life's problems. He and his wife were found in their expensive car, double suicides by carbon monoxide.—*Newsweek*

1482

Money is the most indispensable tool we have, and while it is a duty to remember that money can be a power for evil, we must not fail to lay equal emphasis on money's power for good.—*Presbyterian Life*

1483

The dollar bill has sometimes been called "Home Maker or Breaker Number One." It is true that arguments arise quickly between husband and wife if there is misunderstanding about money. A court judge has reported:

"Quarreling about money is a major reason for America's unprecedented divorce rate. It is difficult to overestimate the vicious part financial trouble is playing in the American home." In one study it was discovered that young husbands attributed 48 per cent of their most serious marital problems to financial difficulties.—John Charles Wynn, *How Christian Parents Face Family Problems*

MORALITY

1484

Morality is simply the forced choice between suicide and abundant life.—Ralph Barton Perry

1485

A Christian may be conservative or reformist and still be Christian. But he stands unequivocally for the supratemporal goods which the temporal order must cherish. Furthermore, he is aware of sin, both in himself and in others; he sees his opponents as men and women who, like himself, are creatures of God and, what is more, are dear in God's sight, and therefore not fit subjects for tyranny. I do not believe that Christians always know what is best to do, and I certainly do not believe that they will agree with one another. But on one thing, and the most important thing, they should be agreed; namely, the nature of the foundation on which the good society should be built.

That is our task: to witness to these things, humbly because we are sinners, confidently because we are citizens of that city of which our Lord is the Master and King.—Alan Paton, *Christian Century*

1486

By moral insensibility I refer to the mute acceptance—or even the unawareness—of moral atrocity. I mean the lack of indignation when confronted with moral horror. I mean the turning of this atrocity and this horror into morally approved conventions of feeling. I mean, in short, the incapacity for moral reaction to event and character, to high decisions and the drift of human circumstance. Such moral insensibility has its roots in World War I; it became fullblown during World War II. The "saturation bombing" of that war was an indiscriminate bombing of civilians on a mass scale; the atomic bombing of the peoples of Hiroshima and Nagasaki was an act committed without warning and without ultimatum. By the time of Korea, the strategy of obliteration had become totally accepted as part of our moral universe. . . . In our world "necessity" and "realism" have become ways to hide lack of moral imagination. . . . One reason for this lack . . . is what must surely be called the moral default of the Christians.—C. Wright Mills, "A Pagan Sermon to the Christian Clergy," *The Nation*

1487

Today the pressure of the rank and file is to "elevate" their leaders. And I assure you that there is very little resistance to this. The consequence is a situation in which the officers are ever farther removed in their way of life from those they represent. Way of life is soon followed by way of thought. Labor leaders become, like other corporation executives, believers in their own indispensability. Believing this, they favor those in the power structure who confirm it; hence the bureaucracy which supports them is increasingly made up of sycophants busy reassuring the "great" men. The process is endless and the result, in extreme, is Dave Beck.—Kermit Eby, *Christian Century*

1488

In first-century Ephesus, Demetrius and his fellow silversmiths stirred up a city-wide tumult over the inroads of Christianity upon their idol-making profits. With similar irresponsibility and avarice, the tobacco industry is diverting $33 million annually into an all-out advertising effort to combat the devasting findings of impartial medical research. But this vigorous propaganda campaign notwithstanding, an estimated 1.5 million smokers swore off cigarettes during an 18-month period beginning in the fall of 1953, according to the U. S. Census Bureau. . . . Tobacco advertisers, eager to enlist new smoking recruits, would like the public to believe that "everybody does it."—Joseph Martin Hopkins, *Christianity Today*

1489

Americans are now faced with immorality paraded in attractive guise by almost every media of entertainment. That the church seldom speaks out against this evil is a strange phenomenon. Why this silence? The Bible says that because of these very things the holy anger of God falls on those who refuse to obey. . . . This is a matter of the first magnitude. . . . Raise the question of moral conduct, and often there is little effective reaction. One does not have to choose one course of righteousness at the expense of another. It is the obligation of the church to show concern in many areas of life. But at the present time, individual Christians and the church are far too silent about the immoral concepts that are gaining ascendency in the thinking and living of the multitudes. For the sake of all concerned, let the church speak up.—*Christianity Today*

MOTHER

1490

History records that France had sixty-nine kings, of which number only three were loved by their subjects. Those three were the only kings who had been raised by their mothers, the others being reared by private tutors, governesses, all disinterested persons.—Charles Allen and Charles L. Wallis, *Christmas in Our Hearts*

1491

Of all the men I have known, I cannot recall one whose mother did her level best for him when he was little who did not turn out well when he grew up.—Frances Parkinson Keyes

1492

I put the relation of a fine teacher to a student just below the relation of a mother to a son, and I don't think I could say more than this.—Thomas Wolfe

1493

The last lines of this portrait remind us that we do not need to praise the true mother God made. The "fruit of her hands"—her house, her clothes, her children, her own works—they praise her in the market place. Her life has stamped itself deeply upon the lives of those about her and in the community. Thank God for mothers like this!—Bartlett L. Hess, *Christian Herald*

1494

Portrait: A mother, who looked as if she had worn her heart to the bone. —Marcelene Cox

1495

Men and women frequently forget each other, but everybody remembers mother.—Jerome Paine Bates

1496

I am one of the poor abused mothers you've wept about. To a few . . . the word "children" may mean:

    C are
    H ubbub
    I llness
    L ack of free time
    D efeat of talent and ambition
    R un-down home
    E nd of fun, extra work
    N oise and nagging

To me, the word has many wonderful meanings, including:

    C ompanionship
    H ope for a better tomorrow
    I nspiration and added interest in my daily life
    L ove and laughter
    D etermination to do my best every day
    R ewards that can't be measured
    E xtra fun, extra enthusiasm
    N ever a dull or lonely moment.
           —Jane K. Shoemaker

1497

Moses never forgot the lessons his mother taught. She so thoroughly shaped his character that in later years he "refused to be called the son of Pharaoh's daughter. . . ." What were the "wages" this mother received? . . . the only reward that motherhood has ever asked; the privilege of loving, and of giving . . . and that she had been a successful mother. The little lad she carried in her arms grew to manhood and blessed the world.—Edwin W. Parker

1498

On Mother's Day one of the girls in the House of Neighborly Service in California was pinning red carnations on the children. Said one little girl: "You'd better give me a white one. As far as church is concerned, I'm an orphan. Mother and Daddy never come with me."—Annual Report Presbyterian Board of National Missions

1499

In the job of homekeeping there is no raise from the boss, and seldom praise from others to show us we have hit the mark. Except for the child, woman's creation is so often invisible, especially today.—Anne Morrow Lindbergh

NATURE

1500

Dr. Willard Fetter, of Akron, reports a scoutmaster as telling his cub scouts to remember "that in the woods we are the guests of the animals and trees and plants." I like that!

A refined person is very careful of the house and furniture where he is being entertained. He handles objects with even more care than if they were his own. Likewise, as guests of God, we are courtesy-bound to conserve the resources of God's good earth, its forests, its soil, its oil, its water power, that we may leave to our posterity a land richer than we found. We . . . sometimes act as if our country's wealth was inexhaustible and also wholly our own. Not so! . . . "The earth is the Lord's and the fulness thereof." Let us not forget that basic truth.—Ralph W. Sockman, *National Radio Pulpit*

1501

No adult can possibly be as wise as a happy child can be. Coming home from church services Sunday night, our family paused in the snow for a moment to study the star-gemmed sky. "Goodness!" breathed our Babe, after an appreciative silence. "If heaven is that beautiful on the bottom, just think how wonderful the other side must be!" —Burton Hillis, *Better Homes & Gardens*

1502

A New York youngster, who was more accustomed to man-made wonders than the marvels of nature, was treated to a vacation in the country. There he saw his first rainbow. The attitude of the child, as he gazed upon the gorgeous phenomenon, was one of wonder and perplexity. "Mother," he finally commented, "it's very beautiful, but what is it supposed to advertise?"— *Capper's Weekly*

1503

Our Father in heaven, Lord of the field and the stream,
The sun and the clouds, we thank Thee for the revelations
Of Thy power in all growing things. We invoke Thy blessing
Upon the efforts of men to harness and control the floods
That they may give unto the fields that which is necessary to sustain life.
The winds are in Thy hand, O God; bridle and bind them,
That they may not come forth to destroy the labors of the ploughman,
Nor to defeat the farmer of his hopes. Grant unto all who dwell
On this Thy Holy Earth wisdom to understand Thy laws,
And to cooperate with Thy wise ordering of this world.
Give to our statesmen the will to make just and righteous laws
Regarding the lands. Give to the farmers the desire to preserve
This Holy Earth that future generations may know its fruits.
Grant that the harvests of these fields may not make men selfish
But that it may bring good health and abundant Christian living
To this people, according to Thy will as revealed in the life
Of Thy Son our Saviour and Lord, even Jesus Christ in whose name we pray. Amen.

—E. Paul Hovey, at dedication of Angostura Dam in the Black Hills

NEGATIVE

1504

So few of us really think: what we do is rearrange our prejudices.—George Vincent

1505

While the noisy axle may receive grease, it may also be seriously considered for replacement because of unusual wear.—Douglas Meador

1506

There is a story about a football player who raced sixty or seventy yards through a broken field for the winning touchdown. . . . A few days later his coach was reviewing films of the game and three times he stopped the projector to point out flaws in the lad's technique. . . . "You should have cut to your right there," he'd say, or "You broke away from your blockers there. . . ." "Yes sir, coach," the player responded as he watched his image cross the goal line. "But how was it for distance?"

1507

The man whose spiritual state lies somewhere in the vasty region between the apostates on the one hand, and the martyrs on the other, reads the words which St. John had for the church of Laodicea and thinks that the judgment was in excess of the crime. The only fault that God could find with the Laodiceans was that they were tepid: . . . We feel uneasy about this decision because most of us are also lukewarm, neither missionaries nor confidence men, neither ascetics nor bon vivants, and we need a little mercy in the matter.—Paul Elmen, *The Restoration of Meaning to Contemporary Life*

1508

Shun idleness. It is a rust that attaches itself to the most brilliant metals.—Voltaire

1509

Too many people are thinking of security instead of opportunity. They seem more afraid of life than death.—James F. Byrnes

1510

The essence of the Christian gospel is anything but negative.—Charles Templeton, *Life Looks Up*

NEIGHBOR

1511

Love your neighbor, but be careful of your neighborhood.—John Hay

1512

We can never be the better for our religion if our neighbor is the worse for it.

1513

It is very easy to manage our neighbor's business, but our own sometimes bothers us.—Josh Billings

1514

When I grow up I am going to have a big house, not with green trees and grass about it like ours, but right in among the crowded little homes of poor people, and be neighbors with them.—Jane Addams

1515

A good neighbor is a fellow whose garden you can view with anticipation instead of jealousy.—Burton Hillis, *Better Homes & Gardens*

1516

It is so much easier to make up your mind that your neighbor is good for nothing, than to enter into all the circumstances that would oblige you to modify that opinion.—George Eliot

1517

What a great deal of ease that man gains who lets his neighbor's behavior alone and takes care that his own actions are honest.—Marcus Aurelius field of human endeavor.—Charles F. Kettering

NEW YEAR

1518

Back in the seventeenth century, Samuel Daniel, a minor poet, wrote two lines that mark his genius and are for us a clue to the year we wish to make. "Unless above himself he can erect himself, how poor a thing is man." It was a striking way of saying that unless we reach for the stars, compete against ourselves, and climb from day to day from where we are to where we can be, we are poor indeed.

Yesterday's mistakes and failures can teach us wisdom and yesterday's triumphs can suggest what is possible. We can make the year ahead glorious. . . .—Harold Blake Walker, *Specialty Salesman*

1519

We do the same as last year: when we have not grown any; when we have no desire to improve; when we have no goal.

1520

The fatality of good resolutions is that they are always too late.—Oscar Wilde

1521

"We are reading the first verse of the first chapter of a book whose pages are infinite. . . ." I do not know who wrote these words. But I have always liked them as a reminder that the future can be anything we want to make it. . . . The past is gone and static. Nothing we do can change it. The future is before us and dynamic. Everything we do will affect it. Each day brings with it new frontiers, in our homes and in our businesses, if we will only recognize them. We are just at the beginning of progress in every

1522

God make your year a happy one— Not by shielding you from all sorrow and pain, but by strengthening you to bear it if it comes. Not by making your path easy, but by making you sturdy enough to tread any path. Not by taking hardships from you, but by taking all cowardice and fear from your heart as you need hardships. Not by granting you unbroken sunshine, but by keeping your face bright even in the shadows. Not by making your life always pleasant, but by showing you where man and his cause need you most and by making you zealous to be there and to help. Not by keeping you from battle, but by bringing you off every field more than conqueror through Christ "Who loves you."—Cleland B. McAfee

1523

In Philippians, Paul says he forgets "the things which are behind" by "stretching forward to the things which are before." One can't forget by keeping his mind on the things he desires to forget, but by engaging his attention with something else . . . forgetting doesn't eliminate . . . the necessity of some remembering . . . but we must forget in the sense of ceasing to give primary attention to certain things. . . . Perhaps . . . if we will only forget ourselves, we will probably forget all things that ought to be pushed far out of the field of active consciousness. For dwelling too much upon successes, failures, sins, sorrows, and unpleasantness is simply thinking too much about ourselves. So Jesus taught that if we forget ourselves by giving ourselves to the Kingdom of God with utter abandon and complete indifference to what happens to us, we will find the pearl of great price.—Ilion T. Jones, *Presbyterian Tribune*

1524

Of seasons and of holidays and of fleeting occasions. . . . We make much of the year ending and the year's beginning, as though the stroke of midnight, by some strange alchemy, transformed the world and all the universe. But with all the changing times and seasons there are in the heavens those things which change not and are eternal.

These are the things that cause the world to keep its balance and cause men to return to moderation, despite the strange doctrine, false teachings, and ill-conceived schemes which trouble this age and generation.—Richard I. Evans, "Unto These Hills"

1525

The famous St. Gotthard Tunnel through the Alps was opened on a New Year's Day. Travelers entering it for the first time had no idea what to expect at the other end. So it is with a new year. As it is entered, no one knows what will have happened when the end is reached—decisions, new responsibilities, disappointments perhaps. Much can occur in 365 days. How desirable it is to begin the new year with God!—Ruth Bernice Mead

1526

As a new year dawns, we stand before an open door. Looking through its arch, we see all things new. Behind us the door is closing—closing forever . . . sealed to everything save our memories. Before us lies the new— "new fields of service for our God and fellow men." . . . A challenge to . . . the best living we can manage to achieve. "No one," said Charles Lamb, "ever regarded the first of January with indifference." No year . . . is likely to be any better than we try to make it . . . any one of us can take a new year and make it worse or better.—E. Paul Hovey, *Today*

1527

It is typical of the insecurity in which the children of men have always lived that every new year is an adventure into which we must, as Abraham of old, go out, not knowing whither we go. . . . The faith by which those live who are informed by a Biblical religion that a Divine Providence does govern, enables them to approach the future with serenity rather than hysteria, knowing that "neither death, nor life . . . nor things present, nor things to come . . . shall be able to separate us from the love of God."—Reinhold Niebuhr

NORMAL

1528

Most of us have never lived in normal times.—Statement of Youth

1529

Life is made up, not of great sacrifices or duties, but of little things, in which smiles and kindnesses and small obligations, given habitually, are what win and preserve the heart and secure comfort.—Sir Humphrey Davy

1530

We let the boys at our camp ranch do as they please, as long as they please to do right.—Jesse G. Arnold

1531

One sign of maturity is the ability to be comfortable with people who are not like us.—Virgil A. Kraft

NOTHING

1532

A hole is nothing at all, but you can break your neck in it.—Austin O'Malley, *Keystones of Thought*

1533

American court procedure proved a little puzzling to the Oriental mind of Lung Poon, although he had spent twenty-four of his sixty-three years in this country. Arraigned on a charge, he understood only with difficulty when his interpreter explained that the judge would appoint an attorney free of charge. Assured there would be no fee, he then demanded assurance that the lawyer would win the case.

That of course was impossible, the court pointed out, so Lung Poon reconsidered his plea. "Something for nothing is never so good," he stated. "I think I plead guilty and save time."

1534

Censorship is like an appendix. When it does nothing, it is quite useless. When it is active, it's dangerous. —Pierre Mendes

OBEDIENCE

1535

No principle is more noble than that of true obedience.—Henry Giles

1536

The first boy in Jesus' parable (Matthew 21:28-31) was at least honest and did not intend to promise what he was not going to fulfill. It was only after he thought about it carefully that he saw that he had not treated his father very well, and that he owed him this day's work in the vineyard. Out of his obedience he found the way to a right relationship with his father. He discovered the real test of any man's life . . . the ultimate test in our Lord's teaching seems to be obedience and little else. If our modern critics regard us as having too much activism in our religion, the answer is that activism seems to be at the very heart of the gospel as it was taught by our Lord.— Gerald Kennedy

1537

We are not here to get our rights; we are not to defend ourselves; we are here to render our service. We are to give rights—not to get them. So we may feel the injustice done to others, where we will not allow ourselves to feel the injustice done to ourselves.— Cleland B. McAfee, *Studies in the Sermon on the Mount*

1538

I was ready to give up. With my cup of coffee sitting untouched before me, I tried to think of a way to move out of the picture without appearing a coward. In this state of exhaustion, when my courage had all but gone, I decided to take my problem to God. With my head in my hands, I bowed over the kitchen table and prayed aloud. The words I spoke to God that midnight are still vivid in my memory. "I am here taking a stand for what I believe is right. But now I am afraid. The people are looking to me for leadership, and if I stand before them without strength and courage, they too will falter. . . . I've come to the point where I can't face it alone."

At this moment I experienced the presence of the Divine as I had never experienced Him before. It seemed as though I could hear the quiet assurance of an inner voice saying: "Stand up for righteousness, and stand up for truth; and God will be at your side forever."—Martin Luther King, Jr., *Stride Toward Freedom*

OBSTACLES

1539

Obstacles are those frightful things you see when you take your eyes off the goal.—Hannah More

1540

What on earth would a man do with himself if something did not stand in his way?—H. G. Wells

OPINION

1541

We pick our friends, by and large, because they agree with us. When you think of it, you rarely associate with anyone who disagrees with you—because the way friendships are formed is around agreement. But the newspapers and the radio intrude upon us with different opinions. As a matter of fact, the only way we occasionally know other people's minds is through the mass media.—Paul F. Lazarsfeld

1542

The difficult part in an argument is not to defend one's opinion, but rather to know it.—André Maurois

1543

The fellow who stands high in his own estimation is still a long way from the top.

1544

Partisanship is what someone else does. When I do it, it is taking a stand.—Roger L. Shinn

OPPORTUNITY

1545

I remind myself of the solemn yet hopeful aphorism that man's extremity is God's opportunity. . . . Why should we not accept with unmistakable conviction the other part of this vital aphorism, that it is God's design to utilize the present time of man's extremity as opportunity?—John R. Mott

1546

The wise man will make more opportunities than he finds.—Francis Bacon

1547

A problem is an opportunity in work clothes.—Henry J. Kaiser, Jr.

1548

A chaotic time such as ours presents not only the *need* of discerning the abiding amid the transitory, but as well the opportunity of discerning it. —Harry Emerson Fosdick

OPTIMIST

1549

Nothing contributes more to cheerfulness than the habit of looking at the good side of things. The good side is God's side of them.—Ullathorne

1550

I believe that if you think about disaster, you will get it. Brood about death and you hasten your demise. Think positively and masterfully, with confidence and faith, and life becomes more secure, more fraught with action, richer in achievement and experience. —Eddie Rickenbacker

1551

A single sunbeam is enough to drive away many shadows.—Francis of Assisi

ORGANIZATION

1552

Organization! What a word! Used as an end in itself, I have seen it become a weight tied to the ankle of progress and initiative. But—used as a means to an end greater than itself, I have seen it serve as wings to lift the spirit of man on his way to Life itself.

1553

Our large organizations endanger and deceive their members, not by indecency and terror, but precisely by amiability and good will. . . . We remain the children of organization, not the masters of it.—David Riesman

1554

The newly elected secretary of the Baptist Church's young people was told one of her duties was to record the minutes of each meeting. Her second day on the job, she was called upon to read the minutes.

"Minutes of the last meeting," she said, "twenty minutes, six seconds." Then she sat down.

1555

One of the reasons why the Ten Commandments are so short and to the point is the fact they were given direct and did not come out of committees. —H. G. Hutcheson, *Gazette,* Augusta, Kansas

1556

Our three-year-old had received her first batch of modeling clay. I showed her how to play with it, and made samples of various simple shapes—a ball, a ring, a triangle—then went about my work.

But our good Methodist daughter felt there was one shape I had not demonstrated. She came into the kitchen bearing a wad of clay. "Please, Mommy," she asked, "make an Official Board."—Mrs. Lyle Williams, *Together*

PARENTS

1557

Children do need to be guided and reminded and corrected—no matter how well disposed they are—and that's the parents' job.—B. Spock, M.D.

1558

There is increasing acceptance of the fact that the job of parent education is not to supply information but to change feelings and attitudes and, in turn, behavior.—Ruth Andrus

1559

Dr. Barbara Biber gave the specialists one of the biggest laughs of the meeting with her story of the middle-aged matron who had never tasted the white meat of chicken. It seems a worthy wife and mother was asked at a dinner party which she preferred, the white or the dark, and threw her host into confusion by saying she really didn't know.

"You see," she told him simply, "when I was a child, my father used to carve the chicken. He'd ask all the adults which they preferred, and of course they said the white meat. So I was always served dark. Now I'm married and my husband carves. He asks the children which they prefer and of course they say the white. And so I've never tasted the white meat of chicken."

The moral of her parable, Dr. Biber was quick to add, is: Parents today, the older ones certainly and many of the younger ones too, represent a transition generation. Under the circumstances, she said, "We must be forgiving of our own errors. We are trying to live a life with our children that we have never tasted."—Dorothy Barclay, *The New York Times Magazine*

1560

There ought to be an organization of Parents Anonymous, those who have fought and won the battle of saying "No!" and sticking to it. Then, when some parent finds himself slipping, he could call for reinforcements.—Marcelene Cox

1561

All parents are amateurs who start out knowing nothing of this complex and delicate job. By the time they have acquired a few rudiments, their children have grown up and the job is over. Parenthood is a profession by no means conducive to learning on the job. There is hardly time for such refinements.

It suddenly becomes a matter of life and death to young Johnny that he be permitted to accompany some friends on a boating trip. Shall his parents grant this desire, which is a matter of almost unbearable importance to Johnny, or shall they follow the dictates of their adult caution, which tells them that Johnny, being unable to swim, stands far too great a chance of drowning?

This is not an easy decision, but it has to be made—and made at once. I sometimes marvel, considering the inexperience of parents and the terrible risks that hinge on their every blundering move, that children ever grow up at all.—Joseph N. Welch, "You Can't Teach Children Anything," *McCall's Magazine*

PATRIOTISM

1562

The degree of our patriotism can be measured by our faithfulness in measuring up to this responsibility. Samuel Johnson once said, "Patriotism is the last refuge of a scoundrel." Although every generation has seen examples of self-seekers wildly waving banners . . . the fact remains that genuine patriotism is a major Christian virtue. . . . Patriotism is not making a loud noise on the Fourth of July. It is not preaching a selfish and narrow Americanism. It is not pride in mere material prosperity. It is not boastful of American superiority. . . . Patriotism is hearing the call of God and following the providential guidance of God amid the perplexing problems of our day. Patriotism is allegiance to the teachings of Jesus Christ. . . . Patriotism is carrying our religious loyalty into all the practical affairs of government.—William P. King, *Adult Student*

1563

To love one's country, it is not necessary to hate others.

PEACE

1564

As we study New Testament Christianity, we are aware that there is an inner core of tranquility and stability . . . it was not mere absence of strife or conflict, [but] a positive peace, a solid foundation which held fast amid all the turmoil of human experience. —J. B. Phillips, *New Testament Christianity*

1565

Peace, as Jesus would identify it, is more than outward conformity to a principle of nonviolence but rather an inward recognition of the principle of good will toward all men. The peace our Lord will share can be received whenever we will make ourselves ready. The world can be full of evil as was the world of Jesus' day—and still we can individually know this peace of our Master. —James O. York

1566

There is still the voice crying through the vista of time, saying to every potential Peter, "Put up your sword." History is replete with the bleached bones of nations; history is cluttered with the wreckage of communities that failed to follow this command. So violence is not the way.—Martin Luther King, Jr.

1567

We seek peace—enduring peace. More than an end to war, we want an end to the beginnings of all wars. . . . Today we are faced with the preëminent fact that if civilization is to survive, we must cultivate the science of human relationships—the ability of all peoples, of all kinds, to live together in the same world.—Franklin D. Roosevelt

1568

Fascism believes neither in the desirability nor the possibility of perpetual peace. War alone brings to its highest tension all human energy and puts the stamp of nobility upon the people who have the courage to engage in it. —Mussolini

1569

If we pulled together as much to put over a siege of peace as we do a spell of war, we would be sitting pretty. Peace is kinda like prosperity: There is mighty few nations that can stand it. —Will Rogers

1570

We should remember that while modern developments have made war more terrible they have also made the consequences of retreat and surrender more terrible.—John Foster Dulles

1571

I have made a pilgrimage to Hiroshima. In the center of the city they have kept the ghostly, twisted ruins of the former exhibition hall and have made it a permanent exhibition of death, idiocy, and shame. A wire fence has been erected around the ruin. As it stands, it is to be the central memorial. On a standard outside, designating the mass of horror, is one word only, inscribed in large, bold letters. The word is Peace.—Charles T. Leber, *Christian World Facts*

PERFECTION

1572

Grandma's remark stuck by me. "Perfection takes only a few minutes longer. . . ." Perfection, after carelessness, too much longer . . . I was thankful I had learned how to make perfect stitches . . . perfection is sewing . . . perfection is developing character . . . takes longer, but it is worth while. "Be ye therefore perfect," said the only perfect man. . . . God has outlined for us the blueprint, the pattern, of perfection for our lives. . . . —Kathleen Barron

1573

Man's sin ever needs a double cure, moral renewal as well as forgiveness, purity of life as well as release from guilt. . . . God's grace is utterly transforming and perfecting and is able to bring man to realize the purpose of life in becoming a child of God.—Paul W. Hoon, *The Interpreter's Bible*

POLITICS

1574

Influencing political life is basically a spiritual matter, and we need to help our ministers to preach a more complete love and to inspire us to a more complete love.—Layman, at a conference on "Churchman as Citizen"

1575

I would rather that the people should wonder why I wasn't president than why I am.—Salmon P. Chase

1576

A church which has nothing to say on political, economic and international issues abandons God and betrays the people.—Alan Walker

1577

Why are the churches in politics? They want to help shape the future conditions of human life and to shape them so that men and women and children may live more abundantly.— Fred Eastman, "The Minister and Politics," *Information Service*

1578

One of the difficult responsibilities of the Christian citizen is that of bearing his share in party politics, and yet doing so from a Christian rather than a secular perspective.—Robert E. Fitch, "Politics in Christian Perspective"

1579

I lean to the idea that politics is an art. When we speak of a science, we think of something that can be measured at all times. There are too many intangibles in politics, like human nature and human progress.—Leonard W. Hall

1580

I believe that politics is a science. It's a scientific approach to handling human beings.—James A. Farley

1581

You can't beat an administration by attacking it. You have to show some plan of improving it.—Will Rogers

1582

A politician was asked how he stood on an issue. He replied: "Some of my friends are for it, some of my friends are against it and I'm for my friends."

1583

No political campaign ever ought to justify putting the Sermon on the Mount and the Ten Commandments in some moral deep-freeze.—Richard L. Neuberger, *Saturday Review*

1584

Directives range from the familiar "The church should stick to religion and stay out of politics," to "Nothing in the sight of God should be outside the church's interest."—Charles Y. Glock, *Information Service*

1585

The American people have a very strong desire to declare themselves on principles. . . . They think and talk politics in terms of men, not issues. . . . Very few Americans have any conception of political parties as the bases

of policy making and integration in government. . . . Because he thinks of politics as essentially corrupt, the average man is reluctant to turn over to government the handling of his responsibilities and rights. He constantly struggles to keep government to a minimum and hold the reins of power in individual hands.—William Muehl, *Politics for Christians*

1586

Members of churches are urged to bring issues . . . on the basis of high Christian principle, to party leaders and candidates for office. They should appeal to the political parties to affirm high standards in their platforms and to observe them in their campaigns. Above all, Christians should recall that they have fallen far short of the goals which have been formulated in the name of our Christian faith. We are challenged by this new opportunity provided by the forthcoming elections to act more truly in line with our Christian duty.—General Board of the National Council of Churches

1587

Surely we are in error if we think that our main business is to exhort the Christian citizen to assume his duties as a citizen, to take part in party politics, to study the issues, and then to vote. That he will do this much we ought to be able to take for granted. The critical issue lies not in his participation in politics but in his transcendence over it, not in conviction but in humility, not in commitment but in retaining the capacity for criticism.—Robert E. Fitch, *Christian Century*

1588

The best Christian thought has never been willing to exclude any area of life from the formulations of theology. . . . The necessity for relating the Christian faith to the political process is no less urgent today than in the past.

If anything, it is more pressing. The obvious reason for saying this is, of course, the constantly increasing role of government in our highly organized and integrated society. Scores of relationships which were only recently personal in character are now carried on through political channels.—William Muehl, *Politics for Christians*

1589

"Should a Christian become active in one of the major parties?" William Muehl asks. The answer: "He most certainly should, unless he can show a compelling reason for choosing some other means of discharging his responsibility to the realm of politics and some more effective means of witnessing to his faith amid the turmoil and need of social complexity. The burden of proof is on the one who stays outside of a party, not the one who goes in." —*Information Service*

1590

No shoulders can carry responsible burdens if they are already loaded with partisan chips.—Governor Abraham Ribicoff

1591

The only ones who know all the answers are politicians out of a job. —Charles E. Wilson

1592

The advice of Prime Minister Robert Menzies, of Australia, to politicians is: "It is better to be dull than crooked."

1593

Every politician in this country who has presumed upon the meanness of the people has come to grief.—John Burroughs

1594

It is our duty as patriots to cast out this un-American doctrine and rebuke those who have raised the torch of intolerance. All believers in any faith can unite and go forward in our political work to bring about the maximum amount of happiness for our people. —Senator George W. Norris

POWER

1595

A hundred years or more ago, our statesmen dealt frankly and confidently with the realities of power. The Monroe Doctrine, the diplomacy of westward expansion, the encouragement of the political separation of this hemisphere from Europe—all involved realistic power considerations. Then came a time when the "consciousness of the power factor" seemed to slip from our minds. Americans wanted their statesmanship, like their architecture in the Victorian Age, impressive and unfunctional, "with the emphasis on outward appearance rather than inner reality." Satisfied with our own borders, we falsely assumed that other people were, or ought to be, satisfied with theirs. Our foreign policy became a vain search for a contractual framework to perpetuate the status quo. We withdrew from the realities of power to a dream world of arbitration treaties and of utopian schemes for disarmament, the outlawry of war, and international organization. We were blind to the things that were happening in the real world of power relationships. Until almost too late, we missed the significance of the rising power of Germany, Japan and Russia. The price we paid was two World Wars and an even more perilous cold one.—Benjamin H. Brown, *The New Leader*

1596

Where there is power . . . men will try to use it for their own ends, good and bad. For a long while Jehovah was not conceived as either good or bad; He was only Force—the lightnings playing about the cloudy head of Sinai. And just as today we employ the force of atomic fission alike to kill or cure, so men used Jehovah.—Joy Davidman, *Smoke on the Mountain*

1597

Power is a relative thing, and no nation, or group of nations, can become relatively stronger without making other nations relatively weaker. If each nation had sought to excel in the arts, in learning or well-being, its success would not have meant failure for the others. But with each nation . . . aiming at an increase in power, we have entered an era of perpetual warfare . . . burdensome and fruitless.—Glenn E. Hoover, "The Century of the Common Man," *Vital Speeches*

1598

The state and the church each has its own sphere in government committed to it by God, and neither may take to itself the jurisdiction of the other. There is, Calvin says in the *Institutes* in the section on discipline, a great distinction between the ecclesiastical and the civil power. For the church has no power of the sword to punish or to coerce, no authority to compel, no prisons, fines or other punishments like those inflicted by the civil magistrate. Besides, the object of this power is not that he who has transgressed may be punished against his will, but that he may profess his repentance by a voluntary submission to chastisement.—T. H. L. Parker, *Portrait of Calvin*

1599

Power is an emotionally charged word. When we possess it we call it *influence,* but when it is held by someone else we are content to use the ugly word. Yet there is nothing wrong with power; it takes power to get things done. Power is the application of intel-

ligence to force. A river may be a terrific force, but it develops power only when directed through a turbine. —Arthur F. Corey, *National Parent-Teacher*

1600

Do you remember who remarked that "in union there is strength"? All the political leaders of the world have realized that, as Longfellow wrote in "Hiawatha": "All your strength is in your union; all your danger is in discord."

The slogan of one ruthless dictator who wanted to conquer Europe was, "Divide and conquer." He knew that when the people of a country quarreled among themselves, they became easy victims of their enemies. Lincoln knew, too, that the Union must be preserved if our great country were to survive and become the kind of nation that our forefathers intended it to become.

All these rulers, however, both the good and the bad, were talking about union for *material* power. Many years before their time, Jesus talked about union for *spiritual* power, which is the greatest force in the world. No material power can destroy a spiritual force, or even make an impression upon it.

PRAYER

1601

Prayer is essentially the outreach of our finite spirits to the infinite and eternal Spirit. A great mystic called it a flight from the vanity of time into the richness of eternity. Prayer is the movement of our whole personality, our emotions, our minds, and our wills toward the one immanent and transcendent Personality. Prayer is not so much an act as an attitude. It is the desire and purpose to cooperate as fully as we can with the will and purpose of God.—Gilbert Cox, *Adult Student*

1602

It has been said that prayer is often "plain, manly determination heading in the right direction." If I could get one message over to the youth of this world, it would be that success in life does not depend on genius. Any young man of ordinary intelligence, who is morally sound, aboveboard in his dealings, and not afraid of work, should succeed in spite of obstacles and handicaps, if he plays the game fairly and keeps everlastingly at it.—J. C. Penney, *Rotarian*

1603

The prayers of an old man are the only contributions left in his power. —Thomas Jefferson

1604

Prayer is not using God; it is more often to get us in a position where God can use us. I watched the deck hands on the great liner *United States,* as they docked that ship in New York Harbor. First, they threw out a rope to the men on the dock. Then inside the boat the great motors went to work and pulled on the great cable. But oddly enough, the pier wasn't pulled out to the ship; but the ship was pulled snugly up to the pier. Prayer is the rope that pulls God and man together. But it doesn't pull God down to us: it pulls us to Him. We must learn to say with Christ, the master of the art of praying, "Not my will; but thine be done."—Billy Graham

1605

Seven days without prayer makes one weak.—Allen E. Bartlett

1606

It takes a lot of courage to ask God through prayer when you know He will reply. Is God such a stranger that I hesitate to ask Him anything? It takes more faith to receive God's answer than to ask of Him in the first place.— Leonard G. Clough

1607

Give me a heart too brave to ask Thee anything.—John Galsworthy

1608

One of the difficulties encountered by United States Ambassador Page during the First World War was the problem of keeping in touch with Washington from London. But we, all of whom are ambassadors of Christ in the world, need have no such difficulty. The channel of prayer is always open, and the Holy Spirit is always at hand to hear and answer.—John H. Jowett

1609

Let us pray for ourselves that we may adjust ourselves and our attitudes to harmonize with this new spirit that proceeds from the United Nations. The story is told that an elderly lady, visiting New York, went to pay her respects to the United Nations. She asked to be shown the UN flag, and remarked, "The United Nations is such a wonderful organization that I should like to display its flag in my living room." When she saw the flag, however, she exclaimed, "Oh, this is a beautiful flag, but it would clash with the color scheme in my living room; can I get it in another color?" The clerk explained that that was impossible, and very politely suggested, "Perhaps it would be easier to change the color scheme in your living room."—Julius Kerman

1610

How deeply rooted must unbelief be in our hearts when we are surprised to find our prayers answered.—Julius Hare

1611

Lypiatt Cathedral had its own distinctive odor. It was as if the prayers of the faithful throughout history had not all ascended to God, but had become wedged in the rafters and gone bad up there.—Joyce Warren, *The New Yorker*

1612

I don't expect God to give me a victory if I pray for one, because the opposing pitcher might be praying for victory, too. But I do pray for strength and courage and foresight to set a good example for the boys who might want to walk in my footsteps. I also pray that I shall not let my teammates down by being careless, lazy, selfish, or inconsiderate. I'm sure that prayer helps me do my job the way I feel it should be done.—Carl Erskine, "Little Leaguer," *Family Circle*

1613

We need to watch our wishes if that saying by Elizabeth Barrett Browning is true: "Every wish is like a prayer to God."

1614

Prayer is blasphemy if it does not alter your life.—Charles Templeton

1615

A prayer in which the Kingdom is never mentioned is no true prayer.—Saying of Ancient Rabbis

1616

Witches are reported . . . to say the Lord's Prayer backward. Are there not many who, though they do not pronounce the syllables of the Lord's Prayer retrograde . . . yet they transpose it in effect, desiring their daily bread, before God's Kingdom come, preferring temporal benefits before heavenly blessings. Oh! If every one by this mark should be tried for a witch, how hard would it go with all of us.—Thomas Fuller

1617

Praying is dangerous business. Results do come.—G. Christie Swain

1618

Do we pray only at night, thinking that like the telegram, the rates are cheaper? It may cost more to pray in the daytime, but again, like the telegram, the message gets there quicker.

1619

Prayer is the chief agency and activity whereby men align themselves with God's purpose. Prayer does not consist in battering the walls of heaven for personal benefits or the success of our plans. Rather is it the committing of ourselves for the carrying out of His purposes. It is a telephone call to headquarters for orders. It is not bending God's will to ours, but our will to God's. In prayer, we tap vast reservoirs of spiritual power whereby God can find fuller entrance into the hearts of men.—G. Ashton Oldham

1620

Edmund Gosse tells in his autobiography, *Father and Son,* how as a boy he wished to go to a birthday party of which his father disapproved. "Lay the matter before the Lord," the elder Gosse admonished, evidently thinking this to be a subtle use of discipline. But when little Edmund emerged, he showed that he too had learned guile, and forthrightly piped: "The Lord says I may go!"—John Charles Wynn, *How Christian Parents Face Family Problems*

1621

Solitude gave God a chance to teach me the power of prayer. God laughs. Who can take freedom from a Christian? We all have a part to play in the world where He is making all the moves. "Truth is on the scaffold"; we would be willing to suffer if we knew truth would win.—Sara Perkins (a missionary captured by the Communists)

1622

The young salesman came to his minister with a problem. "I'd like to get married, sir," the young man confessed, "but I'm not making enough money to support a wife, and my girl is getting tired of waiting. What should I do?"

The minister thought for a while and then suggested that the young man pray for a raise.

"Oh, no! I couldn't do that," was the answer. "My boss doesn't like anyone to go over his head!"—Antonio Martinelli

1623

The practice of alternation was the secret of Jesus' spiritual growth; He alternated between intense activity in ministering to people and periods of withdrawal in solitude, silence and prayer. To His hours of reflection He brought the tragedies and sorrows of His countrymen, and to His days of toil in their behalf He brought power from the hilltop. Concern made it easy to pray, and prayer deepened concern. —Kirby Page, *The Creative Revolution of Jesus*

1624

Adelaide Kerr asked Reinhold Niebuhr, "Is there a right and wrong way to pray?" Dr. Niebuhr answered: "The right prayer concentrates on the glory and majesty of God and sublimates itself. Every prayer we make should begin with thanksgiving, praise, adoration, and reverence for God. Next we should express our repentance and contrition for our mistakes. Then we may pray for our right work and for character: integrity, courage, wisdom and strength. Finally, we should commit our day and our lives to God's will.

"I think it is wrong to pray for success in a business enterprise. It is selfish to pray for yourself. You are using God when you pray for your own ends. It cheapens prayer when people pray for trivial ends like success in a business deal; but it does not cheapen prayer when they pray for what they regard as ultimate ends: integrity, courage and wisdom. I believe that prayer for oneself should be only within the limits of Jesus' prayer: 'Father, if thou be willing, remove this cup from me: nevertheless not my will but thine, be done.' "

1625

Personal prayer, it seems to me, is one of the simple necessities of life, as basic to the individual as sunshine, food and water—and at times, of course, more so. By prayer I believe we mean an effort to get in touch with the Infinite. We know that our prayers are imperfect. Of course they are. We are imperfect human beings. A thousand experiences have convinced me beyond room of doubt that prayer multiplies the strength of the individual and brings within the scope of his capabilities almost any conceivable objective.—Dwight D. Eisenhower

1626

It may be that we should at times say, "let us open our eyes as we pray," rather than the traditional, "Let us close our eyes and bow in prayer." A deaf woman told of "hearing" her minister pray for the first time because he asked them to open their eyes. She read his lips during the sermon but had always dutifully bowed her head and thus had never "heard" his prayers. —E. Paul Hovey

1627

I do a full day of work in the office, run a six-room house with two active sons, and consider it easy. My wife has been ill for years, but my house could stand a "white-glove" inspection any Sunday afternoon. I also have found time to canvass neighbors in support of a school-bond issue, and to serve as treasurer of a Boy Scout troop and as a P.T.A. committeeman. My secret? Two fine sons and organization, partly. But the real answer is that we three take time *every* day for prayer. God does the rest. If everybody would spend a few minutes daily in quiet self-inspection and rearrangement of real values, homes would be homes: places where each member of the family gathers strength for next day.—John Burrill

PREACHING

1628

Preaching . . . means God's way of meeting the needs of sinful men through the proclamation of His revealed truth by one of His chosen messengers. Not as a scientific definition, but as a working description, this account shows why those evangelical preachers looked on their calling as second to no other on earth, and on their preaching as a privilege that angels might covet. Preaching as the proclamation of God's revealed truth means that the man in the pulpit makes known to others what he has received from God, mainly through the written Word, and there through the guidance of the Holy Spirit, in response to the prayer of faith.—Andrew W. Blackwood, *Christianity Today*

1629

It takes a great amount of skill to take the gospel and make it boring, tedious and dull. We can do this only because we have a long background of boring tradition.—Tom Allan

1630

I never see my preacher's eyes
Tho' they with light may shine—
For when he prays he closes his,
And when he preaches, mine!
—Complaint of a "Man in the Pew"

PREJUDICE

1631

If you have any attitude or any thoughts about it, you are prejudiced.

And why not? There are only two ways to be quite unprejudiced and impartial. One is to be completely ignorant. The other is to be completely indifferent. Bias and prejudice are attitudes to be kept in hand, not attitudes to be avoided.—Charles P. Curtis

1632

Prejudices, it is well known, are most difficult to eradicate from the heart whose soil has never been loosened or fertilized by education; they grow there, firm as weeds among stones.—Charlotte Brontë, *Jane Eyre*

1633

I am not unmindful, as a Southerner, of the force of this virus of prejudice. I know, however, that there is a cure for this virus, and that is our faith. As pastor of your souls, I am happy to take the responsibility for any evil which might result from different races worshiping God together, but I would be unwilling to take the responsibility of those who refuse to worship God with a person of another race.—Bishop Vincent S. Waters

1634

The tight skirts of prejudice impede the steps of progress.—Karl K. Quimby

1635

Sometimes man is his own worst enemy . . . this invariably comes . . . with prejudice. We pick up a book which could be helpful, but because we are prejudiced by the title or author we will not read it. . . . There are those in any community who could give guidance to civic betterment, but their offer is met with a shrug and a cynical turn of the head, as if to say, "Can any good thing come out of Nazareth?"

Prejudice is generally incorrect. History shows that prejudices against certain individuals and movements were wrong. The word Quaker was a reproach hurled at the followers of George Fox. Today the word Quaker is a badge of honor. . . . The word Christian was a sneer addressed to the followers of Jesus. Today we bless God to be numbered among them.

People who live with prejudices invariably betray a fear that what they hold may not be true. They are afraid lest someone deprive them of something which they are loath to give up; so they build walls around it. But truth never needs to be afraid of light. It can defend itself and is its own virtue. Prejudice can only be overcome by the constant day by day pressure of good will. Deliberate and constant appreciation of others breaks down ultimately every intolerance.—Archie H. Hook, *The Congregational Way*

1636

An interesting discussion was started at a banquet attended by the late Glenn Frank on the subject of cancer research . . . which continued . . . until two o'clock in the morning. President Frank returned to the University of Wisconsin impressed with the objective and logical thinking of these men. He concluded that if science developed logical objective and analytical thinking such as he had heard, all the students at Wisconsin should take courses in science. Some time later he was in Chicago in attendance at another banquet. It so happened that the men who were at his table that night instead of talking about cancer research, discussed problems in the field of politics and government. Dr. Frank said he could hardly believe his ears for these same men who had been so objective and scientific in the field of cancer research, in the field of politics and government reacted on the basis of prejudices. All of us are more or less limited in knowledge and as a result we react on the basis of prejudice.

1637

Because we have had an experience and found it to be good, we become prejudiced into feeling that way is the only way. Mr. Charles Kettering at one time had to drive by automobile from Dayton to Detroit and return, many times during the year. In conversation with a man from Detroit, he remarked that he could drive from Detroit to Dayton in a certain time. The gentleman contradicted him and said he couldn't drive the trip in that time. However, he accompanied Mr. Kettering and they made the trip in the stated time. When they arrived in Dayton, he said, "Well, of course you were able to do it—you didn't stay on Highway 25." When one gets on Highway 25 he tends to stay on it for he is comfortable.

You have acquired information, knowledge, skills, appreciations and, it is hoped, wisdom which should aid you in overcoming the blocks of prejudice on your highways. Your educational equipment should give you perspective and should assist you in fighting against the pressure of the immediate. There are many opportunities in our world if we realize that the boundaries of our universe are unlimited.—Charles L. Anspach, *Vital Speeches*

1638

A prejudice is a vagrant opinion without visible means of support.—Ambrose Bierce

1639

Those who use their reason do not reach the same conclusions as those who obey their prejudices.—Walter Lippmann

PROBLEMS

1640

Problems come only to the living and the working. . . . There are no issues in the lives of those willing to sleep with their fathers. . . . You either push up issues or you push up daisies.—Douglas Horton

1641

We make a study of a situation and find that it is the parents who are to blame—then we try to do something for the children—when it is the parents who need the treatment.—E. Paul Hovey

1642

The native is a problem; he is never a person.—Trevor Huddleston, *Naught for Your Comfort*

PROGRESS

1643

This much is certain. *Change* is a neutral concept; *progress* is not. It implies a standard of value, a standard of judgment. It means bringing into existence more of this or more of that to which we attach worth. "Whatsoever things are true . . . whatsoever things are pure, whatsoever things are lovely . . . If there be any virtue and if there by any praise, think on these things." And think on them creatively, in such a way as to come to a deeper understanding of their nature and therefore to a greater capacity to be "on their side," helping to increase their proportionate strength in the world as against the things that are false, base, and ugly. Where moral imperative is enacted, growth takes place in the individual. His inborn powers develop through relationships to his environment that are marked by loving, learning, and creating. Wherever the skilled influence of such an individual is exerted, progress takes place in the world—in some measure, large or small. . . . The kingdom of God's fatherhood and of human brotherhood comes a little closer to possessing an earthly location.—Bonaro Overstreet, *National Parent-Teacher*

1644

In the final analysis, there is no other solution to man's progress but the day's honest work, the day's honest activities, the day's generous utterances and the day's good deed.—Clare Booth Luce

1645

There is no greater disloyalty to the great pioneers of human progress than to refuse to budge an inch from where they stood.—William R. Inge

PROPAGANDA

1646

[Propaganda] has always to be directed more and more toward the feeling, and only to a certain extent to so-called reason.—Adolf Hitler

1647

A great Latin word, "propaganda" is falling into disrepute in our day. To "propagate" is to make something increase and multiply. And "propaganda" is just the process and the means of making something multiply and spread abroad. Speak a word in someone's hearing, and that word is planted and grows in his mind and heart, and from him it spreads to some other soul; and so on. All of us are propagandists of good or bad, of purity or uncleanness, of truth or falsehood. And Jesus, in His last Commission, called His followers to spread the greatest, finest propaganda in the world.—*Christianity Today*

1648

Whether it is called brainwashing, public relations, indoctrination, lobbying, psychological warfare, white papers, advertising, paper bullets, or even "directed" education, propaganda has had an ancient if rather disreputable career.—*Newsweek*

PUBLICITY

1649

Publicity is justly commended as a remedy for social and industrial diseases. Sunlight is said to be the best of disinfectants; electric light the most efficient policeman.—Louis D. Brandeis, *Other People's Money*

1650

The public is wiser than the wisest critic.—Bancroft

1651

There is no tyranny so despotic as that of public opinion among a free people.—Donn Piatt

1652

Let a man proclaim a new principle. Public sentiment will surely be on the other side.—T. B. Reed

PURPOSE

1653

When men have no eternal point of view and are dealing with the merely temporal, they cannot even choose realistically or wisely. The man going on a journey has to strip things down to essentials, and he has to choose what is necessary. If he takes more along, he knows that they are the items which can be discarded when necessary. It is the traveler who knows freedom.

We need to be reminded who we are and where we are going. The Book of Hebrews put it very clearly and, after reminding Christians that they are strangers and exiles so far as this earth is concerned, it gave them this wonderful assurance: "Therefore God is not ashamed to be called their God, for he has prepared for them a city."

To put it in another way, God is proud of His pilgrims.—Gerald Kennedy, *The Christian and His America*

1654

A Catholic priest named William Sullivan left his church when he felt his choice had to be made between the institution and the truth. He became minister of the Unitarian Church of Germantown. . . . In his autobiography, *Under Orders,* he stated in the Foreword the moral learned from his long and difficult experience. "So at the end of the long journey," he wrote, "I have come to this: the first article of my creed is that I am a moral personality, under orders." What that man had learned about life was its mobility and its meaning. It was neither a dead end nor an aimless wandering, but a marching toward the heavenly city, conscious of God's demands and purposes for every human life.—Gerald Kennedy

1655

Human beings who take their purpose in life from what the public thinks lean on a swaying reed. They accept the philosophy that economic security will release them from uncertainty about what they are and where they are going. They think they will be happy when they can be sure of higher incomes, better houses, more abundant food, stylish clothes, the latest gadgets, the fastest cars, the fullest social life, the highest professional standing, the finest entertainment. In this materialistic day, it is widely assumed that these are the things that will fill human emptiness with satisfaction.

A child born into a world where security of person and possessions are supremely important is soon impressed with these goals. . . . He learns the major reason for going to school is to prepare himself for a good job . . . there is nothing wrong with trying to improve one's economic situation . . .

but to imbue our children with the belief that their main drive in life should be to get ahead economically, socially, and professionally is to fail to develop in them the resources of mind and heart that will make them responsible members, not only of their own families, but also of the family of man. If we would have our children grow into men and women who are able to obtain the world peace that we have failed to obtain, we must show them how they must first find peace within themselves. . . . Socrates said: "Whether . . . a city exists in heaven or ever will exist on earth, the wise man will live after the manner of that city, having nothing to do with any other, and in so looking upon it, will set his own house in order."—Pauline Frederick, *National Parent-Teacher*

QUESTIONS

1656

The question in the Bible is often a rhetorical device, but is more effective when it is genuine . . . it shows life and thought in action. . . . I listed what I considered the most vital . . . nine in number, and encompass the whole of man's reasoning life on earth, his quest for survival, for meaning, for love, in life, and in the hereafter. They are a way of summing up all we work for and with. . . . I submit them . . . : Will God dwell on the earth? (Solomon's question at the dedication of the temple). What is man (that Thou are mindful of him)? If a man die, will he live again? What is truth? What does the Lord require of you? What shall I do to inherit eternal life? What have I to do with Thee, O Christ? "What will you have me do for you?" Whom shall I send, and who will go for us?

As the heroes of old died without the promise, God having ordained that they without us should not be made

perfect, so it is given us to strive to answer their questions, or at least to ask them again.—Robert L. Eddy, "Question Marks in the Bible," *The Minister's Quarterly*

1657

Questions in the Passion Story. . . . Look at those of Judas: Why was the ointment wasted? How much will you give me? Is it I? Questions to Judas: Do you betray the Son of Man with a kiss? What is that to us? . . . Question of Annas: Are you the Son of God? Of Pilate: Are you the King of the Jews? Don't you know I have the power to free you? What is truth? What evil has he done? Will you have him or Barabbas? The malefactors: Are you the King? Save us and yourself! Have you no respect for God even now? . . . Questions of the resurrection: Why seek ye the living among the dead? Woman, why do you weep?—Robert L. Eddy, *The Minister's Quarterly*

QUIETNESS

1658

An inability to stay quiet . . . is one of the most conspicuous failings of mankind.—W. Bagehot

1659

Margaret T. Applegarth . . . entitles a meditation: "Centering Down." These two words, borrowed from our Quaker friends, seem appropriate for thinking . . . for self-appraisal. . . . A Chaplain led . . . a series of beautiful liturgical worship services, employing . . . periods of silence. He realized that unless we have acquired the art of being still we are certain to miss some of the real values of worship. Many had mountain-peak spiritual experience in these worship periods. However, one person was heard to remark: "Why doesn't he say something or do something?" and another, "This total silence makes me fidgety." Most of us are so accustomed to and so much a part of the babble and confusion in which we live, that we neither sense the need nor know how to use *quiet moments with God*. Truly we need to "center down" deep into our hearts and search for and await the presence of God. "Be still and know that I am God."—Archie H. Hook, *The Congregational Way*

1660

The days in which we live are shot through with the spirit of haste. Everyone is in a hurry. The man of the hour is the man out of breath. The quick lunch and the short story, the swift flight—all these are thoroughly characteristic of the life we live. Half the people you meet are just in the act of leaving something half done in order to rush ahead to tackle something else which will be left half done. "In quietness and confidence shall be your strength."—Charles R. Brown

RACE

1661

Racial segregation as such is morally wrong and sinful because it is a denial of the unity and solidarity of the human race as conceived by God in the creation of man in Adam and Eve.—Archbishop Rummel

1662

We are about to embark on a great crusade. A crusade to restore Americanism . . . and return the control of our government to the people. . . . Generations of Southerners yet unborn will cherish our memory because they will realize that the fight we now wage will have preserved for them their untainted racial heritage, their culture, and the institutions of the Anglo-Saxon race. We of the South have seen the

tides rise before. We know what it is to fight. We will carry the fight to victory.—Senator James O. Eastland

1663

I have from early age been strongly fortified by the philosophy taught me by my maternal grandmother. . . . Your color, she counseled, has nothing to do with your worth. You are potentially as good as anyone. How good you may prove to be will have no relation to your color, but with what is in your heart and your head. That is something which each individual by his own effort can control. The right to be treated as an equal by all other men, she said, is man's birthright. Set a goal for yourself and determine to reach it in spite of all obstacles.—Ralph J. Bunche, *Vital Speeches*

1664

Nobody knows the age of the human race, but all agree that it is old enough to know better.

1665

Understanding does not mean that you have to embrace the Negro or the white person. The Negro or the white person must be judged as a man, with all of his goodness or badness, and the color of his skin makes no difference. He who made us all did not make any mistake when He made us of a different color. If we only used the same intensity to love as we do to hate!—Marian Anderson, *My Lord, What a Morning*

1666

Don't talk about "the white man's rights." No white man, no Negro, has any right because of his color. Whatever moral rights he has are his because he belongs to the human family. Whatever legal rights he has in our country are his because they are guaranteed by our Constitution to everybody, regardless of race, creed, or sex.—Lillian Smith, *Now Is the Time*

RELIGION

1667

Religion should be the motor of life; the central heating plant of personality; the faith that gives joy to activity, hope to struggle, dignity to humility, zest to living.—William Lyon Phelps

1668

You surely cannot argue that a tankful of water containing a thimbleful of whisky is correctly described as whisky. A publican who sold the mixture as whisky would get into trouble. And it is high time that theologians who advertise a mixture one part Christian to ten thousand parts secular as Christian also got into trouble.—D. R. Davies

1669

My religion is something I cherish. I am not in church every Sunday but I hope and believe that I am on good speaking terms with Him. I carry my troubles and I don't sit back waiting for them to be cleared up. I realize that when the time is ripe they will be dissolved, but I don't mean that one should sit inert, waiting for all things to come from above. If one has a certain amount of drive and intelligence and conscientiousness, one must use them. Having made the best effort, one is more likely to get a hearing in an extremity. I believe that I could not have had my career without the help of the Being above.—Marian Anderson, *My Lord, What a Morning*

1670

There are no religious or irreligious types of people. This is a curtain which needs to be swept aside.—David Read

1671

The religious person at his best is never wholly content with himself and at peace with the world, for he knows how far he falls short of what he ought to be and can be. There is a positive and healthy tension between what is and what ought to be that forbids complacency and incites to action.—Harry C. Meserve, *The Atlantic Monthly*

1672

I would not give a farthing for a man's religion if his dog and cat are not the better for it.—Rowland Hill

1673

We do not need more material development; we need more spiritual development . . . we do not need more law; we need more religion. We do not need more of the things that are seen; we need more of the things that are unseen.—Calvin Coolidge

1674

Religion must provide the believer an answer when he asks why there are rich and poor, violence and justice, war and peace, or it will force him to look for an answer elsewhere.—Ludwig von Mises

1675

If your religion cannot stand tearing apart, you had better get one that will.

1676

The task of all religion is to concentrate more on life here than in the hereafter.—William S. Rosenblum

1677

The Christian faith holds that love conquers, that hearts can be strangely warmed, that both new men and a new society are possible here and now and that it is thus that Jesus comes and thus that the Holy Spirit works.—Methodist Council of Bishops

REPENTANCE

1678

It is at the point of—scientism, democracy, nationalism, and capitalism—and their diffusion into an exaltation of scientific and technological achievement, the American way of life, patriotism, and free enterprise, that the identification becomes most common. Add . . . a sense of the dignity of man, humanitarian concern . . . a wholesome respect for law . . . responsible citizenship—and one comes out with what most Americans regard as "acting like a Christian."

Is this judgment mistaken? It is, and it is not. All the achievements and virtues . . . have . . . large elements of goodness. Some . . . can be traced directly to Christian roots. Yet taken as a whole, they do not add up to Christian *agape*. One can believe in every one of them and be a decent . . . citizen, and still not be a Christian . . . the most difficult, task of Christian leaders is to induce people who are virtuous . . . to see that such goodness is not good enough. As long as one identifies Christian ethics with the ethics of Christendom, one does not cry out, "God, be merciful to me a sinner!" or lay hold in humility upon divine grace, or seek in costly self-surrender to follow the path of obedient love.—Georgia Harkness, *Christian Ethics*

1679

I wish there existed someone to whom I could say that I was sorry.— Character in Graham Greene's, *The Quiet American*

RESPONSIBILITY

1680

The account of Adam stirs us to thinking of our own God-given opportunities and responsibilities. All things were Adam's, with very few prohibitions. Life could have been rich and full under God, but he found this freedom to be a two-edged sword. Freedom and obedience to God could lead to purposeful, holy living, but freedom accompanied by disobedience led to chaos and destruction. Faced with this choice, Adam yielded to . . . temptations . . . he disobeyed God. In Adam's story we see represented the rebellion of all mankind. Man has become a spiritual refugee, cast out of his true homeland. . . . The course of every man's life . . . is determined by his use of this God-given freedom of choosing to submit his will to that of his Maker or to flaunt self-will in the face of the Eternal God. A loving Creator has placed a tremendous responsibility upon us and a great opportunity before us—the opportunity to grow as free human beings—but with it the responsibility to choose Him that we may live, and live abundantly. —*Discovery*

1681

In 1954 there were 4,200,000 people who came into the United States to live. These people knew nothing of our way of life, our ideals, or our principles. In fact, they could not even speak our language, and had never heard of our religion. These four million people, were, of course, the babies born in this country that year. These children are the direct responsibility of us as citizens, as parents, as teachers, as civic leaders, and as Sunday school teachers. If we fail, what chance is there for this great republic in the next generation? Our ancestors came to this country looking for freedom, and they found it. But freedom is something that must be earned. With freedom there rests responsibility.— Henry W. Phillips, *The Rotarian*

1682
If you don't have responsibilities, you don't grow strong enough to handle them.—Bishop Alexander P. Shaw

1683
There are voices of greed, racial suspicion, hate, revenge, folly. The world is clearing its throat. Let the men of God speak. We have the Word. We have the responsibility.—Orlo Choguill

1684
If you . . . bring advantages to a great lot of previously underprivileged people, they will rise to their opportunities and, by and large, will become responsible citizens.—Frederick L. Allen, *The Big Change*

1685
No man is completely independent. Each of us is responsible to others and to God. Many of our mental ills are due to our revolt against authority. The only way actually to be free is to submit to controls. Aristotle said; "Freedom is obedience to self-formulated rules." It would be more correct to say that freedom lies in obedience to the laws of God. Insofar as we bend our wills to the will of God, and are responsible to Him, we are free.—Lawrence Fitzgerald

1686
Make no mistake about it, responsibilities toward other human beings are the greatest blessings God sends us. —Dorothy Dix

RIGHT

1687
Always do right; this will gratify some people and astonish the rest.—Mark Twain

1688
I prefer to do right and get no thanks rather than to do wrong and get no punishment.—Marcus Cato

1689
Some things are eternally right and some things are eternally wrong. As one of the Justices of our Supreme Court put it long ago, "The Ten Commandments will not budge."—Edward L. R. Elson, *America's Spiritual Recovery*

SACRED

1690
Truth once found is sacred; it is something that must not be denied, but maintained at whatever cost.—Edgar J. Goodspeed

1691
To have friends whose lives we can elevate or depress by our influence is sacred. To be entrusted with little children is sacred. To have powers by which we can make this earth a more decent place is sacred. To be a child of God is sacred. And honor, honesty, truthfulness, fidelity, and love are sacred.—Harry Emerson Fosdick

SALVATION

1692
The way to be saved is not to delay, but to come and take.—Dwight L. Moody

1693
When a man or a community is confronted with an issue of life and death, the word "save" is likely to be spoken. A child is "saved" from drowning. A man is "saved" from death by penicillin. When a community is confronted by such a measure of internal disorder or of economic chaos as to

threaten its very being as a community, the leader who restores order may earn the title of "saviour of his country." . . . These situations present themselves as ultimate. Everything is at stake. But the issues that have this character are not confined to those in which the bodily life of an individual or the material being of a community is radically threatened. There is another death than the death of the body. A job may be the "saving" of a man, not only or not chiefly because it provides him with a means of existence, but because it restores meaning and shape to his existence. When a man is the victim of alcoholism, Alcoholics Anonymous may be his salvation because it restores his disintegrating manhood to human nature. . . . The rescuer must make of his life a bridge . . . between God and man in his lostness . . . without losing his hold on God.—Angus Dunn, *The Saving Person*

1694

No one today can seriously study the life of Abraham Lincoln without being —in one way or another—emancipated. —J. C. Penney

1695

"Salvation" is one of religion's great words. It is well to see what is its true and full meaning. To some it means a drunkard saved from the ditch, to others escape from hell or reaching heaven . . . this is true, but not enough. Salvation means three things: (1) deliverance from evil, evil of every kind, within and without, now and to come; (2) the gaining of good, good of every kind but especially the highest good, the life with God and all that this brings; (3) the help of God. In a word, salvation is deliverance and life by the help of God . . . "You did he make alive," Paul writes. "That is salvation, being alive to God and to every good which God's world can

bring us."—H. F. Rall, *The Christian Advocate*

1696

We are saved by someone doing for us what we cannot do for ourselves.— Donald Lester

1697

Salvation is not something that is done for you but something that happens within you. It is not the clearing of a court record, but the transformation of a life attitude.—Albert W. Palmer

SCHOOL

1698

One woman said, "We ought to let the teachers teach and the parents parent." She meant that the school has absorbed many functions which belong in other hands. Her list of such functions included the following: instruction in health, safety and athletics; supervising recesses, study and lunch periods; taking care of behavior problems; performing extra paper work and serving on Scout committees.— Joseph H. Fichter, *Commonweal*

1699

We do not need political scholars whose education has been so specialized as to exclude them from participation in current events—men like Lord John Russell, of whom Queen Victoria once remarked that he would be a better man if he knew a third subject, but he was interested in nothing but the Constitution of 1688 and himself.— Senator John F. Kennedy

SCIENCE

1700

The more a real scientist knows, the more reverent he must become. The more thoughtful person tries to penetrate the wonderful workings of God, and the more one knows about them, the more reverent he must be toward the Power back of it all. Scientists believe in the unseen atom because they see evidence of its existence. A true scientist believes in God and worships Him largely for the same reason. A scientist's experiences in life have given him innumerable evidences of God's existence. . . . What man could be a deeply thoughtful bacteriologist or astronomer and not be reverent toward God?—Sidney S. Negus

1701

We must not let science hypnotize us into believing that simply by sitting in front of desks and drawing boards and instruments all day, we are contributing to the character of man. . . . Man must balance science with other qualities of life, qualities of body and spirit as well as those of mind—qualities he cannot develop when he lets mechanics and luxury insulate him too greatly from the earth to which he was born . . . only by placing the character of man above the value of his products . . . measuring scientific accomplishments by their effect on man himself . . . can we retrieve the qualities of mankind.—Charles A. Lindbergh

1702

The final test of science is not whether it adds to our comfort, knowledge and power, but whether it adds to our dignity as men, our sense of truth.—David Sarnoff

1703

Science without religion is lame, religion without science is blind.—Albert Einstein, *The World as I See It*

SELF

1704

It is part of our human nature but there is that within us which always wants to make self the center of its own universe and, in that selfish way, wants to tear God from His throne and deny his brother and advance his own ambition.—Bishop Robert R. Brown

1705

The basic fact of today is the tremendous pace of change in human life. In my own life I have seen amazing changes, and I am sure that in the course of the life of the next generation these changes will be even greater . . . nothing is so remarkable as the progressive conquest of understanding of the physical world by the mind of man today. While there has been this conquest of external conditions, there is at the same time the strange spectacle of a lack of moral fiber and of self-control in man as a whole. Conquering the physical world, he fails to conquer himself.—Jawaharlal Nehru, *The New Leader*

1706

We men are all thieves who have stolen the self which was meant as a part of God and tried to keep it for ourselves alone.—Joy Davidman

1707

Every man brings an egg and every one wants an omelette—but without breaking his own egg. That poses a most difficult situation.—Frank Mar

1708

Lord, make this a better world—beginning with *me!*—Claire MacMurray

1709

The story of the Bible is the story of what God has done to save man from the disaster that has overtaken him through his persistent refusal to recognize God's higher will. In the Old Testament God reveals His true self to pagan man through the agency of a chosen people. In the New Testament He draws man to Him in Jesus

Christ, who took upon Himself our sins on the cross in order to reconcile us to the Father and to be the mediator between us and God. The aim of God throughout is to re-establish communion between man and Himself, so that human will is merged into His will. And this happens when we live together as "the body of Christ." It is thus perfectly clear that it is not my will but God's which is to be done, and that God has given me freedom and power, not to do what I want, but to do what He wants. This is my only security; apart from it I shall be like the totally undisciplined child—nervous, unstable, and drawn by the winds of whim, because I really do not know what I ought to want.—G. Ernest Wright, "The Problem of Self-will," *Growing*

1710

There are times when our children, perhaps unconsciously, see into the heart of life, after the fashion of the little girl who remarked: "Mother, I've had such a happy time today." "Really," her mother answered. "What made today different from yesterday?" The child thought a moment and responded, "Yesterday my thoughts pushed me around and today I pushed my thoughts around."

Those perceptive words of a child picture life as it is, a perpetual struggle between the things that push us around and the inner resources that enable us to push our lives where they ought to go.—Harold Blake Walker, *Specialty Salesman*

1711

"Above all, don't lie to yourself," said Father Zossima, in Dostoevski's *The Brothers Karamazov,* to a young seeker after eternal life. Now psychiatrists are telling us the same thing. When we become adept, they say, at fooling ourselves by means of plausible but untrue explanations of our failures and follies, "mental ill health lies ahead." Of course, we all deceive ourselves at times. J. Pierpont Morgan once said that a man usually has two reasons for what he does—a good reason and the real one. This doubtless overstates the matter somewhat, but, if we have been observant, we must have noticed that most of us fool ourselves part of the time in respect to unwelcome considerations, but that some people do so pretty nearly all the time, until they are virtually incapable of thinking straight about themselves at all.—Eliot Porter, *Forward*

1712

In a letter to a friend, Sherwood Anderson, the novelist and playwright, wrote, "The disease we all have and that we have to fight against all our lives is the disease of self. Let any man, or woman, look too much upon his own life, and everything becomes a mess." By comparison and in contrast consider what Karl Heim says about Johann Sebastian Bach: "The most outstanding characteristic of this artist, and that which distinguishes him at once from men like Beethoven or Richard Wagner, is that he never sought man's recognition of his works. It never entered his mind that his music was so great that it towered far above that of all his contemporaries. He exercised his creative power without being aware of it. It was like the powers which work in Nature unseen. It never occurred to him to ask whether the people in the church would understand his works. It was enough for him that there was One who would understand, God. At the head of his scores he wrote the words "Soli Deo gloria" and "Jesu juva." This creed was illustrated by all his creative work. Because he worked for God alone, without a single thought of winning fame, his art possesses that blessed peace which comes from the grace and compassion of God.—Robert J. McCracken, "The Religiously Self-Made Man"

1713

I have had more trouble with myself than with any other man.—Dwight L. Moody

1714

Everybody thinks of changing humanity and nobody thinks of changing himself.—Tolstoy

SERVICE

1715

The words "servant" and "service" are often used in our everyday life. We call the experts who "service" our cars, "service men"; the clubs we join, "service clubs"; and the time our young men spend in the army is regarded as a time devoted to "military service." But we all feel that such "services" usually have mixed motives; that they are more or less compulsory. And unless something else is added to them, they are but the products of rapid calculations and enlightened self-interest.

That "something else" is exactly the unique quality of Christian service: initiated by a call to "sonship," motivated by thankful obedience, rendered primarily to the "Word of God," and designed to benefit the whole world. It is the greatest unifying factor in human society. The Oberlin Conference . . . rightly stated, "Our hope in seeking unity resides . . . in love to serve our brother and to be served by him as servants together of the Word of God."—Bela Vassady

1716

The soul's supreme need and desire: "We would see Jesus." The law of reproduced life and abiding influence: "Except a grain of wheat fall into the ground and die, it abideth alone, but if it die it beareth much fruit." The law of life's lastingness; give up the love of life for the sake of the life of love. The law of eternal fellowship; "If any man serve me, let him follow me, and where I am, there shall my servant be." The secret of Christ's resistlessness: "I, if I be lifted up, will draw. . . ." We do not know whether the Greeks saw Him. He was sifting out the multitudes again.—Robert E. Speer, *John's Gospel*

1717

Life is like a game of tennis; the player who serves well seldom loses.

1718

We all seem to want organizations which do something for us. We need to do something for them.

1719

What is the greatest right conferred upon man? There have been many to insist that it is the right to command others and be served by them. Until modern times the greatest men were supposed to be kings, and they claimed that they ruled by divine right. A great man could be judged by the number of his subjects, the size of his army, the extent of his wealth and power. But the prophet who wrote the words found in the book of Isaiah recognized a nobler greatness, that of the right to serve. In the language of exultation he tells of the high privilege that had come to him—the right to help others (Isaiah 60, 61:1-6).—E. Leigh Mudge

1720

"What would you say about service to people?" I asked Prime Minister Nehru of India. "Doesn't doing things for people give meaning to life?"

"Yes, service to people can be very important, but only if you do things for people whom you love because you care for them, not for pay—because you are concerned with their welfare. Such service is an aspect of freedom, and can truly give meaning to life," he replied.—Arthur Holly Compton

1721

Angelo Patri tells of a childhood incident in school. The alarm bell sounded, which meant a fire drill, and being nearest the door he went through quickly and was soon out in the yard. The next day the principal sent for him and, when he was seated in the office, there came this sudden question: "You were near the big door yesterday when the alarm rang. Why didn't you hold it open for the others?" Young Patri gulped and explained that he was going on an errand and, besides, Tim was monitor of the door. Then the principal said something Patri never forgot. "You knew the door was to be held open. And you were there. Next time, serve where you are."

1722

How many know of Hetty Green? How many know of Pasteur? Probably no one remembers Hetty Green. She was once the richest woman in the world. Her consuming desire was to make her son the richest man in the world. She bent every effort and used ruthless methods to accomplish her purpose. But she is almost unknown today. Pasteur spent his life in serving humanity. These many years after his death, he is known throughout the world.

SHAME

1723

It is far more shameful to be caught than to be guilty. . . . We are ashamed for the things that men know, not for the things we do.—William Allen White, *Autobiography*

1724

When I look back upon the more than sixty years that I have spent on this entrancing earth and when I am asked which of all the changes that I have witnessed appears to me to be the most significant, I am inclined to answer that it is the loss of a sense of shame.—Harold Nicolson

SIN

1725

The sheep was not lost because it got in the thicket but because it had been separated from the shepherd.—Arthur L. Miller

1726

The spark of sin in our hearts can also blaze up into what put Him on the cross.—Arthur L. Miller

1727

Sin is twisting and distorting out of its proper shape a human personality which God designed to be a thing of beauty and a joy forever.—Walter L. Carson, *Interpretation*

1728

All human sin seems so much worse in its consequences than in its intentions.—Reinhold Niebuhr, *Leaves from the Notebook of a Tamed Cynic*

1729

At least half of the sins of mankind are caused by the fear of boredom.—Bertrand Russell

1730

The sin against the Holy Ghost (Mark 3:28, 29) is continued conscious sin, without repentance. According to the Christian religion, no sin wholeheartedly repented of is unpardonable, but all conscious sin is unpardonable until there is sincere repentance.

SPACE

1731

Indeed, of what avail is it for men to soar into space and at the same time lose the best consolations which our earth has to offer—peace of mind, the ability to love and be loved, the trust in the goodness of life?

Is it the better part of wisdom to be searching out the heavens without first trying to bring a little more heaven to this earth? The tragedy of our times may be summed up in one simple sentence: We have split the atom before we have united mankind.—Rabbi Julius Mark

1732

Is it presumptuous wanting to visit other worlds while our own world is in such an unsettled state of affairs? This argument appears to me without basis in logic or facts. It is doubtful whether an agreement over what a settled state of affairs is, or should be, can be attained at all. If we have to wait for that, we will never have space flight, or for that matter any other major endeavor. But the fallacy goes deeper. Man's life and civilization have been dynamic since the beginning of his time. Nations and civilizations rise and fall (war or no wars), and there is no evidence whatever for the assumption that this will change in the future. We will, therefore, always have our troubles on this planet (space flight or no space flight). Should Portugal, Spain and England have waited until every citizen in their countries was mature, enlightened, and overflowing with neighborly love, before exploring the world? The fundamental notion of this argument is wrong and contrary to our entire development in the past. We grow with our aspirations and by making them come true—not before. Therefore, I believe that space flight will help us to improve our own world—directly and indirectly.—Krafft A. Ehricke, *Think*

1733

Will we lose God in outer space? The quick answer to this question is No. But having said that, it is necessary to go on to say, "But it all depends. . . ." Depends on what? It depends on our ability and our willingness to think greater and deeper thoughts about God, His nature and His purpose, His ways with men and with the world . . . the conception of God must be expanded from that of creator and sovereign ruler of a relatively small area to that of creator and sovereign ruler of the whole vast cosmos. . . . We never get beyond Him, and never can. . . . We need only prepare ourselves to give thanks for still another disclosure of God's loving care for His creation.—W. Norman Pittenger, *Think*

1734

There is beauty in space, and it is orderly. There is no weather, and there is regularity. It is predictable. . . . Everything in space obeys the laws of physics. If you know these laws, and obey them, space will treat you kindly. And don't tell me man doesn't belong out there. Man belongs wherever he wants to go.—Wernher von Braun

1735

Gazing out into God's clear space instead of back into our own murky psychological depths may let fresh air into modern thought. In such air, it may be easier for the spirit . . . to evoke more ready responses.—Bishop John J. Wright

1736

The scientific attempt, as such, a legitimate means of exploration, will neither remove us from nor will it draw us nearer to God. But it will remind the Christian of the cosmic reach of his faith: the work of Christ, mediator of all creation, concerns the entire universe. That faith will inspire the solution of the ethical problems. —Oscar Cullmann

1737

There are indirect religious effects of these developments comparable to those which occurred with the victory of Copernican astronomy. They can immensely increase man's awareness of himself as free, namely free from bondage to any encountered situation, including bondage to the power-field of the earth. But they also can greatly increase man's temptation to confuse his power to progress endlessly into world space with the inner infinity of his spiritual nature and, hence, to lose the vertical line by surrendering to the horizontal one. Finally, the opening of outer space can overcome our terrestrial provincialism and produce a new vision of the greatness of the creation of which earth and mankind, their space and their time, are only a part.—Paul Tillich

SPIRITUAL

1738

One of the loveliest remarks that one person can make regarding another is that which was made by Nathaniel Hawthorne of his wife. Said he, "I never knew what spiritual refreshment meant until I met her." —Douglas Horton

1739

It has always been true that, the more man gains of this world, the more he hungers for and needs the peace found only in the world of the spirit.—Don Allen, "Religion in Hollywood," *Photoplay Magazine*

STEWARDSHIP

1740

Christian stewardship is the matching of gift for matchless gift; our life and its whole substance for the gift of perfect love. And though God's Son and His precious death are matchless —in the strange economy of God our gift returned is made sufficient. My all for His all. Stewardship is your commitment; the asking of God to take you back unto Himself—all that you have and all that you are.—Lawrence L. Durgin, *Mission Today*

1741

An annual budget is not a list of expenses. It is a program of great undertaking for Christ.

1742

This congregation was a 100 per cent Igorot congregation. The problem with this group was that, though they embraced Christianity, they still practiced their pagan religion. They were willing to kill ten carabaos, ten cows, ten pigs, and ten chickens for their pagan feasts and yet they were not willing to give enough support to the work of the church.—Samson Almarez, *Internship Report*

1743

The problem with our giving is that we give the widow's mite, but not with the widow's spirit.—*Survey Bulletin*

SUCCESS

1744

To have faith where you cannot see; to be willing to work on in the dark; to be conscious of the fact that, so long as you strive for the best, there are better things on the way, this in itself is success.—Katherine Logan

1745

. . . Our current difficulties stem far more from our *successes* than from our *failures*. If our forebears had never struck off on their own from Great Britain, if the Founding Fathers had started us off with a less effective Constitution, had we not successfully colonized and developed this great continent, applied ourselves to scientific invention and the perfection of mass production techniques, held the Union together, and won two world wars, our burdens would today be far lighter. Some other great nation and not America would be struggling with predicaments comparable to ours. Walt Whitman had a point when he said: "It is provided in the very essence of things, that from any fruition of success, no matter what, shall come forth something to make a greater struggle necessary."—Dorothy Fosdick, *Common Sense and World Affairs*

1746

You may have success if you do not demand victory.—John Buchan

1747

They never fail who die in a great cause.—Lord Byron

1748

The common idea that success spoils people by making them vain, egotistic and self-complacent is erroneous; on the contrary, it makes them, for the most part, humble, tolerant and kind. Failure makes people bitter and cruel. —W. Somerset Maugham, *The Summing Up*

1749

When a man succeeds, he does it in spite of everybody, and not with the assistance of everybody.—E. W. Howe

1750

If at first you don't succeed, try something harder.—Marcelene Cox

1751

Have a sincere desire to serve God and mankind, and stop doubting, stop thinking negatively. . . . Simply start living by faith, pray earnestly and humbly, and get into the habit of looking expectantly for the best. . . . When you live on a faith basis, your desire will be only for that which you can ask in God's name. . . . By success, of course, I do not mean that you may become rich, famous, or powerful. . . . I mean the development of mature and constructive personality.—Norman Vincent Peale

SUNDAY

1752

When a man labors not for a livelihood, but to accumulate wealth, then he is a slave. Therefore it is that God granted the Sabbath. For it is by the Sabbath that we know that we are not working animals, born to eat and to labor. We are men. It is the Sabbath which is man's goal; not labor, but the rest which he earns from his labor. It was because the Jews made the Sabbath holy to God that they were redeemed from slavery in Egypt. It was by the Sabbath that they proclaimed that they were not slaves but free men.—Sholem Asch, *East River*

1753

Sunday can be the best day of a better week if we desire it, but we must courageously and even ruthlessly change our schedules that now employ Saturday hours in dissipating our strength and treasure; that leave Sunday a day of exhaustion and late sleeping or lounging amid newspapers and sporting gear—the worst day of the week-end! In this hour we need desperately for ourselves, our neighbors, our nation, our world, the presence and power of God. If we are to find God, we must first recover Sunday. —Paul Newton Poling

1754

Does it matter if we miss once? What is important? Does anything ever happen in church or Sunday church school?

What if a big game hunter misses once when a wild animal is charging him? What would have happened if William Tell had missed once? What if John Wesley had missed going to Aldersgate? If Paul had missed going to Damascus? If a doctor missed once with his knife in an operation?

TAXES

1755

It is in peace that our commerce flourishes most, and that our taxes are most easily paid.—Monroe

1756

What you pay in taxes, you cannot give to the church. You can give other money to the church, but not that money. When government increases its "take" out of the American pocketbook . . . it certainly makes contributions to charity more difficult. This inverse ratio of gifts to charity and taxes has gone right on despite the fact that the income tax law is supposed to encourage charitable contributions by making them deductible before paying the tax.—Samuel B. Pettengill

TEACHING

1757

When a teacher sets her class an arithmetic problem, the pupils may imagine that all she cares about is getting the answer. Actually, however, she already knows the answer and isn't in the least interested in it; what she cares about is teaching the pupils. —Joy Davidman, *Smoke on the Mountain*

1758

Like his students, the teacher has his failures, but he has unequaled and creative opportunities to tap new sources of power for good.—William G. Saltonstall

1759

A college class made a study of two hundred children and in the majority of cases predicted a rather dismal future for them.

Twenty years later, another class in the same college looked up the record of those children and found that most of them had turned out surprisingly well.

Then it was discovered that all went to the same school and one little teacher had influenced them all—for good—and had performed a miracle of Christian service.—Donald Lester

TEMPTATION

1760

Temptation is a part of life. No one is immune—at any age. For temptation is present wherever there is a choice to be made, not only between good and evil, but also between a higher and lower good. For some, it may be a temptation to sensual gratification; for others a temptation to misuse their gifts, to seek personal success at the cost of the general welfare, to seek a worthy aim by unworthy means, to lower their ideal to win favor with the electorate, or with their companions and associates.—Ernest Trice Thompson, *The Presbyterian Outlook*

1761

In the three temptations Jesus made His basic decision. He fixed the path and spirit and method of His ministry. He refused to act out of selfish concern; He would not try to force sensational support from God; He would not surrender to Satan for apparent advantage that could only defeat His God-given purpose. He would take up His humble ministry, which would lead to the cross rather than to personal comfort, spectacular power, and worldly success.—Floyd Filson

1762

In the story of Jane Eyre, Rochester pleads with Jane to go away with him to the south of France—a wrong thing for her to do. She stands up against the temptations of his argument, saying, "Laws and principles are not for the time when there are no temptations; they are for such moments as this. . . . If, at my individual convenience I might break them, what would they be worth?"

1763

No man knows how bad he is until he has tried to be good. There is a silly idea about that good people don't know what temptation means.—C. S. Lewis, *The Screwtape Letters*

1764

There is the temptation to shine, the temptation to whine, and the temptation to recline.—G. E. Lenski

1765

Temptation provokes me to look upward to God.—John Bunyan

THANKSGIVING

1766

True thanksgiving means that we need to thank God for what He has done for us and not tell Him what we have done for Him. . . . It is rather sobering . . . to remember that the one person Jesus mentions as going up to the temple to give thanks is picked out, not for praise but for censure. . . . The Pharisee began his prayer with words which are on countless lips . . . at Thanksgiving time, "God, I thank Thee." Yet he left the temple with divine disapproval. . . . Are we not guilty of thanking God that we are not like other people. . . . Let us beware of our boasting. . . . Let us forget how much we have done for God, and remember what He has done for us in Christ, and what He is continuing to do for us every day.—George R. Hendrick

1767

"What does a guest want?"

"I believe," said Augustus, "that . . . a guest wants first of all to be diverted . . . to shine . . . to find some justification for his existence altogether. . . . Signora, please tell me now: What does a hostess want?"

"The hostess," said the young lady, "wants to be thanked."—Isak Dinesen, *Seven Gothic Tales*

1768

The Thanksgiving proclamations of the American presidents for the last two decades have increasingly departed from the original rather purely religious spirit of Thanksgiving, and they have increasingly become congratulations to God for having such very wonderful children in America.—Reinhold Niebuhr

1769

Truly, this is God's country. Nothing can destroy it unless we become unthinkably weak—too weak to lift our hearts to heaven in gratitude for its uncounted blessings.—Burton Hillis, *Better Homes & Gardens*

TIME

1770

Where does time go? These days time is even more elusive than money. If you want to find out where the time goes and then perhaps to save it, you will have to pay close attention to how you manage it. If you want more time for things you really want to do, you can find it somewhere. But you have to want it very much—planning and saving always call for discipline—Lillian M. Gilbreth, *Woman's Home Companion*

1771

If it takes you half an hour to do your lessons and it takes someone else fifteen minutes, take the half hour and do them right.—The mother of Marian Anderson

1772

Time is the most valuable thing a man can spend.—Theophrastus

1773

We can not give anyone our time in the sense that we add to his actual time. We can only take duties and responsibilities from him.

1774

Time is never ripe; time must be cultivated to make it ripe.

TITHING

1775

"You can't figure your tithe?" our pastor asked in his sermon. Then he went on, "I venture to say that if anyone offered you a gift of one-tenth of your year's salary, you could figure it pretty closely in a hurry!"—R. C. Clarke, *The Protestant Church*

1776

Tithing does not "pay off," as some irreverent protagonists would have us believe. God does not promise material blessings to those who live His will; but He does promise peace of mind and soul and closer fellowship with Himself.—William S. Findley

1777

I have learned that tithing is a means to an end. Tithing is not just practiced to secure the blessing of God. "I will open the windows of heaven and pour out such a blessing as there is not room enough to receive." I do not think this is true. In other words, tithing is not a calculated system whereby the tither receives further reward financially for his investment in God. It is not quite that way as I understand it in the Bible. Rather, it is God's way of accomplishing His purpose for us in the world.—Robert B. Munger

1778

Tithing is just the recognition that we are committed to the work of Christ in all areas of life. Only in the church is so much done with so little. Only through the church is so much received for so little given.—Richard K. Smith

1779

Every church has . . . those timid souls who insist that they will give but cannot make a pledge. Some even intimate that there is something religious in relying upon unpledged contributions. Our contention is that the direct contrary is true. A pledge is more than a gift. It is an expression of confidence in the program which is planned. Through it the individual says that he is willing to share in the work that is being planned. He is identifying himself with the project and giving a "clear ahead" signal for the year.

A pledge is much more an act of

Christian faith than giving as the spirit may move. The emotional giver contributes as he finds the money available. The individual who makes a pledge agrees to so organize his life that there will be money available to meet the obligations when due. Givers may help the church treasury; pledgers definitely increase the morale.—*Church Management*

1780

Every family today is tempted to live beyond its means. We all want better clothes, larger houses, newer cars, longer vacations, better education for our children. In order to get more money we are tempted to do things which fall below a Christian standard of values. Likewise, we are tempted to bypass the great opportunities for Christian giving in favor of a further indulgence in the pleasant but unnecessary luxuries of life.—*Split Level Family*

TOLERANCE

1781

"In a republic," Theodore Roosevelt once said, "we must learn to combine intensity of conviction with a broad tolerance of difference of conviction." Conviction is not incompatible with tolerance. Tolerance without it can be a negative state of mind—not knowing what one believes. Tolerance with conviction makes a combination in which each strengthens the other—a continuing willingness to test one's own ideas, a determination to allow others the freedoms he demands for himself.—*Christian Science Monitor*

1782

Man is always inclined to be intolerant toward the thing, or person, he hasn't taken time adequately to understand, and consequently, you get quite inconceivable things cast into

your teeth from people who don't understand.—Bishop Robert R. Brown

1783

Whoever kindles the flames of intolerance in America is lighting a fire underneath his own home.—Harold E. Stassen, *Where I Stand*

1784

Tolerance does not lie in denying the possibility of truth or its claim on man, as some would have it. To deprive a man of the right to live according to the truth as he understands it is to rob him of all that makes life human. Tolerance does lie . . . in truly grasping what the other person understands by truth and judging him as a person not by one's own standards but by his own, however misguided they might be. This does not mean indifferentism. Each man has to serve the truth and we may well believe that some men who think they are serving the truth are in fact bound to superstition or ignorance. False ideas have no claim on tolerance. The central figure in tolerance is the person, infinitely worthy of respect.—John Cogley, *Commonweal*

TROUBLE

1785

Trouble. . . . Why do we fear it? Why do we dread ordeal? Every good thing the human race has experienced was trouble for somebody. Our birth was trouble for our mothers. To support us was trouble for our fathers. Books, paintings, music, great buildings, good food, ideas, the nameless joys and excitements which add up to what we call "a good life" came out of the travail of countless hearts and minds.—Lillian Smith, *Now Is the Time*

1786

Sure the world is full of trouble, but as long as we have people undoing trouble we have a pretty good world.—Helen Keller

1787

The art of living lies not in eliminating but in growing with troubles.—Bernard Baruch

1788

If trouble comes, it'll keep our religion from getting rusty. That's the great thing about persecution; it keeps you up to the mark. It's habit, not hatred, that is the real enemy of the church of God.—Charles T. Leber, *Is God There?*

TRUTH

1789

The Bible and our faith . . . give us the religious basis for the freedom to criticize, which guarantees the reality of education, and of progress in social experiment and experiences as well. After all, do we not most of us agree with the words of that curious eighteenth century writer, William Paley, who remarked, "Truth results from discussion"?—Ursula W. Niebuhr, "Man's Freedom Under God"

1790

A lie, repeated endlessly, can be sold to many; but what is often overlooked is that truth, by the process of repetition, can be sold more easily than lies.—George Gallup, *Saturday Review*

1791

Great truths announce their presence before they are formulated. . . . Neither truth nor righteousness is ever in haste.—William J. Tucker, *The Making and the Unmaking of the Preacher*

1792

The smallest atom of truth represents some man's bitter toil and agony.—H. L. Mencken

1793

The trouble with man is twofold. He cannot learn truths which are too complicated; he forgets truths which are too simple.—Rebecca West, *The Meaning of Treason*

1794

You should never wear your best trousers when you go out to fight for freedom and truth.—Henrik Ibsen

1795

Overheard in a midtown bookstore: "It isn't authentic, of course, but it was worth reading just for the information in it."—*The New Yorker*

1796

When the truth is in your way, you are on the wrong road.—Josh Billings

UNDERSTANDING

1797

Man masters nature not by force but by understanding . . . in the four hundred years since the Scientific Revolution, we have learned that we gain our ends only with the laws of nature; we control her only by understanding her laws.—J. Bronowski, "Science and Human Values," *The Nation*

1798

If you keep your head while others are losing theirs . . . then maybe you don't understand the situation.

1799

Ignorance of others' real intentions may increase fright and distrust. But understanding of these intentions does not necessarily reduce fright or augment trust. The American Revolution took place not because we misunderstood British intentions, but because we knew them well enough to know that we must oppose them.—Dorothy Fosdick

UNIVERSITY

1800

The university which fails to offer its students a chance to be introduced to the great truths and the history of religion along with their other courses, and an opportunity to participate in the finest kind of worship experience, is neglecting its responsibility. But a philosophy of religious education which says, "This you must believe," will not work, because it is contrary to the pattern of exploration the students are following in their other fields of study. What is needed is an intelligent presentation of religion which will convince young people that commitment to God's purpose for mankind can be a soul-satisfying experience.—Mildred McAfee Horton

1801

Kierkegaard . . . said that in the matter of faith every generation has to begin again. The people awakening to the significance of religion in the university would be inclined to agree with this statement. None of them works under the illusion that faith can be handed on from one generation to the next, or is concerned therefore for the transmission of dogma. What they are saying is that we must get over an entirely unacceptable notion that faith is a matter of indifference. Faith is something given, not won, and no man can claim to be educated without inquiring into what it is, without studying its manifestations in human history, not least in the literature of religion, and without trying to find a way into its life-giving influence.—Nathan M. Pusey

1802

Said Carlyle, "The true University of these days is a Collection of Books." While one may quarrel with Carlyle's statements about some other things, one finds him in good company in speaking thus. And I venture to say that the best educated man is the man with the best store of ideas which he knows how to use, and with the best knowledge about their source. . . . The library of a college is second only to the faculty. Indeed, without an adequate library a college can hardly sustain an adequate teaching faculty or adequate activity in the minds of its students. . . . To many, a book is a natural enemy rather than something to be welcomed—an outreach of the author's mind. Nevertheless, the adventure does take on excitement for many students every year, and it is the ferment of ideas on a campus which lends vitality to the whole effort.—J. L. Zwingle, *Park College Record*

1803

The university is a place where inquiry is pushed forward, and discoveries verified and perfected, and rashness rendered innocuous, and error exposed, by the collision of mind with mind and knowledge with knowledge. It is the place where the professor becomes eloquent, and is a missionary and a preacher displaying his science in its most complete and most winning form, pouring it forth with the zeal of enthusiasm, and lighting up his own love of it in the breasts of his hearers. It is the place where the catechist makes good his ground as he goes, treading in the truth day by day into the ready memory, and wedging and tightening it into the expanding reason. It is a place which wins the admiration of the young by its celebrity, kindles the affections of the middle-aged by its beauty, and rivets the fidelity of the old by its associations. It is a seat of wisdom, a light of the world, a minister of the faith, an Alma Mater of the rising generation.—Cardinal Newman

VICTORY

1804

Nothing in history has turned out to be more impermanent than military victory.—Harry Emerson Fosdick

1805

What is victory? Victory is that which must be bought with the lives of young men to retrieve the errors of the old. Victory is a battered thing courage must salvage out of the wreckage which stupidity has wrought. Victory is redemption purchased for men's hope at a cost so terrible that only defeat could be more bitter.—Gordon R. Munnoch, "We Are Debtors to Sacrifice"

VIRTUE

1806

The whole of virtue consists in its practice.—Cicero

1807

Wisdom is knowing what to do next; virtue is doing it.—David Starr Jordan

VISION

1808

Vision is of God. A vision comes in advance of any task well done.—Katherine Logan, *The Upper Road of Vision*

1809

The Pilgrims stayed because they were able to see the eternal in the temporal, and the invisible in the visible, and because among them the material was dominated by the spiritual.—Daniel L. Marsh, *The American Canon*

1810

The problem is not that we have exhausted our frontiers. The problem is that we fail to recognize them! And as our vision shortens, our pessimism deepens. Eternally right was that optician who plastered across his window . . . the slogan: "You can't be optimistic if you've got a misty optic." The failure of today's youth—reflecting, I'm afraid, the malignant myopia of us oldsters—is to see that—just as in other eras the frontiers have been geographical—today they are personal. Today, the frontiers are within.—Clarence Hall

1811

Other people can't make you see with their eyes. At best they can only encourage you to use your own.—Aldous Huxley

1812

It is all very well to try to adjust young people to society, but it is far more important that they be given some vision of the nature, ends, and purposes of that society.—Grayson Kirk

1813

Generations are like dwarfs—seated on the shoulders of giants—see more than the ancients and more distant.—Bernard of Chartres

1814

Closely related to initiative is that subtle factor which I have called vision. Others describe it as creativity or imagination. I believe it was Edison who said invention is 99 per cent perspiration and 1 per cent inspiration. The point is, of course, that without the 1 per cent, all the sweat would be wasted or spent on some wholly unrelated work. I can think of no epoch in recorded history when the situation offered such free rein to men of vision, nor when vision was so desperately needed if we are to provide the foundation required for the full enjoyment of tomorrow.—J. B. Medaris, "Your Tomorrow," *Vital Speeches*

1815

We are unable to comprehend fully some ideas and truths until we see them incarnated in a person. What does courage or sacrifice or goodness mean to us until we see it displayed in some life? In Jesus we see the attributes of God in action, being lived and practiced by a Person. We begin to understand the love of God when we see it being lived and expressed in the life of Jesus. God has revealed Himself adequately to us in the Person of Jesus Christ. When we confess our faith in Christ, we are affirming our belief as to the kind of God we worship.—Earle W. Crawford, *Pulpit Preaching*

1816

Justice Chase was one time on a train that took him through the town that was the birthplace of Patrick Henry. He got off the train at this place and stood on the platform witnessing the beauty of the scenery, and he exclaimed: "What an atmosphere! What a view! What glorious mountain scenery! No wonder that Patrick Henry grew here!" An old resident of the place heard him and said: "Yes, sir, but as far as I have heard, that landscape and those mountains have always been here, but we haven't seen any more Patrick Henrys."—Katherine Logan, *The Upper Road of Vision*

1817

Vision does not come by inspiration. It comes from knowledge, intelligently cultivated.—Robert A. Weaver

1818

A vision foretells what may be ours. It is an invitation to do something. With a great mental picture in mind we go from one accomplishment to another, using the materials about us only as steppingstones to that which is higher and better and more satisfying. We thus become possessors of the unseen values which are eternal.—Katherine Logan

1819

Cowles was a little lad. One day he tried to reach something on the mantel and found it was beyond him. He came down from stretching on tiptoe and said to his mother: "I am not very big, am I, Mamma? I can't reach very high." His mother reached out, as she noted the serious look on his face, and said to him, "No, you are not very big now, my son, but you will grow and some day you will be a big man like your papa." He stood erect as the faith within him spoke: "Mamma, I feel a man pushing inside of me *now!*"—Katherine Logan, *There's Something Better*

1820

Churches deny their faith when they venture only so far as they can be sure that they can see the way.—Roswell Barnes

1821

Christ came to open closed eyes, to make sightless eyes to see, to give glory and grace to human life. To accept Him as Friend and Saviour is to enter a bright and spacious world through magic doors flung open by His pierced hands.—Thomas McDormand

1822

The farther backward you can look, the farther forward you are likely to see.—Winston Churchill

1823

All the powerful things in the world are invisible—honor, character, love, your power to visualize and make dreams come true. They are lights within, casting their rays around you so that you can find your way. Open your eyes with faith so that you can see them.—Celia Caroline Cole

1824
Dreams are to be condemned only when they are a lazy substitute for an effort to change reality; when they are an incentive they are fulfilling a vital purpose in the incarnation of human ideals. To kill fancy in childhood is to make a slave to what exists, a creature tethered to earth and therefore unable to create heaven.—Bertrand Russell, *Education and the Good Life*

1825
In discussing the cause of the collapse [of the Czarist regime] Raymond Robbins used an unforgettable phrase, "the indoor mind." He had been describing how the privileged class in Russia had gone the round of their isolated and self-sufficient life, sheltered wealth and careless gaiety, with the silken curtains drawn across the windows through which they did not see the ominous forces moving in the dark night of the common life of Russia. They had, he said "the indoor mind." That is the cause of every collapse in man's personal and public life. Over against this, place the outward looking, outward reaching minds of the Master of Men who came not to be served, but to serve.—Theodore Cuyler Speers

1826
A blind man's world is bounded by the limits of his touch; an ignorant man's world by the limits of his knowledge; a great man's world by the limits of his vision.

1827
Christ's insight was one which future generations may rediscover but can never upset.—V. G. Simkhovitch, *Toward the Understanding of Jesus*

1828
We are living in a new era in the land of beginning again. The boundary of your dreams is the measure of your success. Dare to dream.—Elma Easley

1829
The Bible is a window in this prison-world through which we may look into eternity.—Timothy Dwight

1830
It is all right to dream of things you are going to do, but begin work right away.—Briggs, *Ideals*

1831
Getting your imagination captured is almost the whole of life. The minute the eyes of your heart are enlightened, the minute your imagination gives you the picture of your path, your goal, your aim—it is as good as done. The way to become the architect of your fate, the captain of your soul, is to have your imagination captured.—Rufus Jones

1832
Only one expection do I know, and that is the most tremendous war song I can recall. Even an outsider in time of peace can hardly read it without emotion. I mean, of course, Julia Ward Howe's "Battle Hymn of the Republic," with the choral opening line: "Mine eyes have seen the glory of the coming of the Lord."—A. Conan Doyle, *Through the Magic Door*

1833
A working definition of vision . . . is the capacity—to see what others do not see—to see further than they see—to see before they see.—John R. Mott, *American Magazine*

VOCATION

1834
Once two topics—sex and politics—could be guaranteed to make for live discussions among young people. Now

a third—vocations—has been added.
—Alexander Miller

1835

I believe business is meant to be a channel of God's power, the main and chief extension of the church in the world. God may never have any other access to certain people except that one who believes in Him happens to work alongside them. When they see peace, poise and power they will become curious and be persuaded that religion is not a "racket," but a source of light. Obviously, life and deeds have to precede words—the life and deeds, not of a great and mature saint, but of a sinner who has quit bluffing and is trying to do what God wants him to do. The spiritual opportunity that confronts a man in any kind of job whatever is unlimited, if he has the imagination to see it, and the courage to grasp it.

It is a very great task to attempt to make business Christian throughout, to serve God effectually on the daily job, and to make our profession or business work for God. Our daily work, like our human nature, cannot be made statistically good. No hope can come from the superimposition upon business of "systems" which sound and look good, but do not reckon with the ever-present problem of human nature. We can only hope to make real progress in the Christianizing of business by the Christianizing of the men who manage and work in it. If this is carried far enough, these men will use their freedom to obey God more fully in their business relations. I am convinced that God enters the business scene in two ways: first, through converted men whose hearts He has touched and changed and who carry His Spirit with them at all times; and second, in human relationships that are different because He has become third party to them. Slowly Christian persons and Christian rela-

tionships permeate the business situation. Prayer, good will and fellowship are a powerful combination. The Spirit of God uses them to change man's mere self-interest into the wider interest of the whole. Slowly, but (under these conditions) steadily, "the kingdoms of this world become the Kingdom of our Lord and of His Christ."—Samuel M. Shoemaker, *The Experiment of Faith*

1836

Man is born to live, not to prepare for life. Life itself, the phenomenon of life, the gift of life, is so breathtakingly serious!—Boris Pasternak, *Doctor Zhivago*

1837

Personal life is at a discount today. People work keenly, putting everything into their work, but many complain that their personal life is barren; so that one wonders why women who do not have to work have such a strong urge to do it. It almost seems that work has come to have a value that is unreal, and we take it as a drug, exciting and deadening. Women drive themselves when they are not driven by necessity, and everyone insists upon being exhausted. It is disturbing to see women so caught by activity, for the individual bond that used to matter most to women is a quality that is now doubly precious. The devotion we have all seen in woman makes one dare to say that as she tends to half relinquish her personal role, moving out into the impersonal world and allowing society to do what she was given by nature to do, we are almost faced with being contained in the crowd as a substitute for being loved.—Florida Scott-Maxwell, *The Greatness of the Task*

1838

God does not look kindly on us when we take advantage of Him. The job,

the work, the toil still has to be done.
—Edward Mooney

1839

No race can prosper until it learns that there is as much dignity in tilling a field as in writing a poem.—Booker T. Washington

WANTS

1840

When the gods are angry with a man they give him what he asks for.—A Greek saying

1841

In this world there are only two tragedies. One is not getting what one wants, and the other is getting it. The last is much the worse; the last is the real tragedy.—Oscar Wilde

1842

Knowing what you want is not the easiest thing in the world. Yet if you go up to a friend and ask, "Have you given any thought today to what you really want?" you probably will get this reply, "Don't be silly, I know what I want. My only problem is how to get it."—Howard Whitman, "What Do You Really Want?" *Pageant*

1843

Someone once said cryptically that the two most important things in life are to get what you want and then enjoy it. But do you know what you want? Few people do. A psychologist put the figure at one out of ten and another psychologist disagreed with him. He said it was more like five out of a hundred. The thinking of the rest of the population is decidedly fuzzy on the subject.—Constance Foster, "Do You Know What You Want?" *Your Life*

WELCOME

1844

On Francis E. Clark's old home in Auburndale, Massachusetts, the word "Welcome" was written in twenty-three different languages. God, in Christ Jesus, says "Welcome" in the warm, glowing letters of love. Yet men and women turn their backs upon Him, and show a greater love for the things of the world than for God.

1845

People may still beat a path to our doors. But they may not lift the latch and walk in unless they feel they are welcome; unless they feel our business is a friendly place with a sincere interest in improving the American scene.
—John A. Barr

WORDS

1846

The five most important words:
 I am proud of you.
The four most important words:
 What is your opinion?
The three most important words:
 If you please.
The two most important words:
 Thank you.
The least important word:
 "I."

—Zion's Herald

1847

While the word is yet unspoken, you are master of it; when once it is spoken, it is master of you.—Arab proverb

WORK

1848

Work is love made visible. If you bake bread with indifference, you bake a bitter bread that feeds but half man's hunger.—Kahlil Gibran[1]

1849

The Egyptians utilized 20 per cent of their national potential for twenty years to build the Great Pyramid. If we applied the same percentage of national effort for the same time, we could put the pyramids into orbit. I want to go on record that I am not advocating it.—Fred Whipple, Director of Smithsonian Astrophysical Observatory

1850

Nothing is worse for those who have business than the visits of those who have none.

1851

To take a job and make it grow is better than to take another's job away from him. No position is small when it is held by a big man. Success is better measured by growth than by displacement.—Ralph W. Sockman

1852

Without work life would be worthless and aimless, and work should still be the principal aim of the worker, but they would make an effort all their own, not under compulsion.—Sidney Hillman

1853

God gave man work, not to burden him, but to bless him, and useful work, willingly, cheerfully, effectively done, has always been the finest expression of the human spirit.—Walter R. Courtenay, *The Pulpit*

1854

To all Employees:

Due to increased competition and the keen desire to remain in business, we find it necessary to institute a new policy.

Effective immediately we are asking that somewhere between starting and quitting time and without infringing too much on the time devoted to lunch period, coffee breaks, rest periods, story telling, ticket-selling, golfing, auto racing, horse selections, window-gazing, vacation-planning and rehashing of yesterday's TV programs, that each employee try to find some time that can be set aside and be known hereafter as The Work Break.

WORRY

1855

Jesus once said, "Don't worry." . . . That's good advice; but . . . notice . . . Jesus is talking about people who are worrying about themselves. He is not talking of those who are anxious about the welfare of others. . . . The more you worry about other people's welfare, the less you will worry about your own. To "get away from ourselves," we need only to get into the lives of those around us, yes, and those far from us, with whom we are bound up in the bundle of life. . . . Isaiah once made a joke about people who are too self-centered. He said, "The bed is shorter than that a man can stretch himself on it and the covering is narrower than that he can wrap himself in it." Sounds uncomfortable, doesn't it? That's the man whose life is not big enough. He is cramped into too small a place . . . so you should worry, not about yourself . . . but about the concerns of those who have no claim upon you except that they are in trouble and in need.—Alvin E. Magary, *Your Life*

1856

Why worry? is a question that any worrier should be well qualified to

[1] Reprinted from *The Prophet* by Kahlil Gibran with permission of the publisher, Alfred A. Knopf, Inc. Copyright 1923 by Administrators C.T.A. of Kahlil Gibran Estate, and Mary G. Gibran.

answer. But just ask a worrier! The average worried woman can't really explain, or else she relates so many troubles—most of them obscure, imagined, or future—that it's impossible to pin her down to one real worry. Actually, there is no "good cause for worry." There are countless problems calling for constructive thought and sound planning—and there are countless men and women whose lives are constantly shadowed by worry. But the real problems and the chronic worriers seldom get together.—Ernest Dichter, M.D.

1857

In Eden, where the human race began, God supplied man's every need, and to crown his joy, God fellowshipped with man daily. After sin came, worry came too, for worry is a by-product of sin. The guilty conscience feared to meet God. . . . To worry is not to trust God's ability or willingness to help, and has serious consequences on body, mind and soul. Worry is anxious, fearful, fretful contemplation of situations over which we are powerless, forgetting that God is powerful. Saying, "Everybody does it," does not make worry right, neither is that statement the truth, for devout Christians seek and really find release from it.

1858

Some time ago a businessman drew up what he called a "Worry Chart," in which he kept a record of his worries. He discovered that 40 per cent of them were about things that probably would never happen; 30 per cent concerned past decisions that he could not now unmake; 12 per cent dealt with other people's criticisms of him; 10 per cent were worries about his health. He concluded that only 8 per cent of them were really legitimate.—Francis C. Ellis, *The Pulpit*

1859

The American people are so tense that it is impossible even to put them to sleep with a sermon.—Norman Vincent Peale

1860

A businessman, who had had many worries and had successfully emerged from his difficulties, says that one red-letter day in his life was when his bank agreed to stand behind him and support him. He says that just to know that he had such backing gave him poise and confidence and enabled him to do better.

How much peace and confidence ought to fill the souls of those who realize that the God who led His people is also behind them! A bank may fail, but God cannot fail.—Archer Wallace

1861

Very few people really enjoy worrying. There is no need to describe all the misery which worry causes. What we want to know is: How can I stop it? . . . We can begin by using common sense and eliminating three sorts of things . . . from our worry-list. First are the things that are going to happen anyway. What cannot be stopped or delayed by thinking or by action of any sort may as well be accepted. . . . Second, don't worry over what has already happened. . . . What is done is done and not even God can make it different. . . . Learn the lessons of disaster. But don't fret your mind over it. Third, don't worry about the bad things that may happen but which in any case you cannot possibly prevent . . . if things are beyond your control by planning or action, then you certainly cannot control them by worrying.

But you cannot resist this temptation by merely resolving, "I will not worry." There is no casting our anxiety and leaving your mind a blank . . . the practical cure is . . . recommended by Jesus . . . replace worry by trust . . . "Let not your heart be troubled," said Jesus. The word means literally to be torn apart, to be divided. Put all your heart in one place; "Believe in God." The cure for worry is a deeper knowledge of God.—Kenneth J. Foreman, "How to Stop Worrying," *Presbyterian Outlook*

1862

It's easier to get ulcers from what's eating you than from what you eat. —Robert S. Kerr

1863

If you are standing upright, don't worry if your shadow is crooked.— Chinese proverb

WORSHIP

1864

Man worships because God lays His hand to the dust of our experience, and man miraculously becomes a living soul —and knows it and wants to worship. . . . Once an individual has met his God, the curtain between heaven and earth is thinned to gossamer and he cannot but make plans to live in the presence of that God, returning ever and again to acknowledge Him.— Douglas Horton

1865

Worship is pictured at its best in Isaiah when the young prophet became aware of the Father; aware of his own limitations; aware of the Father's directives; and aware of the task at hand.— David Julius

1866

The whole history of the worship of God has been one of a widening circle: Adam—Joseph—Moses—Samuel —David—Peter—Paul—Timothy—Au-gustine — Luther — Calvin — Wesley — Carey—Judson—and all others.

1867

At Vicksburg, Mississippi, an engineer showed me an almost dry channel. He explained that once the great Mississippi River flowed there but now it had been changed into another channel, which had been dug. The flow of the river could not be stopped, but it could be diverted. So with our worship of God. Man is incomplete without an object of worship; the yearning of his soul demands attention.—Charles L. Allen, *God's Psychiatry*

1868

A man who bows down to nothing can never bear the burden of himself. —Dostoevski

1869

Worship is the act of rising to a personal, experimental consciousness of the real presence of God which floods the soul with joy and bathes the whole inward spirit with refreshing streams of life.—Rufus Jones, *The World Within*

WRONG

1870

In one sense you are right about this notion. Practice does make perfect, but you fail to observe that it perfects your errors just as rapidly and intensively as it does your successes. That is why some men who practice golf year after year get worse instead of better. After reaching a certain degree of proficiency, most people never improve in any skill. They practice their errors until they become perfect in them.—*Religious Digest*

1871

Falsehood often lurks upon the tongue of him who, by self-praise, seeks to enhance his value in the eyes of others.—James Gordon Bennett

1872

No matter how big and tough a problem may be, get rid of confusion by taking one little step toward solution. Do something. Then try again. At the worst, so long as you don't do it the same way twice, you will eventually use up all the wrong ways of doing it and thus the next try will be the right one. —G. F. Nordenholt

1873

If you think the world is all wrong, remember that it contains people like you.—Gandhi

YOUTH

1874

Every child grows in his own pattern and at his own rate and everyone is different—that's what makes us individuals.—Eleanor Metheny

1875

The first years of man must make provision for the last. He that never thinks never can be wise. Perpetual levity must end in ignorance; and intemperance, though it may fire the spirits for an hour, will make life short or miserable. Let us consider that youth is of no long duration, and that in maturer age, when the enchantments of fancy shall cease, and phantoms of delight dance no more about us, we shall have no comforts but the esteem of wise men, and the means of doing good. Let us, therefore, stop, while to stop is in our power: let us live as men who are some time to grow old, and to whom it will be the most dreadful of all evils to count their past years by follies, and to be reminded of their former luxuriance of health only by the maladies which riot has produced. —Samuel Johnson, *Rasselas*

INDEXES

TOPICAL INDEX

(ITEMS ARE LISTED BY SELECTION NUMBER)

INDEX FOR SPECIAL DAYS
AND OCCASIONS

(ITEMS ARE LISTED BY SELECTION NUMBER)

Church-Centered Days and Occasions

Christmas and Advent
90, 334, 347, 383-434, 601, 666, 1056, 1115, 1118, 1193

Easter and Lent
335, 338, 343, 344, 345, 347, 348, 349, 351, 355, 358, 362, 364, 695, 711, 732, 749, 753, 754, 809-825, 915, 994, 1064, 1077, 1334, 1365, 1396, 1657, 1693, 1709, 1726, 1761

Communion and Lord's Supper
258, 450, 470, 497, 591-604, 1038

Missions
7, 27, 29, 30, 31, 100, 108, 115, 122, 138, 169, 243, 245, 258, 262, 343, 344, 442, 443, 444, 451, 521, 525, 555, 569, 588, 606, 673, 740, 916, 917, 929, 930, 931, 972, 1115, 1146, 1239, 1298, 1473, 1474, 1507, 1803

Bible
27, 64, 68, 133-157, 205, 219, 262, 276, 305, 346, 441, 480, 499, 558, 643, 645, 767, 803, 1004, 1072, 1113, 1245, 1269, 1291, 1489, 1527, 1656, 1709, 1777, 1789, 1829

Pentecost
126, 140, 443, 444, 450, 477, 495, 501, 521, 551, 811, 958, 1151, 1253-1256, 1608, 1628, 1677, 1730

National and Patriotic Occasions

Independence Day
2, 5, 58, 72, 290, 542, 583, 588, 636, 842, 858, 1025, 1057, 1058, 1069, 1281, 1380, 1382, 1385, 1390, 1562, 1563, 1720, 1781, 1789

Lincoln's Birthday
2, 68, 282, 587, 708, 1033, 1069, 1191, 1306, 1600

Flag Day
71, 679, 1046-1051

Memorial Day
5, 58, 61, 66, 71, 72, 92, 538, 678, 680, 745, 829, 840, 1035, 1046, 1059, 1069, 1244, 1380, 1383, 1385, 1390, 1444, 1562, 1567, 1570, 1571, 1597, 1804, 1805

School and Civic Occasions

Commencement and Talks to Young People
2, 5, 7, 12, 13, 14, 15, 16, 17, 20, 23, 33, 38, 88, 158, 288, 290, 294, 576-578, 679, 795, 986, 1000, 1001, 1206, 1211, 1212, 1284, 1285, 1286, 1346, 1357, 1362, 1363, 1369, 1397, 1406, 1414, 1444, 1457, 1461, 1468, 1472, 1481, 1505, 1518, 1546, 1547, 1552, 1597, 1636, 1637, 1640, 1643, 1655, 1660, 1684, 1701, 1705, 1707, 1711, 1715, 1721, 1732, 1734, 1739, 1745, 1746, 1747, 1749, 1750, 1759, 1762, 1771, 1774, 1783, 1785, 1796, 1800, 1801, 1802, 1803, 1805, 1807, 1810, 1816, 1833, 1836, 1842, 1843, 1846, 1851, 1854, 1873, 1874, 1875

P.T.A.'s, Service Clubs, and Similar Groups
2, 7, 14, 15, 16, 51, 59, 60, 65, 68, 69, 70, 94, 99, 103, 105, 151, 158, 164, 237, 239, 240, 241, 242, 267, 270, 287, 291, 292, 314, 315, 319, 321, 328, 459, 469, 537, 539,

INDEX OF CONTRIBUTORS AND PERSONS MENTIONED

(ITEMS ARE LISTED BY SELECTION NUMBER)

Sperry, Willard, 12
Spinoza, 775
Spock, B., 1557
Stassen, Harold E., 1783
Steere, Douglas, 1346
Stern, Karl, 1451
Stevenson, Adlai E., 61
Stevenson, Robert Louis, 694, 1197
Stockwell, F. Olin, 29
Stone, Harlan, 1379
Strickland, Frances L., 1295
Strunsky, Simeon, 319
Studebaker, J. W., 656, 881
Sun Yat-sen, 587
Sullivan, William, 1654
Sumner, Charles, 288
Swain, G. Christie, 1617
Swaim, J. Carter, 74, 1225
Sweazey, George, 597, 1131
Sweetser, Arthur, 546
Swift, Jonathan, 233, 1103
Sylvester, Robert, 863

Taft, Charles P., 524
Taft, Larado, 914
Taft, Robert A., 551
Tagore, 1457
Taine, H. A., 904
Talkington, H. L., 745
Taylor, Herbert J., 540
Tebbetts, George, 1027
Tell, William, 1754
Teller, Edward, 1251
Temple, William, 595, 1257, 1339
Templeton, Charles, 126, 368, 375, 377, 739, 744, 919, 1138, 1283, 1403, 1510, 1614
Tennyson, Alfred Lord, 540
Thackeray, William M., 1056
Thomas, 695
Thomas, Emrys, 1306
Thompson, Dorothy, 1268
Thompson, Ernest Trice, 1760
Theophrastus, 1772
Thoreau, Henry David, 46, 106, 226
Thorne, Guy, 1294
Thorndike, 1363
Tillich, Paul, 457, 1437, 1737
Tittle, Ernest F., 508
Tocqueville, 124
Tolstoy, 156, 1714
Tomlinson, H. M., 146
Tong, Hollington K., 842
Toynbee, Arnold J., 699, 905, 995
Townsend, Atwood H., 268
Trueblood, D. Elton, 976
Truman, Harry S., 260, 551

Tucker, William J., 373, 847, 950, 1139, 1791
Turgenev, 256
Tyler, John, 370
Tyndall, John, 947

Ullathorne, 1549

van Dyke, Henry, 1296
Van Gogh, 106
Van Doren, Mark, 858
Van Kirk, Walter, 909
Varvenargues, 907
Vassady, Bela, 1152, 1715
Verne, Jules, 156
Victoria, Queen, 1699
Vincent, George, 1504
Vieth, Paul H., 831
Voltaire, 780, 1170, 1212, 1508
Von Braun, Wernher, 1734
Von Mises, Ludwig, 1674
Von Thadden, Reinhold, 984

Wagner, Hughes, 926
Wagner, Richard, 418, 1712
Walker, Alan, 1576
Walker, Harold Blake, 1039, 1309, 1518, 1710
Wallace, Archer, 256, 288, 289, 344, 740, 1237, 1294, 1860
Wallace, R. C., 120
Wallis, Charles L., 604, 1490
Walz, Rew, 485
Warburton, 161
Ward, Artemus, 556
Ward, Barbara, 973
Ward, W. Ralph, Jr., 14
Warne, F. W., 344
Warren, Earl, 1385
Warren, Joyce, 1611
Washington, George, 68, 654, 1015, 1050, 1069
Washington, Booker T., 266, 1407, 1839
Waters, Vincent, 1633
Waugh, Alec, 302
Wayland, H. L., 167
Weaver, Robert A., 1817
Weatherhead, Leslie D., 121, 123, 883, 1219
Webb, Bert, 648
Webster, Daniel, 154, 331
Webster, J. B., 1236
Webster, Noah, 147
Weigle, Luther A., 1382
Weiss, Paul, 636
Weitz, Martin M., 875
Welch, Joseph, 1350, 1561
Wells, Corinne U., 1109